The State of the Parties

People, Passions, and Power

Social Movements, Interest Organizations, and the Political Process

John C. Green, Series Editor:

Forthcoming

The State of the Parties

*The Changing Role of Contemporary
American Parties*

FOURTH EDITION

Edited by John C. Green
and Rick Farmer

ROWMAN & LITTLEFIELD PUBLISHERS, INC.
Lanham • Boulder • New York • Oxford

ROWMAN & LITTLEFIELD PUBLISHERS, INC.

Published in the United States of America
by Rowman & Littlefield Publishers, Inc.
A Member of the Rowman & Littlefield Publishing Group
4501 Forbes Boulevard, Suite 200, Lanham, Maryland 20706
www.rowmanlittlefield.com

P.O. Box 317, Oxford OX2 9RU, United Kingdom

British Library Cataloguing in Publication Information Available

Library of Congress Cataloging-in-Publication Data

The state of the parties : the changing role of contemporary American
parties / edited by John C. Green and Rick D. Farmer.—4th ed.
p.   cm.—(People, passions, and power)
Includes bibliographical references (p.   ) and index.
ISBN 0-7425-1821-3 (cloth : alk. paper) — ISBN 0-7425-1822-1 (pbk. :
alk. paper)
1. Political parties—United States.   I. Green, John Clifford, 1953–
II. Farmer, Rick D., 1958–   III. Series.
JK2261 .S824   2003
324.273—dc21   2002153816

Printed in the United States of America

∞ ™ The paper used in this publication meets the minimum requirements of American
National Standard for Information Sciences—Permanence of Paper for Printed Library
Materials, ANSI/NISO Z39.48-1992.

Contents

Tables and Figures

Tables

Figures

Preface

The research effort that produced this book is the product of more than a decade of scholarship. The first edition originated from research coordinated at the Ray C. Bliss Institute of Applied Politics in 1993 on the changing role of political parties in American politics. The second edition reflected the impact of the 1994 elections and the third edition reviewed the effects of the 1996 campaign. The present, fourth edition considers the impact of the 2000 election and subsequent events.

From the beginning of this effort, our goal was to bring together party scholars from around the nation to discuss the state of American party politics and new avenues of research. On each occasion, we have been privileged to field a "dream team" of contributors, and although the roster differs a little each time, the team has been strong, including a mix of veteran and emerging scholars. Taken together, the essays in this volume offer insight into the "state of the parties" as the twenty-first century begins.

The development of this volume was greatly aided by the staff of the Bliss Institute. Janet Bolois was not only instrumental in compiling the chapters and managing the layout, but has also honed the unique skill of putting up with the editors—no simple task, to be sure. Kimberly Haverkamp deserves special mention for her invaluable assistance with logistics, and Jason Haas provided a careful reading of the manuscript and a critical eye. As before, we owe a debt of thanks to Jennifer Knerr and her associates at Rowman & Littlefield, especially Alden Perkins. Finally, we would surely be remiss if we did not acknowledge our families, principally Lynn Green and Marjean Farmer. Without their unwavering support and encouragement *The State of the Parties* would not have been possible.

The State of the Parties in an Evenly Divided Nation

John C. Green and Rick Farmer

When future historians evaluate the 2000 and 2002 elections, they are likely to be impressed by the unusually close division between the major political parties. No doubt they will cite the now common refrain "we are a fifty-fifty nation." Of course, such historians will have two advantages over contemporary observers: a broader perspective on the factors that produced such an electoral tie, and how the tie ultimately was broken. We can anticipate their insights by investigating a question of our own: What is the state of American political parties at the turn of the new century?

Answering this perennial question has added urgency because parties are central to the political standoff and its potential resolution. Indeed, some analysts believe that party weakness is partly responsible for the evenly divided politics of 2000 and 2002, while others see the parties as responding with some success to the many problems that beset the nation. But nearly everyone sees strong parties as critical to resolving these divisions in a productive fashion. Thus, like anxious physicians, scholars take the pulse of the parties, looking for signs of vitality or frailty, and then debating the diagnosis and potential remedies.

This collection represents a regularly scheduled examination of the state of parties, the fourth in a series of such efforts (Shea and Green 1994; Green and Shea 1996, 1999a). Here, a group of established and emerging scholars considers the state of the parties from a wide variety of perspectives, revealing some troubling weaknesses as well as some encouraging signs of strength. This mixed assessment reflects in part the volatility of contemporary politics. Thus, it is useful to briefly catalogue the recent stresses on the American polity.

A Volatile Era

The even division in 2000 and 2002 was the product of a decade of unusual events, for which the stage was set circa 1990. The decades-long Cold

War with the Soviet Union had ended and new foreign policy challenges were in the making, aptly symbolized by the Persian Gulf War. Meanwhile, global trade and cybernetic technology were generating a torrent of changes on the American economy, putting new pressures on the government, including the federal budget and entitlement programs. And long-simmering disputes over cultural issues, such as abortion, gay rights, and public education, were about to boil over. A decade of "divided" government between a Republican president and Democratic Congress (and most state governments) left many issues unresolved, including reform of the campaign finance laws and the growth of party "soft money."

The volatility began in 1992, with the defeat of an incumbent president, George H. W. Bush. Such an occurrence would be worthy of note in its own right, but more dramatic events overshadowed it. Of special note was Ross Perot's independent campaign for president, which garnered 19 percent of the popular vote. Perot then fashioned the Reform Party out of his movement and ran in 1996 election. Taken together, these two campaigns mark one of the most successful minor party efforts in American history. Minor parties became an important part of national politics throughout the 1990s.

The 1992 winner was William Jefferson Clinton, marking the ascension of the baby boom generation to the presidency. Although receiving far less than a majority of the popular vote, Clinton restored the Democrats to power after twelve years in the political wilderness. When combined with Democratic control of the Congress, the 1992 election produced a rare result in contemporary politics: unified party government. However, Democratic control was short-lived. In 1994, the Republicans made an extraordinary comeback, winning control of both houses of Congress for the first time in forty years and scoring major gains among the nation's governors and state legislatures. Indeed, this dramatic election ushered in a new period of close party competition across the country.

The 1994 election elevated another baby boomer, Newt Gingrich, to the post of Speaker of the House of Representatives. Gingrich was the first Republican to occupy that office since 1954. Republican control of Congress generated a new form of "divided government," between a Democratic president and a Republican Congress instead of the other way around. In 1996, the Republicans failed to win the White House, and Bill Clinton was reelected in a remarkably placid election given the nature of the times. However, the Democrats received less than a majority of the popular vote and failed to recover the Congress or many state offices.

Once again, Bill Clinton's success was short-lived as he was beset by scandals, including questionable campaign finance practices involving party "soft money," and of course, his affair with White House intern Monica Lewinsky. The latter scandal sparked an acrimonious debate that produced yet another anomaly: the Democrats gained seats in the House of Representatives in the 1998 midterm elections, one of the few instances in which the party of the president has done so. Although the Republicans remained in control of the Congress, Speaker Gingrich resigned (pursued by his own personal scandals). The Republican House of Representatives then impeached Clinton—only the second such occurrence in American history—but the Republican Senate acquitted Clinton in 1999.

As if this roller-coaster ride were not enough, the decade ended with one of the closest presidential elections in American history. It was a rematch of sorts: The Democrats nominated Vice President Al Gore, the heir-apparent to Bill Clinton, and the Republicans nominated Texas Governor George W. Bush, the son and political heir of former president Bush (defeated in 1992 by Clinton and Gore). Although most analysts expected Gore to win easily, he eked out just a tiny plurality of the popular vote and was edged out in the Electoral College in a controversy of historic proportions. In fact, Bush's razor-thin Electoral College majority depended on disputed ballots in Florida and a margin of less than six hundred votes. After thirty-six days of bitter partisan wrangling, the U.S. Supreme Court ruled in favor of Bush by a 5-4 margin, putting him in the White House. Minor party candidates may have influenced the outcome of the contest, especially Green Party candidate Ralph Nader, who probably cost Gore Florida and other close states.

The 2000 election was a "perfect tie" (Ceaser and Busch 2001) in terms of congressional and state elections as well. For example, the Democrats reduced the Republican margin in the House of Representatives to just a handful of seats, and won enough Senate seats to produce the first 50-50 tie in history, broken by newly elected Vice President Richard Cheney in favor of the Republicans. This brief and unusual instance of unified Republican control was soon shattered when Republican Senator James Jeffords of Vermont became an independent, putting the Senate in Democratic hands. The 2000 election had its own campaign finance controversy: Bush became the first major party candidate to bypass public financing in the primaries and win the election.

Of course, all of these political events paled next to the terrorist attacks of September 11, 2001. Nearly three thousand Americans perished in the hijacking of four commercial airliners and subsequent crashes into the World Trade Center in New York, the Pentagon in Washington, D.C., and a field near Shanksville, Pennsylvania. It was the largest foreign attack ever on the continental United States. This calamity was compared to the surprise attack on Pearl Harbor that led the United States into World War II, and it had a dramatic effect on national politics, spawning a brief moment of national unity. President Bush's response to 9/11 brought him high levels of public approval and the longest sustained period of presidential popularity on record. Foreign affairs returned to the forefront of national politics for the first time in a decade, including aggressive opposition to terrorism at home and abroad, war (in Afghanistan), and rumors of war (in Iraq). These events may influence national politics for years to come.

Another stress on the political system occurred in the spring of 2002 when the Congress passed campaign finance reform. The Bipartisan Campaign Reform Act (BCRA) represented the culmination of a decade of intense debate, and was the first major change in the federal campaign act in decades. Among other things, BCRA restricted party soft money and raised the amounts of hard money that can be contributed to candidates and parties. It went into effect the day after the 2002 midterm election, although litigation may delay or alter its implementation. BCRA will have a major impact on the state of the parties, for good or ill.

The Volatility Continues: The 2002 Elections

The 2002 congressional election continued the pattern of electoral volatility. Early on, most analysts believed that the historic pattern of the party in the White House losing in Congress would prevail, thus allowing the Democrats to maintain control of the Senate and retake control of the House of Representatives. Certainly the weak state of the economy and other problems such as corporate scandals supported this expectation. And the war on terrorism did not appear as much of an impediment to the historic trend: After all, Franklin Delano Roosevelt's Democrats lost forty-two seats in 1942, less than a year after the attack on Pearl Harbor.

Instead, the Republicans achieved a solid victory in the 2002 election, restoring the precarious Republican control of the federal government won in 2000. In fact, in many respects the 2002 election was a continuation of the "perfect tie," but with a very small—rather than tiny—edge for the Republicans. Relatively small changes at the polling booth made a big difference in terms of the control of government. Overall, the Republicans received just 51 percent of the votes cast (the Democrats received 44 percent and the rest went to minor party and independent candidates). Overall, the GOP will control 51 percent of the Senate, 52 percent of the House, 52 percent of the governors, and just over half of the state legislators. While the proclamation of a "mandate" for Bush by commentators of all partisan stripes is probably overstated, there is no doubt that the results validated the Bush presidency. In the words of David Broder, Bush is no longer an "accidental" president (2002).

By Election Day 2002, attention focused on control of the Senate, and the available evidence suggested the contest would be very close. Most analysts expected a Democratic victory because the Republicans were defending more seats, and, due to the departure of a phalanx of conservative Senators, five of these seats were open: North Carolina (Jesse Helms), South Carolina

(Strom Thurmond), Tennessee (Fred Thompson), Texas (Phil Gramm), and New Hampshire (Bob Smith was defeated in the GOP primary). In addition, there were at least two vulnerable Republican incumbents running for reelection: Wayne Allard in Colorado (with a lackluster legislative record) and Tim Hutchinson in Arkansas (a "family values" candidate who had divorced his wife and married a staffer). Democrats had a smaller number of vulnerable senators, including Jeanne Carnahan in Missouri (filling out the term of her deceased husband) and Paul Wellstone of Minnesota and Tom Johnson of South Dakota (both regarded as too liberal for their states). Some analysts gave the GOP a slim chance against Max Cleland in Georgia and Mary Landrieu in Louisiana.[1]

On November 5, the Republicans held all of their open seats, retained Colorado, won an upset in Georgia, and took close contests in Missouri and Minnesota. The Minnesota outcome was marred by tragic circumstances. Incumbent Democrat Paul Wellstone died in an airplane accident ten days before the election and was replaced on the ticket by former vice president Walter Mondale, who had once represented Minnesota in the Senate. Mondale lost in a short campaign fraught with conflicting emotions, including grief over Wellstone's tragic death and anger over the strident partisanship demonstrated at a public memorial service.[2] All told, the Republicans were guaranteed a majority of fifty-one seats in the Senate.

Democrats took some solace in holding on to South Dakota, where the prestige of the Democratic Senate leader and South Dakotan Tom Daschle was on the line, and by winning the Republican-held seat in Arkansas. Their spirits brightened further on December 7, when Mary Landrieu retained her Louisiana Senate seat in a run-off election, 51 to 49 percent. The run-off was required because state law requires a majority to win an election, and Landrieu received just 46 percent against three Republican candidates on November 5. The Republicans had hoped for such a run-off because in the past their candidates have done well in such contests. Although control of the Congress was no longer in doubt, President Bush and the Republican establishment campaigned vigorously for the Republican candidate, Susan Terrell. This intense support allowed Terrell to improve dramatically over the 27 percent she received on November 5, but she fell short of winning. Meanwhile, Landrieu maintained a fragile "bi-racial coalition" of African Americans and moderate whites to eke out a narrow victory.

By Election Day, most analysts believed it would be difficult for the Democrats to take back control of the House of Representatives. The culprit was the redistricting after the 2000 census: Republicans obtained a small gain from the redrawing of district lines, but more importantly, the new districts largely protected incumbents of both parties, producing very few competitive races. Still, many observers felt the GOP would lose a few seats. Instead, the Republicans gained seats, winning at least 229 (up from 223).

As a result, Richard Gephardt chose not to run for reelection as Democratic Majority Leader in the House of Representatives. This departure is reminiscent of Newt Gingrich's resignation after the 1998 election, when the Democrats picked up five seats. The 1998 and 2002 results suggest that perhaps the historical pattern of congressional losses by the party holding the White House is coming to an end.

The Democrats did make important gains in the 2002 gubernatorial races, taking nine open state houses from the Republicans. These victories included the industrial states of Illinois, Michigan, Pennsylvania, and Wisconsin, plus Republican strongholds Arizona, Tennessee, Wyoming, and Oklahoma. They also won New Mexico and Maine, where an independent governor was retiring, and retained California, despite the unpopularity of Governor Gray Davis. These victories may lay the groundwork for a successful presidential campaign in the future.

However, the Republicans also did well in the 2002 gubernatorial races, taking eight state houses from the Democrats, including Democratic strongholds Maryland, Vermont, Hawaii, and Georgia, and winning New Hampshire, South Carolina, Alabama, and Alaska. The Republicans also won Minnesota, where Governor Jesse "the Body" Ventura was retiring, and Jeb Bush, the president's brother, was reelected as governor of Florida despite intense Democratic efforts to defeat him. All of these changes left the Republicans with a slim advantage over the Democrats in governorships (26 to 24). These results point to the even division of the nation, and suggest that two-party competition has spread to all regions and nearly every state.

One of the brightest spots for the Republicans was the unexpected and sweeping victory in Georgia. Winning the governorship was especially important, since Georgia was the last of the Southern states to elect a Republican governor in the modern era. Republicans won the Senate seat, three open House seats (despite a pro-Democratic redistricting plan), and did very well in state legislative races. The Georgia results reveal the continuing Republican realignment in Dixie (Halbfinger and Yardley 2002). However, the Democratic victories in key Southern races, such as in Louisiana on December 7, show that they can still win close races.

In addition, the GOP made dramatic gains in state legislative seats (Lee 2002). Indeed, the Republican pick-up of 177 seats represents the first gain in state legislative seats during a midterm election by a president's party since 1938, and will give the Republicans a slight majority of all state legislators for the first time since 1952. These gains plus a postelection shift to the GOP by three Georgia state senators, gave the Republicans control of the state legislatures in 21 states and the Democrats control in 16, with twelve states divided. Here, too, the 2002 election produced an even division between the parties and reveals the spread of two-party competition. This pattern is especially evident in the combined control of governorships and state legislatures: The Republicans have unified control in just 12 states and the Democrats in 8, with 29 states divided.

All analysts agree that President Bush was the big winner in the 2002 election. He put the prestige of his office on the line by campaigning for Republican candidates in close races. This effort ended with a seventeen-stop, fifteen-state campaign tour in the last five days of the campaign. In a fashion advocated by political scientists—but frowned upon by campaign consultants—the president asked voters to elect Republican candidates to help him fashion policy in Washington D.C. These efforts, in tandem with Bush's 63 percent approval rating, helped generate a surge of undecided voters for the Republican cause, especially in states he carried in the 2000 election. One analysis calculated that where Bush campaigned, the GOP won 21 of 23 House seats, 12 of 16 Senate seats, and 11 of 22 gubernatorial contests (Milbank and Allen 2002). Bush was the first president since FDR in 1934 to win seats in both the House and Senate in a midterm election.

Bush's last-minute barnstorming was part of a broader strategy that included recruiting candidates and raising money. Indeed, Bush raised a total $141 million for the 2002 races. As a consequence, GOP party committees were able to outspend the Democrats five to three to assist their candidates. In addition, the party implemented a "72-hour Task Force" to increase turnout in key races. Nationally, turnout was 39 percent, up from 1998, and appeared to have been high among Republican constituencies and low among Democratic constituencies, such as African Americans. In this regard, the results of the December 7 run-off in Louisiana reveal the limits of the Republican efforts: Bush's campaigning made the run-off election very close, but did not secure a victory.

Aside from support for Bush, the policy content of the election was far from clear. Polls revealed that the economy was the most important concern of voters, but here the Democrats enjoyed only a small advantage. It may be that the one-year anniversary of 9/11 and the debate over a potential war with Iraq kept the public from focusing on economic questions, to the advantage of Bush and the GOP. It is also possible that the Democrats did a poor job in presenting an alternative platform to that of the president. Interestingly, foreign policy issues were not especially salient to the public, although they may have helped Republicans at the margins. Democrats enjoyed their usual advantage among the small number of voters who were concerned with social welfare and the environment.

In this context, minor parties experienced mixed success. On a positive note, minor parties posted the best electoral performance since 1934 (*Ballot Access News* 2002). The Green and Libertarian parties were successful at the local level (now holding a total of 171 and 538 offices, respectively). Minor party and independent candidates continued to be common and probably determined the outcomes in close races (the Oklahoma governorship is a good example). But on a negative note, Independence Party nominee Tim Penny was unable to succeed Jesse Ventura in Minnesota, and in New York, the Liberal, Green, and Right to Life parties lost ballot status in that state's unique fusion-party system.

The State of the Parties, 2000–2002

The essays that follow investigate the state of the parties in this volatile era within six categories: the party system, party finances, party services, party in government, party responsibility, and minor parties.

The Party System. The first section of the book considers the state of the broader party system, beginning with A. James Reichley's overview of the 2000 and 2002 elections (chapter 2). Reichley places these events in the context of partisan eras, defined by sixty- to seventy-year "supercycles," instead of the more common thirty-year generational cycles. From this perspective, the recent campaigns and the political instability of the 1990s can be understood as a transition from one party era to another. However, the equipoise between the major political parties obscures the details of the new era. Reichley notes that both the Republicans and Democrats bring special strengths to the struggle to secure a majority coalition. Initially, September 11 benefited George W. Bush and the Republicans, and Reichley sees the economy as a case of the "dog that didn't bark" in the 2002 elections, giving the GOP an initial advantage in resolving the partisan division. However, it is unclear whether this advantage will persist in the long term. Overall, Reichley finds the "much abused" two-party system to be exhibiting "signs of renewed vitality."

Paul Beck reviews the state of party coalitions in the electorate over the last forty years (chapter 3). He finds the 2000 elections and preceding decade to be a "tale of two electorates," one highly partisan and evenly divided between the Democrats and Republicans, and one nonpartisan and highly volatile. The two electorates arose from a slow decay of public support for the Democrats without comparable gains in support for the Republicans. This situation presents the major party organizations with a difficult challenge: Appealing to their strong constituencies in the first electorate tends to alienate potential supporters in the second electorate. The 2000 campaign represents the culmination of these trends, with sharp partisan divisions occurring alongside relatively low turnout. Many of these trends appeared to continue in 2002. Like Reichley, Beck inventories the ways in which each party might triumph over the other, noting that the size of the second electorate will render long-lasting success difficult.

John Jackson, Nathan Bigelow, and John Green look at the state of party elites using surveys of national party convention delegates from 1992 to

2000 (chapter 4). They find an interesting pattern of attitudes: clear and polarized issue positions *between* the major parties, and the dominance of centrist factions *within* the parties. These often stark differences reflect the attitudes of Beck's highly partisan electorate, and help explain the near-even results of the 2000 election. At the same time, however, party elites had worked out the tensions of the 1990s so that centrist factions dominated the conventions in 2000: the "New Democrats" of Clinton and Gore, and the GOP "moderates" of George W. Bush. Like Reichley, the authors note that either centrist faction could produce victory—or defeat. The 2002 election will surely renew the internal debate among Democratic factions, while offering the Republicans a chance for consolidation.

David Ryden considers the state of party law with his review of relevant U.S. Supreme Court cases (chapter 5). Without a doubt, the most controversial of these cases was *Bush v. Gore,* the decision that resolved the 2000 election and allowed George W. Bush to occupy the White House. Ryden notes that this ruling may produce unintended consequences for the party system, including benefits for the Democrats. A case with more immediate impact on party organizations was *California Democratic Party v. Jones,* where the Court upheld the "association rights" of parties against state regulation. Yet another important set of cases concerned campaign finance reform, an area of considerable interest as the Supreme Court considers challenges to the constitutionality of the BCRA. All of these cases have important implications for the issues raised in the previous three chapters and those in the next section of the book. Ryden concludes these cases have further "constitutionalized" the electoral process. Despite predictions to the contrary, the 2002 elections have not produced a raft of postelection litigation thus far.

Party Finances. The major parties played an extraordinary role in financing the close 2000 election, including the national, congressional, and state party committees. The 2002 campaign represented a continuation of these patterns. Party soft money was critical to this expanded role. The chapters in this section document the state of party finance, setting a useful baseline against which to judge the future impact of the Bipartisan Campaign Reform Act, which took effect the day after the 2002 election, and is facing a court challenge.

Anthony Corrado, Sarah Barclay, and Heitor Gouvêa describe the state of party finance in the 2000 presidential campaigns (chapter 6). They find that the Democratic and Republican national committees spent a minimum of $80 million in broadcast advertising on behalf of their presidential tickets, and if other less well-documented expenditures were included, the total could easily have surpassed $100 million. Much of this expenditure was soft money that allowed for the largest *party* contribution to the presidential campaign in recent memory. Indeed, in 2000 the only effective limits on party spending were "how much they were willing to spend to capture the Oval Office." The authors conclude that if upheld by the courts, the soft money restrictions in BCRA will cause the national parties to alter the ways they spend money in presidential campaigns.

Robin Kolodny and Diana Dwyre continue the theme of party adaptation in their description of the state of party finance in congressional elections (chapter 7). They note that the congressional parties shifted their patterns of expenditures to maximize the impact on the elections. In 2000, this "committee shuffle" produced dramatic transfers of soft and hard money to state parties, where the appropriate mix of funds paid for extensive "issue advocacy" television ads in key races, and equally dramatic declines in other forms of campaign spending. This highly centralized effort may well change if the courts uphold BCRA. Kolodny and Dwyre suggest that the congressional parties may once again alter their spending patterns in pursuit of congressional majorities.

Ray La Raja investigates the impact of soft money on the organizational strength of state parties (chapter 8). He finds that, contrary to conventional wisdom, soft money was also used to build state party organizations, and that the state parties were not just conduits for soft money spending on behalf of candidates. Soft money not only allowed parties to expand their technical infrastructure, but to recruit and train candidates and provide them with sophisticated campaign assistance. La Raja concludes that if BCRA significantly reduces the flow of money, it may harm state party organizations. As part of his research effort, La Raja produces an updated measure of state party strength, which is presented in an appendix.

Sarah Morehouse and Malcolm Jewell sound a similar theme when they focus on the state of party finances in the states, concluding that they are "independent partners" in the money relationship with the national parties (chapter 9). Indeed, they find that the state parties they studied raised approximately three-quarters of all of the funds spent within their borders. Here, too, the findings contradict conventional wisdom: Viewed from the vantage point of the states, the major parties are not in decline, but are vital and autonomous organizations. Morehouse and Jewell conclude that the provisions of BCRA may well strengthen the partnership between the national and state parties.

Party Services in the States. Much of the money raised and spent by party organizations in 2000 and 2002 was directed toward sophisticated services. The chapters in the next section investigate the activities of state and local parties.

Peter Francia, Paul Herrnson, John Frendreis, and Alan Gitelson investigate the state of party campaigning in state legislative elections, using surveys of candidates (chapter 10). Reinforcing the conclusions of the previous chapters, the authors find that the "battle for the statehouse" has been "congressionalized." As in congressional campaigns, parties provide a wide range of services to their legislative candidates, including technical assistance and voter mobilization. The authors conclude that both kinds of party services have a positive impact at the polls. The Republican gains in the 2002 state legislative races point to the importance of these activities.

Rick Farmer and Rich Fender turn to a new kind of activity, the state of party web sites (chapter 11). They note that the Internet is the communication medium of the future, and for parties to stay relevant, they must learn to use it. In 2000, state parties were "casting a weak net" by failing to take advantage of these opportunities. The parties did a better job at providing substantive content than they did in exploiting the technical capabilities of the Internet. In this regard, the state party web sites are behind competing organizations, such as the news media. Larger state parties are on the leading edge in web site development, but even there, much more innovation is needed to fully enter the cyber age.

Melanie Blumberg, William Binning, and John Green present a case study of the state of local party activity in the 2000 campaign (chapter 12). The authors observe that Al Gore's narrow loss of Ohio was among the many reasons for the near tie in the Electoral College, and one of the reasons for this defeat was the weakness of local party organizations. The case in point was Mahoning County, a Democratic stronghold, where a strong and well-led local party helped Clinton and Gore win big in 1996. But a combination of local organizational problems, weak leadership, and a poorly executed Coordinated Campaign led to a turnout lower than expected. This disappointing performance reveals how the "grassroots matter" even in modern, media-driven campaigns. The Mahoning Valley was once again in the spotlight in 2002 when James Traficant ran for Congress from a federal prison cell. Although he received some 27,000 votes, the Democratic nominee, twenty-nine-year-old Tim Ryan, won the race with the help of traditional grassroots campaigning.

David A. Dulio and James A. Thurber investigate what is commonly assumed to be a serious problem: the tensions between campaign consultants and parties (chapter 13). Using surveys of consultants and state party leaders, the authors find that these actors have a symbiotic relationship with one another. Indeed, both consultants and party leaders recognize a practical division of labor in modern campaigns, with consultants providing the technical expertise and party leaders providing services that require extensive staff. So, for example, consultants dominate media and message development, while parties provide voter registration and get-out-the-vote efforts. The authors conclude that consultants and parties are "partners past, present, and future." In many respects, the 2000 and 2002 campaigns were examples of this partnership.

Party in Government. The 2000 and 2002 elections produced a near tie in the U.S. Congress as well as the presidential race. The next set of chapters reviews the state of the parties in Congress. Jeffrey Stonecash considers the most direct political result: the struggle to gain ascendancy in the House of Representatives (chapter 14). Echoing the points made by Reichley and Beck, the author catalogues the dilemmas facing each party. The Republicans believe the country has shifted to the right on government activism and cultural issues, and that this shift will expand their slim margins in the House. In contrast, the Democrats believe that growing economic inequality plus increasing ethnic and racial diversity will allow them to win back the House. But if either party guesses wrong, then the efforts to mobilize their own base will, in effect, aid the other party's quest for power. The first round in this competition, the 2002 campaign, went to the GOP by a slight margin, but the long-term dilemmas remain unresolved.

Larry Schwab investigates the "unprecedented Senate": the first time ever that an election produced an exactly even division between the parties (chapter 15). Initially, the tie-breaking vote of Vice President Cheney gave the Republicans control, but then the defection of Senator Jeffords put the Democrats in charge. Contrary to the expectations of many observers, neither moderate nor bipartisan coalitions dominated the operation of the Senate. The principal reason was that the ideological makeup of the body changed little despite the changes in partisanship. From this vantage point, the Republican capture of the Senate in 2002 may make little difference in the behavior of the Senate. The author notes, however, that the rules adopted during the 50-50 division may have set a precedent by ceding power to the minority party.

Lawrence Butler reviews the situation in the House of Representatives, which, although closely divided, remained in Republican hands after 2000 (chapter 16). Using a novel concept of party government, "single party legislating," and a new measure of roll-call voting in the House, the "Majority Party Strength Index," the author reviews the claim that the congressional parties have become more cohesive in recent times. This analysis finds a strong trend toward party government up through 1996, but thereafter a sharp drop occurs. This drop coincides with the fall of Republican Speaker Newt Gingrich and the term of Speaker Dennis Hastert. It is possible, then, that the trend toward party government has abated and a new era of weak congressional parties has begun. It will be interesting to see if the Republican congressional gains after 2002 affect this trend. The author's approach to studying roll-call voting adds a new perspective to the debate over party government.

Party Responsibility. The year 2000 marked the fiftieth anniversary of the publication of "Toward a More Responsible Two-Party System," the report of the Committee on Political Parties of the American Political Science Association (1950), which greatly influenced party scholarship. The chapters in this section consider the state of party responsibility. (For a fuller discussion of the report, see Green and Herrnson 2002.)

Gerald Pomper offers a provocative argument that the United States is moving toward a parliamentary form of government, a trend reinforced by the 2000 election (chapter 17). The chief cause of this development was an increase in party responsibility, including meaningful party programs backed by party elites, officeholders, and strong organizations. Greater responsibility allows the parties to overcome the separation of powers and produce something resembling the party government in a parliamentary system. Pomper concludes: "Perhaps this new form of American government is both inevitable and necessary," echoing some of the issues raised by Reichley. The united Republican control of government after the 2002 election will provide a useful test of Pomper's thesis.

Daniel Shea offers a different perspective on the state of party responsibility (chapter 18). He notes two trends in party development, which continued in the 2000 election: organizational revitalization and voter withdrawal. Shea notes the substantial growth of the resources of party organizations, as reported in the chapters on party finances and services. He also documents the decline in citizen attachment and participation in the political process, reflecting the evidence presented by Beck and Stonecash. However, the most common formulations of party responsibility argue that strong organizations should be associated with strong citizen engagement, and not the other way around. In a provocative argument, Shea suggests that organizational revitalization may be at least partially responsible for citizen disengagement. Some aspects of the 2002 campaign, such as Bush's campaign on behalf of Republican candidates, appear to represent a departure from Shea's thesis. However, the continued low levels of citizen engagement tend to support his argument.

John Coleman offers a new perspective on the state of party responsibility (chapter 19). The debate over the character of American political parties has tended to equate responsibility with functionality, with critics arguing that the lack of party responsibility produced poor government, while defenders argue that "irresponsible" parties produced government that worked. Coleman argues that responsibility and functionality are better thought of as separate dimensions of party, rather than end points of a single dimension. This insight suggests a fourfold classification of American party eras in terms of the relative degree of responsibility and functionality. Coleman concludes that contemporary parties exhibit a higher degree of both characteristics than in the immediate past. The 2002 elections may represent a continuation of this tendency.

Minor Parties. The last set of chapters is concerned with the state of minor parties in 2000. John Berg offers an analysis of the Green Party, whose presidential candidate, Ralph Nader, may well have made a difference in the close election (chapter 20). Indeed, Berg asks if Nader was a "spoiler or a builder." Although there is some evidence for both effects, Berg concludes that on the whole, the Nader campaign helped build the Green Party. While it is unlikely that the Greens will elect a president, they may well help transform the debate in American politics, with the potential for eventual changes in public policy. The performance of the Greens in the 2002 election supports this argument. In this sense, Nader and the Greens are following a well-trodden path of minor parties in the two-party system.

Ronald Rapoport and Walter Stone report this kind of minor party impact in their analyses of Ross Perot and the Reform Party, which influenced presidential elections in the 1990s but declined precipitously under Pat Buchanan in 2000 (chapter 21). The authors argue that this insurgency had a dramatic effect on political debate, and particularly on the Republican Party. Indeed, they show that much of the Reform Party activist corps was absorbed into the GOP by the 2000 campaign. Overall, the chapter demonstrates the dynamics of minor parties in the two-party system. The experience of the remnants of the Reform Party, the Independence Party, in the 2002 Minnesota gubernatorial campaign is a further example of this dynamic.

Theodore Lowi calls for a "deregulation" of American democracy by reducing the legal supports that, in his view, maintain the two-party "monopoly" (chapter 22). Here he offers the latest version of his famous argument for a "responsible three-party system" in America. For Lowi, a genuine third party will contribute to both the responsibility and functionality of American politics. Achieving this goal requires a full-scale assault on the laws governing ballot access, single-member districts, and voting systems. If democracy were deregulated in this fashion, the fluctuation of citizen concerns and government performance would create and alter parties to fit the contemporary circumstances. Needless to say, Lowi disagrees with Reichley's assessment about the renewed vitality of the two-party system.

Unanswered Questions

The evidence presented here suggests that the state of the parties is in flux, as one might expect in a period of volatile politics. The even division of the 2000 and 2002 elections is evidence of this pattern in its own right, but behind this equipoise are several important trends. Party organizations are strong, party elites are ideologically distinct, and party elected officials are, on the whole, programmatic. In contrast, many citizens are alienated from the political process, parties are often ineffective in mobilizing them, party government is hardly complete, and potential challenges to the party system are numerous.

These conclusions prompt three sets of questions central to any full diagnosis of the state of the parties and prescriptions for improvement:

- Will the parties be able to maintain their organizational prowess in the near future, especially their financial resources? Will the Bipartisan Campaign Reform Act of 2002 pass constitutional muster? If so, how will a ban on soft money affect the national parties and the relationship between the national and state organizations? Will the parties adapt to new communications technologies, and will they find ways to effectively reengage the public in the political process?
- Will the recent policy coherence of the major parties continue in the future or will it decline as the parties return to "politics as usual"? Will party responsibility become the norm, moving American government toward a parliamentary form of government? Or will the limits of party responsibility spawn continued minor party revolts, perhaps culminating in the deregulation of American democracy?
- Will the even division between the major parties be broken, and which party will prevail? Will the impetus of September 11 give George Bush and the GOP an edge for the foreseeable future? Or will domestic troubles and the increasing diversity of the nation eventually push the Democrats to the fore? What will the next party era look like and will it put an end to this volatile era?

Notes

1. Republican prospects in other states failed to materialize. Senator Max Baucus (D-MT) was thought to be too liberal for his state, but his Republican opponent withdrew after claiming that campaign advertising implied he was gay. Senator Tom Harkin (D-IA) surmounted accusations that he was too liberal as well as an ethics flap to win handily. The ethical troubles of New Jersey Democratic Senator Bob Torrecelli offered the GOP a good opportunity to pick up a seat. However, Torrecelli withdrew and the Democrats were able to replace him with former Senator Frank Lautenberg. This move was controversial because it appeared to violate the letter of New Jersey election law—which was set aside by the New Jersey State Supreme Court, one of the most liberal in the nation. The Republicans appealed to the U.S. Supreme Court, which refused to get involved, thus averting yet another controversial decision involving elections. Lautenberg won the fall contest handily.

2. Another potential ballot dispute occurred in Minnesota's general election, where absentee ballots cast for the late Senator Wellstone were disallowed.

Part One

The Party System

2

The Future of the American Two-Party System at the Beginning of a New Century

A. James Reichley

The new century has brought signs of renewed vitality in that much-abused and frequently written-off institution, the American two-party system. Many thoughtful scholars, while acknowledging the indispensable value of parties to politics and government, continue to find the two major parties severely weakened players in national politics. But others detect evidence of sustained effectiveness and relevance—even resurgence.

In the 2000 presidential election, party identifiers voted for their party's candidate "more than in any election since modern polling has been measuring the electorate"—91 percent of Republicans for George W. Bush and 86 percent of Democrats for Al Gore (Ceaser and Busch 2001, 166). While the share of avowed party identifiers remains only about 60 percent of the total electorate, adding voters who acknowledge "leaning" toward one party or the other brings this figure to almost 90 percent (Weisberg and Hill 2001). Party remains by far the best predictor of voter choice. Ticket splitting in voting for president and Congress has sharply declined. In 2000, more than 80 percent of voters for Bush or Gore cast straight-party ballots for president and the U.S. House (Hetherington 2001).

Party unity on roll-call votes in both the Senate and House rose steadily during the last two decades and now hovers around 90 percent—almost 50 percent higher than in the early 1970s. About two-thirds of voters "perceive important differences between the parties"—up from 46 percent in 1972. Voters are better able to identify the major parties with distinctive ideological directions (Hetherington 2001).

Third parties play significant roles in a few state, congressional, and local elections, but Ross Perot's startling 19 percent of the popular vote in the 1992 presidential election has not been repeated, and third-party voting declined steadily in 1996 and 2000.

None of this, of course, should be interpreted to mean that parties or the party system are out of the woods as effective political institutions. Both major parties remain substantially less popular with the voters than they were in the 1960s. Self-identified independents in 2000 reached just over 40 percent of the electorate—an all-time high (Weisberg and Hill 2001). The recently enacted campaign finance reform, if declared constitutional, will weaken the role of national parties and party committees in congressional elections—though parties at the state level may actually become more important (see chapters 6–9). L. Sandy Maisel, while viewing the party as "the vital linking institution" in American government, finds that "the role of parties in elections remains in doubt" (1999, 493). John Kenneth White and Daniel Shea conclude, more pessimistically, that "Americans are beset with a public life that is marked by the failure of parties to reestablish their connection with the voters" (2000, 314).

Nevertheless, signs of party resurgence indicate that the two-party system will continue to be the major arena in which American political life is conducted. "The party decline thesis," Marc Hetherington writes, "is in need of revision" (2001). Probing the current dynamics of the two-party system should therefore provide important clues to the future direction of American politics.

A Durable System

In earlier volumes in this series, I argued that the two-party system—which is unusual in developed democracies—is anchored in the United States by constitutional and statutory provisions governing methods of election (Reichley 1996; 2000). Most democratic polities, even in relatively homogeneous countries such as Sweden and the Netherlands, have tended to divide into three or more major parties. Maurice Duverger pointed out years ago (in his formulation known as Duverger's Law) that polities maintaining single-member, first-past-the-post systems of election, principally the United States and Britain and its dominions, tend to foster the development of two major parties. Systems including two rounds of elections or using some form of proportional representation usually produce a multiplicity of parties (Duverger 1954, 217).

Even polities such as Britain, Canada, and Australia, however, which, like the United States, use the first-past-the-post system, have generally had at least one significant minor party represented in parliament alongside the two major ones. Why have enduring minor parties with substantial impact been so rare in the United States?

The first-past-the-post system pushes us toward a two-party system. But the thing that really has kept this system locked in place has been the institution of the Electoral College for electing presidents.

Quite contrary to the Founders' intention, the Electoral College, as long as most states retain the at-large system for choosing electors (not required by the Constitution), regularly limits the presidential candidates with a real chance of winning to the nominees of the two major parties. Perot's 19 percent of the popular vote in 1992 did not earn him a single vote in the Electoral College. The system even makes it improbable that a minor party could hold the balance of power between the two major parties, as has sometimes occurred in Britain and Canada. Constitutional change to eliminate the Electoral College would entail a political effort that is unlikely to be forthcoming. Even the hotly contested 2000 election, in which Al Gore won the popular vote but lost narrowly in the electoral vote, produced surprisingly little movement to replace the Electoral College.

The high visibility of the presidential contest shapes our entire political system. As long as the Electoral College confines the real presidential competition to the candidates of the two major parties, the United States will probably continue to have a two-party system in most congressional and state elections.

Reinforcing the effects of the Electoral College and first-past-the-post elections, representatives of the two major parties have taken pains to enact election laws that strongly favor major party candidates. Public financing of presidential election campaigns heavily advantages the Republican and Democratic nominees. At the state level, barriers against third-party candidates are even more severe. In Pennsylvania, for example, major party candidates for the state senate need only 2,000 signatures on petitions to get their names on the ballot, whereas minor party candidates require 29,000 (reduced from 56,000 by court order).

A major national calamity or conflict might lead to the creation of a new major party, as the struggle over slavery gave birth to the Republicans in the 1850s. Barring such a catastrophe, it is probable not only that we will continue to have a two-party system, but also that the Republicans and Democrats will be the main competitors. After all, even the Great Depression of the 1930s failed to put enduring cracks in the two-party system, though for a time it spawned some successful third parties at the state level, such as the Farmer-Labor Party in Minnesota and the Progressives in Wisconsin.

Short-Term Cycles

Examination of American political history under the two-party system reveals two series of broad cycles that appear to be inherent. The first is a series of short-term cycles that is relatively simple and emerges clearly from empirical data. The second is a chain of long cycles, which is more complex and much more controversial. Many political scientists and historians doubt that long cycles even exist—or, if they ever did, that they still operate.

The short cycles are generated by a tendency among voters to grow bored or dissatisfied with a party in power, even if no major failures or misdeeds have occurred, after eight to twelve years. The normal result is for the incumbent party to be voted out, often by a large majority, and the former opposition installed.

The "throw the rascals out" cycle operates to some extent even under multiparty systems, but is particularly pronounced in countries with the two-party system, probably because this system inhibits formation of new ruling coalitions of the kind that incumbent parties are sometimes able to put together when a multiplicity of parties are available.

In the United States the normal incumbency span translates into two or three presidential terms. From the 1950s through the 1990s, the Republicans and Democrats regularly alternated in control of the White House, with four two-term spans, one three-term (the Reagan-Bush years), and one that was confined to a single term (Carter).

Going back further, since the present two-party system was formed in the 1850s, the average duration of party control of the White House has been eleven years. The only markedly longer periods of party dominance were the twenty-four-year tenure of the Republicans during and after the Civil War, and the twenty-year period of Democratic supremacy during and after the Depression. Both of these exceptions reflect the effects of the long cycle, which I describe below.

Similar cycles appear to operate for the governorship in states with competitive two-party systems. In the seven most populous states with historically competitive systems, the average period of party control of the governorship from 1950 to 2000 was a little more than eight years. In Pennsylvania, Ohio, and New Jersey, the two parties alternated in control of the governor's office with almost rhythmic regularity. In New York, Illinois, and Michigan, parties tended to hold gubernatorial dominance for somewhat longer periods, but alternation nevertheless occurred. In California, the two parties exchanged control of the governorship every eight years until the Republicans won four consecutive terms in the 1980s and 1990s, giving way to the Democrats under Governor Gray Davis in 1998. Cyclical party turnover now seems to be developing in some of the Southern states where the Democrats used to enjoy one-party dominance, such as Texas, Virginia, and Florida.

The impulse of voters to change party control of government at regular intervals is both understandable and rational. After two or three terms of party control of a nation or state, enough things are likely to have gone wrong to give voters a taste for change. This tendency may sometimes be unjust to the party in power, but it at least keeps incumbent parties on their toes, seeking to come up with policies or solutions that will cause voters to relent and give them "four more years."

From 1954 to 1994, regular shifts in party control did not occur in Congress. Between the Civil War and the Eisenhower administration, control of Congress normally accompanied, or slightly preceded, the presidential cycle. In only four two-year periods did the president's party not control at least one house of Congress (under Hayes, 1879–1880; Cleveland, 1895–1896; Wilson, 1919–1920; and Truman, 1947–1948). From 1954 to 1994, however, the Democrats controlled the House of Representatives without interruption and the Senate for all but six years. As a result, Republican presidents during this forty-year span regularly confronted Congresses controlled by their partisan opposition, producing the famous deadlock that disrupted the policy-making process. After the 1994 election, the shoe was on the other foot, with a Democratic president facing a Republican Congress—creating even more spectacular instances of deadlock. Whether the 1994 turnover will lead to more normal alternation in party control of Congress remains to be seen.

Long Cycles

Beyond the usual two- to three-term alternation in party control of the presidency, the existence of long-term party cycles in American political history becomes less clear. If such cycles exist, however, they are bound to have important effects on both politics and government, and therefore must be included in any overall consideration of the two-party system.

Probably the best known of the theories of long-term political cycles is that of the historian Arthur Schlesinger Jr. (1986, 32–33), carrying on work begun by his father. Schlesinger's theory is more closely related to ideology than to parties, but it also has party manifestations. According to Schlesinger, throughout American history regular alternations between spans of liberalism and conservatism have occurred, each lasting about sixteen years, or four presidential terms. The most recent spans have been the liberal one launched by John Kennedy in 1960, and its conservative successor, which began in the late 1970s. Right on time, Schlesinger claimed after the 1992 election, Bill Clinton initiated a new liberal span.

Like most cyclical theories, Schlesinger's theory seems to work better in retrospect than as a predictive tool—though even in retrospect it requires some rather odd combinations, such as bunching Richard Nixon and Gerald Ford with Kennedy and Lyndon Johnson in a common liberal era that began in 1960. The Republican landslide in the 1994 midterm elections seemed to bring a premature end to the new liberal era under Clinton. Perhaps Clinton's reelection in 1996 might be interpreted as getting the new era partially back on track. But George W. Bush's arrival in the White House in 2001, by however narrow a margin, can hardly be seen as a continuation of liberalism.

Among political scientists, who generally have been more open to cyclical theories than historians, most theories of long cycles are linked to the concept of "realigning elections" introduced by V. O. Key (1955). Realigning elections, Key claimed, have periodically purged American politics and government of accumulated detritus and opened the way for new departures. Key's work has been carried on by, among others, Walter Dean Burnham (1970), Gerald Pomper (1970), Paul Allen Beck (1974), and James Sundquist (1982). In most versions of this theory, realigning elections, ending the dominance of one political party, and ushering in normal party control by another, have occurred every twenty-eight to thirty-six years. The root of these cycles appears to be social upheaval coupled with generational change.

There is some dispute over which were the actual realigning elections, but general agreement places realignments at or just before the elections of Thomas Jefferson in 1800, Andrew Jackson in 1828, Abraham Lincoln in 1860, William McKinley in 1896, and Franklin Roosevelt in 1932. (Some scholars drop the elections of Jefferson and Jackson on the ground that the party system did not achieve full development until the 1830s.)

A puzzle for believers in the theory of realigning elections is the apparent failure of one to occur on schedule in the 1960s. Burnham argues that a realignment *did* occur with the election of Nixon as president in 1968 and the creation of a new Republican majority in presidential politics. Certainly the shift of the South away from the Democrats at the presidential level after 1968 was a major change in national politics. But if this was a realignment, why did it not produce a change in control of Congress or in most of the major states, as previous realignments had done?

The theory of long-term cycles that I have proposed in earlier volumes deals with this problem—and some of those that rise from Schlesinger's rival formulation—by proposing that long cycles in their fullness have actually covered not sixteen years (Schlesinger), or twenty-eight to thirty-six years (the political scientists), but *sixty to seventy years* (Reichley 2000). Truly realigning elections, in my view, have occurred only three times in American history: 1800 (Jefferson), 1860 (Lincoln), and 1932 (FDR). (2002 may turn out in retrospect to have been a realigning election, as discussed below, but that of course remains to be seen.)

The elections of Jackson in 1828 and McKinley in 1896, coupled with their subsequent administrations, were important political events. But they were in fact restorations and climaxes of eras that had begun approximately thirty years before, rather than true realignments or, in the broader sense, new political departures.

Jackson won in 1828 after a period of about ten years in which national politics had been in flux and the old hegemony of Jefferson's party appeared shaken. But Jackson was clearly in the line of Jefferson and was so recognized at the time. Martin Van Buren, one of Jackson's principal lieutenants and his successor as president, wrote: "The two great parties of this country, with occasional changes in name only, have, for the principal part of a century, occupied antagonistic positions upon all important political questions. They have maintained an unbroken succession" (Van Buren 1967, 2). Jackson carried every state Jefferson carried in 1800 and lost every state Jefferson lost. Jefferson's narrow victory over John Adams in 1800 was converted into Jackson's landslide triumph over John Quincy Adams in 1828 by the addition of new Western states in which the Democrats were strong. So the 1828 election and Jackson's subsequent triumph over forces in Congress led by Henry Clay *restored* the dominance of the (renamed) Democrats instead of bringing in a new majority party.

Similarly, McKinley's victory in 1896 followed a period during which Republicans and Democrats had taken turns controlling the federal government, or dividing control, and in which there had been no clear majority party. The 1896 election represented a rallying of the forces, temporarily in eclipse, that had made the Republicans the clear majority party from 1860 to 1876. McKinley won through renewal of the coalition of Northeastern and Midwestern states on which the Republican Party had been founded. William Jennings Bryan, his Democratic opponent, swept the South, the Democrats' principal stronghold since the end of Reconstruction. Bryan also tapped the farmers' revolt and the silver issue in the West to win some of the Western states, normally Republican, that had been admitted to the Union since the Civil War. But within a few years most of these were back in the Republican column where they remained until the Great Depression of the 1930s. The 1896 election, therefore, did not displace the former majority party but renewed and strengthened the party that had become dominant after the last major realignment.

The mystery of why no true realignment occurred in the 1960s is thus explained: it was not due. What actually happened in the 1960s was the renewal and climax of the cycle dominated by liberalism and the Democratic Party that began in the 1930s. In 1964, Lyndon Johnson decisively defeated Barry Goldwater, representing a radical version of the laissez-faire economic doctrine that had prevailed during the preceding cycle. The movement of the South away from the Democrats at the end of the 1960s was an early sign of the breakup of the New Deal cycle—similar to the move of the Northeast away from the Democrats in the 1840s, and the swing of major Northern cities away from the Republicans in the era of Woodrow Wilson.

Briefly summarized, each of the sixty- to seventy-year cycles moved through roughly similar phases: (1) a breakthrough election in which the new majority gained power under a charismatic leader (Jefferson, Lincoln, FDR), followed by an extended period during which the majority changed the direction of national life and enacted much of its program; (2) a period of pause during which the new majority lost some of its dynamism, and forces that dominated the preceding cycle staged a minor comeback (John Quincy Adams, Cleveland, Eisenhower); (3) a climactic victory by the majority party over a more radical expression of the ideology of the preceding cycle (Jackson over Clay, McKinley over Bryan, Johnson over Goldwater), followed by enactment of remaining items in the majority party's program; and, finally, (4) the gradual decline and ultimate collapse of the majority party, opening the way for a new realignment and a new majority.

The phases of the sixty- to seventy-year cycles correspond roughly to some of Schlesinger's sixteen-year spans. The long-cycle theory, however, explains why the Jeffersonians after 1800, the Republicans after 1860, and the Democrats after 1932 held onto power for longer than Schlesinger's theory would predict. These were all periods covered by the initial phase of the long cycle, during which the majority is fresh and holds the support of the public through an extended series of elections. The separate cycles posited in the twenty-eight- to thirty-six-year theory correspond neatly to the rise and decline segments of the long cycle.

Political cycles are probably rooted, at least partly, in generational change. Schlesinger argues that his sixteen-year spans reflect the succession of political generations. Members of the political generation of John Kennedy, for example, were putting into effect values and attitudes acquired during their youth in the liberal environment of the 1930s. The Reaganites of the 1980s were applying views they had developed during the relatively conservative 1950s (though many of the Reaganites regarded themselves as revolting *against* Eisenhower's moderate Republicanism). Members of the generation of the 1990s, in this theory, should have been eager to reintroduce the liberal values with which Kennedy inspired them during their college years in the 1960s (Schlesinger 1986, 33–34).

Schlesinger's analysis, like his larger cyclical theory, captures part of the truth. Genuinely major changes in political direction, however, seem to occur *only after persons whose political values and party loyalties were formed by the last major realignment, including many who were in childhood at the time, have largely passed from the political scene.* So long as generations whose party ties were shaped by the Civil War remained politically active, even voting in substantial numbers, the normal Republican majority in national elections was hard to shake. Similarly, party loyalties formed by the Depression and the New Deal have been exceptionally durable. In the 1990s, the generation whose attitudes were most deeply marked by the New Deal era, roughly those born from 1905 to 1930, included a sharply declining share of the total electorate—already less than 15 percent in 1996. This, I think, is a major reason for the presence of a large segment of voters who have felt no particular loyalty to either of the major parties whose images and agendas were formed in earlier times.

The last two major realignments, in the 1860s and 1930s, came at times of massive traumas within the larger social system—the Civil War and the Great Depression. The first realignment, in the 1800s, coincided with huge territorial growth and population migration. Probably a major realignment requires *both* an electorate in which the ties of many to the existing party system have grown weak *and* extraordinary social upheaval. We certainly now have the former. Deep and prolonged economic troubles could provide the political shock setting off realignment, as they did in the 1930s. But the causes of social upheaval need not be primarily economic—those of the 1800s and 1860s were not. Possibly responses to threats to national security or an ecological crisis may form the basis for a new realignment. Or continuation of current trends toward moral and social disorder and decay could bring it on. Or there could be a combination of factors—the Republican realignment of the 1860s responded to emergence of a new industrial economy and homestead settlement of the West, as well as abolition of slavery and the Civil War. The point is that the political system is now open, as it was not in the 1960s when the hold of the New Deal alignment remained strong, to transformation by a new political shock.

The End of Realignment?

In earlier volumes of this book published in the 1990s I argued that, since we are now more than sixty years beyond the last major realignment (under my version of the long-cycle theory), conditions exist within the electorate that make a new realigning election possible. I also predicted that, while both major parties had qualities that might equip them to become the new majority party, the Republicans on the whole had the best chance to profit from realignment.

Instead, the 2000 election brought a polity almost perfectly balanced between the two parties, with the Republicans regaining the presidency by award of Florida's disputed electoral votes through a one-vote majority on the Supreme Court, a narrow Republican majority in the House, and an evenly divided Senate (later broken by defection of Republican Senator Jim Jeffords of Vermont to independent status and voting with the Democrats)—the *Perfect Tie* in James Ceaser and Andrew Busch's account of the election (2001). Is it now time to consider whether major realignments have become a thing of the past, as was forcefully argued in the 1990s by proponents of the dealignment thesis (Shafer 1991; Ladd 1991)?

Perhaps. Let it first be said, however, before exploring the deeper wellsprings of current politics, that there is little reason to believe that the present, almost exact division between the parties shown by the 2000 election is likely to last. Recent politics have been, if nothing else, volatile—and volatility does not favor continuation of even balance more than any other disposition of forces.

Some analysts, while conceding this point, maintain that durable realignment, making one major party or the other the normal majority party, is now unlikely (Stanley and Niemi 2001). Both major parties, they point out, have for more than two decades fallen far short of winning committed support from a majority of voters (Weisberg and Hill 2001). The probable outlook, in this view, is that the major parties, or candidates elected under their labels, will take turns holding the White House for a term or two, with the opposition party often winning midterm elections. Independents will have a real chance of breaking through the major party monopoly to win the chief executive office, as Perot briefly seemed to have a chance at doing in the summer of 1992, and as occurred in the gubernatorial contest in Minnesota in 1998. In other words, the short-term cycle, under which party control of the executive branch frequently changes and divided government is common, will be the prevailing pattern of American politics for the foreseeable future.

This prospect is possible—even likely—lacking any transforming shock to the political system. The apparent instability of the current system, however, conceals forces that may under some circumstances produce a period of relative consistency in political direction. Unlike the indifference toward parties that characterized the 1970s, about two-thirds of voters, including many who do not avow a party identification, now see "important differences between the parties" (Hetherington 2001). Both major parties have been making gains within constituent groups among which they were formerly weak. In 2000, these gains about evenly balanced out, producing electoral standoff. There is no reason to believe, however, that such balance in the effects of competing trends will continue. Conditions, therefore, still exist under which a new realigning election is possible—and if anything, they have ripened.

Democratic Assets

Which party would gain normal majority status through realignment has seemed uncertain. Several factors, however, had improved the outlook for the Democrats—at least before the catastrophic events of September 11, 2001.

For one thing, the Republicans had not followed through on what appeared their best opportunity to achieve durable realignment. Growing public discontent with the Democrats was unleashed in the midterm election of 1994. The Republicans in that year carried everything before them, not only winning majorities in both houses of Congress for the first time in forty-two years, but also sweeping the governorships of most major states, often by huge majorities, and substantially increasing their strengths in state legislatures and local governments. As Ceaser and Busch (1997) convincingly argued in their account of the 1996 election, if the Republicans had not won the midterm election in 1994, Bill Clinton almost surely would have been defeated for reelection in 1996. As matters turned out, however, voters by 1996 had seen enough of Republicans in power at the national level to give Clinton a second term.

George W. Bush's victory in 2000 seemed less an affirmation than an expression of moral disapproval of Clinton and reaction against Gore's inept campaign—neither of which brought Bush a majority of the popular vote or clear title to Florida's crucial electoral votes. The protracted postelection struggle in Florida, and the disputed settlement of the election by the Supreme Court, hardened partisan loyalties on both sides, making it difficult for Bush to establish a firm base among a majority of the national public during the early months of his presidency.

The Democrats in the 1990s consolidated their remaining bases and made gains among some groups with whom they formerly had been weak. African Americans, Jews, Hispanics, labor union members and their families, and unmarried women continued to give overwhelming majorities to Democratic candidates, including Gore in 2000. Asian Americans, who in the 1980s had been predominantly Republican, and even in the 1996 election gave a small majority to Bob Dole over Clinton, swung heavily to Gore in 2000. Democrats remained competitive in many of their old Southern strongholds, holding solid support among blacks and winning enough white votes to elect personable and well-financed candidates like Senator John Edwards in North Carolina and Governor Mark Warner in Virginia. The rapidly growing body of self-identified seculars—15 percent of the electorate by 2000—heavily supported Democrats, giving Gore 65 percent of their vote.

Democrats had gained strength among more affluent voters and those with advanced education, particularly among graduates of elite private institutions. Among the small minority who tell pollsters they are "upper class," 56 percent voted for Gore to 39 percent for Bush. Even among the much larger upper-middle class, which remained predominantly Republican, a substantial minority, particularly among suburban women, the famous "soccer moms," had trended Democratic. Many such voters hold liberal views on such issues as abortion, gun control, and the environment. As the Democrats under Clinton moved toward the center on economic issues, and fear of crime declined, traditional Republicanism began to lose some of its attraction.

Partly because of these shifts, Gore in 2000 was able to carry heavily populated suburban counties around New York, Philadelphia, Cleveland, and Detroit, and suburban communities in Cook County, Illinois, outside Chicago—all bulwarks of Republican support during most of the twentieth century. In Pennsylvania and Michigan, Gore's unusual suburban strength was sufficient to win those states' crucial electoral votes—sending the 2000 election into overtime.

Perhaps most promising of all for Democratic political fortunes, the American economy, after almost two decades of record growth (briefly interrupted at the beginning of the 1990s), in the spring of 2001 fell into recession. Economic downturns, particularly if prolonged, almost always have helped the party out of power in the White House. They helped the Democrats in 1992, 1982, and 1958, and the Republicans in 1980. And of course the last major realignment was caused by the Depression of the 1930s. The effects of deep or continuing recession under a Republican administration on a public used to economic good times could restore the Democrats as the normal majority party in national politics for at least a generation.

Democratic leaders in the summer of 2001 believed they had Bush and the Republicans in a trap. Polls showed that substantial majorities among the voters supported Democratic proposals on health care, the environment, energy, and education. Disappearance of projected federal budget surpluses, caused at least in the near term by the oncoming recession, could be blamed on the large tax cut that Bush had pushed through Congress. Bush could not fund the domestic priorities favored by the public without violating the mythical "lockbox" constructed by both Democrats and Republicans, which, defying economic logic, prohibited use of the Social Security surplus even in time of recession. Thus, from this perspective, voters were bound to turn toward the Democrats.

Citing these and other factors, John B. Judis and Ruy Teixeira argue in their book *The Emerging Democratic Majority* (2002) that a prolonged period of dominance by the Democrats, given effective leadership and concentration on popular issues, is virtually certain. The Judis-Teixeira thesis rests on several predictions, including: continued weakening of traditional religion; maintenance of overwhelming Democratic majorities among African Americans, Hispanics, and Jews; permanent alignment of a large majority of women with the Democrats; some restoration of Democratic strength in the South, particularly Florida and Virginia; and conversion of independent or ticket-splitting suburban professionals to firm Democratic allegiance. Many of these predictions seem possible, but most are either questionable or unlikely—as the results of the 2002 midterm elections showed.

Republican Opportunities

Even before the change in national direction manifested by the 2002 election, there was substantial evidence that the underlying long-term trend toward the Republicans that began in the 1980s may not yet be over. The strong swing to the Republicans among white evangelical Protestants, and the less marked but nonetheless substantial movement among Catholics, both heavily Democratic groups before the 1970s, have shown no signs of abating (Stanley and Niemi 2001). In 2000, Bush won 76 percent of the vote of white evangelicals and slightly more than half of the vote of non-Hispanic Catholics. White evangelicals make up about 25 percent of the total electorate and non-Hispanic Catholics about 22 percent—both formidable voting blocs. As John Green and his associates have shown, swings toward the Republicans among both evangelicals and Catholics have come mainly from "more observant" church members—those who attend church regularly and hold more traditional religious views (Green et al. 2001). The very fact of their institutional loyalty probably makes them more cohesive in voting and more readily motivated for participation in campaigns. (Judis and Teixeira disparage the importance of these groups, arguing that many people tend to exaggerate their church attendance. But even claiming church attendance probably indicates underlying social attitudes. The fact is that reported church attendance is a good predictor of voting.)

The Bush administration has worked hard, through political outreach and social policies, to maintain and expand the growing Republican base among evangelicals and Catholics. Both groups strongly support Bush's faith-based initiative, which would provide increased government funding for nondiscriminatory provision of social services by religious institutions.

National leaderships of most mainline Protestant denominations, historically the grassroots base of the Republican Party outside the South, have been highly critical of Republican administrations since the 1980s. But mainline Protestant laities remain predominantly Republican, giving Bush about 60 percent of their vote in 2000. A survey in 2000 by the Presbyterian Church (USA), the largest Presbyterian denomination, found that 55 percent of Presbyterians nationally regard themselves as Republicans, 25 percent as Democrats, and 17 percent as independents (Reichley 2002).

Recent political behavior indicates that strongly observant members of most religious groups—often with long records of political as well as religious hostility toward each other—have been coming together in support of Republican candidates. In 2000, among the 42 percent of voters who reported usually participating in religious services at least once a week, 58 percent voted for Bush and 40 percent for Gore—a spread almost twice the size of the much reported gender gap. Moral disapproval of Clinton in 2000 was particularly strong among regular participants in religion, and no doubt helped move the more observant of many faiths to vote for Bush. But moral concerns seem likely to be an important factor in American elections for a long time to come.

Some religious groups, as noted above, remain overwhelmingly Democratic in their political allegiances. Jews voted about 80 percent for Gore; African Americans, more politically organized through their churches than any other ethnic group, about 90 percent; and Hispanics, predominantly Catholic but including growing numbers of evangelical Protestants, about 70 percent.

Some Jews, attracted by Bush's staunch support for Israel against Palestinian terrorism, have reportedly been drawn toward the Republicans. In 2002, Republican Governor George Pataki in New York swept some predominantly Jewish districts in New York City that he had heavily lost in earlier elections. Many Jews, however, were concerned by the Bush administration's identification with the religious right and its support for relaxation of barriers between church and state. In 2002 most Jews continued to vote Democratic.

Some African American church leaders, on the other hand, have been among the strongest advocates of the Bush administration's faith-based initiative. Some younger black activists, both religious and secular, appear restive with the undeviating Democratic loyalty prescribed by the established African American political leadership. Although many blacks were outspokenly bitter over the way the 2000 election was settled, polls taken in the spring and summer of 2001 found about 20 percent of blacks approving Bush's performance. According to David Bositis of the Joint Center for Political and Economic Studies, "Black generation Xers—or at least a very significant portion of them—would appear to be a fairly conservative and potentially Republican-leaning group" (Morin and Dean 2001). In 2002 Democratic majorities were little dented in predominantly black areas, but black turnout was down—perhaps indicating reduced mobilization among African Americans for the Democratic Party, or even willingness among some to consider supporting selected Republicans in future elections. If Republicans won only 20 percent of the black vote, up from the recent 10 percent, states like Pennsylvania, Michigan, Florida, and Ohio would move from marginal to leaning Republican.

Bush's 30 percent showing among Hispanics in 2000 was actually 10 percent better than Bob Dole managed in 1996. But Republicans must do much better among Hispanic voters in order to protect their bases in Texas and Arizona and remain competitive in Florida and New Mexico—and perhaps even regain competitive status in the critical battleground of California.

Surveys show that many Hispanics, like blacks, are socially conservative. These sentiments are fed by the traditional attachments of most Hispanics to Catholicism, as well as by newer ties among many Hispanics in the United States to evangelical Protestantism—now about one-third of the total Hispanic population. Hispanics moving into the middle class seem less inhibited than blacks or Jews against voting Republican or even becoming active in the Republican Party (Skerry 1993, 277). But association of Republicans with what were perceived as oppressive restrictions on immigration and immigrants, which occurred particularly in California under the administration of Republican Governor Pete Wilson, preserved Democratic loyalties among most Hispanics throughout the 1990s.

Bush in his race for reelection as governor of Texas in 1998 won almost half of the Hispanic vote. Running against Gore for president in 2000, he held onto about 40 percent of the Hispanic vote in Texas. As president, Bush has made highly publicized efforts to strengthen ties between the United States and Mexico. Republican strategists aim to win 38 to 40 percent of the Hispanic vote for Bush in 2004—a share that would probably guarantee his reelection (Edsall 2001).

Beside Hispanics, Republican aspirations are focused on suburban voters, now 43 percent of the electorate compared with 29 percent urban and 28 percent rural. In 2000 Bush lost older suburban areas like Nassau and Westchester Counties, New York; Bergen County, New Jersey; Montgomery and Bucks Counties, Pennsylvania; and Oakland and Macomb Counties, Michigan. But he won heavily in what Michael Barone calls the "fringe" suburbs—areas farther out that are now growing rapidly and exhibit more conservative attitudes, such as Chester County, Pennsylvania; Howard County, Maryland; Douglas County, Colorado; and Forsyth County, Georgia.

Even in the older suburbs, Democratic preferences have not solidified—most continue to vote Republican in most state and local elections. Many voters in the older suburbs cast ballots for Gore because they associated economic good times with the Clinton-Gore record and were less morally troubled than many other Americans by Clinton's behavior, and because they were unsure of Bush's intellectual or personal capacities to handle the job of president. In 2002, business-friendly Democratic candidates for governor in Pennsylvania, Michigan, Illinois, and Wisconsin were elected through large majorities won in metropolitan suburbs. But in all of these states, except Illinois, suburban voters turned around and helped Republicans maintain or increase majorities in state legislatures. Bush's theme of "compassionate conservatism" seems well-tuned to political attitudes among suburban independents. New Republican senators elected in 2002 from Minnesota, Missouri, New Hampshire, and Georgia were handpicked and promoted by the Bush White House in part because of their appeal to suburban voters.

Reconciling socially liberal suburbanites with antiabortionists and gun owners, who have become among the firmest pillars of Republicanism, or with coal miners and industrial workers who turned to Bush in 2000 out of fear of the economic effects of extreme environmentalism, will not be easy. But the resulting coalition would be no more ideologically diffuse than those that made the Republicans the majority party in the latter part of the nineteenth century or entrenched the Democrats under the New Deal.

A Political Turning Point?

All of these factors may ultimately seem minor beside the impact of the terrible events of September 11 and their aftermath. The full effects of these tragedies, shaping foreign, military, and federal budgetary policies for years to come, will go far beyond any influence they may have on shifting the direction of party politics. The resulting changes in political alignments may themselves, however, have major and enduring consequences.

The immediate response to the tragedies of September 11 among most Americans was, in addition to personal shock and grief, strong expressions of national solidarity. Public opinion surveys found a remarkable upsurge of confidence in the underlying goodness of American life and a renewed sense of national purpose and direction. For many years polls had regularly shown a large majority of Americans believing that the country's "moral climate" was "on the wrong track." A Fox News poll in December 2001 found 59 percent convinced that the nation was headed morally "in the right direction," and only 29 percent the other way. Other national polls produced similar results.

The public's sense of restored moral confidence was widely tied to religion. Most national religious bodies and leaders supported the administration's promise to bring the perpetrators of the terrorist attacks to justice, and associated themselves with some version of the "just war" tradition, while cautioning that military actions should not be carried out in a spirit of vengeance and should be carefully planned to avoid unnecessary civilian casualties. The Gallup Poll in December 2001 found the belief that religion was increasing its influence in American life rising from a steady level of about 40 percent to 71 percent. Bush consistently cast the war against terrorism in religious and moral terms. "As we struggle to defeat the forces of evil," he said early in 2002, "the God of the universe struggles with us."

By the early spring of 2002, some of these signs of renewed moral confidence and belief in religious revival had begun to fade. Although Bush's approval rating remained above 70 percent, the Pew Research Center's national survey in March found the share of the public "satisfied with the way things are going in this country" at 50 percent, down from 65 percent in January. Those believing religion was increasing its influence in America had fallen back to 37 percent (Reichley 2002).

Indications of continued reaching toward religious faith, however, remained strong. Among the 55 percent who believed that religion was losing influence, 84 percent said this loss was a "bad thing." Pew, in March, found

61 percent believing that "children raised with religious faith are more likely to grow up to be moral adults," and 58 percent agreeing "the strength of American society is based on the religious faith of its people."

At least in the short term the political effects of the war against terrorism and concern for homeland security clearly helped Bush and the Republicans. Bush's job approval ratings remained stratospherically high for months after the war was launched. The Social Security "lockbox" was demolished without complaint, the deficit issue almost vanished, and Congress hastily approved vastly increased expenditures to finance the war in Afghanistan, for homeland security, and to benefit the families of victims of the terrorist attacks. Polls taken early in 2002 found the Republicans with around a five percentage point advantage in party identification over the Democrats—the first time in more than seventy years the Republicans had held a definite, though small, edge among party identifiers. Among the groups swinging toward the Republicans were suburban women, whom the Democrats had come to regard as a cornerstone of their hopes for returning to national dominance. A *Washington Post*–ABC News poll at the end of January 2002 found voters between ages 18 and 30 favoring Republicans over Democrats to deal with "the nation's problems" by 50 to 37 percent.

A *Wall Street Journal*–NBC News poll taken in June 2001 found Democrats preferred over Republicans by large margins for dealing with health care, the environment, energy, Medicare, Social Security, and, to a lesser extent, education (White 2002). But the same poll showed Republicans favored over Democrats by 55 to 14 percent for dealing with defense, and by 40 to 18 percent moral values. After September 11, it turned out that defense and moral values had moved to the top of the public's agenda.

Some Democrats took solace that the impact of September 11 had caused a sharp rise of public confidence in government, which they interpreted as favorable to expansion of federal domestic programs. But the *Washington Post*–ABC News poll at the end of January 2002 found 54 percent preferring "a smaller government with fewer services." Apparently what most voters had in mind when they expressed increased confidence in government were firefighters, police, the military services, and George W. Bush.

2002: The Dog That Did Not Bark

By most of the normal rules of American politics, 2002 should have been a good year for Democrats. The economy, after the brief 2001 recession, remained sluggish. By the fall of 2002, the stock market had lost almost 30 percent of its value since Bush became president. Consumer confidence was at its lowest level since 1993. Unemployment was rising. Amid charges of insider skulduggery, several major corporations had gone bankrupt, wip-

ing out employees' savings in their stock funds. Under such economic conditions, the party holding power in the White House almost always has suffered substantial losses in midterm elections. Instead, George Bush became
the first president since Franklin Roosevelt in 1934, at the height of the New
Deal realignment, to lead his party to gains in both houses of Congress in
midterm elections. The state of the economy in 2002 became, as in one of
the celebrated cases of Sherlock Holmes, "the dog that did not bark."

The extent of Republican success in 2002 should not be exaggerated.
Bush's party made only small gains in both congressional houses (though
these were enough to give Republicans firm control of both executive and
legislative branches for the first time since 1954 under Eisenhower.) Capture
of important governorships in Pennsylvania, Michigan, Illinois, and Wisconsin, and retention of California (by a surprisingly small margin) gave the
Democrats powerful bases for future political operations.

The depth of the Republican victory, however, indicated that enduring
political change may be underway. The Republican surge in the last days
before the election, spurred on by Bush's relentless campaigning, showed
that swing voters, as of 2002 at least, trusted Republicans more than Democrats to guide the nation through a dangerous world. The CBS–*New York
Times* poll at the end of October found *independents* approving Bush's performance as president by 60 percent to 27 percent, and viewing Republicans
favorably by 50 percent to 35 percent. Even on the economy, 54 percent of
all voters approved Bush's leadership, and Republicans were favored over
Democrats by 41 percent to 37 percent as "more likely to make sure the
country is prosperous" (perhaps reflecting a tendency among voters once
they have made a party choice to bring all of their attitudes into line with
their overall decision).

At the state legislative level, the all-important training ground for future
political leadership, the Republicans gained about 200 seats, breaking the
historic trend in which the president's party had lost an average of 350 seats
in midterm elections since 1938 (Lee 2002).

The Republicans, moreover, seemed to be off to a head start with future
generations. A survey by the *Washington Post*, the Kaiser Foundation, and
Harvard University, released in October 2002, found that among young
adults 18 to 29, 43 percent chose the Republicans as the party they "trust to
do a better job in coping with the main problems the nation faces over the
next few years," compared with 38 percent Democrats. On two important
Bush administration initiatives, 61 percent of the 18 to 29 age group supported "a plan in which people who chose could invest some of their Social
Security contributions in the stock market" and 58 percent favored "providing parents with tax money in the form of school vouchers to help pay for
their children to attend private or religious schools." On the other hand, 55

percent believed that "gays and lesbians should have the legal right to get married."

The same survey found that among younger voters, the gender gap had given way to a small Republican advantage among women. In the 18-to-37 age group, 34 percent of women and 32 percent of men identified themselves as Republicans. In the same age group, 30 percent of women and 23 percent of men said they were Democrats. The rest were independents, other, or undecided (and probably not voting).

After the 2002 election, American politics remained in flux. Continued economic troubles, a protracted war bringing heavy casualties, failures in homeland defense, or simply Republican excess or neglect could easily restore the Democrats to power. But the Republicans had faced a severe political test and passed it successfully. From a series of such victories, great realignments are made.

3

A Tale of Two Electorates: The Changing American Party Coalitions, 1952–2000

Paul Allen Beck

For several decades, the party loyalties of the American electorate have been undergoing contrasting changes. On the one hand, there has been a slow but steady change in the composition of the Democratic and Republican Party coalitions—what V. O. Key (1959) originally referred to as a "secular realignment." Some see the realignment as beginning as early as the 1960s (Aldrich and Niemi 1995; Carmines and Stimson 1989), whereas others believe that it occurred as recently as 1994 (Burnham 1996). On the other hand, fewer Americans now claim party loyalties than did prior to the mid-1960s (Wattenberg 1998). Even though this partisan "dealignment" appears to have been concentrated in the late 1960s and early 1970s, and an overwhelming majority of Americans remain identified with a party, it has left a larger portion of the electorate as nonpartisans than at any time since the development of the American two-party system. The story of recent American electoral politics revolves around this confluence of realignment and dealignment. It is a tale of two electorates.

One electorate is partisan and ideologically polarized. It has been shaped since the 1950s, which is a convenient benchmark for comparison, by a steady erosion of Democratic loyalists and recent gains in Republican identifiers that have recovered the Republican Party's 1950s share of the electorate.[1] By 2000, these two party electorates were essentially equal in electoral influence, with the smaller GOP group attaining parity through its somewhat higher rates of turnout. The two parties' coalitions also have been reshuffled to a significant degree since the 1950s. By the beginning of the twenty-first century, Democratic loyalists were more dominant among blacks, women were more Democratic than men, and Catholics were less Democratic than they had been fifty years before. By contrast, Republican identifiers now outnumber Democrats among the overlapping groups of white Southerners and white fundamentalist Protestants. These changes have transformed the nature of the two parties and have made them more ideological opposites than they were in the 1950s.

The other electorate is independent and nonpartisan, sometimes even fiercely antipartisan. More inclined to respond to short-term factors involving the candidates and their campaigns, it is available for temporary mobilization on behalf of either a major party candidate or a third-party or independent candidate—or for demobilization into nonvoting. Its members also come from many of the groups that have played prominent roles in the realignment of the parties, which signifies the incompleteness of a group-based account of American politics. In 2000 this pool of nonpartisan potential voters was more numerous than either self-identified Democrats or Republicans. With parity in party strength within the partisan electorate, this nonpartisan electorate now holds the balance of power between the parties, and election outcomes depend even more than before on short-term factors.

Theoretical Considerations

Detailing the story of the development of these two contrasting electorates and their effect on American politics is the task of this chapter. Before providing the details of this story, though, the ideas on which it depends need to be made more explicit. The vote outcome of any election is best seen as the joint product of long-term predispositions of the electorate toward the parties and short-term orientations toward the issues and candidates of the day (Campbell et al. 1966, chapter 2). Long-term predispositions are embodied in enduring party loyalties (Campbell et al. 1960, chapter 6). Most voters possess these loyalties, even amidst today's largely unprecedented dealignment (Bartels 2000). Voters holding these loyalties seem to be readily aware of them, because they report them more reliably than any other political orientations in responding to survey questions (Converse and Markus 1979).

When the distribution of these enduring party loyalties changes in a significant way, so that the coalitions of party loyalists are transformed or the balance between the parties is altered (and the former usually leads to the latter), we speak of the electorate as having "realigned" (Key 1955; Campbell et al. 1966, chapter 4). Analyses of aggregate vote patterns suggest that the American electorate has realigned at regular thirty- to forty-year intervals throughout much of American history (Burnham 1970; Sundquist 1982). When the share of the electorate professing party loyalties declines and more voters are basing electoral decisions necessarily on election-specific factors, the process is described as a "dealignment" (Inglehart and Hochstein 1972; Beck 1977, 1992). This pattern is more easily discernible in survey data on party loyalties than in aggregated vote results, but there are telltale signs of dealignment in vote patterns prior to the availability of surveys (Beck 1979).

This theoretical perspective focuses attention on the distribution of party loyalties, including their presence or absence, as the fundamental character- istic of an electorate at any particular time and on changes in these distribu- tions as the principal dynamic in electoral politics. It relegates actual votes to the background—as consequences of enduring partisanship and immedi- ate, and temporary, candidate or issue-specific forces. Much of the criticism of the realignment concept (Shafer 1991) is the result of a failure to distin- guish, first, between these enduring loyalties and temporary, election- specific forces and, second, between the dynamic processes of realignment and dealignment (Beck 1979). Of course votes, as actual political behavior, are far more consequential in an immediate sense than is partisanship. Yet, patterns of votes down the long American ballot and over time reflect the underlying anchor of partisanship. Therefore, in looking for trends in elec- toral behavior, attention necessarily focuses upon partisanship and the more or less fixed partisan characteristics of an electorate that define different electoral eras or party systems (Chambers and Burnham 1975). It is the na- ture and origins of the contemporary electoral era, seen from the perspective of party loyalties, that is the focus of this chapter.

This realignment theory perspective also draws upon the long tradition of viewing party coalitions in social group terms (Berelson, Lazarsfeld, and McPhee 1954; Lipset and Rokkan 1967; Axelrod 1972; Sundquist 1982; Pe- trocik 1981; Stanley and Niemi 1999). Electoral politics of course is much more complicated than can be conveyed by a group focus. Few social groups, especially in the American two-party system, march in block to the tune of a party or from party to party. That realization was one of the princi- pal contributions of both *The American Voter* (Campbell et al. 1960) and the rational-choice approach (Fiorina 1981). Nonetheless, in understanding changes in the party coalitions from one time point to another, a group ap- proach can be highly beneficial.

Changing American Partisanship: Realignment amidst Dealignment

Since the mid-1960s, two important changes have taken place in the party loyalties of the American electorate. First came a decay or dealignment of partisan loyalties, especially within the Democratic Party coalition that had dominated American electoral politics since the 1930s. It was followed, most noticeably in the early 1980s but foreshadowed somewhat earlier, by the reshuffling of the major party coalitions and a slight growth of Republi- can Party loyalists after their dealignment-era decline. Together these two changes have altered the social composition of the American parties in significant ways.

Figure 3.1 reports the party identifications of the electorate from 1952 to 2000.[2] From relatively stable levels during the 1950s and early 1960s, with Democrats outnumbering Republicans by a five to three margin, the partisan strength of both parties eroded, starting after 1962 for the Republicans and 1964 for the Democrats. The GOP had recovered its 1950s level of party loyalty in 1994, only to fall slightly from that apex for the rest of the decade. In 2000, even after winning both houses of Congress and the presidency, albeit by razor-thin margins in the most controversial election since 1876, the Republicans still were unable to attract more loyalists than either their Democratic opposition or nonpartisan independents. Indeed, they began the twenty-first century with no more loyalists as a percentage of the American electorate than they had in 1952.

That Republican identifiers are no larger a portion of the electorate today than they were in the 1950s is ignored by those who have seen the recent years as a time of pro-GOP realignment. The Republicans are better positioned electorally than in the 1950s and early 1960s. But the reasons are Democratic decay, Republicans' higher turnout rates at the polls, and the disappearance of the solid South as a dependably Democratic voting block—rather than any nationwide realignment to Republicanism. The current GOP hold on the House and the presidency, as well as on many of the state governments, consequently rests on shaky foundations.

It has been the Democratic Party that has borne the major brunt of the

Figure 3.1   Party Loyalties of Americans, 1952–2000

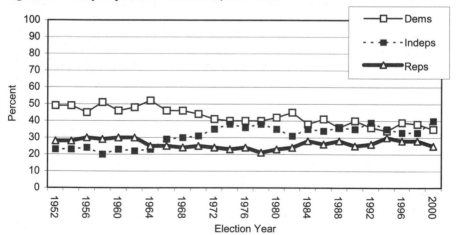

changes since the early 1960s. Erosion in its loyalist base first became visible in 1966 and, despite a few temporary surges, typically in midterm elections, has continued through 2000. The beneficiary of these declines in partisanship has been the amorphous category called "independents." After being outnumbered by both Democrats and Republicans through 1964, independents have become more numerous than Republican loyalists ever since. They came close to comprising a plurality of the electorate in the mid-1970s and again in the mid-1980s, and, beginning in 1992, they attracted a plurality of the electorate in three of the following six election years. Within the range of sampling error these changes can be said to have produced an electorate almost evenly balanced among Democrats, Republicans, and independents by the turn of the century.

Partisan Changes in Key Groups within the Electorate

To gain a better appreciation for how changes in partisan loyalties have transformed the American party system, it is necessary to disaggregate the movements of the entire electorate into the behavior of particular groups. Table 3.1 contains the divisions among Democrats, Republicans, and independents of seven groups that were divided noticeably along partisan lines either in the New Deal party system in place in the 1950s or in the system that replaced it.

As it is with many dominant coalitions (Burnham 1970; Sundquist 1982), the roots of the post-1964 Democratic decay are found to a considerable degree within the political tensions of its original formulation. At its core, the New Deal Democratic majority was based on an alliance of white Southerners and liberal Northerners. Such an alliance could remain intact only so long as economic issues dominated the political agenda and the South was left alone to pursue its traditional segregation of blacks and whites. Once Southern autonomy was challenged over civil rights, the loyalties of both white Southerners and African Americans were put in motion. New Deal politics were largely organized around economic policy and social class issues. As the agenda of American politics shifted to embrace new social and moral issues, the partisanship of other key groups in the American population was challenged. The success of the New Deal welfare state in overcoming the problems of the Great Depression in the 1930s and lifting ethnic minorities and workers into the middle class undermined the subsequent attraction of the Democratic Party to many of its beneficiaries, especially their children and grandchildren (Beck 1974). Moreover, the new issue agenda that emerged, like newly electrified poles of an electromagnet, yielded different party coalition clusters than before.

Table 3.1 Changing Partisan Loyalties of Key Groups, 1952–2000

Year	White Southerners			African Americans			Catholics			Union Households			Men			Women			White Fundamentalists		
	Dems	Inds	Reps	Dems	Inds	Reps	Dems	Inds	Reps	Dems	Inds	Reps	Dems	Inds	Reps	Dems	Inds	Reps	Dems	Inds	Reps
1952	77	12	11	64	21	16	56	26	18	55	23	22	48	26	26	49	21	30			
1954				62	20	19	53	27	21	59	20	21	51	24	25	48	22	30			
1956	68	16	16	61	16	23	52	27	21	52	27	21	46	28	26	44	22	34			
1958	68	17	15	62	18	21	58	25	17	63	20	17	49	23	28	52	18	30			
1960	60	18	21	50	31	18	61	23	16	57	28	15	43	29	28	49	19	32	48	22	30
1962	57	22	21	70	14	16							50	24	26	47	20	32			
1964	66	20	15	77	15	7	58	25	17	64	23	13	50	26	24	54	21	26	55	18	27
1966	55	29	16	62	28	9	55	29	17	56	25	18	46	24	24	47	26	26	46	28	26
1968	50	37	13	88	10	2	53	32	15	51	30	19	43	32	25	48	28	24	42	31	27
1970	43	38	19	78	18	4	52	31	17	54	31	15	42	34	23	45	29	26	42	33	26
1972	47	34	19	69	23	8	51	35	14	46	39	15	37	39	23	44	32	24	38	36	26
1974	47	34	19	68	29	3	48	36	16	45	42	13	35	43	22	43	34	23	40	36	24
1976	45	34	21	71	24	4	50	35	15	47	40	12	37	42	20	42	32	26	36	36	28
1978	41	38	20	68	27	5	50	36	14	50	36	14	38	44	18	42	34	23	37	39	24
1980	43	34	23	75	20	5	43	38	19	46	39	14	38	40	22	44	32	24	42	34	24
1982	49	29	22	79	19	2	55	29	16	50	32	18	39	35	26	50	27	23	40	32	28
1984	37	38	24	65	31	4	43	36	21	46	35	19	34	39	28	41	32	28	33	34	32
1986	40	34	26	74	22	4	45	33	22	47	34	20	37	38	25	44	30	26	37	32	32
1988	34	40	26	64	30	6	38	36	26	43	37	20	30	42	29	40	32	28	32	37	30
1990	37	42	20	64	31	5	45	33	23	50	31	20	36	36	27	43	34	23	35	36	29
1992	32	42	26	66	29	4	41	39	20	45	38	17	32	40	28	40	37	23	28	39	33
1994	32	33	35	62	33	6	40	36	24	44	36	20	30	38	33	39	32	29	30	32	39
1996	36	34	30	66	31	3	43	33	24	43	39	18	34	34	32	44	32	24	37	29	34
1998	33	34	33	73	23	4	40	33	27	43	37	20	35	37	28	41	34	25	28	36	36
2000	24	40	36	68	29	3	35	40	25	46	36	18	30	41	29	39	38	23	23	38	39

Note: Entries are percentages of the group members who identify as Democrats, independents (pure + leaners), and Republicans, respectively. Within each group, these percentages sum to within rounding error of 100 percent across the (three) columns.

The Countermovements of White Southerners and African Americans

By the 1950s, the Democratic alliance between white Southerners and liberal Northerners was beginning to fray. Southern autonomy on matters of racial policy had become untenable to many Northern Democrats, and a movement to secure equal rights for blacks was emerging in the South. Once the national Democratic Party moved to champion civil rights for Southern blacks in the early 1960s and the GOP took the opposite position in 1964 (Carmines and Stimson 1989), the die was cast. White Southerners began to desert their traditional party's candidates as early as the 1950s.[3] This desertion was manifested first in voting Republican for president. As long as Democratic candidates for state and local offices continued to reflect their region's mores, they retained the support of its white voters. Over the years, however, Republicanism steadily penetrated down the ballot as old-time Democratic officeholders retired and new, more mainstream party candidates replaced them (Black and Black 1987; Beck 1992).

It was not too long before the civil rights revolution in the South and the opposing postures of the parties toward it began to affect party loyalties. As the first columns of table 3.1 show, Democratic loyalties already were declining within the white Southern electorate in the 1950s; the reasons at first had little to do with race (Beck 1977). As race became the most salient regional issue, though, this erosion of the solidly Democratic South continued with only occasional and partial reversals through the early 1990s. By 2000, Democratic loyalists among white Southerners had fallen to what undoubtedly is their lowest point in the history of the party. The Democratic share of this group is less than one-third of what it was fifty years before. The days of a solid South, built upon the Democratic commitments of its white electorate, are gone.

The GOP has been able to capitalize upon this Democratic decay to a considerable degree. Steadily, with only occasional slight reversals in the mid-1960s, 1990, and 1996, it gained a stronger base of party loyalists among white Southerners. By the 1990s, there were roughly equal numbers of Republicans and Democrats within this group. By 2000, with another surge in GOP loyalists and decline in Democratic loyalists, white Southerners had become significantly more Republican than Democratic. Republican advances have been especially pronounced within the new generations of white Southerners, many of whom have rejected inherited Democratic loyalties (Beck 1977; Beck 1982). If generational replacement proceeds unimpeded, the Republican share of the Southern white electorate may continue to grow, although it soon may reach its upper bound.

It took several decades for the Republicans to outnumber Democrats among white Southerners, and they remain far short of dominance. At first, in the 1960s, the breakup of the solid South featured a surge of independents, reaching levels that were to be more or less sustained over the next twenty years. In their flight from Democratic loyalties, many white Southerners seemed to take refuge in nonpartisanship. Perhaps this shift is a phase in the natural journey of partisan realignment for a group. Older members first defect in their voting, as many white Southern Democrats did in presidential contests in the 1950s. Next, they desert their traditional party identifications, but cannot bring themselves to convert to the other party, even if they are consistently voting for its candidates, as easily as newer members of the electorate can. Over time, as the inexorable process of population replacement works it way, the group's partisan loyalties are brought into line with their votes.

The undeniable consequence of the changes in partisanship among white Southerners through 2000 is a realigned Southern party system—more Republican than ever before, yet still competitive. The story of Southern electoral change is complex (Black and Black 1987), and it is important not to readily accept a monocausal racial politics explanation of it. Many Southern whites have changed partisan loyalties due to racial issues, yet many others are drawn to the Republican Party for reasons that have little to do with race (Beck 1977). Large numbers of Northerners moved to the South, bringing their traditional GOP loyalties with them. With the modernization of the Southern economy has come an expanding middle class, which as early as the 1950s was drawn to the GOP for many of the same reasons that middle-class Northerners were. The return of religious fundamentalism to the political arena, with its focus on moral and social conservatism, also has been a part of the Southern equation in recent years. More than elsewhere in the nation, it has further eroded the white working-class base of the Democratic Party in the South.

The changes in the South have had enormous consequences for party politics at the national level. Without a solid South, which had comprised the most loyal share of its vote since the 1870s and given it a regional "lock" in the Electoral College, the Democratic Party is no longer dominant in American politics. Important changes have occurred in the party coalitions outside of the South, to be sure, but they pale in comparison to the changes wrought in the South.

The movement away from the Democratic Party by white Southerners is paralleled, and has been inextricably linked, to a consolidation of African American support for the Democrats, as shown in the next three columns of table 3.1. Since 1952, African Americans inside and outside of the South have become the most dependable Democratic loyalists (Gurin, Hatchett, and Jackson 1989; Tate 1993). They began the era with widespread Democratic loyalties, although they were not nearly as devoted to the party as white Southerners. Moreover, the early figures are somewhat illusory, for more than one-half of all African Americans lived in the South in the 1950s, and few of them were permitted to participate in elections because of the state registration laws and practices of that era (Matthews and Prothro 1966). Not only were Southern blacks mobilized into politics in the 1960s, so that their Democratic loyalties became more consequential, but the positioning of the parties on opposite sides of the civil rights divide by the mid-1960s pushed most of the remaining black Republicans out of the GOP.

Discussions of possible growth in black Republicanism in recent years ignore the fact that the "party of Lincoln" enjoyed much more support in the African American community a generation ago than it does today. Survey data occasionally exhibit slight up-ticks in black Republicanism that probably reflect sampling error, but the long-term trend was a steady erosion of Republican loyalties from the 1950s into the early 1970s, then stability at bare trace levels, with only one African American in thirty-three professing Republican loyalties. No group within the modern American electorate contains proportionately fewer GOP adherents. Instead, what votes the party garners from black Americans surely come largely from independents, who themselves are far less numerous among African Americans than they are within the white electorate.

Democratic Decay among Catholics and Labor and Their Contrasting Consequences

Like Southern whites, Catholics and labor unions were core constituencies of the Democratic majority established in the 1930s. Catholics had long been attracted to the Democratic Party in the nation's cities, where they were heavily concentrated, but it took the events of the 1920s—the party's choice of a Catholic as its presidential nominee in 1928, the Great Depression, and Roosevelt's policies of the 1930s—to consolidate their loyalties. Labor unions were empowered by New Deal legislation in the 1930s, which secured the Democratic loyalties of their members. As the next two sets of columns in table 3.1 show, the legacy of these partisan commitments was present in the 1950s and 1960s, when Catholics and people in households containing a union member favored the Democrats over the Republicans by margins of about three to one.

From these parallel baselines, the partisan loyalties of Catholics and union families followed a familiar spiral for a while, and then diverged. Beginning in the late 1960s, the two groups joined in the general dealignment of the American electorate. They contributed to the declines in Democratic and Republican loyalists and the increases in independents through the 1970s. The dealignment of these two groups seems to have halted by 1980—a bit later than it had ended for the electorate as a whole. For union families, the ensuing period was a time of little net change in partisanship.

By contrast, Catholics turned in a Republican direction beginning in 1980, and their movement came at the expense of Democratic loyalties. The net exchange of Democratic for Republican loyalties among Catholics is not large, but it is noticeable.

These changes in partisan loyalties leave Catholics and union families still more Democratic than Republican by the beginning of the twenty-first century. Union households now are over two to one Democratic, down from what they were in the 1950s and 1960s, but nonetheless decisively unbalanced. It is dealignment, rather than realignment, that best characterizes their movement. By contrast, Catholics underwent elements of first dealignment, then realignment, to the point that they show an almost equal balance between Democrats and independents, and a Republican minority that has grown to almost rival them. Union families are no more Republican, on net, at the end of the period than they were at the beginning, but more Catholics are supportive of the GOP than was the case a half-century ago. The emergence of religious issues as powerful shapers of partisan loyalties, it seems fair to surmise, has affected many Catholics just as it has affected many Protestant fundamentalists (see below).

An Emerging Gender Gap in Partisan Loyalties

After years of no differences between men and women in partisan preferences, scholars and commentators have identified a consistent gender gap in recent decades in both partisanship and voting (Abramson, Aldrich, and Rohde 1998). The next six columns in table 3.1 show the extent of the gender gap in partisanship. The partisan loyalties of men and women began to diverge in the 1970s and had become significantly different by the 1980s and 1990s, especially where Democratic loyalties were concerned.

Comparison of the party loyalties of men and women over time yields insight into what has happened, although exactly why it has happened defies simple explanation. Both groups joined in the post-1964 dealignment. Republican loyalties eroded to about the same extent between both groups. Democratic loyalties declined between both as well, albeit at different rates, with the decline coming earlier and reaching deeper among men. This shift left women somewhat more Democratic than men by the mid-1970s. Beginning in the 1980s, Democratic loyalties among women stabilized, with no further losses or Republican gains for the most part; but the decline in Democratic loyalties and growth of Republicanism continued among men. By the turn of the twenty-first century, men were equally likely to be Republican or Democrat, while almost twice as many women were Democrats as were Republicans.

The gender gap, then, is the work of a substantial pro-GOP shift in the partisan orientations of men in the 1980s and 1990s at the same time most women were resisting the movement away from the Democrats. Scholars have been unable to attribute these changes to so-called women's issues and now consider them a result of different expectations about the role of government (Miller and Shanks 1996; Kaufman and Petrocik 1999) as well as myriad other forces. The gender changes are modest compared to those of Southern whites and even African Americans, but what makes them important is the size of the groups involved.

The Delayed Realignment of White Fundamentalist Protestants

Another important change in group party loyalties since the 1950s is a result of the growing importance of religion in American politics. Rather than the Protestant versus Catholic conflict of earlier times, contemporary religious politics has revolved more around the importance of religion in one's life. The GOP has been the traditional home for Protestants, especially in the North before the 1960s, but the party in earlier times represented middle-class "high church" Protestants better than their more fundamentalist and lower-status brethren. Recent years have witnessed the ascendancy of white Protestant fundamentalists in Republican nomination politics and its party organizations and policy-making circles. This new influence of fundamentalists is typically attributed to the group's growing Republicanism.

The changes in party loyalties of white Protestant fundamentalists, presented in the last columns of table 3.1, however, do not quite fit these first impressions.[4] The group has become more Republican than Democratic (Leege and Kellstedt 1993), but only *after* it became more influential in GOP circles. Early on, white fundamentalists joined in the dealignment of the broader electorate, with its deeper erosion of Democratic than Republican loyalties. As the axis of American politics turned to religious and social questions, though, the Democratic loyalties of fundamentalists continued to decline—reaching their lowest point in the series (slightly more than 20 percent of the electorate) in 2000. The decline was not as steady or as sharp as that of Southern whites, particularly Southern white fundamentalists, but it has been persistent. During the time of dealignment, Republican loyalties among white fundamentalists fell off as well. They did not regain their 1960 high point (occasioned because the 1960 Democratic nominee was a Catholic) until 1984. The sharpest growth in Republican loyalties in this group, though, came recently—in the last decade of the twentieth century. By 2000, it had left Republicans tied with independents as the identification of choice for white Protestant fundamentalists.

What is surprising, given their considerable weight in the inner circles of Republican politics for some years, is the delay of a Republican surge in partisan loyalties among white fundamentalists. Strongly courted by GOP candidates since Richard Nixon in 1968, for two decades white fundamentalists seemed to resist becoming Republicans. Only in the early 1990s, then again in 1998 and 2000, have they been significantly more Republican than Democratic in professed party identifications. By 2000, this gap had widened considerably, with continued decline in Democratic identifications, but its significance is challenged by a recent surge of independents. What began as a story of Democratic dealignment seems only of late to have become a story of pro-Republican realignment among white Protestant fundamentalists.

Putting Everything Together

An important part of the story of partisan change in the American electorate during the past half-century can be told by the overall trends in party identification and the patterns for the seven groups discussed above. Overall the electorate has dealigned, becoming less partisan and more independent since the 1950s and early 1960s. The dealignment occurred during the ten-year period between Lyndon Johnson's reelection in 1964 and the immediate aftermath of the departure of Richard Nixon from the White House in 1974 under the threat of impeachment. The percentage of independents in the American electorate at the turn of the century is little different than it was in 1974, but they now may be more numerous than either Democrats or Republicans.

The seven groups I analyze in this chapter present a more variegated picture. White Southerners and white Protestant fundamentalists (and many Americans are both) have realigned from being overwhelmingly Democratic to marginally more Republican by century's end. At the same time, African Americans have become even more attached to the Democratic Party. Two other key groups within the Democratic coalition that emerged from the 1930s, Catholics and labor union households, remain more Democratic than Republican, but their loyalties to the party of Franklin Roosevelt and John Kennedy have eroded, contributing to the dealignment. Democratic (and Republican) loyalties among women have eroded as well, while those of men were realigning to the point that they are now as Republican as they are Democratic.

In describing these changes, I addressed in passing the question of why they took place. In a nutshell, changes in the political world—chief among them the Democrats' support for integration in the South, the traumas of Vietnam and urban riots, the replacement of class-based economic conflict by divisions over civil rights, social policy, and religion—tore the majority Democratic coalition apart. Such centrifugal pressures are hardly surprising as a dominant party coalition ages, its raison d'être undermined by both its successes in fulfilling its agenda and its failures to keep crosscutting issues off the table (Beck 1979).

Although some scholars resist calling the result in this case a realignment, when seen in all of its complexity it certainly possesses key realignment characteristics—changes in the nature of the party coalitions, new issues dominating the political agenda, and differences in who exercises governmental power. It also exhibits signs of realignment in yet another way. The hallmark of a newly aligned party system, one may logically surmise (Beck 1982), is that ideology and partisanship are more strongly linked than they have been before. As measured straightforwardly by the correlation (r) between respondents' self-locations on seven-point ideology and party identification scales, the connection between ideology and party loyalty has strengthened between 1960 and 2000. What we used to describe in 1960 as a remarkably nonideological party system now appears to have been only a snapshot of an electorate at the end of one party system and the beginning of another. Today's highly polarized parties in Washington and the state capitals are now paralleled by more ideologically polarized party electorates than we have experienced in decades.

What we miss here to complete a realignment scenario are two important ingredients. First, this "realignment" is not as broadly encompassing as past realignments have been. More than one-third of the electorate, virtually 40 percent in 2000, is unwilling to join the new two-party arrangement by choosing a major party as the object of their loyalty. Second, for all of its successes since 1968 at the presidential level and from 1994 to 2000 with the Congress, the Republican Party has not been able to become the party choice of a majority of Americans. Through 2000 at least, the GOP has fallen far short of achieving the gains expected for the ascendant party in realignment. Nor have more voters been mobilized into politics by the realignment, as they were in past realignments (Burnham 1970). Rather, with the exception of the Perot-induced boost in 1992, turnout has declined to where only half of the American electorate casts a presidential ballot (Nichols, Kimball, and Beck 1999) and far fewer participate below the presidential level.

Instead of a decisive realignment, then, partisan changes in recent years have yielded a Democratic Party no longer in command of the loyalties of the dominant share of the electorate, and an enlarged group of political independents who are not dependable supporters of either party. There has been some recent Republican growth to be sure, but it has not been sufficient to recapture the levels of Republicanism of the 1950s, hardly a halcyon era for the GOP in terms of party loyalties.

Conclusion

The result of the 2000 presidential election—with George W. Bush's Electoral College victory turning on a U.S. Supreme Court decision about how to count votes in Florida's "dead heat" contest amid Bush's popular vote defeat nationwide—reflects the state of Americans' partisan loyalties as they entered the new century. It is indeed a tale of two electorates—the one partisan, the other nonpartisan.

By 2000, about 60 percent of the electorate was composed of Democratic and Republican partisans, somewhat below the mid-60s average percentage from 1992 to 2000. Like the 2000 results in Florida, the partisan battle comes close to being a "dead heat." With the realignment of the party coalitions, these partisans also have become more ideologically polarized than in earlier times. Such polarization was evident in the 2000 presidential contest and especially its contentious aftermath, from the partisan warfare over the Florida vote through the first eight months of the Bush presidency. The tragic events of September 11 and the "rally around the flag" politics of a nation under attack temporarily muted partisan divisions, but the political battle between two parties with opposing policy dispositions and ideologically polarized partisans has reappeared.

The other electorate, about 35 percent of eligible voters from 1992 to 2000 and up to 40 percent in 2000, is nonpartisan. It opts out of Democratic or Republican identification when asked and, even where it may vote rather consistently for one party's candidates, it is unwilling to commit to that party for the long term. Not only is this electorate less involved in politics than its partisan counterpart, it also seems inclined to withdraw from the political fray as the major parties become more polarized—unless an attractive non–major party alternative is on the ballot. These nonpartisan voters are moved by the candidates and issues of the moment, not by the long-term positioning of the parties, and they add a considerable element of volatility to the electoral arena.

It is a combination of realignment and dealignment that most aptly characterizes contemporary electoral politics in the United States. The realignment has changed the major parties, reshuffling their loyalists along more ideological lines. But the dealignment has prevented either of these more ideological parties from dominating the political world—as is evidenced by persistent divided government, fluctuations in presidential voting from election to election, and slender margins of party control over governmental institutions. Nonpartisans hold the balance of power in the contemporary electorate between equally balanced major parties and provide fertile ground for non–major party candidates. The dilemma for the major parties and their candidates is that what mobilizes their partisan core voters repels the nonpartisan electorate, potentially either costing them the election or, if victorious, a mandate to govern.

This new electoral system may have reached its equilibrium state—a so-called sixth party system (Aldrich and Niemi 1995). If so, it is a highly dynamic equilibrium characterized by considerable election-to-election volatility, which is the work of election-specific movements of a large nonpartisan electorate around an almost fifty-fifty "normal vote" baseline (Converse 1966). Yet it is easy to locate strong pressures toward disequilibria on the contemporary scene. First, as the ascendant party in this system and holder of the presidency in a time of national trauma, the GOP might simply ride the wave of its current momentum into partisan dominance and a more clear-cut realignment; the 2002 results may be an early sign of this. Its decades-long inability to turn its opportunities into more sizable gains in partisan loyalists, however, raises doubt about whether the GOP can build a Republican majority. Second, continued ideological polarization within the partisan portion of the electorate—after an interlude of the rally-around-the-flag unity in the aftermath of the terrorist attacks—may increase popular disenchantment with the current system among nonpartisan voters and deepen the dealignment. This scenario would promote continued electoral volatility and might even buoy the prospects for minor party or independent candidates.

We must not let speculation about the future, however, distract us from the realities of the past and present in characterizing the contemporary electoral scene and the changes that produced it. The story of our current party system can best be told in terms of the relative sizes, compositions, and electoral tendencies of its two electorates—one partisan and about evenly divided, the other estranged from party politics. They shape the prime characteristics of party politics and American politics in our time.

Notes

I am grateful to Steve Greene and Andy Tomlinson for their research assistance on earlier versions of this chapter; to Quin Monson for advice on how to code religious denominations; and to the Taft Lectures at the University of Cincinnati and the Ray Bliss Institute at the University of Akron for providing venues for presenting these analyses. I am also appreciative of the National Election Study at the University of Michigan for its continuing in-depth surveys of the American electorate and its work in combining them into a cumulative series of election surveys that facilitate comparative analysis. The data for this study come from the cumulative series of the National Election Studies (Miller and National Election Studies 1999), plus their 2000 study. In some years, weights must be applied to the data to correct for unrepresentativeness in the sampling frame. This chapter uses these weights for this purpose in 1970, 1994, and 1996. Poststratification weights are also available to make the demographic characteristics of the samples better approximate those of the adult electorate, but those weights were not applied here.

1. Not only were the 1950s the first decade in which reliable survey data were available for the measurement of partisanship, but this decade also is conventionally considered the last of the New Deal party system that had dominated American politics since the 1930s.

2. In the NES (National Election Study), party loyalties are measured by two questions. The first is "Generally speaking, do you think of yourself as a Republican, a Democrat, an independent, or what?" The second question asks Democrats and Republicans to say whether their loyalty is strong or not so strong, and independents are asked if they are closer to the

Democratic or Republican Party. The analysis in this chapter relies solely on answers to the first question, which divides respondents into Democrats, independents, and Republicans, with the handful of people who profess loyalties to another party excluded. Independents who claim, in response to the second question, that they are closer to one of the parties are assumed to be making a short-term choice, not an enduring partisan commitment, so they are retained as independents in this chapter.

3. Southerners are defined as residents of the eleven states that had seceded from the Union on the eve of the Civil War to form the Confederacy. The 1954 study does not allow us to identify the eleven-state South used for other years.

4. Religious preferences are coded from the denominational categories provided in the NES data. Prior to 1960, the codes were not adequate to differentiate Protestant fundamentalists from nonfundamentalists. A more detailed coding scheme was devised for the 1960 study but, by 1988, it had become apparent that this code was not detailed enough to adequately reflect differences among the various religious groupings that had emerged, so a new code was introduced for the 1990 and subsequent studies. Given these coding changes, representing improved conceptualization and operationalization of religious differences in American society, comparisons across the years are challenging. The identification of Protestant fundamentalists in this chapter uses the "translation table" from the cumulative series codebook and incorporates new codes for 1996, 1998, and 2000. It omits the data from the 1950s and 1962 because religious denominations were not coded adequately to differentiate Protestant fundamentalists from nonfundamentalists.

4

The State of Party Elites: National Convention Delegates, 1992–2000

John S. Jackson, Nathan S. Bigelow, and John C. Green

The 2000 election has been dubbed the "perfect tie" (Ceaser and Busch 2001). At the presidential level, George W. Bush and Al Gore almost evenly split the popular and electoral votes. Similar divisions appeared in the congressional contests, leaving the House and Senate almost evenly divided as well as many state legislatures and local governments. Just as importantly, the 2000 elections were a draw between the major political party organizations and their elites, the people most responsible for organizing and executing these campaigns. This equipoise between the major parties is especially interesting because it came at the end of the "Volatile Nineties," a period of significant political turmoil (Green 1999).

This chapter reviews the attitudes of a key set of party elites: delegates to the national party conventions. Convention delegates offer a window on the conflicts between and within the major parties. Because the national conventions have become carefully planned media events, we use surveys of delegates in 1992, 1996, and 2000 to peer behind the image making and into the heart of major party coalitions. We find that the "perfect tie" in 2000 was associated with an interesting combination of attitudes among the delegates: clear and polarized issue positions between the major parties plus the dominance of centrist factions within the parties. This combination reflects a resolution of the political tensions from the Volatile Nineties and outlines the prospects for each party breaking the "perfect tie" of 2000 in the future.

National Convention Delegates: Theory and Practice

National convention delegates represent "the presidential elite" of the major political parties (Kirkpatrick 1976). These women and men leave their homes all across America for a week once every four years and come together at a giant convention hall in some big city to formally nominate a presidential and vice-presidential candidate—and also enact the party's platform, plan the fall campaigns, tend to the organizational business of the party, and celebrate its shared traditions, symbols, and culture (Jackson 1992; Buell and Jackson 1991; Freeman 1986). Indeed, for the week of the national convention, the delegates are the national parties sitting in plenary session (Baer 1993).

Because many delegates are selected in presidential primaries, they are closely linked to their party's presidential candidates and the issues they advocate. But because the delegates are selected by geography, they are also representatives of the party leaders and activists back home, who are far too numerous to fit into the convention hall (Miller 1988; Jackson and Clayton 1996). In both capacities, delegates represent the activist base of the major parties, whose efforts link candidates to the party's mass followers and mobilize voters for the general election (Eldersveld and Walton 2000, 148). Although the national conventions do not exercise the same level of discretion over presidential nominations as in the past, they encapsulate the mix of enduring tendencies and new developments relevant to party coalitions in a particular campaign.

Eldersveld's research has documented the openness and diversity of party organizations, which house a multiplicity of often loosely allied groups (Eldersveld 1964; Green, Jackson, and Clayton 1999). But despite this openness and diversity, the major parties are regularly able to develop considerable coherence in terms of ideology and issues, and present voters with reasonably clear alternatives at the ballot box (Eldersveld 1982; Miller, Farah, and Jennings 1986; Baer and Bositis 1988). The tension between such diversity on the one hand, and coherence on the other, is captured in the well-known distinction between "pragmatic" and "responsible" parties.

Pragmatic parties are focused on winning elections, controlling public offices, and using the levers of power to reward their coalition members. Issues and ideologies are potent tools for mobilizing activists and voters, but they are secondary to getting and holding political power (Herring 1940; Epstein 1986). As a result, pragmatic parties tend to avoid controversial issues when possible. In contrast, responsible parties are primarily focused on ideology and issues for their own sake. Such parties seek to win elections, control public offices, and use political power for the purpose of enacting desirable public policy. As a result, responsible parties tend to take clear stands, inviting controversy (Committee on Political Parties 1950; Schattschneider 1942).

Overall, scholars have found that the major parties have moved away from the pragmatism that characterized them for most of American history, toward greater responsibility (White and Mileur 1992; Pomper 1999; Herrnson and Green 2002). Party elites have become steadily more ideological, as defined by the level and type of government intervention in private life. In this regard, the Democrats have become increasingly "liberal" (that is, on balance in favor of government intervention) and the Republicans steadily more "conservative" (on balance opposed to government intervention). However, these tendencies cover several types of issues that are often inconsistent with one another. Such issues include long-standing economic disputes, such as enacting national health insurance, and also newer social controversies, such as restricting abortion. Many liberals, for example, support government intervention in the economy, but oppose it with regard to social policy. Likewise, many conservatives oppose government economic intervention, but favor regulation of social life. Thus, a key aspect of increased party responsibility has been fierce debates over the meaning of "liberalism" and "conservatism."

In this regard, scholars and pundits have noted other combinations of ideological thinking: libertarians and populists (Maddox and Lilie 1984). Libertarians are opposed to government intervention in both economic and social life in the name of individual liberty. Populists are in one sense the opposite, supporting government intervention in both economic and social life wherever "the people" (usually defined as the majority of citizens) want it. Despite their consistent views on government—or perhaps because of it— neither libertarianism nor populism have supplanted the liberal-conservative cleavage in national politics, although they have influenced its development. The libertarian commitment to individual rights is found among liberals (civil and women's rights) as well the conservatives (gun owning and property rights). Meanwhile, the populist critique of elites appeals to the left (hostility to corporate elites) and the right (hostility to media elites). Interestingly, both left- and right-wing populists regularly share a disdain for politicians and other government officials—especially those associated with policies they dislike.

Despite the increase in party responsibility, pragmatism has not entirely disappeared: the dominant actors in modern campaigns—candidates, their managers, consultants, and advisors—still want to win elections (Menefee-Libey 2000). Beyond personal incentives (many of these elites will personally hold office if their party wins), such pragmatism is a response to the costs of increased party responsibility and the fierce controversies it generates, including the alienation of voters, decreasing turnout, the deadlock in government policy making, and the rise of minor parties (Dionne 1991; also see chapter 2). A common expression of this pragmatism is a call for "moderation" among party elites, including proposals to soften the tone and image of party ideology and creatively repackage its key elements. Unlike party pragmatism in previous eras, these efforts presumed that ideology and issues played a dominant role in the party coalitions. Indeed, these tendencies arose from the nexus of increasingly responsible party elites and candidate-centered politics.

Three patterns of conflict dominated party politics in the Volatile Nineties. First, the party elites and their interest group allies became increasingly polarized along liberal-conservative lines on some issues. If nothing else, liberals set the terms of debate among the Democrats and conservatives played the same role among Republicans. Each party risked becoming identified in the popular mind by its most doctrinaire elements: the Democrats with a resurgent labor movement, buoyed by public employees plus environmentalists, feminists, and gay rights advocates; the Republicans with independent businesses, antitax advocates, property rights advocates, gun owners, and Christian conservatives.

Second, there were significant attempts to moderate—but not reverse—the ideological polarization within the parties. This pragmatism regularized conflict between each party's doctrinaire and "centrist" wings. An important example was the effort of the "New Democrats" to move their party away from doctrinaire liberalism. For example, Bill Clinton's "new covenant" program in 1992 sought to encourage greater personal responsibility and government fiscal discipline in order to achieve basic liberal goals of a more inclusive and just society. Based in the Democratic Leadership Council, New Democrats Clinton, Al Gore, and Joe Lieberman won the presidential and vice-presidential nominations in 1992, 1996, and 2000. Similarly in the GOP, a collection of self-described "moderates" sought to mitigate their party's hard-edged conservatism. An example is George W. Bush's "compassionate conservatism" program in 2000, which advocated some welfare spending and social tolerance in order to achieve conservative goals of a more stable and virtuous society. Strongly supported by the business community, the Bushes—father and son—and Bob Dole won the GOP presidential nominations in the 1990s.

Third, a series of populist revolts erupted within and outside of the major parties (Hertzke 1993). Among the Democrats, Reverend Jesse Jackson's 1988 presidential bid and the campaigns of Jerry Brown in 1992 and Bill Bradley in 2000 were good examples. Even President Clinton proclaimed that the "era of big government" was over, and enlisted Al Gore in the task of "reinventing government." In the 2000 general election campaign, Gore stressed populist themes of his own, arguing he was for "the people, not the powerful."

This populist tendency was even more pronounced among Republicans. Reverend Pat Robertson's 1988 presidential campaign expanded the presence of Christian conservatives in the GOP, followed by Pat Buchanan's 1992 and 1996 presidential bids, the 1996 and 2000 campaigns of Alan Keyes, and Gary Bauer's 2000 campaign. Newt Gingrich's 1994 "Contract with America" contained numerous populist elements, including term limits for Congress, as did John McCain's 2000 presidential bid, with its stress on banning soft-money donations.

Populism was also evident outside of the major parties in the term limits, Patriot, and militia movements. Ross Perot's presidential forays in 1992 and 1996 and his Reform Party expressed some strong populist tendencies, especially in his attacks on governing elites. Jesse Ventura stressed some of the same themes in his successful bid for governor of Minnesota in 1998. Similarly, Ralph Nader's 1996 and 2000 Green Party campaigns had more than a hint of populism, particularly assaults on corporate elites. Libertarianism was much less of a factor in the party conflicts of the 1990s, perhaps because many of the populist revolts were strongly antigovernment.

The Delegate Surveys

This chapter is based on surveys of delegates to the Republican and Democratic National Conventions of 1992, 1996, and 2000. In each year, a systematic sample of the delegates' names was randomly drawn from the lists of all delegates provided by the national parties. An almost identical questionnaire and methodology was used in each study. Each questionnaire was initially mailed one week after their respective national conventions ended in each election year. Within six to eight weeks, a single follow-up was sent. The receipt of questionnaires was then cut off on the national election date.

In general, there was a good response for a mailed questionnaire, ranging between 40 and 50 percent for each of the studies, well within the range of other similar studies of political elites (Jackson, Brown, and Bositis 1982; Jackson 1992; Jackson and Clayton 1996).[1] An examination of the known characteristics of the delegate population to those who returned the questions revealed no systematic differences, except for the Democrats in 2000. In that case, the percentage of all African-American delegates in the convention population compared to the survey respondents revealed a shortage of responses. As a result, the Democratic delegates were weighted in order to compensate for the shortage of African-American delegates. These samples can be used to generalize to the total population of all delegates to the national conventions in 1992, 1996, and 2000.

The delegate surveys contained eight identically worded Likert-scale items that allow us to measure change in party attitudes over time. Self-identified ideology was asked in all three surveys (a five-point scale) as well as seven issues: government services, national health insurance, aid to minorities, school vouchers, defense spending, term limits (all seven-point scales), and abortion (a four-point scale). While these questions hardly exhaust the controversies of the Volatile Nineties, they do provide a baseline against which to judge changes in party coalitions culminating in 2000. We begin by reviewing each of these items over time (collapsing each item into liberal, moderate, and conservative positions for ease of presentation). Then we subject these items to factor analysis to identify underlying dimensions of opinion (using the full range of the items). Finally, we use the results of the factor analysis to develop a crude measure of factions within the major parties and follow their progress in the 1992, 1996, and 2000 elections.

Attitudes of Party Elites, 1992–2000

A good place to begin describing the attitudes of national convention delegates is with self-identified ideology. Figure 4.1 displays the results of the Democratic and Republican delegates in 1992, 1996, and 2000. Here the delegates' views resemble the results of previous delegate studies (see Jackson, Brown, and Bositis 1982; Jackson and Clayton 1996; Green, Jackson, and Clayton 1999). The Democrats predominantly identified themselves as "liberals" and the Republican delegates overwhelmingly identified themselves as "conservatives." However, self-identified liberals accounted for only a slight majority for the Democrats in all three conventions, actually declining a bit when 1992 is compared to 2000. In contrast, a very large majority of the Republicans called themselves conservatives in all three years; the 2000 figure represented an increase over 1992, but a decline over 1996.

The party elites also differed in the number of self-identified moderates: Democratic moderates ranged from two-fifths to almost one-half over the period, while the comparable Republican figure was much lower, varying between one-sixth and one-quarter. This self-perception is interesting, for, as we will see, Democratic delegates are as strongly liberal on most issues

Figure 4.1 Self-Identified Ideology

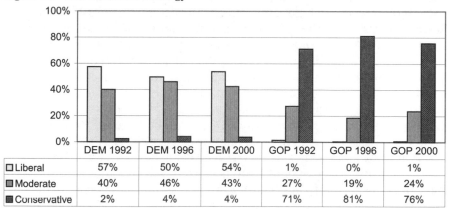

	DEM 1992	DEM 1996	DEM 2000	GOP 1992	GOP 1996	GOP 2000
☐ Liberal	57%	50%	54%	1%	0%	1%
▨ Moderate	40%	46%	43%	27%	19%	24%
▧ Conservative	2%	4%	4%	71%	81%	76%

as the Republicans are conservative. It could be that these figures reflect the negative connotations associated with the "L" word during this period. In contrast, the "C" word was something of a badge of honor among Republicans.

Compared to the benchmark studies of the 1940s and 1950s, the two parties' elites have separated themselves sharply along the liberal-conservative continuum (David, Goldman, and Bain 1960; McClosky, Hoffman, and O'Hara 1960). In the 1990s, there was almost no ideological "misidentification" in either party (i.e., Democrats claiming to be "conservative" or Republicans regarding themselves as "liberals"). The legendary conservative Southerners were no longer a key element among the Democrats, and the liberal Republicans from the Northeast were also a thing of the past. Variants of liberalism and conservatism have taken the places of these historic party factions.

Although the 1990s may not have ushered in the ideal of responsible parties, the party elites were sharply divided along ideological lines. The parties are no longer the pragmatic, electoral-driven organizations that dominated American party politics for a hundred years between the 1850s and the 1960s. Indeed, the ideological patterns since the 1960s are now firmly in place and the rhetoric of ideological polarization in the 1990s was largely a variation on this theme. The GOP delegates that nominated Bob Dole in 1996 were indeed quite conservative, as widely reported at the time, but only by a modest margin compared to their counterparts in 1992 and 2000. By the same token, the claims of party "moderation" in the 1990s, first among the Democrats under Bill Clinton and then the Republicans under George W. Bush, occurred within this strong ideological framework.

The major parties are now consistently composed of two very different groups of elites: one that describes itself as moderate to liberal, and the other that sees itself as solidly conservative. Given their very different value systems, it is not surprising that analysts and practitioners alike now routinely note (and some decry) high levels of interparty conflict in Washington, D.C. Specific issues reveal the scope of such differences among the party elites.

Economic Issues. One the most enduring divisions between the major party elites concerns the proper role of the federal government in economic matters. Democrats, particularly liberals, have long tended to favor more government services and are willing to pay higher taxes in return. In contrast, Republicans, particularly conservatives, have tended to prefer fewer government services and lower taxes. Of course, both parties have made exceptions to these tendencies with regard to particular constituencies. These questions were front and center in the 2000 campaign. Governor Bush advocated a massive tax cut, but also an increase in selected domestic spending areas, arguing the projected budget surplus could accommodate both. Vice President Gore proposed a careful list of new programs and a much smaller tax cut—and attacked Bush for being fiscally irresponsible. Figure 4.2 shows the views of party elites on the provision of government services.

The party elites were quite polarized on this issue. Democrats favored continuing a high level of government services by large majorities, increasing from three-quarters of the delegates in 1992 to more than nine of ten in 2000. In contrast, the Republicans strongly favored fewer government services and lower taxes by large margins. In 2000, however, the Republican opposition to government services dropped sharply, from over 80 percent in the previous years to about 60 percent. And the proportion of Republicans with a neutral position on this question in 2000 was almost four times greater than the Democrats (23 to 6 percent). So, Bush appears to have had some support from GOP party elites in his attempt to moderate the Republican approach to government services with his modest education and "faith-based" initiatives. Gore's more balanced approach enjoyed some support among the Democratic Party elites.

There was even greater interparty polarization on national health insurance, the subject of major party feuding since the New Deal era. In the first Clinton administration, there was a national debate on this issue, led by First Lady Hillary Rodham Clinton, which resulted in a complex and controversial plan. Although the Clinton plan died without a formal congressional vote in 1993, the issue was part of the 2000 campaign in other guises, including proposals for the regulation of Health Maintenance Organizations (HMOs), a prescription drug benefit, and the future of the Medicare and Medicaid programs. On all of these topics, the two parties' proposals divided along predictable lines, with the Democrats preferring governmental solutions and the Republicans favoring private enterprise–based approaches to these complicated issues.

Figure 4.2   Government Services

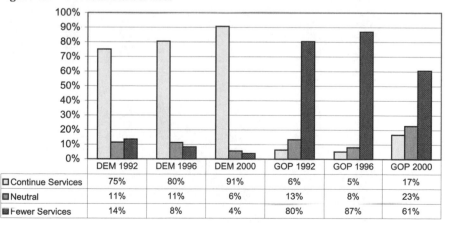

	DEM 1992	DEM 1996	DEM 2000	GOP 1992	GOP 1996	GOP 2000
☐ Continue Services	75%	80%	91%	6%	5%	17%
▦ Neutral	11%	11%	6%	13%	8%	23%
▪ Fewer Services	14%	8%	4%	80%	87%	61%

Figure 4.3 displays the differences between the party activists' positions from 1992 to 2000. The differences could hardly be more striking. Between 70 and 80 percent of the Democratic delegates favored national health insurance, and never fewer than 77 percent of the Republicans opposed it. Here the Democrats moderated a bit, with supporters dropping from over four-fifths in 1992 to less than three-quarters in 2000. But the Republicans went in the opposite direction, moving from some three-quarters to roughly nine of ten opposed. Indeed, there were few delegates neutral on this topic in either party, although Democrats outnumber Republicans in this regard (16 to 6 percent).

Providing help to minority groups, such as affirmative action for African Americans and other victims of prejudice, has long been controversial. Although not strictly an economic issue, by the 1990s it was closely linked to economic views (Carmines and Stimson 1989). African Americans are one of the strongest constituencies of the Democratic Party, reflecting its role in the passage of landmark civil rights legislation in the 1960s as well as continued support for programs that aid minorities. By contrast, the "party of Lincoln" has opposed many of these initiatives since the 1960s, further solidifying minority support for the Democrats. In 2000, Bush sought to mitigate this situation by some policy moderation and extensive symbolism. An example of the latter was the large number of minorities that made prime-time appearances at the 2000 Republican National Convention—in sharp contrast to the very small number of minorities among GOP delegates. Bush's strategy certainly failed at the ballot box, where he received the fewest African American votes of recent GOP presidential candidates. Gore

Figure 4.3   National Health Insurance

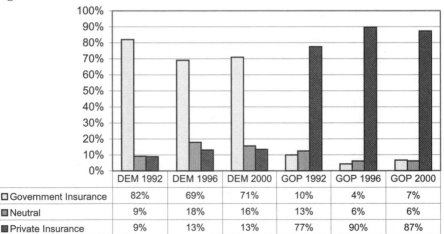

	DEM 1992	DEM 1996	DEM 2000	GOP 1992	GOP 1996	GOP 2000
☐ Government Insurance	82%	69%	71%	10%	4%	7%
▨ Neutral	9%	18%	16%	13%	6%	6%
■ Private Insurance	9%	13%	13%	77%	90%	87%

stressed traditional Democratic positions on these issues and benefited from very high African American turnout.

Figure 4.4 reveals that the two parties were dramatically polarized on the issue of aid to minorities. From 1992 to 2000, roughly three-quarters of the Democratic delegates supported help for minorities, and one-sixth or less opposed such aid. A majority of the GOP delegates opposed such aid in all three years, but its size varied considerably. For example, in 1992, just 50 percent opposed minority aid, a figure that rose to three-quarters in 1996, and then declined to 60 percent in 2000. A large minority of Republican delegates supported minority aid in 1992 and 2000, and these delegates, plus the moderate white voters they represent, may have been the real targets of Bush's symbolism.

Defense Spending. Defense spending is both an economic issue, related to budget priorities, and a foreign policy issue, reflecting perceptions of the threat to national security. For these reasons, the party positions on defense spending vary considerably over time. The 1990s began with the much publicized end of the Cold War and the dramatic American victory in the Persian Gulf; by the end of the decade, the United States was facing new realities in the international system. George W. Bush made defense spending an issue in the 2000 campaign, and he issued a clarion call for an increase in defense spending and a "rebuilding of the U.S.'s defense readiness." He also excoriated the Clinton-Gore administration for its alleged neglect of the defense establishment during their eight years in office. Perhaps as a result of the Bush critique, Gore at times during the campaign suggested that he would increase defense spending even more than Bush proposed. This apparent convergence did not appear among the party elites, as can be seen in figure 4.5.

Figure 4.4   Help for Minorities

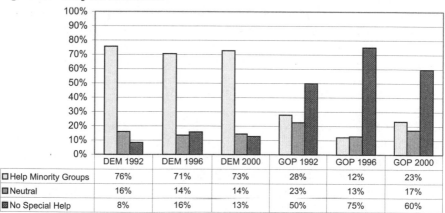

	DEM 1992	DEM 1996	DEM 2000	GOP 1992	GOP 1996	GOP 2000
Help Minority Groups	76%	71%	73%	28%	12%	23%
Neutral	16%	14%	14%	23%	13%	17%
No Special Help	8%	16%	13%	50%	75%	60%

Figure 4.5   Defense Spending

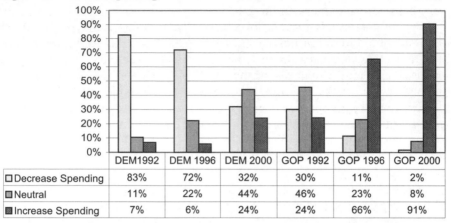

	DEM1992	DEM 1996	DEM 2000	GOP 1992	GOP 1996	GOP 2000
☐ Decrease Spending	83%	72%	32%	30%	11%	2%
▣ Neutral	11%	22%	44%	46%	23%	8%
▪ Increase Spending	7%	6%	24%	24%	66%	91%

The parties essentially reversed patterns on defense spending in the 1990s. In 1992, some four-fifths of Democratic delegates favored a decrease in defense spending, while their GOP counterparts were deeply divided, with less than one-third favoring fewer defense dollars, almost one-half neutral, and only one-quarter for an increase. By 1996, the party elites had polarized, with nearly three-quarters of the Democrats favoring defense cuts, and some two-thirds of the Republicans favoring more money for defense. In 2000, it was the Democrat delegates who were divided, looking very much like the GOP in 1992. Meanwhile, the Republican delegates overwhelmingly supported Bush's call for a defense expansion. Of course, the parties' positions on defense spending could change again dramatically in the wake of the September 11, 2001, terrorist attacks.

Social Issues. Social issues were an important source of party conflict in the 1990s. It is hard to think of an issue that has been more contentious over the past twenty-five years than abortion. The 1973 Supreme Court decision in *Roe v. Wade* that legalized abortion was one of the signal achievements of the women's movement—and a key factor in mobilizing Christian conservatives into politics. Once underway, the abortion debate pushed pro-choice advocates toward the Democrats and pro-life activists toward the GOP. In 2000, Gore strongly supported "a woman's right to choose," while Bush advocated an ambivalent position, promising to sign a ban on certain "late term" abortions, but backing away from a broader commitment to overturn *Roe v. Wade*, which had been a plank in the GOP platform since the 1980s. Figure 4.6 helps account for these positions.

Abortion produced something close to consensus results among Democrats. In 2000, 90 percent of the delegates endorsed the strongest pro-choice

Figure 4.6 Abortion

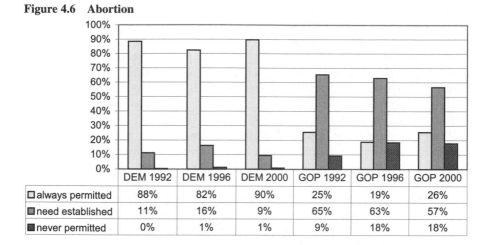

	DEM 1992	DEM 1996	DEM 2000	GOP 1992	GOP 1996	GOP 2000
☐ always permitted	88%	82%	90%	25%	19%	26%
▤ need established	11%	16%	9%	65%	63%	57%
▦ never permitted	0%	1%	1%	9%	18%	18%

position by saying that an abortion should always be permitted—up from 88 percent in 1992. In 1996, this figure declined to 82 percent because the proportion of Democrats who would accept some restrictions on abortion increased. Virtually no Democrats believed that abortions should be banned. In contrast, the Republicans were much more divided. In 2000, one-quarter of the delegates held the strongest pro-choice position, nearly three-fifths accepted some restrictions, and almost one-fifth believed abortions should never be permitted. The 2000 numbers represented a small shift toward the pro-choice position from 1996 and 1992, where support for some restrictions was more popular. These patterns are at variance with a common perception that the GOP is solidly pro-life and the Democrats are divided on the issue. This perception may reflect the vocal activism of pro-life forces in the 1990s, especially Christian conservatives, who have become one of the strongest Republican constituencies.

Another contentious social issue in the 1990s was school choice. One proposal in this regard was for government vouchers that parents and students in inadequate public school systems could use to take their business elsewhere, just as the American consumer would if he or she were dissatisfied with a product or service. Republicans and conservatives—and some inner-city minorities—favored school choice, while liberals and Democrats opposed it. Both parties have strong constituencies with clear positions on this question: Christian conservatives in the GOP and teachers' unions among the Democrats. The school choice issue is partly a question of religious values, but it also represents a populist distrust of certain elites, from teachers to school boards to bureaucrats and legislators. In 2000, Bush expressed cautious support for vouchers and Gore adamantly opposed them in favor of improving the public schools.

As figure 4.7 shows, party elites were deeply and increasingly divided on this issue. In 2000 and 1996, well over 80 percent of Democratic delegates opposed school choice, and just one-tenth or less supported it. This pattern represents a substantial change from 1992, when opposition was limited to 52 percent of the Democrats, while 33 percent of them supported school choice. In all three conventions, nearly 80 percent of the Republican delegates were in favor of school choice. Given that the Supreme Court recently upheld the constitutionality of some form of school vouchers, this issue is likely to remain on the political agenda for years to come.

Term Limits. In contrast to school choice, legislative term limits was an issue of the early to mid-1990s that faded by 2000. Term limits was a classic populist issue because it targeted the prerogatives of a class of elites— legislators—regardless of their politics or performance. The term limits movement arose alongside Ross Perot's presidential campaign and eventually produced legislative term limits in seventeen states (Farmer, Rausch, and Green 2002). One provision in Newt Gingrich's 1994 "Contract with America" was term limits for Congress, but the provision did not pass. Initially, conservatives and Republicans favored term limits in principle but also pragmatically, as a way to help break the long-term grip of the Democrats on Congress and in many state legislatures. However, Republican victories in congressional and state legislative elections in 1994 appear to have reduced support for term limits. Liberals and Democrats tended to oppose terms limits on both philosophical and practical grounds. The issue was not prominent in 2000.

Figure 4.7   School Choice

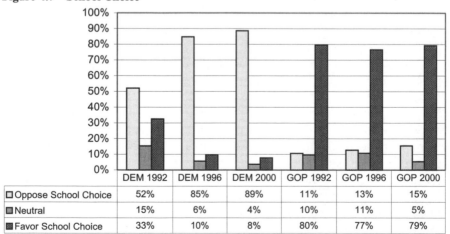

	DEM 1992	DEM 1996	DEM 2000	GOP 1992	GOP 1996	GOP 2000
☐ Oppose School Choice	52%	85%	89%	11%	13%	15%
▨ Neutral	15%	6%	4%	10%	11%	5%
▩ Favor School Choice	33%	10%	8%	80%	77%	79%

Figure 4.8 shows that Democratic opposition was strong and became stronger in the 1990s. In 1992 nearly two-thirds of the delegates opposed term limits, a figure that rose to three-quarters by 1996 and 2000. The small minority of Democrats who backed the idea fell from one-quarter in 1992 to one-sixth in 2000. The Republican delegates experienced greater change on the subject. In 1992, nearly three-quarters of the Republicans supported term limits. By 1996, support had fallen to a bare majority, and by 2000, to just over one-third. Opposition rose from one-fifth in 1992 to over one-third in 1996—and to a majority in 2000.

Issue Dimensions, 1992–2000

How did these attitudes fit together among Republican and Democratic delegates in 1992, 1996, and 2000, and how did the structure of opinion vary over time? To answer these questions, we performed a factor analysis on self-identified ideology and the seven issue questions for all three surveys combined by year and party.[2]

Table 4.1 reports one result of this analysis, combining both sets of party elites. The first column shows the results from 1992–2000, and the next three columns replicate the analysis for each year. The pattern is the same throughout. As one might expect, self-identified ideology, and the economic issues of government services, national health insurance, and help for minorities have the highest loading overall and in each election. The social issues were modestly less polarizing overall, but abortion and school choice be-

Figure 4.8   Term Limits

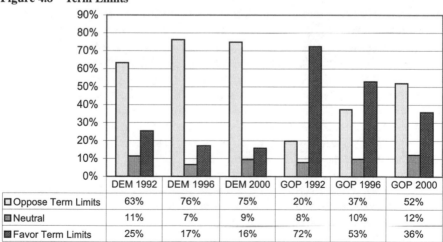

	DEM 1992	DEM 1996	DEM 2000	GOP 1992	GOP 1996	GOP 2000
☐ Oppose Term Limits	63%	76%	75%	20%	37%	52%
▨ Neutral	11%	7%	9%	8%	10%	12%
■ Favor Term Limits	25%	17%	16%	72%	53%	36%

Table 4.1   Structure of Opinion, National Convention Delegates, 1992–2000

Factor Loadings	1992–2000	1992	1996	2000
Liberalism-Conservatism	.87	.87	.88	.87
Maintain government services	.85	.83	.87	.86
Support national health insurance	.83	.82	.83	.83
Support minority assistance	.75	.74	.77	.73
Oppose school choice	.75	.66	.82	.81
Support abortion rights	.73	.69	.73	.76
Decrease defense spending	.68	.67	.78	.76
Oppose term limits	.50	.60	.54	.37
Eigenvalue	4.5	4.4	4.9	4.7
% variance explained	57%	55%	61%	58%
Weighted N	3000	1000	1000	1000

Source: Surveys by authors.

came more so between 1992 and 2000. Defense spending and term limits were less important overall, largely because of the dramatic changes in the pattern of opinion we have noted: defense spending became more polarizing by 2000 and term limits became less so. There should be no doubt that the major party elites were strongly polarized along liberal-conservative lines, and became more so during the Volatile Nineties.

The Internal Structure of Democratic Opinion. A different picture emerges, however, when we look at the structure of opinion among each party's delegates. Table 4.2 looks at the Democrats. In all three years, two dimensions of opinion emerge from the analysis. The first dimension might be called "welfare liberalism" (column A in all three years), and it is made up of self-identified ideology, national health insurance, help for minorities, and defense spending. Delegates on one end of this dimension of opinion strongly identified as liberals and supported the central priorities of the welfare state: national health insurance, help for minorities, and reduced defense spending (presumably to free up funds for domestic support). Delegates on the other end of this dimension were less likely to identify as liberals, and were skeptical of expanded national health insurance, increased aid to minorities, and reduced defense spending. (Of course, among Democratic delegates the "least liberal" were moderate rather than conservative.)

There was some change over time in the contents of welfare liberalism. With the exception of defense spending, the strength of all of these items declined over the period as the Democrats moved toward a consensus on these matters. The development of consensus also helps explain the idiosyncratic patterns of two staples of liberalism: government services and abortion. The government services item changes the most: in 1992 and 1996 it

Table 4.2   Structure of Opinion, Democratic National Convention Delegates, 1992–2000

	1992		1996		2000	
Factor Loadings[a]	A	B	A	B	A	B
Liberalism-Conservatism	.74	—	.61	—	.55	—
Maintain government services	.45	—	.50	—	—	− .58
Support national health insurance	.66	—	.59	—	.57	—
Oppose schools choice	—	.70	—	.81	—	.63
Support minority assistance	.71	—	.71	—	.60	—
Support abortion rights	—	− .42	.40	—	.35	—
Decrease defense sending	.60	—	.66	—	.65	—
Oppose term limits	—	.75	—	.81	—	.65
Eigenvalue	2.2	1.3	2.4	1.2	2.1	1.0
% variance explained	27%	16%	30%	15%	26%	14%

Legend: A = traditional liberalism, B = antigovernment populism

[a]*Positive signs indicate that liberal positions are correlated with opinion dimensions; negative signs indicate that conservative positions are correlated with opinion dimensions. Factor loadings less than .35 are omitted for ease of presentation. See text for details.*

Source: Surveys by authors.

loaded with welfare liberalism, but at a much lower level than the other items, and by 2000 it was hardly part of this dimension at all. Abortion also had a variegated pattern: it loaded modestly level with welfare liberalism in 1996 and 2000, but in 1992 did not. Both these measures made a brief contribution to the second opinion dimension to which we now turn.

The second dimension can be cautiously labeled as "antigovernment populism" and at its core are school choice and term limits (column B in all three years). We use the term "antigovernment" to distinguish the targets of this populism, public officials, as opposed to populism targeted at corporate officials, which is more popular on the left, but for which we lacked consistent measures in the delegate surveys.[3] Despite its limitation, this measure reveals that hostility to government elites was part of the structure of opinion among Democratic delegates in the Volatile Nineties.

In 1992, abortion loaded modestly on the populist dimension, and so did government services in 2000, but both had negative signs. Thus in these years the small minority of delegates with moderate positions on abortion and government services tended to also support school choice and term limits—while the pro-choice, pro-government majorities among their fellow delegates strongly opposed these policies. Overall, clear divisions between economic and social issues did not characterize the Democratic delegates in the 1990s. Instead, there was a major welfare liberalism dimension and a secondary populist one.

The Internal Structure of Republican Opinion. The Republican delegates had a much more complex structure of opinion, changing substantially over the period. As can be seen in table 4.3, there were three dimensions of opinion in 1992 and 1996, and just two in 2000. Readers accustomed to thinking of the Democrats as more diverse than the Republicans may find this result surprising, but other studies of Democratic and Republican elites in the 1980s found similar patterns (see Green and Guth 1991). To adequately capture this complexity, we resort to a special labeling convention based on the content of the issue dimensions.

The 1992 and 1996 Republican conventions were characterized by bitter disagreements between economic and social conservatives. In both years, three economic issues loaded together (government services, national health insurance, and help for minorities), which can be called "economic conservatism." In both years abortion defined "social conservatism," although slightly different versions of these kinds of conservatism appeared in 1992 and 1996.

In 1992, economic conservatism was the most important dimension of opinion and it included conservative ideology (column A1). Social conservatism played a secondary role and included school choice—also cutting defense spending and moderate ideology (note the positive signs in column B1). This finding may reflect the new activists brought into the GOP by Pat Buchanan and Pat Robertson, many of whom did not partake of a broader conservatism. However, by 1996 social conservatism included increased defense spending and conservatism (column B2), and this dimension became

Table 4.3   Structure of Opinion, Republican National Convention Delegates, 1992–2000

	1992			1996			2000	
Factor Loadings[a]	*A1*	*B1*	*D*	*B2*	*A2*	*D*	*C*	*D*
Liberalism-Conservatism	−.49	.64	—	−.70	—	—	−.70	—
Maintain government services	−.76	—	—	—	−.75	—	−.61	—
Support national health insurance	−.68	—	—	—	−.77	—	−.64	—
Oppose school choice	—	−.40	−.59	—	—	−.66	—	−.70
Support minority assistance	−.81	—	—	—	−.64	—	−.67	—
Support abortion rights	—	−.85	—	−.78	—	—	−.55	—
Decrease defense spending	—	.48	−.50	−.66	—	—	−.65	—
Oppose term limits	—	—	−.76	—	—	−.75	—	−.75
Eigenvalue	2.6	1.2	1.0	2.5	1.1	1.1	2.7	1.2
% variance explained	32%	15%	13%	31%	14%	14%	34%	15%

Legend: A1 = economic conservatism 1992; A2 = economic conservatism 1996; B1 = social conservatism 1992; B2 = social conservatism 1996; C = combined conservatism 2000; D = antigovernment populism

[a]Positive signs indicate that liberal positions are correlated with opinion dimensions; negative signs indicate that conservative positions are correlated with opinion dimensions. Factor loadings less than .35 are omitted for ease of presentation. See text for details.

Source: Surveys by authors.

the most important of the issue dimensions. Meanwhile, economic conservatism was relegated to second place in 1996 and only included the three economic questions (column A2).

All of this complexity was reduced sharply in 2000 when the three economic items, abortion, conservatism, and defense spending, all loaded together into what might be called "combined conservatism" (column C). The factor loadings for all of the items except ideology were lower than in the previous years, especially abortion, suggesting a degree of compromise among GOP elites. Thus, the division between economic and social conservatives in 1992 and 1996 was bridged, at least for the moment, in 2000.

One constant from 1992 to 2000 was an "antigovernment populism" factor (column D in each year), which included term limits and school choice, and in 1992 defense spending as well. Thus by 2000, the structure of opinion among the Republican delegates mirrored that of the Democratic delegates: a major combined conservatism dimension and a secondary populist one.

Factions among Party Elites, 1992–2000

To better visualize this structure of opinion among the delegates, we created a crude measure of factions among the party elites.[4] Here we dichotomized the issue dimensions produced above at the mean and then crosstabulated them to produce groups of delegates with various combinations of "high" and "low" scores. For the Democrats, the two issue dimensions produced four such groups. For the Republicans, such a strategy produced potentially eight groups, but upon inspection we combined three of them that were very similar, for a total of six factions.[5]

Democratic Factions. The four Democratic factions represent various combinations of welfare liberalism and antigovernment populism. The most recognizable of these groups we labeled the "Traditional Liberals" because they scored high on welfare liberalism and low on populism. The Traditional Liberals contained a lion's share of the interest group and social movement activists, including feminists, environmentalists, and labor union activists, and tended to be "bicoastal" in residence. Another group was essentially the opposite, scoring low on welfare liberalism and high on antigovernment populism; we called this group the "Traditional Centrists." Drawn heavily from the South and the Midwest, the Traditional Centrists contain more delegates with business occupations.

The other two factions represent additions largely peculiar to the 1990s. We call one the "Populist Liberals" because they score high on welfare liberalism, but also high on antigovernment populism. African Americans are more common in this group, and they tended to come from large metropolitan areas around the country. With some caution, we label the remaining faction the "New Democrats"; they scored low on welfare liberalism (consistent with the fiscal restraint of the Democratic Leadership Council [DLC]) as well as low on the populist dimension (fitting with the progovernment vision of the DLC). Although these groupings—and their labels—must be viewed with caution, they allow us to observe the changes in the makeup of the Democratic convention delegates in the Volatile Nineties. Figure 4.9 shows the relative size of these factions from 1992 to 2000.

The 1992 Democratic convention was a low point for the Traditional Liberals in the 1990s: they made up only about one-fifth of delegates that year. This situation may reflect some discouragement with liberal activism left over from three straight presidential defeats at the hands of Ronald Reagan and his vice president, George H. Bush (1980, 1984, and 1988). However, the Traditional Liberals rebounded in 1996, rising to more than one-third of delegates, and then declining to a bit under one-third in 2000. This change reflects the polarization of the Democratic elites on economic issues we observed above.

The journey of the Traditional Liberals was influenced by the rise and fall of the Populist Liberals. In 1992, they were the single largest faction, making up more than two-fifths of the total. No doubt these delegates were influenced by the populism sweeping across the nation and the critique it offered of welfare liberalism. However, this faction declined sharply after 1992, falling to less than one-sixth of the delegates in 1996 and then to less than one-tenth in 2000. This decline was propelled by the decline in support for school choice and, to a lesser extent, term limits.

The Traditional Centrists made up about one-quarter of the delegates in 1992, outnumbering the Traditional Liberals. They remained essentially unchanged in 1996 and then declined in 2000, ending the period with a little more than one-sixth of the delegates, barely more than one-half the size of the Traditional Liberals in 2000. The decline of school choice hurt this faction, but it was buoyed by the shift in defense priorities among Democratic delegates.

The Traditional Centrists had to compete with a novel "centrist" faction during this period, the New Democrats. This faction was quite small in the 1992 convention, accounting for about one-eighth of the delegates. This suggests that Bill Clinton and Al Gore were first nominated by a variety of other groups, but they apparently made numerous converts: the New Democratic delegates more than doubled by 1996, making up more than one-quarter of the total, and then expanded to more than two-fifths in 2000, to become the single largest faction among the Democrats.

Thus, the national convention that nominated Al Gore for president was quite different than the one that first nominated him for vice president. New Democrats and Traditional Centrists made up more than three-fifths of dele-

Figure 4.9   Democratic Factions, 1992, 1996, and 2000

1992 Democratic Faction Groups

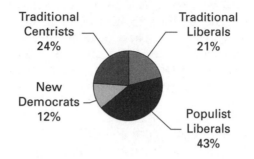

1996 Democratic Faction Groups

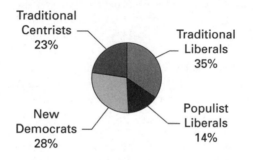

2000 Democratic Faction Groups

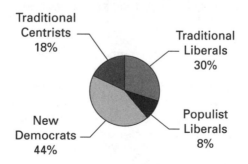

gates in 2000, whereas in 1992, the Traditional and Populist Liberals made up two-thirds of the delegates. In political terms at least, the DLC and Bill Clinton reshaped Democratic elites to offer a more moderate and reformulated approach to a liberal agenda. The key appears to have been a new view of government, which defused the populist tensions that had invaded even the Democrats in the early 1990s. These patterns offer some perspective on Al Gore's populist rhetoric in the 2000 campaign. Having largely remade the party in the image of the DLC, Gore may have needed to reach out to Traditional Liberals in the context of a very close election.

Republican Factions. The GOP was rife with factions in the early 1990s, representing both the successes and failures of the Reagan-Bush era. We find six factions, ranging in rough order on conservatism, which are displayed in figure 4.10: Traditional Conservatives, Populist Conservatives, Populist Moderates, Moderates, Libertarians, and Progressives.

The Traditional Conservatives scored high on both economic and social conservatism, but low on antigovernment populism; the Populist Conservatives scored high on all three dimensions, adding strong support for school choice and especially term limits to conservative positions on the other issues. Much of the Christian Right is found among the Populist Conservatives, but so were elements of the hard right, such as gun owners and antitax advocates.

A similar division occurred among the historic rivals of the hard right, the more moderate conservatives. This division produced the Moderates and the Populist Moderates: the former scored low on economic or social conservatism and also low on populism, while the latter had a similar moderation but high scores on populism. These two factions contained much of the traditional business and professional constituency of the party. (Of course, these "moderates" were conservative compared to the Democratic delegates.)

The Libertarians scored high on economic conservatism and low on social conservatism, and they also scored high on populism, largely on the grounds of personal liberty. Finally, the Progressives harkened back to the once potent "liberal Republicans": they scored low on all of the issue dimensions.

Much as among the Democrats, the populism of the 1990s rearranged the factions within the GOP. The Traditional Conservatives made up only one-twentieth of the delegates in 1992, largely because of the Populist Conservatives, who made up one-fifth of the total. However, the Traditional Conservatives made a rebound in 1996, more than tripling in size to make up over one-sixth of the delegates, and they grew further to about one-quarter of the delegates in 2000. These increases were fueled in part by the decline in support for term limits, especially after the GOP victories in the 1994 elections. However, the Populist Conservatives maintained one-fifth of the delegates in 1996 before declining to less than one-tenth in 2000.

Figure 4.10   Republican Factions, 1992, 1996, and 2000

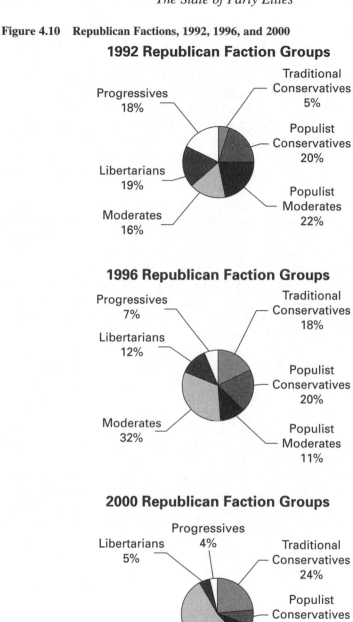

1992 Republican Faction Groups

Traditional Conservatives 5%

Progressives 18%

Populist Conservatives 20%

Libertarians 19%

Populist Moderates 22%

Moderates 16%

1996 Republican Faction Groups

Progressives 7%

Traditional Conservatives 18%

Libertarians 12%

Populist Conservatives 20%

Moderates 32%

Populist Moderates 11%

2000 Republican Faction Groups

Progressives 4%

Libertarians 5%

Traditional Conservatives 24%

Populist Conservatives 7%

Moderates 53%

Populist Moderates 7%

The Moderates experienced a similar trajectory. In 1992, they made up about one-sixth of the delegates, and were eclipsed by the Populist Moderates with more than one-fifth. However, the Moderates made a big comeback in 1996, doubling in size to almost one-third. Much of this gain appears to have been at the expense of the Populist Moderates, whose numbers were cut by one-half, falling to about one-tenth of the total. This trend continued in 2000, when the Moderate faction expanded to an outright majority of the GOP delegates, and the Populist Moderates declined to less than one-tenth. So, the long-standing debate over how conservative the GOP should be was submerged briefly by a surge of populism in 1992, but then resurfaced once the surge subsided.

Both the Libertarians and Progressives suffered dramatic declines over the period. Each made up almost one-fifth of the delegates in 1992 and fell steadily to less than one-twentieth by 2000, with the Libertarians declining somewhat more slowly. The merging of the economic and social conservatism in 2000 sharply reduced the distinctiveness of these small factions. In fact, if the 2000 survey were analyzed by itself, most of these delegates would be in the Moderate faction, largely because of their strong pro-choice position on abortion. Thus, the Moderates may actually have approached some three-fifths of the 2000 delegates.

Thus, the national convention that nominated George W. Bush was quite different from the one that renominated his father. In 1992, the Republican delegates were deeply divided, with no single faction making up as much as one-quarter of the total. The bitter public confrontation between the economic and social conservatives, exemplified by Pat Buchanan's "culture wars" speech at the convention, may have doomed the party to defeat. Although buoyed by the unexpected 1994 victory, these kinds of divisions still hampered the GOP in 1996. But in 2000, the Moderates were in the ascendancy, having made a fragile peace with both conservatives and populists. Whether George W. Bush produced this combination or was a product of it, this fragile detente allowed the Republicans to return to presidential competitiveness in 2000. The key feature of this "compassionate conservatism" is compromise on social issues and government services focused around the ideal of a vigorous private sector. Whether this gambit succeeds or not remains to be seen, but it is possible that President Bush could remake the Republicans in the same fashion as President Clinton remade the Democrats.

The State of Party Elites in the New Century

What do the attitudes of party elites tell us about the state of the parties? Three conclusions come to mind. First, Democratic and Republican party elites are sharply polarized along liberal-conservative lines, and with a few exceptions became more so in the 1990s. In this sense, the major parties have moved toward the "responsible party" model, a shift that appears to be part of a broader change in American politics. After surveying all such evidence, Pomper concludes the United States is developing "institutions of semi-parliamentary, semi-responsible government" (see chapter 17; Pomper 1999). Our evidence documents some of the contours of this new and uniquely eclectic model of the American party system at the beginning of the twenty-first century. The "perfect tie" in 2000 may have been partly due to the fact that each major party offered real choices to the voters on a variety of issues, and the country was deeply divided on these choices.

Second, candidate-centered pragmatism played an important role within the context of such ideological polarization. Within both parties, there were concerted efforts to moderate—but not reverse—the dominant ideological tendencies. The rise of the New Democrats and the Republican Moderates among delegates from 1992 to 2000 bespeaks the impact of such efforts. Both parties found ways to come to terms with the populist uprisings of the early 1990s, and by 2000, new factions were in the ascendancy. The New Democrats sought to make government more "responsible" to win elections, and they produced two (and almost three) presidential victories. Meanwhile, the GOP Moderates sought to make the conservative forces behind the party's dramatic congressional and state victories more "responsible" so they could regain the White House, and they succeeded, albeit by the slimmest of margins. So, another reason for the "perfect tie" in 2000 was that each party had moderated its internal disputes enough to make a plausible case to the voters.

Finally, we can raise some useful questions about how the "perfect tie" might be broken among party elites in the early years of the new century. Will the New Democrats be able to maintain the support of the Traditional Liberals without losing their hard-won commitment to fiscal discipline and personal responsibility? And can the party remain competitive if elements defect to the Green Party or some alternative minor party? Having finessed the antigovernment populism of the 1990s, can the New Democrats handle a rise of anticorporate populism? Similarly, can Bush's "compassionate conservatism" move beyond rhetoric to substantial changes in policy? Can the GOP Moderates survive some of the contradictions built into the Bush coalition, especially the special emphasis on the private sector? And will the Traditional and Populist Conservatives remain cooperative without major—and controversial—concessions on social issues?

Answering these questions is complicated by the potential for new issues to arise, such as those associated with the war on terrorism. However, it will be the party elites who will rise—or fail—to meet these challenges, whatever they may be. The two parties provide evidence of both continuity and change as they adapt to the new challenges and conditions while trying to preserve their distinctive values. These party elites will lead and define the two parties as they face the first decade of the twenty-first century.

Notes

1. In the 2000 survey, we received 475 usable returns for the Democrats, for a response rate of 48.7 percent, excluding undeliverable mail; for the Republicans, we received 432 usable returns, for a response rate of 45.5 percent, excluding undeliverable mail.

2. For purposes of this analysis, we used the full range of the survey items. So that the number of cases in each of the studies did not bias the results, we weighted each set of party delegates and each year equally. We performed a principal components analysis with a varimax rotation.

3. Items for the individual surveys suggest that opposition to corporate elites is likely to be strongly associated with welfare liberalism.

4. Here we define factions by issue positions rather than membership in or affect toward factional organizations. Of course, issue positions and affiliation with such organizations are highly correlated (Baer and Dolan 1994; Green, Jackson, and Clayton 1999).

5. For these purposes, we used factor scores generated by pooling all three surveys. For the Democrats, the results are straightforward because the same two-factor solution emerged in the pooled data. The Republicans were more complicated: the pooled data generated a three-factor solution, with an economic conservatism factor (government services, national health insurance, and help for minorities), social issue conservatism (ideology, abortion, and school choice), and populism (term limits, school choice, and defense spending). We used factor scores from this analysis to define the GOP factions.

5

Out of the Shadows, but Still in the Dark?
The Courts and Political Parties

David K. Ryden

In contemplating the state of American political parties, the U.S. Supreme Court looms large. A historic 2000–2001 term memorably demonstrated an ever-growing challenge for the parties: the constitutionalizing of the electoral process and the judicial shaping of the world in which parties operate. Once upon a time, the High Court routinely declined to intervene in a host of questions overtly political in nature. But since its piercing of the "political question" barrier some forty years ago in *Baker v. Carr*, 369 U.S. 186 (1962), the Court's entry into the electoral realm has been steadily and inexorably growing. Recent terms show a Court no longer merely stumbling occasionally into the "political thicket," but rather a Court that is now "head gardener," pruning and shaping the political process. It now habitually thrusts itself into the electoral arena, reshaping practical politics in dramatic and often unintended ways. The culmination of this trend, of course, was the Court's hand in bringing the 2000 presidential election to a merciful end in *Bush v. Gore*. Despite the protestations of many, the case was an aberration only in the circumstances that forced the election into the courts in the first place. Arguably it was the logical extension of the Court's increasingly proactive and assertive regulation of the electoral process.

A brief glance back reveals the extent of the constitutionalizing of the electoral process. The roster of Supreme Court decisions from the past few years reaches far and wide, including hot-button questions like term limits, campaign finance regulation, and the role of race in redistricting. It touched on a host of other political issues—ballot initiatives, statistical sampling for census purposes, participation in party conventions, ballot issues for third parties, and patronage.

Nevertheless, the 2000 term elevated to a new level the Court's role as a prime force in shaping electoral politics. *Bush v. Gore,* 121 S. Ct. 525 (2000) marked the Court's most dramatic intervention into the political process in modern American history. This enormously controversial decision will forever be grist for the academic mill. But even as *Bush v. Gore* dominated the headlines, several other decisions held important legal ramifications for political parties. In *California Democratic Party v. Jones,* 530 U.S. 567 (2000), the Court rejected a ballot-induced state law imposing blanket primaries on the state parties. In *FEC v. Colorado Republican Federal Campaign Committee,* 121 S. Ct. 2351 (2001), the Court upheld existing Federal Election Campaign Act (FECA) limits on what political parties could spend in coordination with their candidates.

These decisions demonstrate the challenge the presence of the Court presents for the major parties. They reveal a Court driven by pragmatic considerations, aiming for satisfactory political outcomes over doctrinal neatness. Yet, even as the Court displays only sporadic cognizance of the character and function of parties, its decisions significantly shape party behavior. The future success and relevance of parties will rest in no small part on how they react to this formidable judicial presence.

Judicial decisions impact parties on multiple levels. One group of questions relates to the *legal-contextual effects:* How do cases change the constitutional backdrop, or how do legal frameworks influence how parties operate? A second set of questions relates to the *functional effects:* How do the cases impact parties' capacity to perform the variety of tasks and functions they bring to democratic politics? Finally, the cases have *competitiveness effects:* How do they directly and indirectly affect the level, nature, and intensity of competition between the two major parties? These sets of effects are not mutually exclusive, but overlap and interact. They depend on how the parties themselves react and respond to judicial edicts. A change in the legal environment of parties may influence (for better, worse, or both) their functional capabilities. Party organizations will likely counter or adapt to those changes for immediate or long-term competitive gain. The decisions vary widely in nature and degree of impact on these three levels.

Several theoretical models are useful in ascertaining the import of Supreme Court decisions on parties. While none furnishes a consistent framework for analysis, they equip us with a working language for dissecting judicial action impacting the parties. One approach to the Court's party jurisprudence is the *responsible party model.* Responsible parties are marked by (1) a clearly defined ideological identity and policy orientation, (2) candidates who embrace that intellectual dimension of the party and campaign on it, and (3) discipline in pursuing the party's policy platform by those members elected to office. In this view, strong party systems are essential organizational tools of representative politics. Responsible parties institutionalize public opinion, discern and reflect majority sentiment, and channel opinions into policy outputs. Representation comes through the competing agendas and programs that rival parties present to voters. The result is competitive elections that grant authority to those in power, and ensure their accountability to the governed.

A second model stresses *the hierarchical/populist duality* of parties. Contemporary controversies reflect the tension between the participatory role of individual members and the mass of voters, on one hand, and the collective and organizational role of party leaders on the other (Maveety 2001, 30). The two roles are often at odds: The activists frequently run counter to the populist tradition of expanding and enlarging the role of voters at large and the interests of the organization. They entail fundamentally divergent visions of what makes a strong and vital democratic system.

The third analytical model is the tripartite description of parties traditionally employed by party scholars. The *party-in-government* refers to their governing capacity, and the extent to which government actions result from the partisan makeup of the legislative and executive branches, and policy conflict, competition, and compromise between them. Strong parties-in-government exhibit discipline and unity as they pursue explicit policy agendas, manage the legislative process, and dominate the ranks of government. The *party-in-the-electorate* refers to the partisan attachments among the electorate, and the strength and durability of those attachments. It refers to the parties' standing among the voters—the bond or connection that they are able to maintain with citizens. Finally, the *party organization* includes the party entities, associations, and activists standing between the party-in-the-electorate and the party-in-government. Party organizations work to mobilize and expand the party presence in the electorate, to translate it into success at the voting booth, into majority status in government. The effects of judicial action cannot be accurately assessed without isolating the aspect of *party* at issue.

Bush v. Gore: Does Party-in-Government Now Include the U.S. Supreme Court?

The significance of *Bush v. Gore* for the parties, while indirect, was nevertheless complex and potentially enormous. From a party perspective, the momentous decision is akin to a pebble tossed in a pond, with its implications for the parties rippling outward in a multiplicity of directions.

The conclusion is unavoidable: The Supreme Court determined the winner of the 2000 presidential election. On the most elementary level, it carried the most direct partisan impact imaginable by deciding the contest for the highest elected position in the country, putting the executive branch of the federal government in the hands of one party and denying it to the other.

Many critics found the Court guilty, not just of politicking, but also of overt partisanship. The decision was "intensely partisan" (Foner 2001), a "nakedly partisan" (Hertzberg 2000) grab at "a political outcome" (*The New Republic,* 2000). The five-justice majority was openly equated with the Republican Party; *Bush v. Gore* was the result of "right-wing Republican control of the Supreme Court," reflecting "a decisive preference by the judges for one party over another" (Kennedy 2001). The Court wielded judicial power in "the interests of a particular political party and [to] install its candidate in power" (Balkin 2001; see also Greenhouse 2000).

Some distance from the case and the intense passions the postelection battle generated should enable us to dispense with the notion of the Court as part of the "party-in-government." The Court cannot be understood from a conventional party analysis, and to conclude from *Bush v. Gore* that the Court and the political parties are equivalent is woefully simplistic. The justices' behavior, even if influenced on some level by party politics, was not necessarily impelled by the desire for an explicit partisan outcome. Indeed, the charges of partisan motive reveal less about the Court than its accusers, whose partisan blinders seemed to have prevented them from recognizing other reasonable bases for the outcome.

One persuasive explanation is that the members of the Court were guided by competing judicial principles that naturally aligned with the respective parties. The opinions reflected two decidedly different ideological views among judges of the democratic process, views that happened to coincide with the party positions. For the majority in *Bush v. Gore,* the emphasis was on order, stability, and participation channeled through established rules and forms of engagement (parties, for example). The recount exercise unfolding before them in the various Florida counties offended their understanding of procedural order and fairness. The minority, in contrast, valued openness, inclusion, and maximum individual participation. Hence the desire to count every vote, even if it meant messy recounts in Florida (Pildes 2001).

A second explanation attributed the decision to pragmatism rather than partisanship. According to this view, the outcome was not only defensible, but was the least undesirable of a number of unpalatable options. While weakly reasoned, the majority opinion ending the recount process was justifiable, even praiseworthy. The decisions to first stay and then end the recount altogether, while distasteful, avoided worse alternatives sure to follow—heavy-handed interference by the Republican-controlled Florida state legislature and the passing of the matter to the U.S. Congress.

The majority was roundly abused for snatching the conflict from popularly elected, accountable representative bodies. *Bush v. Gore* was said to reveal an arrogant judiciary distrustful of the political process and disdainful of the parties around which state legislatures and Congress are organized. Were the Court so contemptuous of parties and party-run legislative bodies, it would be highly troublesome.

But precedent suggests the majority is not nearly as dismissive of parties or the political process. The *Bush v. Gore* majority has been far more willing to explicitly acknowledge the benefits of strong parties. Meanwhile, those in the *Bush* minority have generally shown little regard for parties, preferring instead populist understandings of individual political rights and unmediated participation.[1]

The majority was more likely animated, not by its contempt for parties, but by its cognizance of the public's disdain for them. It correctly foresaw that an election decided by legislatures and their partisan majorities would not be accepted by a public that holds parties in such low esteem. The Court was equally aware of its own institutional standing relative to Congress, and its ability to absorb and withstand damage the decision might inflict. It was willing to sacrifice some of its short-term institutional legitimacy to assure greater acceptance for the eventual presidential winner. In this view, *Bush v. Gore* was a judgment born out of pragmatic objectives of legitimacy and public acceptance. One pair of commentators put it this way:

> The Court had a stopping point at its disposal, and it finally was the actor that took the opportunity to use it and bring the 2000 election to an end. . . . The Court knew, for better or worse, that it had the reservoir of respect to end the contest without entering a real crisis, and that it was perhaps the only institution at that point in a position to do so. (Ceaser and Busch 2001, 209–210)

Notwithstanding Justice Stevens' mournful dissent predicting the demise of the Court, hindsight suggests the Court's calculations were accurate.

Bush v. Gore, the Legal Environment, and the Implications for Parties. The implications for parties extend well beyond the immediate selection of the president. While *Bush v. Gore* did not directly alter the legal-structural framework for party operations, it could trigger subsequent changes in that legal regime. For example, the Court's doctrinal reliance on the Equal Protection Clause, if taken at face value, could have substantial repercussions for voting rights. Seven justices found that the selective hand recounting of ballots in the absence of consistent standards violated the equal right to vote, and to have one's vote count, including the manner of its exercise. This could require much greater vigilance on the part of courts and legislatures to ensure equity in voting practices and procedures.

Such inequities disproportionately affect those belonging to Democratic voting blocs. A postelection precinct-by-precinct study by the *Washington Post* found that rejected ballots, antiquated voting equipment, and other disparities most heavily impact poor, minority, and Democratic neighborhoods (Mintz and Keating 2001). An adjustment to the constitutional backdrop—by broadening the future application of equal protection to the mechanics of voting processes—would work a competitive advantage for Democrats.

Consider *Department of Commerce v. U.S. House of Representatives,* 119 S. Ct. 765 (1999). In that case, the Court vetoed the Clinton administration's plan to implement statistical sampling in the 2000 Census to more accurately count population for reapportioning U.S. House seats. Conventional methods have traditionally undercounted millions of citizens, especially low-income minorities and urban dwellers. *Bush v. Gore*'s standard of "equal treatment and fundamental fairness . . . in the electoral process" could obligate states redrawing district lines to use sampling for a more accurate count. The undercount (estimated at 2–4 percent) is far larger than the minuscule number of Florida ballots at issue in the recount (0.7 percent of the state's total ballots). Might not the Court's finding of a denial of equal protection in Florida require it to revisit the Census undercount issue (Klain 2001)? A reversal could position Democrats to make considerable gains in the House in future elections (Ryden 2000).

As currently comprised, the Court would unlikely reach such a result. Nor would it construe equal protection so broadly in other circumstances, given its attempt to limit its holding to the specific circumstances. Nevertheless, *Bush v. Gore* may not be so easily confined in the future. A more sympathetic treatment of equal protection claims in the voting context could create "the potential for future mischief" (Mansfield 2001) or worse, "an explosion of federal lawsuits after every close election" (Rosen 2001).

The Florida fiasco also prompted widespread demands for changes in the election laws themselves. Many called for reconstituting or abolishing outright the Electoral College. Others sought uniform voting procedures, standardized equipment, and other improvements to the election machinery and voting methods. Changes to the Electoral College or large-scale federalizing of the voting process could seriously alter the strategic shape and nature of party campaigns and activities, and perhaps the competitive balance between the parties.

However, the likelihood of major electoral reform legislation has dimmed considerably since the 2000 election. Talk of amending the Electoral College has dissipated almost completely. Other reforms have been slow in coming. On the federal level, Congress is on the verge of modest voting reforms that would offer block grants for certain election improvements, tying the availability of federal funds to mandated machine and ballot standards (Seligson 2001a). At the state level, the results have been even more modest, despite hundreds of proposed bills. Florida passed the most significant legislation, outlawing punch cards and butterfly ballots, rewriting the rules for recounts and registration, and providing state-of-the-art machines and uniform ballots (Seligson 2001b). Otherwise, only a handful of other states wrought any meaningful change in their election laws. Thus, it appears *Bush v. Gore* is unlikely to work far-reaching change in the statutory regime that frames party activity.

Bush v. Gore and Partisan Competition: How Will the Parties Respond?
Bush v. Gore may also impact partisan competition between Democrats and Republicans. The case could act as a catalyst, driving party responses that in turn influence party competition in upcoming elections. A presidency stolen from Democrats by a partisan judiciary could be an effective strategy to mobilize the party-in-the-electorate to vote in future elections (Rosen 2001).

It is difficult to gauge the staying power of the intense passions aroused by *Bush v. Gore.* One wonders whether the Court will be a "devil" Democrats can run against. From casual observation, it is striking how quickly *Bush v. Gore* passed from the scene. The general public did not greet the decision with widespread outrage or anger, as did academic and party elites. The weakened links between the parties and the electorate meant that anger and disappointment from the decision did not run very deep. The case hardly made a dent in the Court's general approval ratings. Even among Democrats, the resentment has gradually dissolved. After a precipitous plunge of some thirty percentage points after *Bush v. Gore,* the Court's approval rating among Democrats rose from 42 percent to 55 percent over the next nine months (*Gallup News Service* 2001).

Certainly the potential of *Bush v. Gore* as a turnout tool for Democrats lost much of its punch with the postelection recounts performed by various news services. As the extended battle in Florida dragged on, many expected that a full count would inevitably produce a victory for Gore. Instead, the news organizations' recounts were inconclusive at best, and offer some support for Bush's win. While the *Miami Herald/USA Today* recount produced numerous possible outcomes, the paper concluded that "under almost all scenarios, Bush still would have won" (Merzer 2001; see also Driscoll 2001).

Intervening events also have dampened the doubts many harbored as to President Bush's legitimacy. The impulse for national unity in the face of the terrorist acts of September 11 and subsequent events squelched anti-Bush sentiments. Partisanship was shelved, at least temporarily, and Bush was transformed into a legitimate president, even in the eyes of many Democrats. While Democratic support for Bush will surely wane, the charge of illegitimacy is weakened by the events that have transpired.

Two final observations are worth noting. First, the interplay between the Court and political parties is likely to become a more reciprocal affair. Senate Democrats are likely to act with greater partisanship on Bush's judicial nominations. Some academics have urged them to rebut any efforts by Bush to appoint more conservative judges. A partisan freeze on the judicial appointment process is not what an overburdened and understaffed federal judiciary needs, nor is it consistent with long-standing traditions surrounding the "Advise and Consent" power of the Senate. Nevertheless, Democratic senators can make a strong case for asserting their role in the confirmation process in the face of a closely divided government and a politicized judiciary, especially when serious ideological differences exist between Democrats and the nominee.

The other potential impact of the 2000 election may be to bring the Court back into the public consciousness. A more realistic grasp of the political and pragmatic considerations that inform the Court's work is a desirable thing. It might even resurrect as a meaningful campaign issue the future direction of the Court and the candidates' likely appointments to the bench. With retirements anticipated among the current Court, and given its frequent ideological polarization, future appointments should have been front and center as a campaign issue in 2000; instead they were relatively low on the campaign radar screen. That the election was ultimately determined by the Court in a 5-4 vote is one of the rich ironies of political and legal history.

Parties, Primaries, and Voters

In *California Democratic Party v. Jones,* 530 U.S. 567 (2001), the Court's rejection of a mandatory blanket primary modestly revised the legal backdrop in favor of "responsible" and "hierarchical" parties at the expense of broader and more inclusive public participation. In the process, it enhanced the functional capacity of parties to couple their electoral identity with their ability to govern. The preference for closed over open or blanket primaries implicitly rests upon the "responsible party" notion of parties and party membership. If parties are to serve a programmatic purpose—by offering a policy platform that voters can hope to see enacted into law—they require a means of securing candidates who will campaign on those stances and pursue them in office.

Blanket primaries do the opposite. They strip party affiliation from primary voting, depriving parties of control over the ideological or policy commitments of those who will carry forward the party label. Opening up primaries to voters unaffiliated with the party dilutes the party choice of candidate. It destroys the link between what parties stand for and what they can deliver should they win. By eroding partisan coordination of policy making, blanket primaries threaten the intellectual coherence of parties. In *Jones,* the Court gave the parties a small measure of protection by allowing them to delineate who can vote in the primary.

These pro-party arguments often come across as abstract musings without practical application. But the 2000 Republican presidential primaries gave concrete illustration to the practical repercussions of open versus closed primaries. John McCain's challenge to eventual winner George W. Bush was built largely on primaries that were open to non-Republican voters. There, he was the overwhelming choice among crossover Democratic voters and preferred by independents. Where voting was limited to Republican Party affiliators, Bush dominated. The respective performances of President Bush and Senator McCain since the election make the point. Bush has proven himself largely in tune with established Republican orthodoxy (tax cuts, strong defense, traditional morality), while McCain has grown even more independent. Had a system of open primaries led to a McCain nomination, the presence of the Republican party-in-government would have been less united and consequently weakened.[2]

The case's *functional effects* for parties, while real, are relatively modest. Given the rarity of blanket primaries (only three states), the party victory in California is at most a rear-guard action against further erosion of a function already eviscerated by commonplace open primaries. Although the arguments for party autonomy apply with significant force to open primaries, the constitutional demise of open primaries is unlikely, given the cautious, incremental nature of this Court.

Parties and the Perils of Campaign Finance Regulation

The campaign finance cases are decidedly more complicated in their implications for political parties, though they are more notable for what they failed to do than anything they accomplished. Pro-party scholars had eagerly anticipated the *Colorado Republican Federal Campaign Committee v. FEC,* 518 U.S. 604 (1996) case as a vehicle by which the Court might sweep away all financing restrictions on parties. This case was the second time Colorado's 1986 U.S. Senate race was before the Court. During the race, the state Republican Party had run radio ads against Democratic Congressman Tim Wirth, the declared candidate for the seat. Since the GOP did not yet have a declared candidate, it counted the ads as operating costs rather than party "coordinated expenditures" limited by the Federal Election Campaign Act (FECA). The Federal Election Commission (FEC) sued when Democrats complained that the cost of the ads exceeded FECA limits. The Republican Party defended with a frontal challenge to all campaign spending limits on parties, claiming a violation of the First Amendment.

In *Colorado Republican Party I, Colorado Republican Federal Campaign Committee v. Federal Election Commission* (Colorado 1; 518 U.S. 604 [1996]), the Court sided with the Republican Party by a 7-2 vote, but decided the case on narrowly circumscribed grounds. Avoiding the broad question of whether parties could be subject to any spending restrictions, the Court found no coordination with a candidate (since the party had no declared candidate when the ads ran). Hence the spending was the functional equivalent of independent spending and not subject to limitation. However, four justices within the majority expressed a willingness to dispense with party restrictions altogether. In so doing, they invoked a "responsible party" model of politics; the elevated financing role for parties would legitimately give them leverage over candidates to ensure their loyalty to the party platform. *Colorado Republican Party I* left party proponents eagerly anticipating the next case to see if Justice O'Connor could be convinced to join the pro-party forces.

In the interim between the two Colorado cases, the Court decided *Nixon v. Shrink Missouri Government,* 120 S. Ct. 897 (2000). The state law at issue in *Nixon* closely resembled the FECA, presenting the Court with an opportunity to revisit the much-maligned 1976 *Buckley v. Valeo,* 424 U.S. 1, decision, which had nevertheless survived as the basic constitutional framework for campaign finance regulations. The criticisms of *Buckley* centered on the constitutional distinction between contributions (which could be limited) and expenditures (which could not). The plaintiffs challenged the $1,000 statutory contribution limit on free speech and associational grounds, contending it kept them from running competitive campaigns. The Court rejected the claim, reaffirming the basic regulatory approach crafted in *Buckley. Nixon* signaled that broad-scale challenges to *Buckley* and the current legal regime would likely be unsuccessful (Hasen 2000, 26).

The six-member majority opinion also suggested it might not be so friendly to eliminating constraints on parties. Emphasizing the danger of *the appearance* of corruption, the *Nixon* Court remarked, "[l]eave the perception of impropriety unanswered, and the cynical assumption that large donors call the tune could jeopardize the willingness of voters to take part in democratic governance."

Limits were warranted, not just to guard against corruption, but by voters' perceptions (warranted or not) that politicians are too beholden to well-heeled interests.

Five years after its predecessor, *Colorado Republican Party II, Federal Election Commission v. Colorado Republican Federal Campaign Committee* (Colorado II, 121 S. Ct. 2351 [2001]) put the question of party-coordinated expenditures squarely and unavoidably before the Court. The encore presentation of the case sorely disappointed those seeking a purge of all constraints on the parties' role in financing elections. In a narrow 5-4 split, the Court upheld FECA limits on party expenditures made in coordination with their candidates (with the four justices who concurred in *Colorado I* dissenting here). The majority opinion explicitly rejected the "responsible party" justifications put forth by the state Republican Party (and the four dissenters). Instead, it expressly equated parties with other political players. To Justice Souter, coordinated party spending "functionally unite[d] parties with other self-interested political actors" rather than distinguished them (p. 2364). Parties are "in the same position as some individuals and PACs [Political Actions Committees], as to whom coordinated spending limits have already been held valid" (p. 2366). Party-coordinated spending posed the same risk of corruption as when other entities spent in coordination with a candidate.

So what are the ramifications of these decisions for parties? No area of election law is fraught with greater uncertainty in forecasting future developments. Changes in campaign spending rules are sure to have consequences both expected and unintended. Moreover, candidates, parties, and outside groups react and adapt with alacrity to changes in the legal regime. The ramifications of these cases are difficult to predict, hinging in large part on the responses of political actors. Litigation over the Bipartisan Campaign Reform Act (BCRA), passed in 2002, is a case in point.

Easiest to decipher are the immediate effects on partisan competition, of which Democrats are the clear beneficiaries. The hard money limits upheld in *Nixon* (on contributions) and *Colorado II* (on coordinated expenditures) disfavor Republicans, who traditionally are better at raising hard money from individual donors. Had the Missouri law (and the FECA limits on hard money by extension) fallen, it would have opened a wide Republican advantage in raising hard money.

More difficult to predict are the legal-structural effects and their impact on the performance of party functions. Had the coordinated party expenditure limits fallen, conventional "responsible party" wisdom holds that greater influence would have accrued to parties over their candidates, enhancing their intellectual component and strengthening the link between partisan organizations and parties in government. The influence of parties on candidate selection and election would have continued to expand, giving the parties greater control over their members once in office (Wallison 2001).

Instead, *Colorado II* dampens coordination between parties and candidates, further complicating the linking of candidates to coherent national policies. While the majority viewed parties' coordinated funding of candidates as corrupting, to "responsible party" types, it allows some intellectual compatibility between partisan organizations and candidates running under their label. How else is a party to advance its core principles and positions? Taken together, the two Colorado cases discourage spending arrangements that allow strategies and messages to be tailored, synchronized, and melded together. They fly in the face of the responsible party model, simultaneously encouraging unlimited independent spending by parties over coordinated spending between candidate and party.

Consideration of these decisions leads inevitably to the central issue of soft money. At this point, educated speculation can quickly turn to wild conjecture. Nevertheless, some tentative observations on the soft money front are in order. First, these cases do nothing to quell the demand for, or diminish the role of, soft money. By upholding the puny hard money caps, *Nixon* guarantees the continuing thirst for soft money. *Colorado II* further ensures the premium on soft money at the expense of hard. If parties could spend unlimited amounts of hard money on their candidates, they would put greater efforts into raising it. The incentives to raise hard money would increase and the need for soft money would abate (Wallison 2001). Until hard money is easier to raise, the manic pursuit of soft money and other deep-pocketed sources will continue.

Second, if the soft money ban in BCRA stands judicial scrutiny, the functional effects of *Nixon* and *Colorado II* will be amplified. The combination is likely to badly undercut parties' ability to raise and expend significant resources. The beneficiaries will be nonparty groups to whom those funds will be redirected (Samuelson 2001), diminishing parties relative to rival special interests. It will also weaken competitiveness of elections by hampering the ability of parties to target races for special attention and spending. Elections will become even more secure for incumbents. Hence the charge that McCain-Feingold is only a thinly veiled incumbency-protection act.[3]

This raises the central question of the constitutionality of a soft money ban, and how the Court will resolve the inevitable challenge. While *Nixon* and *Colorado II* provide no conclusive answers, they do lend credence to the rationale usually extended for banning soft money. In each instance, the majority articulated a general interest not only in preventing actual political corruption, but also in avoiding its appearance. Large soft money contributions undeniably generate perceptions of corruption among the public, even if actual corruption has not been proven.

These cases, and the entire campaign finance debate, demonstrate the dialectic interplay between the Court and party organizations. Judicial action triggers party responses on a political level; the cases have second- and third-order effects, as the parties react to changing legal contexts to gain the competitive edge. These produce the next round of legal challenges that may bring the Court back into the arena. Consequently, party responses carry both risks and opportunities.

The *Colorado* cases reveal the peril of exploiting legal openings too successfully. The removal of limits on independent party expenditures produced a deluge of soft money spending in subsequent election cycles. The expansion of party influence on an otherwise candidate-centered electoral system was discernible (Magleby and Holt 1999). But the parties' very success in exploiting the decision fueled the cries for banning soft money, arguably pushing the ever-cautious Justice O'Connor into the pro-regulation camp in *Colorado II.*

Party responses to judicial action are determined by immediate concerns of electoral competitiveness, not abstract visions of responsible parties. Had coordinated expenditure limits been set aside, Republicans with their larger base of hard money donors would have overwhelmed Democrats in hard money fundraising. It would have left soft money the lone remaining weapon in the Democrats' arsenal, meaning instant death for reform efforts such as

BCRA. With Democrats far less vulnerable on the issue of hard money, they were more receptive to a soft money ban. The passage of BCRA will trigger the next round of partisan responses, followed eventually by the judgment of the Court. And so the dance will continue.

In the end, questions abound as to what campaign finance reform means for parties and their ability to function in a more responsible mode. Their heightened status as campaign financing actors has led to greater influence overall—in coordinating national, state, and local organizations; in articulating and advancing a more coherent party image and identity; in supporting and servicing their candidates; and in enhancing the competitiveness of the party system (Maisel and Bibby 2000, 22). Important party functions are enhanced by their capacity to expend substantial financial resources on campaigns and elections.

However, a knee-jerk race to the courthouse to challenge any and all restrictions on party funding may not serve the long-term interests of the parties. Parties must be conscious of public attitudes even as they react to changes in the legal context. Genuine party renewal is not possible without stronger links to voters and the public. Parties are already viewed as suspect, if not patently corrupt, by much of the public. The escalation of soft money has hardened the bond between party organizations and moneyed elites, while widening the disconnect between parties and the public. The banning of soft money contributions coupled with the modest increase in hard money limits (like BCRA) could reinfuse parties' links to parties-in-the-electorate; the parties' intellectual/ideological identity might better reflect rank-and-file affiliators rather than the political interests of the well-heeled (Briffault 2000, 666). It is unrealistic for partisan organizations to heed such considerations, given their focus on winning the next round of elections. But it certainly compels party scholars to weigh in and advance the cause of parties before the Court even when the organizations themselves cannot.

Stepping Back: Observations on the Relationship between the Court and Parties

These cases, particularly *Bush v. Gore,* brought the Court out of the political shadows. However, in terms of a consistent view of parties, the Court is still in the dark. What conclusions are to be drawn from the spate of cases impacting the political parties? First, *this Court is incurably pragmatic,* avoiding bright-line standards and overarching philosophical frameworks that might guide its consideration of parties. Doctrinal standards are manipulated to strike palatable and satisfactory political outcomes (Maveety 2001, 37). The Court bears the mark of Justice O'Connor, the key "swing vote" on the Court: cautious, fact-specific, narrow in application. Conflicts are likely to be judged by their anticipated ramifications for the electoral process. Unfortunately, the complexity of these cases and their crosscutting implications for parties and politics make such predictions exceedingly difficult. The effect on parties' abilities to carry out in fact the functions attributed to them in theory are elusive indeed. The most astute party experts and political observers cannot agree on how decisions will play out in practice or how parties might react.

Second, *we cannot expect a neat doctrinal treatment of parties*. The key attributes of the historical constitutional context are the Framers' antipathy toward parties and the absence of textual guidance. Party systems and traditions developed outside the constitutional framework. This lack of formal constitutional standing for parties has deprived the Court of the means necessary for doctrinal consistency. Parties' hazy constitutional status ensures that they are "unlikely to conform very neatly to lawyerly doctrinal categories" (Maveety 1991, 187). The uncertainties are heightened by the lack of a widely accepted normative understanding of parties, their roles, and functions. No consensus exists among legal minds or political scientists on a constitutionally grounded, "responsible party" approach. It is no wonder the Court has struggled to integrate parties into its traditional modes of analysis. Instead, the relationship between parties, the Constitution, and the Court has been marked by ambiguity and ambivalence.

Third, *the Court has shown itself willing to intervene in the electoral process to advance the interests of institutional and democratic legitimacy*. The Court in its relations to parties is often akin to a parent acting in the best interest of the child who does not know what is good for him. Parties seeking short-term electoral gain rarely match the "responsible party" model. Yet the Court will not sit back and let parties undermine their own legitimacy or that of the political process. What legitimacy demands will vary with blocs of justices in differing circumstances, however. The concern for the majority in *Bush v. Gore* was the perceived public legitimacy of the presidency. For the majority in the campaign finance cases, it was the threat to the legitimacy of the electoral process from public perceptions of corruption.

If one can categorize these cases, it is along those discernible impulses that blocs of justices within the Court are inclined to follow. They reflect two divergent sets of constitutional values underlying the democratic process. The *hierarchical* side is characterized by the desire for order, stability, and a mediated political process controlled through institutions such as parties. The *populist* view is informed by values of openness, equality, and maximum individual participation. Justices Thomas, Scalia, Rehnquist, and Kennedy are aligned with the former; hence their amenability to "responsible party" arguments and their willingness to cite the functional role of parties. The more liberal justices are aligned with the latter view. They are inclined to subordinate parties to individualistic, unmediated popular participation.

In *California Democratic Party v. Jones,* 530 U.S. 567 (2000), the hierarchists in the majority favored a party-controlled process; the populist minority preferred broadened voting rights. In *Bush v. Gore,* the hierarchists were appalled at the chaotic, disorderly recount process at issue; the populists sought to count every vote. In the campaign finance cases, the prevailing majority (the populists) were driven by a perception that the voices of average voters were drowned out by big money and big parties, hence the need for limits. The minority (the hierarchists) saw campaign spending as another way for parties as mediating institutions to perform channeling and aggregating functions in mass elections.

At this point, the limits of pragmatism and the peril of a doctrinally thin jurisprudence are joined. The Court's constitutional treatment of parties is the doctrinal equivalent of trying to fit a square peg into a round hole. The justices, even those pro-party in orientation, inevitably fall back on a rights-based analysis that is a poor fit for the parties. Even favorable party treatment is based upon right to association, speech, and assembly. Without linking those rights to party functions, the outcomes are sure to be ad hoc and random. A functional approach to party-related claims, in contrast, would inform pragmatic considerations with the contributions made by parties to democratic systems (see Issacharoff 2001). It would necessitate identifying the functions served by parties, examining how they are performed within a particular legal or constitutional context, and how the Court's decision might impact them.

Free-form pragmatism untethered to theory or function is inadequate. The more active the Court is in these matters, the greater the unforeseen repercussions. The theoretical case for parties—that they are critical to the essential constitutional values of authority, accountability, responsiveness, and representativeness—should be vigorously made. Then those theoretical assertions should be examined in the light of the empirical reality. Political scientists have much of relevance to contribute by empirically examining electoral processes, policy outcomes, and other behavior of party officials on organizations and the government itself.

The pro-party arguments are hard to make. They tend toward the abstract. Parties perform the functions ascribed to them imperfectly at best. Yet parties are an indispensable means of meshing and melding individuals, groups, and states into a representative pluralistic democracy. They are uniquely constituted to pursue multiple democratic aims of aggregation, consensus, compromise, choice, and competition. The challenge is to articulate these academic, abstract arguments in practical terms applied in specific constitutional contexts.

In sum, the constitutionalizing of the electoral process presents complex challenges for partisan organizations. The Court will to continue to influence party activities in a variety of ways, as it molds the constitutional framework for the electoral process. Party responses in turn will determine how well or poorly they carry out democratic functions for which we have long given them credit. How well these unlikely partners perform will have no small bearing on the ongoing evolution of the American democratic experiment.

Notes

1. Compare the explicitly pro-party Scalia dissents in the patronage cases (see *Rutan v. Republican Party of Illinois,* 497 U.S. 62 [1990]) or the Thomas and Kennedy concurrences in the first *Colorado Republican Party* campaign finance case with any of the opinions on the other side in those cases.

2. Blanket primaries are problematic on a theoretical "responsible party" level as well. The more open the primary is to any unaffiliated voter, the less the likely distance between the two major party nominees. The heightened role of hedgers, crossover voters, and nonideological voters minimizes real distinctions between the primary winners. The result is diminished meaningful choice in the general election, as open primaries produce more moderate centrist candidates. The blurring of party identity undermines the "responsible party" goals of competing partisan visions for voters, party loyalty and discipline within government, and ultimately accountability.

3. Opinions abound as to the likely impact of a soft money ban generally. Pro-party advocates foresee diminished parties relative to interest groups (Eilperin 2001). It would "cripple the parties" (Saleton 2001), "eliminat[ing] virtually all state and local party get-out-the-vote efforts and voter registration drives" (Fund 2001). "PACs could even displace the political parties, whose budgets would be decimated by the elimination of soft money" (Berke 2001a). Veteran Washington observer David Broder predicts the weakening of parties at least in the short term (Broder 2001), as does the U.S. Senate's greatest defender of soft money, Mitch McConnell, who predicts the loss of soft money will mean the loss of the balancing effect of parties and the ultimate fragmenting of American politics (McConnell 2001).

Others reject such gloomy projections (Dionne 2001). They see it as a blessing in disguise. Rather than parties simply thriving as fundraising service organizations at the service of candidates, it would force parties to appeal to their rank and file as sources of money. Norman Ornstein, a coauthor of McCain-Feingold, argues that "returning parties' funding and focus to the hard money . . . will channel their efforts away from media buying and back to genuine, broad-based party building and grassroots efforts." It would "revitalize parties by shifting their focus back to basics" (Ornstein 2001).

Part Two

Party Finances

6

The Parties Take the Lead: Political Parties and the Financing of the 2000 Presidential Election

Anthony Corrado, Sarah Barclay, and Heitor Gouvêa

Recent innovations in campaign finance and the changing dynamics of the presidential selection process have expanded the role of parties in the financing of presidential campaigns. With the growth of soft money and the advent of issue advocacy advertising, parties have become an important source of funding in the race for the White House. Their role has become particularly prominent in recent elections, as the party nominees have found it increasingly difficult to accommodate the financial demands of the presidential selection process under the provisions of the Federal Election Campaign Act (FECA) and its public funding program. Consequently, party committees have assumed greater responsibility for fulfilling the financial and strategic aspects of the contest for our nation's highest office.

While the role of parties in the presidential race has been expanding for some time, the 1996 election featured a major change in tactics that heralded a new era in party finance. In this election, the Democratic and Republican parties supplemented the coordinated expenditures made on behalf of their respective nominees with substantial expenditures in the form of issue advocacy advertisements that were designed to advance the electoral prospects of the party's presidential ticket. These ads, because they did not "expressly advocate" the election or defeat of a specific candidate, were exempt from the limits governing party expenditures made in coordination with a candidate. Furthermore, the ads were funded with a combination of hard and soft money, with most of this additional spending coming from soft money accounts. This strategy thus allowed the parties to circumvent the FECA restrictions on their finances and transcend their limited role in federal elections prescribed by federal law. More importantly, it allowed the party committees to play a substantial role in delivering candidate-specific broadcast messages to the electorate on a scale that was unprecedented in any of the presidential campaigns conducted since the implementation of the FECA in 1976.

The parties' use of issue advocacy advertising in 1996 was a bold innovation; by the election of 2000 it had become a standard approach. The party
organizations were therefore able to pursue a more coordinated and integrated strategy on behalf of their candidates during the 2000 campaign, a
strategy that relied heavily on unregulated funding. The purpose of this
chapter is to explore party activity in the 2000 presidential race to provide a
better understanding of how parties participate financially in national elections in the new regulatory environment that emerged after the 1996 campaign. It also seeks to provide some insight into how parties use hard and
soft money resources to assist candidates and address some of the strategic
problems generated by the presidential selection process.

The New Realities of the Regulatory Environment

The role of parties in the financing of a presidential campaign is principally determined by the regulations governing party funding and the strategic context of the race. In recent election cycles, both of these factors have
evolved in ways that have encouraged parties to expand their role. An increasingly lax regulatory structure has provided party committees with
ample opportunities to spend substantial sums of money on the presidential
race, and the strategic context has provided them with the incentive to do
so. While the strategic factors ultimately determine the level and timing of
spending, the regulatory factors have been most important in defining the
financial activities parties undertake.

Party committees are given a limited role in presidential campaign financing under the terms of the FECA. Their primary role is to provide direct
assistance to their nominees in the form of coordinated expenditures. In
2000, the Democratic and Republican national party committees were each
allowed to spend up to $13.7 million in coordination with, or on behalf of,
their respective nominees (FEC 2000a). These expenditures must be funded
with "hard money," or monies raised in accordance with federal contribution limits. Such spending can be devoted to a wide array of purposes that
expressly advocate the election of a presidential candidate, including polling,
direct mail, broadcast advertising, and voter persuasion and mobilization efforts. The most common use is to pay for broadcast advertisements that complement the messages distributed by the candidates and their campaigns. In
this way party committees make the most of their spending, since advertising
allows them to reach a greater share of the electorate with limited dollars.

Since 1980, party committees have also provided indirect assistance to
presidential candidates in the form of generic party activities or "party-
building" efforts. Originally, these activities were to be governed by the
1979 amendments to the FECA, which allowed party organizations to spend

unlimited amounts of hard money on certain activities specified in the law that were considered to be essential to "party-building" or the promotion of "grassroots volunteer efforts." The law specifically prohibited party committees from paying for broadcast advertisements or other mass public communications under this provision, but it did permit voter identification and turnout programs, the production of campaign paraphernalia such as buttons and bumper stickers, and the printing of slate cards and other get-out-the-vote materials that listed the names of candidates for federal, state, and local office. However, as a result of a number of regulatory decisions issued by the Federal Election Commission (FEC), the parties were allowed to deviate from the restrictions of the statute and finance these activities with a combination of hard and soft money funds, based on allocation formulas that were eventually standardized through rules adopted in 1991 (Corrado 1997b). Consequently, parties began to rely on their soft money revenues as a principal component of their federal election–related activity.

In recent elections, the FECA's relatively simple schema for party funding in presidential campaigns has been replaced by increasingly sophisticated and complicated financial schemes that revolve around the parties' continuing efforts to exploit their ability to spend soft money in ways that benefit a presidential candidate. The most recent innovation emerged in 1996, when first the Democratic Party and then the Republican Party supplemented the finances of their presidential hopefuls by spending millions of dollars on issue advertisements that featured President Bill Clinton or his Republican challenger, Robert Dole. The parties claimed that these advertisements were not campaign expenditures subject to FECA restrictions because they did not use the "magic words" associated with "express advocacy" such as "vote for" or "vote against," that most previous court decisions had deemed necessary for the application of federal limits (Potter 1997). The committees therefore paid for the advertising with a mixture of hard and soft money, but mainly soft money.

The Democrats did most of the issue advertising conducted by the party committees in 1996 during the prenomination phase of the campaign. While the national party organizations had engaged in issue advocacy advertising before the 1996 election (mostly during the debate over Clinton's healthcare proposal in 1993 and 1994), they had never before used such advertising in a significant way to influence the election of a presidential candidate. But the Democrats decided that they could use such advertising to promote President Clinton's reelection prospects by highlighting his agenda and accomplishments. Accordingly, they embarked on a massive advertising effort that would not have been possible under the spending limits of the public funding program.

From July 1995 to June 1996, the Democratic National Committee (DNC) and state Democratic Party committees spent millions of dollars on ads designed to help Clinton's reelection. According to estimates by Common Cause, the Democrats spent $34 million on pro-Clinton ads prior to June of the election year, including $12 million in federally regulated hard money and $22 million in soft money (Common Cause 1996). This tactic allowed the party to function as a surrogate campaign committee; the party distributed the president's message in the early stage of the election and thereby allowed his campaign committee to conserve resources for later use.

The 1996 Democratic Party ad campaign, combined with an uncontested nomination contest, provided Clinton with a significant financial advantage over the prospective Republican nominee, Robert Dole, in the months leading up to the national nominating conventions. By the end of March, Dole had all but reached the expenditure ceiling imposed on publicly funded nomination candidates, while Clinton's committee still had more than $20 million left to spend (Labaton 1996). To address this imbalance, the Republican Party stepped in to assist Dole, providing a sort of "bridge financing" for the "bridge period" between the effective end of the nomination contest and the conclusion of the presidential nominating convention, when Dole would receive the public subsidy for the general election campaign. In May, the Republican National Committee (RNC) announced that the party would spend $20 million on advertising between June and August "to show the differences between Dole and Clinton and between Republicans and Democrats on the issues facing our country" (Republican National Committee 1996).

In 1996, the major parties spent a combined total of more than $65 million on advertising, not including the coordinated expenditures they were allowed to make in accordance with the FECA (Corrado 1997a). These activities pushed the borders of federal law and essentially rendered the regulations imposed on candidates meaningless, at least as far as the party nominees were concerned, since it suggested that the candidates could rely on party monies to assist their campaigns, regardless of any spending and contribution limits. With respect to the parties, it suggested that these committees could use soft money, in combination with hard money, to directly assist their respective presidential nominees, without having to wait until after the presidential nominating conventions (the official beginning of the general election period under the FECA) and without triggering the coordinated spending limits. It also suggested that party committees could work with their presidential standard-bearers to raise soft money that could be used to pay for advertising that benefited their campaigns. In sum, parties could easily evade the restrictions placed on their financial activity by federal law.

Whether such actions were permissible under federal law was a very uncertain matter in 1996. While party lawyers claimed that their activities were legal and beyond the scope of federal regulation, their arguments were based on gray areas in the law that had not been litigated in the courts or definitively interpreted by the FEC. Whether federal regulators would permit such activity was a question that was yet to be determined as the election came to an end.

In the aftermath of the 1996 election, the FEC took no action to prohibit or even deter the new financial strategies employed by the party committees. The FEC Audit Division, based on a detailed examination of the expenditures made during the nomination period, felt that the party ads should be considered campaign expenses and recommended that the Clinton and Dole campaigns be penalized for exceeding spending limits and receiving "excessive contributions" from the party committees (FEC 1998b, 1998c). But the commission voted 6-0 against the recommendation that the candidates be asked to repay $25 million to the U.S. Treasury for violating the law (FEC 1998a). The agency's Office of General Counsel also recommended an enforcement proceeding, based on its conclusion that the Democratic Party's ads were coordinated with the Clinton campaign and therefore constituted illegal soft money expenditures and campaign contributions (FEC 1998a). The FEC failed to act on this recommendation also, as it reached a 3-3 deadlock on the matter, ending any further action. In rendering these decisions, the FEC did not set forth a position on whether soft money–funded party-issue ads that featured a federal candidate were permissible under the law. Nor did the agency state whether a party could coordinate its issue ads with a candidate. The commission simply left the law in limbo, albeit in a much lighter shade of gray, since the lack of any sanction in effect approved such activity with respect to future elections.

Similarly, Congress and the Department of Justice conducted major investigations of party finances, but neither took actions to prevent similar practices in the future. Thus, despite the major controversy sparked by soft money contributions and party funding in the 1996 election, no changes were made in the regulatory structure to stem the use of soft money for issue advertising before the start of the 2000 campaign. Instead, federal regulators essentially gave the party committees further incentive to use the issue advertising strategy, since they signaled an unwillingness to take action against the practice.

The FEC did make one minor change in the rules governing party finance before the beginning of the 2000 campaign, a change that sought to address one of the factors that stimulated the move to issue advertising: the problem of financing campaign activities during the "bridge" period between the effective end of the nomination process and the national nominating conventions.

The front-loading of the presidential primary calendar has produced presidential nomination contests that are decided earlier and earlier in the election year. In the most recent presidential races, the nominee has essentially been selected prior to the beginning of April, and the prospective nominees have begun their general election campaigns months before the national party conventions. But the spending limits imposed by the presidential public funding program, which were established more than twenty years ago, are not designed to accommodate this front-loaded primary process, especially in a hotly contested race. For example, in 1996, Dole's inability to continue to spend substantial sums due to the restraints of the expenditure limits was one of the primary reasons why the RNC initiated its issue advertising campaign (Corrado 1997a).

In an attempt to address this problem, the FEC eased some of its restrictions to facilitate the option of greater spending from June 1 of the election year to the start of the party conventions. During this period, candidates who accept public funding can allocate salary and overhead expenditures equal to no more than 15 percent of the primary spending limit to the general election expenditure ceiling. The agency also eased the rules on party spending, expressly granting parties the option of making coordinated expenditures on behalf of a candidate before that candidate formally receives the presidential nomination (FEC 2000c).

Party Finance in the 2000 Presidential Election

At the outset of the 2000 election cycle, party committees had greater opportunities and flexibility with respect to the financial strategies they could employ than they had in any previous election since the adoption of the FECA. As in previous years, they could spend a limited amount of hard money on coordinated expenditures during the general election period and a combination of hard and soft money on generic party activities. In 2000, they could also make coordinated expenditures prior to the national nominating conventions. Another alternative was to follow the model established in 1996 and spend combinations of hard and soft money either before the nominations were determined or throughout the course of the general election on issue advocacy advertisements. Moreover, because there was greater certainty about the options available to them, party leaders could better plan and integrate their strategies than they could four years earlier, when issue advertising was an emerging tactic that evolved during the course of the election.

The post-1996 regulatory environment thus substantially altered the role of party organizations in the strategic and financial conduct of a presidential campaign, since it allowed these committees to evade the FECA limits. Instead of being restricted to a limited amount of coordinated spending, party committees might now take advantage of various strategic alternatives. In the context of a race in which an incumbent is seeking reelection, a party committee could conduct an early advertising campaign designed either to promote the incumbent's chances or, conversely, to undermine the prospects of a likely general election challenger. In the context of a competitive nomination campaign or open race, a party could provide bridge financing to supplement the depleted resources of the winner of the party nomination. Even if the apparent nominee still has ample amounts left to spend after wrapping up the nomination, the party could spend funds in the hope of providing the margin needed for a party victory in the general election.

Further, the parties could now coordinate their use of soft and hard money resources over the course of an election cycle. Instead of being confined largely to grassroots, general election types of activities, such as voter mobilization efforts and slate cards, soft money could now be used throughout the election year to pay for mass public communications. Moreover, by relying on soft money to pay a share of the costs of issue ads, parties could reserve their limited coordinated spending for use in the key periods close to Election Day, when a strong election message might be most useful. They even had the option of forgoing any coordinated spending at all. Instead, they could combine their hard money with soft money to broadcast only issue ads, thereby expanding the "bang for the buck" their hard money would provide. For example, instead of spending the $13.7 million allowed for coordinated expenditures, a party could use that $13.7 million in addition to soft money to pay for more than $30 million in issue advertising, depending on the committee making the expenditure and the allocation formula for soft money spending in the applicable state.[1]

Given the strategic advantages offered by soft money alternatives, it is not surprising that the parties in 2000 continued to build on the approach established in 1996, placing great emphasis on the solicitation of soft money and the use of issue advocacy advertising. The parties had strong incentives to pursue this strategy. First, such funding was free of any restrictions (other than the allocation formulas that dictate the ratio for mixing hard and soft money to make the total sum spent on any particular advertising purchase). They could therefore spend unlimited sums on issue ads that were, for all intents and purposes, comparable to coordinated ads, the only difference being that issue ads did not include any of a handful of "magic words."

Second, the major party committees were very successful in soliciting soft money funds and increasing their hard money receipts; they therefore had the resources available to spend. The Democratic and Republican national committees raised almost twice as much soft money in 2000 as they did four years earlier. In all, the party committees raised more than $495 million in soft money, with about $250 million solicited by the Republican committees and $245 million by the Democratic committees. When hard money is included, total revenues exceeded $1.2 billion, or approximately $300 million more than in 1996, with the Republicans surpassing the Democrats by a margin of almost $200 million (FEC 2001). So the parties had the revenues needed to wage extensive advertising campaigns.

Third, the strategic context of the race was also conducive to party spending. Competitive races spur spending, and the 2000 race proved to be one of the closest contests for the White House in American history. From an early point in the election year, most observers predicted a tight race between Governor George W. Bush of Texas and Vice President Al Gore, although no one could have anticipated the extraordinary final outcome. Both candidates had secured their party's nomination before the end of March, so they had a long period to campaign against each other. Neither wanted to lose any momentum that might have been gained by a primary victory and neither wanted to cede any potential advantage to the other. So campaigning continued throughout the late spring and summer, and the parties began their general election campaigning well before the conventions began.

Without an incumbent in the race, both parties decided to wait until the general election candidates were determined before beginning their advertising campaigns. The RNC did spend some money early in the election year, broadcasting two issue ads in the last two weeks of January that criticized statements made by Gore in a New Hampshire candidate debate. The ads claimed that Gore would apply a "litmus test" to his appointees for Joint Chiefs of Staff if he were president. But the party spent a relatively small sum on the ads, spending about $10,000 in the first week and then running the ad only on selected cable stations and three local stations in New Hampshire during the second week (*National Journal* 2000a, 2000b). No additional party ads were broadcast until the major parties began campaigning in earnest at the beginning of June.

By the middle of March, the Gore campaign was already beginning to think about the overall spending limit, while Bush, who became the first nominee to forgo public funding and finance his winning nomination campaign solely with private contributions, was free to spend as much as he could raise. In late March, Gore had about $10 million left to spend and Bush had $10 million in available cash. But Bush would go on to raise an additional $20 million before his campaign was over, while Gore faced the constraints imposed by the spending ceiling (Shogren 2001). Bush thus enjoyed a significant resource advantage at the onset of the general election campaign, which helps to explain why the Democratic Party took the lead in initiating the advertising campaigns conducted during the bridge period leading up to the conventions.

The Democrats

Despite the fact that Gore had earlier said that the Democrats would not run soft money–financed advertisements unless the Republicans did so first, the Democrats initiated the party "air war" in early June, as soon as the presidential primary season ended. Although the Gore campaign had some money in the bank, they did not have the resources needed to maintain a core campaign operation, mount a convention program, *and* finance broadcast advertisements. In fact, the disclosure reports filed with the FEC by the Gore 2000 Committee show no expenditures for media advertising in June and July, and only about $35,000 for media consulting. Lacking resources of his own, the vice president had to rely on the party to distribute his campaign message through the summer.

The Democrats sought to justify their action by claiming that potential groups that favored Bush, including an organization called "Shape the Debate" and a missile defense organization called the "Coalition to Protect America Now," were broadcasting an estimated $2 million in anti-Gore advertising (Doyle 2000a). Yet the first ad broadcast by the party did not confront these messages; instead it promoted Gore's plan for a prescription drug benefit. It was aired in fifteen states, all of which were expected to be swing states in the presidential contest (*National Journal* 2000c). The states targeted were Florida, Georgia, Illinois, Iowa, Kentucky, Louisiana, Maryland (for Delaware audiences), Michigan, Missouri, New Mexico, Ohio, Oregon, Pennsylvania, Washington, and Wisconsin. Less than two weeks later, the DNC sponsored a second ad, this one running on Father's Day weekend, featuring a montage of Gore, his father, and his son, with statements made by Gore regarding fatherhood (*National Journal* 2000e). This ad was shown in the same fifteen states as the first spot, as well as Arkansas and Maine.

The Democrats broadcast at least ten other ads in support of Gore between the middle of June and the first week of September. In late June, the party sponsored a second health care spot, as well as ads that targeted black and Hispanic voters. A spot in Spanish that was broadcast on the Univision cable channel in Florida, Illinois, Wisconsin, and New Mexico claimed that Gore would fight for Social Security, Medicare, child health care, and "world class public schools." Another ad broadcast on Black Entertainment Television promoted Gore's support for a patient's bill of rights. This spot was aired in Florida, Illinois, Louisiana, Michigan, Missouri, Ohio, and Pennsylvania. All of these states were considered critical presidential election battlegrounds.

In July, the Democrats sponsored an ad featuring the vice president at a town hall meeting touting his "Crime Victim's Bill of Rights." The ad ran in the same seventeen states where the Father's Day ad was broadcast. By this point, the party had spent an estimated $14 million on presidential-election-related advertising that targeted voters in traditionally Democratic states or electoral swing states (*National Journal* 2000g).

This effort was followed by at least four ads released around the time of the Republican National Convention that focused on the themes the Republicans were expected to highlight in their convention message. These ads primarily attacked Bush's record and that of his vice-presidential nominee, Richard Cheney. For example, the first ad in this series recalled votes Cheney cast while serving in Congress against the Clean Water Act, Head Start, and the School Lunch Program. The next criticized Bush's record as governor of Texas, stating that he "opposed health coverage for 200,000 more children" and "appointed a chemical company lobbyist to enforce the environmental laws." In all, the Democrats purchased an estimated $3.5 million in advertising time to broadcast these spots, which aired in the same seventeen states they had been targeting since June (*National Journal* 2000i).

After the Republican convention, the party did not resume its ad campaign until the first week of September, when it broadcast two ads, one heralding Gore's drug plan and the other criticizing Bush's health care record. These ads were broadcast in response to a Republican Party ad released at the end of August, which claimed that Bush had a better prescription drug plan than Gore. The Democrats aired these spots in the nine states (Arkansas, Delaware, Louisiana, Michigan, Missouri, Ohio, Pennsylvania, Washington, and Wisconsin) that the Republicans had targeted in their own media spending (*National Journal* 2000j).

The Republicans

Even though Bush had plenty of money to mount a substantial advertising campaign on his own, his campaign committee spent relatively little money on media during the months of June and July. According to campaign disclosure reports filed with the FEC, the Bush for President Committee spent less than $104,000 on media expenses in June, including a payment of $100,000 to Maverick Media, a firm that produced at least one of the RNC issue ads. In July, the campaign committee spent about $2.9 million, including a payment of $2.76 million to National Media, Inc., a firm that produced at least three of the RNC issue ads.

Most of the advertising aired on Bush's behalf between June and September took the form of issue advertising financed by Republican Party committees. Once the Democratic assault had begun in June, the Republicans quickly responded with ads of their own. Within a few days of the broadcast of the first Democratic ad, the Republicans announced their own advertising drive. On June 10, the RNC unveiled a $2 million advertising campaign focused mainly on the same states the Democrats were targeting. The only difference was that the initial Republican ads were broadcast in Maine and Arkansas, in addition to the fifteen states initially selected by the Democrats. The first ad released by the Republicans presented Bush's proposal to allow workers to invest part of their Social Security payroll taxes in the stock market (Doyle 2000b). A few days later, a second ad on the same issue was released, but this version featured a voice-over by Bush and an appearance by Bush at the end of the message (*National Journal* 2000d). Later in the month, the party broadcast two other ads on Bush's Social Security plan, one that ran in the seventeen states targeted by Democrats and another in Spanish that aired only in New Mexico (*National Journal* 2000f).

The RNC ran one additional ad during the summer months. In mid-July, it released a spot touting Bush's plan to improve education. The party did not report the size of the media buy accompanying this ad, but the spot ran in all of the seventeen states that were the locus of Democratic advertising, as well as in California, Nevada, and New Hampshire. Besides serving as a "counterpunch" to the Democrats' efforts, this ad was designed to draw attention to one of Bush's major issues—education reform—in advance of the Republican convention (*National Journal* 2000h).

Party Financial Strategies

It is difficult to determine the exact amount the two major parties spent in support of their nominees during the summer months. The lack of specific disclosure data in FEC filings and the national committees' practice of transferring funds to state party committees to take advantage of allocation ratios make detailed accounting difficult. However, a sound sense of the scope of party spending can be discerned from estimates developed by the Brennan Center for Justice. These estimates, which are based on detailed analyses of media spending in seventy-five media markets that cover 80 percent of the population, provide a baseline for analyzing party strategies, especially with respect to the role of soft money financed advertising as compared to coordinated communications in the 2000 campaign.[2]

According to the Brennan Center survey, the major parties spent a conservatively estimated total of $79.1 million on television advertising in the top seventy-five media markets during the period from June 1 through Election Day (Brennan Center 2000c). Of this amount, an estimated $48 million, more than half of the total, was spent from June 1 through September 13 (Brennan Center 2000a). This represents a substantial increase over the amounts spent by the party committees during the comparable period in 1996. On a party basis, the Democrats spent an estimated $25.7 million, while the Republicans spent approximately $22.3 million.[3]

The amount spent on advertising during this bridge period is particularly noteworthy because it includes no party coordinated expenditures. Neither party took advantage of the relaxed regulations on coordinated spending that the FEC adopted to encourage hard money spending in advance of the formal general election period. According to the disclosure reports filed by the party committees with the FEC, the Republicans did not begin to make coordinated expenditures on media advertising until September 15; the Democrats' first disbursement occurred on September 11 for an ad that ran the following week. None of the money spent on media advertising prior to mid-September represented coordinated hard money funds; instead, it represented the expenditure of hard and soft money on issue ads, and the major share of the spending came from soft money contributions.

Both parties thus followed similar strategies in 2000. They used issue ads to promote their nominees throughout the summer and into the initial weeks of the general election campaign. This allowed them to reserve their limited coordinated expenditures, which could be used to expressly advocate the election or defeat of a candidate, until the latter weeks of the election when voter attention was likely to be most focused on the presidential contest and when the states that were still undecided could be clearly determined. And when they finally spent these coordinated funds, they devoted the lion's share to even more advertising.

The RNC spent a total of $13.2 million on coordinated expenditures in support of George Bush (see table 6.1). Of this amount, $11.1 million, or about 84 percent of the total, was spent on media, with an additional $310,000 spent on ad production and testing. The only other major expense, totaling $1.2 million, was for polling, which included state surveys and state and voter-tracking surveys.

The distribution of these media purchases is impossible to determine precisely from the FEC disclosure reports, since the parties only need to report the amount of any expenditure and the date on which it is made, which does not necessarily mean that that was the date on which the money was spent, or that it was used to buy advertising time in the period immediately following the expenditure. For example, monies could be paid to a media-buying firm on a certain date, but those monies might be used to buy time or reserve ad slots to be used at a later time in the campaign. Even so, the

Table 6.1   RNC 2000 Presidential Coordinated Expenditures by Type

Purpose of Expenditure	Total Amount (in millions)	Percent of Total
Media	$11.10	83.8
Polling[a]	$1.21	9.1
Mailing	$0.61	4.6
Ad Production and Testing	$0.31	2.3
Focus Groups	$0.01	0.08
Transportation and Lodging	$0.002	0.02
Subtotal Media	$11.10	83.8
Subtotal Nonmedia	$2.14	16.2

[a]Referred to as polling, state and voter surveys, and state and voter tracking in FEC reports.
Source: Reports on coordinated expenditures filed with the FEC by the Republican National Committee.

available data on media buy expenditures is instructive. With respect to coordinated expenditures, the RNC reported a media purchase expense of $7.2 million on September 15, a purchase of $3.6 million on September 28, and a $300,000 purchase on October 24. So they reserved their coordinated spending until the last seven weeks of the election.

The Democrats also spent most of their coordinated monies on media advertising. In all, the Democrats disbursed $13.8 million in coordination with their presidential nominee (see table 6.2). Of this amount, $10.1 million, or about 73 percent of the total, was spent on media. Like its Republican counterpart, the DNC devoted a substantial share of its coordinated monies to the costs of polling that was done throughout the general election period. The party spent more than $1.9 million on survey research, which represented about 14 percent of total coordinated spending. The Democrats also spent a significant amount, $1.1 million, on a telephone-based get-out-the-vote effort in the final two weeks of the election.

With respect to the distribution of media spending, the Democrats basically split their media buying between mid-September and the last two weeks of the election. On September 11, the party transferred $4 million to its media consultant for advertising. On October 20, the party purchased $3.8 million in media. The $2.3 million remaining from the $10.1 million media total was mostly spread over the weeks that fell between these two peaks. If all forms of coordinated spending are considered, including media and nonmedia spending, then more than half of the Democrats' coordinated spending, over $7 million, is reported as occurring in the period from October 20 to the end of the campaign.

Table 6.2   DNC 2000 Presidential Coordinated Expenditures by Type[a]

Purpose of Expenditure	Total Amount (in millions)	Percent of Total
Media	$10.10	72.8
Polling[b]	$1.95	14.1
Telephone	$1.10	7.9
Printing Services	$0.24	1.7
Travel Expenses	$0.21	1.5
Legal Services	$0.27	1.9
Subtotal Media	$10.10	72.8
Subtotal Nonmedia	$3.77	27.2

[a]The total spent on coordinated expenditures by the DNC, according to FEC reports, is $13.53 million. This disagrees with the total of $13.87 million reported herein. In the last report the DNC filed with the FEC in December of 2000, the committee reported an aggregate total of $13.53 million on behalf of Gore. The DNC filed additional reports in February and May of 2001 listing additional coordinated expenditures on behalf of Gore. However, the aggregate total for DNC coordinated expenditures was not increased from December's $13.53 million. Hence the difference between the table and the FEC reports.

[b]Referred to in FEC reports as political consulting fees.

Source: Reports on coordinated expenditures filed by the Democratic National Committee with the FEC.

These data demonstrate the relative reliance that parties placed on hard money "express advocacy" advertising, as opposed to soft money–supported "issue advocacy" advertising. Combined, the DNC and RNC spent about $27.1 million on coordinated expenditures, including more than $21.2 million on media advertising and production. Even if the assumption is made that all of this $21 million in advertising was done in the top seventy-five media markets, which is not a safe assumption, that leaves approximately $58 million of the $79 million tracked by the Brennan Center unaccounted for. In other words, the party committees spent almost $3 on issue advertising for every $1 spent on coordinated advertising. This estimate provides a strong indicator of the extent of soft money spending in connection with the presidential race, and of the preferences parties gave to issue ads over express advocacy ads in communicating messages to the electorate. Overall, the amount of soft money spent on issue ads, which constitutes the major share of issue ad dollars, was substantially greater than the amount of hard money spent in the form of coordinated expenditures.

The data also provides an understanding of how the party committees integrated their financial strategies and communications approaches in connection with the presidential contest. During the bridge period from June 1 to September 13, the parties relied exclusively on issue ads. In the mid–general election period from September 13 to October 16, and in the final weeks of the election, they relied on a mix of coordinated ads and issue ads. Overall, the Brennan data indicate that Republican Party committees spent a total of at least $22.5 million on advertising from mid-September through November 7 in the top media markets. Of this amount, only $11.1 million could have been in the form of coordinated advertising, since this was the total amount the Republicans spent on coordinated media. This suggests that an equivalent amount was spent on issue advertising during the last seven weeks of the campaign. The Democrats, however, apparently relied almost exclusively on coordinated advertising during this period, since their total coordinated media spending is roughly equivalent to the total amount of Democratic Party advertising identified by the Brennan Center in the period from mid-September through Election Day.

While these communications programs were the largest component of the parties' programmatic activities (as distinguished from administrative expenses and fundraising expenditures), they were not the only form of party activity in the election. Both major parties also spent millions of soft dollars in combination with hard dollars on voter identification, absentee ballot efforts, and voter turnout programs as part of their voter mobilization campaigns conducted in coordination with state and local party organizations. How much of this spending was specifically targeted for the presidential race is difficult to determine from disclosure reports. But it is safe to assume that presidential voting was a high priority in these efforts and that tens of millions of dollars were spent on these activities to influence the outcome of the White House race.

Conclusion

The Democratic and Republican Party committees spent substantially more money on the 2000 presidential race than they had in any previous election since the FECA was adopted. At a minimum, the parties spent close to $80 million on broadcast advertising in the top seventy-five markets and another $5.9 million on nonmedia coordinated expenditures. If the amounts spent on voter identification and turnout programs related to the presidential general election are included, the total amount of party spending easily surpassed the $100 million mark, not including any related administrative and fundraising costs. In contrast, the party nominees, George Bush and Al Gore, each received $67.6 million in public funds to finance their general election campaigns and spent an additional $18.6 million in compliance monies for total combined spending of almost $154 million, not including the recount battle (Corrado 2002).

Consequently, in 2000, the amounts provided to the presidential contenders in public monies served as a floor rather than a ceiling with respect to campaign spending. The provisions of the FECA provided the base for the financial activity that took place in the election; the law had little effect on the level of spending that took place or the sources of funding used to pay for election-related campaigning. In effect, the availability of the issue advocacy option eviscerated the FECA's restrictions on publicly funded candidates and coordinated party support. The only restraints on presidential campaign finance, as far as the parties were concerned, were the limits of how much they were willing to spend to capture the Oval Office.

In terms of broadcast advertising and the communication of campaign messages to the electorate, the 2000 election signaled a dramatic change in the relative role of candidates and party organizations. For the first time since the FECA was adopted, the parties took the lead in communicating with the electorate during the general election campaign. According to the analyses conducted by the Brennan Center for Justice, the parties spent $79.8 million on advertising from June 1 through November 7, with the Republican Party disbursing an estimated $44.7 million on ads supporting Bush, and the Democratic Party expending about $35.1 million on ads supporting Gore. This sum exceeded the total amount spent during the same period on broadcast advertising in these same markets by the candidates themselves by at least $12.7 million (Brennan Center 2000c). In every previous election since 1976, candidate spending on broadcast communications greatly exceeded the amounts spent by party committees. And given the ability of party committees to capitalize on the issue advertising option and thereby circumvent the restraints of the coordinated spending limits, it is likely that party communication expenditures will continue to outpace comparable candidate spending for the foreseeable future, absent fundamental changes in the rules that govern the present system.

Given the narrow margin of victory in the 2000 race, it is reasonable to assume that party spending had an important effect in determining the final outcome. At least one analysis based on focus-group research and national surveys conducted by the Center for the Study of Elections and Democracy has shown that voters made little distinction between the party issue ads and the ads paid for by candidates (Magleby 2001a). Nearly 90 percent of the respondents in their national survey believed that "the party ads were trying to persuade them to vote for or against a candidate, and 94 to 95 percent saw the purpose of the ads as helping or hurting a candidate." Only about 2 percent of respondents said "that the party soft money ads had as their primary objective or purpose 'to promote a particular political party.'"

This finding is supported by the content of the ads the parties financed. These communications primarily presented the central themes and issues advanced by the candidates. The ads focused on the issues of prescription drug benefits, Social Security reform, education, and other topics that formed the centerpiece of the candidates' respective platforms. For the most part, they prominently featured the candidates and made little mention of the party. The Brennan Center research, for example, found that almost 92 percent of all party ads (not just those that featured the presidential race) never even identified the name of a political party, let alone encouraged voters to register with the party, to volunteer with a local party organization, or to support the party (Brennan Center 2001).

This use of soft money in the presidential race reinforced the concerns about the role of soft money and issue advocacy in federal elections that have animated campaign finance debate in recent years. Accordingly, it was one of the principal problems Congress sought to address in adopting the Bipartisan Campaign Reform Act of 2002 (P.L. 107-155), the first major revision of federal campaign finance law since the passage of the FECA. The BCRA, which was enacted in March 2002 and was scheduled to take effect November 6, 2002, will prohibit national party committees and federal officials or candidates from soliciting, raising, directing, transferring, or spending soft money (Section 101). The law also redefines "federal election activity" to include any public communications that refer to a clearly identified federal candidate and promotes, supports, attacks, or opposes that candidate for federal office, regardless of whether the communication expressly advocates a vote for or against the candidate (Section 101). Under the provisions of the act, any advertisements sponsored by party committees that feature a presidential candidate will have to be financed with hard money.

If these restrictions on party finance are upheld by the courts, party committees will have to employ a different financial strategy in 2004, since they will no longer have the soft money option for financing candidate-based advertising.[4] Generally, the law offers party committees a choice of spending hard money in a coordinated manner or in a manner independent of a candidate. Section 213 of the statute requires that parties make a choice between these approaches by the time of a party's nomination of a candidate.

As in previous presidential campaigns, parties will be allowed to sponsor hard money–financed coordinated advertisements in support of their respective nominees. But these expenditures, which could be used during the bridge period between the end of the primaries and the start of the general election, would be subject to strict spending ceilings. These limits, recently upheld by the Supreme Court in *Federal Election Commission v. Colorado Republican Federal Campaign Committee* (*Colorado II;* 121 S. Ct. 2351 [2001]), would only allow parties to spend about one-third of the amount they spent in 2000.

Given the restrictions on coordinated spending, parties may instead attempt an independent spending approach. Although parties are generally thought to be linked to their presidential nominees, the Supreme Court in *Colorado Republican Federal Campaign Committee v. Federal Election Commission* (*Colorado I;* 518 U.S. 604 [1996]) ruled that party committees can act independently of their candidates, as long as they do not meet the standards for determining "coordination" set forth in federal campaign finance regulations. Although final regulations for determining what constitutes "coordination" under the new law will have to be decided by the FEC, parties should be able to pursue an independent spending approach, as they have done in some U.S. Senate races in 1998 and 2000. In this way, the national party committees could spend unlimited amounts of hard money in support of their nominees, and thus free themselves of the spending limits that accompany coordinated efforts.

State parties will be able to provide further assistance to presidential candidates, but they will also be limited in their use of soft money. Just as in the case of national party committees, any advertisements broadcast by state committees that promote or attack a presidential candidate will have to be financed with hard money. But state parties will still be able to spend a combination of hard and soft money for voter registration and get-out-the-vote efforts. However, if these efforts are conducted in the last 120 days prior to an election and mention a federal candidate, they must be paid for with funds raised under federal contribution limits.

The new rules may therefore lead parties to act independently of presidential candidates and spend less money on broadcast advertising in connection with the race for the White House. But they may also encourage parties to devote resources to voter registration, voter identification, and voter mobilization, since soft money can be used to defray these costs. In other words, the parties may move away from the pattern exhibited in 2000 and place greater emphasis on grassroots voter mobilization as opposed to broadcast advertising, thereby returning to the pattern of party activity found in presidential elections prior to the advent of issue-advocacy advertising in 1996. Regardless of the particular strategy they decide to pursue, the national committees will continue to play an important role in the financing of presidential elections.

Notes

The authors wish to acknowledge the support of The Pew Charitable Trusts, which funded the research on which this chapter is based. The opinions expressed herein are those of the authors and do not necessarily reflect the views of The Pew Charitable Trusts.

1. Under FEC rules, party committees must abide by allocation formulas in making expenditures of soft money on certain types of activities that can affect federal and nonfederal elections. The allocation formulas are designed to reflect the federal and nonfederal shares of the expenditure. The formulas differ based on the type of party activity and the level of the party committee making the expenditure (federal or state committee). In general, in a presidential election year, national party committees must pay at least 65 percent of the costs of voter drives, administrative expenses, or issue advertisements with federally regulated funds (hard money). For state or local party committees, this proportion is often reversed, with as much as 65 or 70 percent of such costs paid with nonfederal funds (soft money). The percentage of soft money that can be used by a state or local party varies, since it is based on the composition of a state's general election ballot. The percentage used by a state party is based on the proportion of federal offices to the total offices on the general election ballot. The soft money share can thus range from 25 percent to 70 percent or more, but it is often almost twice the share allowed the national party committees. For this reason, national party committees often transfer monies to state party committees for issue advertising purchases, which allows them to spend more soft money than hard money on these expenditures.

2. The Brennan Center for Justice data are based on a detailed analysis of the political advertising aired from June 1 through Election Day in 2000. Campaign Media Analysis Group (CMAG), a commercial firm that advises advertisers and reporters, compiled the data using technology that monitors political advertising by the major national broadcast networks and twenty-five leading cable networks in seventy-five media markets reaching over 80 percent of the population. CMAG reported the average cost of the time slot in which each ad aired. This captured the cost of the media buy, but not the amount spent on production and placement.

3. The figures on party issue advertising expenditures are based on the authors' calculations from the data reported by the Brennan Center. The data reported are adjusted to reflect the totals for the time period discussed, rather than the aggregate totals from June 1 reported by the Brennan Center.

4. The ban on soft money and restrictions on party advertising are among the provisions facing a constitutional challenge at the time of this writing. See *McConnell v. Federal Election Commission,* D.C.C. Civ. No. 02-582 (2002).

7

The Committee Shuffle: Major Party Spending in Congressional Elections

Robin Kolodny and Diana Dwyre

While the major political parties have come to play a larger role in the financing of federal elections over the past two decades (Aldrich 1995; Herrnson 1988, 2000b; Dwyre and Kolodny 2002), they have not always spent their money in the same ways. In the 1996, 1998, and 2000 elections, the national party congressional campaign committees (CCCs) dramatically shifted their patterns of campaign spending. The CCCs spent much less hard money directly on candidates than in the past. Instead, CCCs transferred large amounts to the state parties or allowed the parties' national committees, the Republican National Committee (RNC) and the Democratic National Committee (DNC), to assume some critical spending. These changes accompanied an expansion of soft money and issue advocacy in congressional elections, enabling the parties to spend millions of dollars to run issue advocacy advertisements and conduct voter mobilization activities to promote their candidates (Dwyre and Kolodny 2002).

In this chapter, we explain how and why the CCCs changed their spending in the late 1990s, and what these patterns reveal about the strategic role of parties in congressional elections. First, we describe the hard money expenditures of the CCCs, the national party committees, and state party committees in the aggregate. Next, we look at how the rise of soft money influenced these spending patterns. Finally, we discuss how party spending may change again if the new Bipartisan Campaign Reform Act (BCRA) withstands litigation and takes effect in the 2004 election cycle.

Congressional Campaign Committees and Forms of Spending

The four CCCs are the only party committees charged solely with electing members of Congress. The two committees for the House of Representatives are the Democratic Congressional Campaign Committee (DCCC) and

the National Republican Congressional Committee (NRCC); their two counterparts in the Senate are the Democratic Senatorial Campaign Committee
(DSCC) and the National Republican Senatorial Committee (NRSC).

In the late 1970s, the CCCs raised relatively little money, particularly
the Democrats, and spent much of it on incumbents in safe seats, who generally had little trouble raising funds from other sources, such as political action committees (PACs). By the mid-1980s, this incumbent protection strategy was replaced with a greater focus on maximizing the number of seats
won in Congress by targeting spending on the most competitive races, including challengers and open-seat races (Kolodny 1998; Dwyre 1994; Jacobson 1985/1986; Herrnson 2000b). This change in strategy was due in part to
the entrepreneurial activities of the House CCC chairs, Democrat Tony
Coelho and Republican Guy Vander Jagt, who modernized their committees
and enforced a good deal of discipline on the process of distributing resources (Kolodny 1998).

The spending patterns of these strategically oriented CCCs were influenced by three factors: the competitiveness of congressional elections (Kolodny and Dwyre 1998; Aldrich 1995; Schlesinger 1991), the legal and regulatory environment under the Federal Election Campaign Act (FECA)
(Herrnson 1988), and financial resources derived from exploiting the
FECA's hard and soft money systems (Glasgow 2000a; Herrnson 2000b; Jacobson 1985/1986).

In the late 1990s, changes in all three of these factors had an impact on
the CCCs. After 1994, the struggle to control the House and Senate became
intensely competitive. The new viability of the Republican Party at the congressional level not only encouraged stepped-up GOP electoral activity; it
forced the Democrats to retool their methods and fundamental assumptions
about electoral politics. Meanwhile, changes in the legal and regulatory environment offered the CCCs new avenues for spending money in congressional campaigns. For instance, Supreme Court decisions in the mid-1990s
allowed CCCs to engage in new kinds of expenditures. And after 1996 the
CCCs learned to use soft money, funds that are not subject to the same level
of scrutiny as traditional electioneering funds, in ways that helped their candidates.

Thus, the CCCs had numerous avenues for spending money in congressional campaigns by the late 1990s. First, they could spend hard money, including direct contributions to candidates as well as coordinated and independent expenditures made on behalf of candidates. Second, they could
transfer hard money to other party committees, especially state parties,
which could spend it to benefit candidates. And third, they could spend soft
money on nonelectoral expenses, such as operating costs, or transfer it to
state parties. The combination of transferred hard and soft money helped pay
for issue advocacy ads on behalf of candidates. It is worth explaining these

various kinds of spending in more detail before we consider the patterns of CCC expenditures over time.

Hard Money. "Hard" or "federal" money is regulated under the FECA (until November 6, 2002, when it will be regulated under the Bipartisan Campaign Reform Act, or BCRA), which sets limits on the amounts that can be raised by the CCCs and other national party committees: a maximum of $20,000 per year from an individual or $15,000 per year from a PAC. In addition, hard money cannot be raised directly from corporations, labor unions, federal contractors, or foreign nationals.

The FECA also sets limits on the direct contributions the CCCs and other party committees can make to congressional candidates: a national party committee may contribute up to $5,000 per election (primary, general, runoff, and special) to a House candidate and $17,500 to a Senate candidate. State party organizations may give an additional $5,000 to a House or Senate candidate per election. None of these limits included an adjustment for inflation, so they have declined in real value since their enactment in 1974.

In addition to direct contributions, CCCs and other party committees also may make coordinated expenditures on a candidate's behalf, with the candidate's knowledge and consent. The FECA allowed national and state party committees to make coordinated expenditures of $10,000 in House races and a figure based on state population for Senate races, adjusted for inflation each election cycle. By 2000, the coordinated expenditure limit was a total of $67,560 ($33,780 each for the national committee and the relevant state committee) in a House race and in a Senate race it ranged from a low of $135,120 for the least-populous state to a high of $3.3 million for California (FEC 2000a).

One of us (Kolodny 1998, 137–143) has argued that the invention of "agency agreements" between the national and state party committees was the key to the financial invigoration of the CCCs in the past twenty years. An agency agreement permitted a state party committee to cede its coordinated expenditure limit to a CCC, thus allowing the latter to effectively double its expenditures in individual U.S. House races. The Supreme Court sanctioned agency agreements in *Federal Election Commission v. Democratic Senatorial Campaign Committee et al.* (454 U.S. 27 [1981]). Apart from agency agreements, party committees have been permitted to make unlimited transfers of hard money to other federal and state party committees. State parties can use these funds in a variety of ways, and as we will see below, these hard money transfers can be mixed with soft money to assist candidates.

As a result of the Supreme Court's decision in *Colorado Republican Federal Campaign Committee v. Federal Election Commission* (518 U.S. 604 2309 [1996]), political party committees have been permitted to make "independent expenditures"—that is, hard money dollars spent to support or defeat a candidate, but *without* the candidate's knowledge or consent. Although the Court had long allowed independent expenditures for PACs and individuals on First Amendment grounds, most observers were surprised when this logic was applied to political parties. Indeed, the authors of the FECA did not believe that political parties were capable of true independence from their candidates. And party operatives have noted that they had great difficulty keeping their independent expenditure activities separate from their other spending activities.[1] There is no limit on the size of independent expenditures, but there must be no coordination with the candidate—otherwise the expenditure would not be "independent."

Finally, all hard dollar receipts, contributions, and expenditures must be fully disclosed to the public through reporting to the Federal Election Commission (FEC), which posts the reports and summaries of party receipts and expenditures on its web site. Despite these many restrictions, hard money has one important advantage for parties and candidates: There are very few restrictions on what can be purchased with the funds. So the CCCs and other actors have a great deal of discretion over how they actually spend hard money in campaigns.

Soft Money. "Soft" or "nonfederal" money is money that can be raised by the national parties from virtually any source (including corporations and labor unions) in unlimited amounts. Soft money contributions to the national parties are reported to the FEC, but soft money spending is difficult to trace. It is allowed under the FECA (as amended in 1979) for the purposes of "party building," such as generic party advertising, get-out-the-vote drives, and routine administrative expenses borne by any party organization (e.g., the cost of office space, equipment, supplies, and employees).

After 1996, national party committees, including the CCCs, found ways to centralize and coordinate the raising of soft money (Biersack and Haskell 1999). One obvious advantage of soft money is that it can be raised more easily than hard money, due to the lack of limits on its size and sources. However, soft money is much more difficult to spend than hard money. Under the FECA, soft money cannot be used in any direct way to influence the outcome of an election for federal office. The national party committees, including the CCCs, spent some soft money for nonelectoral purposes such as routine operating expenses, but the bulk was transferred to state party committees to be spent under state law and FEC rules.

Under FEC rules, any state party activity that influences federal elections must be paid for with a combination of hard and soft money, according to ratios set by the FEC. The ratios generally reflect the proportion of federal races on a state's general election ballot. The CCCs' ratio is a minimum of 65 percent hard money and 35 percent soft money, though the percentage may be adjusted upward (to include more hard money) depending on actual disbursements. Typically a state party's ratio will allow for more soft money spending than the national party's ratio, so the national parties often transfer hard *and* soft money to a state party to take advantage of the more favorable state ratio (see chapter 9).[2]

Issue Advocacy. The FECA restrictions apply only to money involving "express advocacy" of the election or defeat of a candidate, and not to spending that involves "issue advocacy." The distinction between "express" and "issue" advocacy ads originated in the Supreme Court decision *Buckley v. Valeo* (424 U.S. [1976]). In a now famous footnote, the Court indicated that the following terms satisfied their strict express advocacy test: "'vote for,' 'elect,' 'support,' 'cast your ballot for,' 'Smith for Congress,' 'vote against,' 'defeat,' 'reject.'"[3] If an advertisement does not contain these "magic words" (and is not coordinated with a candidate), it is considered "issue advocacy," and the FEC ruled that parties may use a mix of hard and soft money to pay for such advertisements. This distinction has been further refined in subsequent litigation (West 2000, 39–61).

National and state party committees can pay for issue advocacy ads that involve candidates if express advocacy words are avoided. However, the FEC requires that the parties use a mix of hard and soft money to pay for such ads. Sometimes the parties are able to spend more than the candidates—and sometimes against the candidates' wishes (Dwyre and Kolodny 2002). Many observers regard the legal distinction between express advocacy and issue advocacy to be specious, since issue ads differ very little from the advertising used by candidates (Herrnson and Dwyre 1999).

Changes in Congressional Campaign Committee Spending

Table 7.1 lists the hard money expenditures of the CCCs, the national committees, and all state/local committees for both major parties from the 1988 to 2000 election cycles. All amounts are expressed as a percentage of total hard money disbursements in this table.[4] We will first consider each form of hard money expenditures by the CCCs, and then seek to the explain changes in the patterns.

Hard Money: Contributions to Candidates. Table 7.1 shows that since 1988, all four CCCs have moved away from using direct contributions to candidates as a disbursement strategy. The two senatorial campaign committees have never had very high levels of their disbursements go to direct contributions: the NRSC has remained at around 1 percent, while the DSCC has declined from a high of 2.6 percent in the 1988 cycle to a low of 2000's 0.7 percent.[5] Still, both the NRSC and DSCC reduced their total contributions to about one-half of that allowed by law in the 1998 and 2000 cycles. The House committees behaved a little differently, giving around 5 percent of their disbursements as contributions in the late 1980s, a figure that fell to

Table 7.1   Direct Contributions, Coordinated Spending, and Independent Expenditures by Party Committees as a Percentage of Total Disbursements

	NRSC	NRCC	Republican State & Local	RNC	DSCC	DCCC	Democratic State & Local	DNC
Direct Contributions								
1987–88	1.2%	4.7%	1.1%	0.4%	2.6%	5.4%	1.7%	0.3%
1989–90	1.0%	2.8%	2.4%	0.4%	2.5%	4.9%	1.7%	0.2%
1991–92	1.0%	2.1%	1.2%	1.0%	2.3%	6.6%	1.2%	0.0%
1993–94	1.0%	3.0%	1.5%	0.6%	2.0%	5.1%	1.7%	0.2%
1995–96	1.1%	1.7%	1.1%	0.3%	1.8%	3.9%	1.0%	0.0%
1997–98	0.5%	1.1%	1.4%	0.4%	0.8%	1.7%	0.8%	0.0%
1999–2000	0.8%	0.7%	0.5%	0.2%	0.7%	1.2%	0.5%	0.0%
Coordinated Expenditures								
1987–88	16.2%	12.2%	0.1%	9.2%	38.1%	19.4%	16.6%	17.2%
1989–90	11.4%	8.2%	0.4%	0.1%	25.7%	31.6%	10.4%	0.6%
1991–92	23.1%	15.1%	1.4%	13.7%	44.1%	32.7%	17.8%	17.3%
1993–94	16.7%	15.0%	1.6%	5.5%	46.5%	39.9%	16.2%	−0.8%
1995–96	0.5%	10.0%	0.5%	11.8%	27.3%	21.5%	10.5%	6.3%
1997–98	0.1%	7.1%	8.4%	3.7%	0.0%	12.0%	12.0%	9.2%
1999–2000	0.0%	3.9%	1.3%	12.6%	0.3%	5.3%	7.9%	11.1%
Independent Expenditures								
1995–96	14.7%	0.0%	0.2%	0.0%	4.5%	0.0%	0.7%	0.0%
1997–98	0.4%	0.0%	0.1%	0.0%	3.7%	0.0%	1.0%	0.0%
1999–2000	0.5%	0.6%	0.4%	0.0%	0.3%	3.9%	0.9%	0.0%

around 1 percent in 2000. The change for the DCCC has been especially dramatic: the high of 6.6 percent in 1992 declined steadily to 1.2 percent in 2000. Direct contributions were never very important for the DNC and RNC, and they declined further over the period. This pattern held for both parties' state and local committees as well. Of course, since direct contributions to candidates were limited to $5,000 for House candidates per election or $17,500 for Senate candidates, and they are not adjusted to increase with inflation, as the parties raise and then spend more hard money, the proportion of that money that they spend on direct contributions would naturally go down.[6] Nevertheless, this decline in direct contributions indicates a change in spending strategy by the CCCs.

Hard Money: Coordinated Expenditures. The coordinated expenditures by CCCs in Table 7.1 show an even more dramatic shift than direct contributions to candidates. All four of the congressional campaign committees hit a six-cycle low in the proportion of their disbursements made through coordinated expenditures in 2000. This decline began in the 1996 election cycle for all four committees, the first cycle in which the use of soft money became widespread. Indeed, the NRSC essentially stopped making coordinated expenditures in 1996, and by 1998, the DSCC had as well (showing the most dramatic decline in coordinated expenditures, from a 1994 high of 47 percent of all disbursements). The DCCC and NRCC have continued with some coordinated expenditures (around 5 percent of total disbursements), but this figure represents a real drop for both organizations, especially the DCCC. Since coordinated expenditures are indexed to inflation, there is no natural inclination for them to decline as a proportion of overall spending, as was the case with contributions. During this period, the CCCs also largely discontinued the use of agency agreements for coordinated expenditures made with state and national committees as a primary means of assisting candidates.

The DNC and RNC also made coordinated expenditures, particularly in presidential elections years, and although there has been a good bit of variation, they do not show the same pattern of decline. Democratic state and local committees were more active in coordinated expenditures than their Republican counterparts, but there was also a decline over the period, especially in 2000. The Republicans also showed a decline in 2000, from their high point in 1998.

Hard Money: Independent Expenditures. As Table 7.1 shows, the NRSC made a significant effort to spend independently in 1996, using 14.7 percent of its total hard money disbursements for this purpose. Since that cycle, however, none of the CCCs made significant use of this type of spending. In the 2000 cycle, only the DCCC made an effort at independent spending, using 3.9 percent of its total disbursements for this purpose.[7] Given these modest amounts, it is unlikely that the recent legality of independent expenditures by parties accounts for the drop in contributions and coordinated expenditures. Neither the national committees nor the state and local committees were active in independent expenditures. It is surprising how little use the CCCs have made of this opportunity to make unlimited independent expenditures. Perhaps this result reflects the fact that independent expenditures must be made with hard money.

Total Direct Hard Money Expenditures. When we combine the CCCs' three direct methods of hard money spending on congressional candidates, we find a significant decline, as can be seen in figure 7.1. All four CCCs were shifting away from direct hard money expenditure strategies by the 1996 cycle, and the trend continued to 2000. If the congressional campaign committees in Washington were not spending hard money directly on candidates, then just where was this money going? Two possibilities come to mind: more hard dollars were spent on party operating expenses, or more hard money was transferred to the states.

Party Operating Expenses. Figure 7.2 shows the proportion of hard money disbursements spent on operating expenditures by the CCCs. The

Figure 7.1   Percentage of CCC Hard Money Spent on Contributions to Candidates, Coordinated Expenditures, and Independent Expenditures

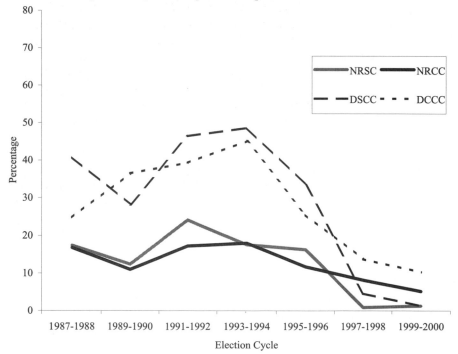

data are only for the last three election cycles, but it is clear that after adjustments in 1998, all of the CCCs spent less of their hard money on operating expenditures. Why? Because they have been using more soft money instead of all hard money to pay for their administrative costs, such as salaries for permanent staff, rent, supplies, routine office expenses, and fundraising expenses. Of course, operating expenses for the purposes of party building, not issue ads, was the initial justification for increased soft money use by the national party committees.

Table 7.2 shows how soft money expenditures for operating expenses have increased along with hard money expenditures. Since the proportion of expenses paid for with soft dollars increased, the proportion of hard money needed for such expenses decreased, especially in 2000. Thus, soft money has allowed the CCCs to shift hard money away from operating expenses.

Transfers to States Parties. Until recently, transfers from the CCCs to state party committees appear to have been fairly limited. Indeed, figure 7.3

Figure 7.2   Percentage of CCC Hard Money Spent on Operating Expenditures

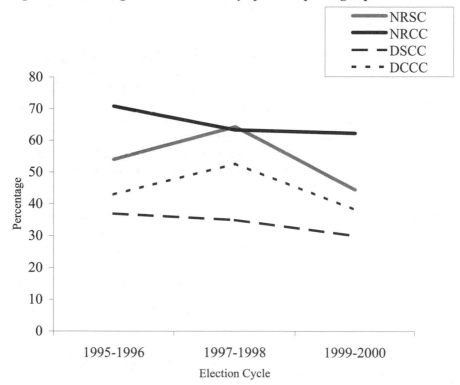

Table 7.2 Operating Expenses for the CCCs

	Hard Money	Soft Money
NRSC		
1993–1994	$18,819,766	$ 649,879
1995–1996	37,992,630	8,106,748
1997–1998	41,111,183	11,227,390
1999–2000	26,666,696	9,901,006
DSCC		
1995–1996	5,022,164	2,301,920
1997–1998	6,844,887	4,273,660
1999–2000	8,181,948	7,448,921
NRCC		
1993–1994	10,308,085	583,802
1995–1996	58,992,129	9,176,416
1997–1998	48,173,593	7,584,607
1999–2000	67,114,364	24,293,925
DCCC		
1995–1996	7,171,423	3,305,725
1997–1998	11,580,702	5,583,796
1999–2000	16,554,840	14,008,257

shows that during the 1994 election cycle (the first cycle with reliable data for transfers), the CCCs transferred almost no money to the state and local parties. However, starting in 1996, the DSCC and the DCCC began to send more of their hard money to the states—just over 15 percent of total disbursements. By 1998, the NRSC and NRCC began to make such transfers. The DSCC then transferred a full 34 percent of its hard money disbursements to state parties in 1998, increasing that amount to over 58 percent by 2000. All of the CCCs increased their hard money transfers to the states to significant levels in 2000.

This dramatic increase in CCC hard money transfers to state and local parties helps explain the decrease in direct spending on congressional candidates—as more money went to the states, there was less to spend on candidates directly. Why did the CCCs begin to transfer significant sums to the state parties, and just what did the state parties do with all of this money?

The central reason that the national parties transferred so much hard money to state parties is that many states were a more hospitable environment for spending soft money. Figure 7.4 shows the dramatic increase in national party *soft money* transfers to state parties. Combined with the significant increase in hard money transfers shown in figure 7.3, it is clear that the national party committees did much of their spending through the state parties. Indeed, David Magleby reports "congressional party senior staff indicated . . . that national to state transfers represent well over 90 percent of

Figure 7.3   Percentage of CCC Hard Money Spent on Transfers to State and Local Parties

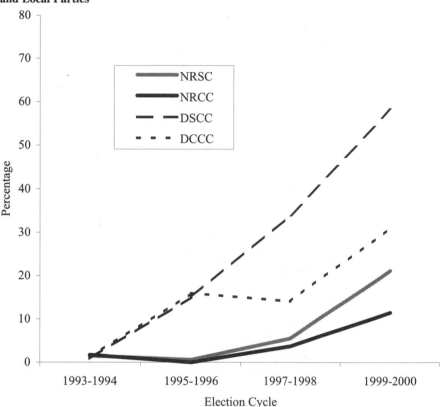

what they spend for congressional candidates" in the 2000 cycle (2001a, 21). The DNC and RNC also made large transfers in the presidential election years for much the same reason.

These national committee transfers to state parties came under a great deal of criticism. Indeed, once national party soft money was transferred to a state party committee, it became extremely difficult to trace exactly how that money was eventually spent. The national committees disclose this money to the FEC as transfers to state parties, but each state has different reporting requirements and different rules regarding soft money use, making expenditures difficult to track (Dwyre 1996; Morehouse 2000).

The need to combine soft money with hard money in order to spend it on federal campaign activities has been a very significant factor behind the recent changes in national and state party spending patterns. The national parties spent less hard money, and the state parties increased their hard

Figure 7.4   National Party Committee Soft Money Transfers to State Party Committees (millions of dollars)

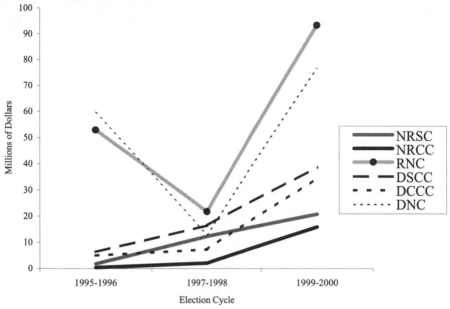

money spending, in order to comply with the matching requirements that allow the parties to spend their abundant supplies of soft money on activities during elections such as voter mobilization efforts, mail campaigns, and issue advocacy ads.

The Committee Shuffle: State and National Committees Spend for the CCCs

Figure 7.5 shows how much hard money the CCCs transferred to all party committees: state parties, the national committee (RNC or DNC), or the party's other CCC (i.e., House or Senate campaign committee). Although figure 7.5 is somewhat incomplete (because it reports only transfers out and does not deduct money that is transferred in to those committees from other committees), it still reveals something interesting: with one exception (the NRCC), transfers from the CCCs increased significantly, and by 2000 constituted a large portion of their disbursements. The NRCC spent more of its money directly, sponsoring a large number of issue ads for GOP House candidates nationwide, rather than transferring money to the state parties for this purpose.

Figure 7.5   CCC Hard Money Transfers to All Party Committees as a Percentage of Total Disbursements

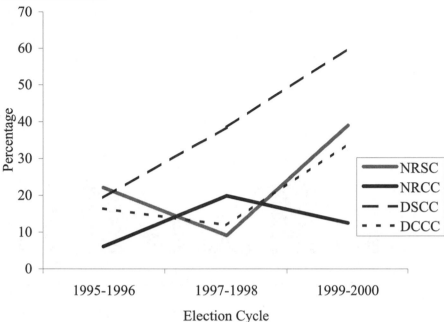

Figure 7.6 shows that when all congressional direct spending is added together, the overall level of spending is remarkably stable, with the exception of Democratic coordinated expenditures in 2000, which is below the levels of the previous two cycles, and the Republican foray into independent expenditures in 1996. As the direct hard money expenditures of the CCCs declined, they were compensated for by expenditures from the national committee and state party committees. How and why did this "committee shuffle" happen?

According to interviews with several key party staff members who worked during the 2000 elections, the amount of money parties could devote to candidate campaigns in coordinated expenditures was smaller than the amount that could be spent through issue advocacy expenditures with a hard/soft money mix. Indeed, the CCCs all but abandoned the use of coordinated expenditures so that they could legitimately claim that they were not "coordinating activities" with their congressional candidates, a requirement for issue advocacy spending. Interviews with media consultants who worked during the 2000 election revealed that the national parties were careful not to hire the same media firm to make hard money campaign ads and soft money issue advocacy ads for the same congressional candidate (Oxman

Figure 7.6   Total Direct Spending on Congressional Candidates, All Federal Party Committees (National Party Committees, CCCs, and State Party Committees)

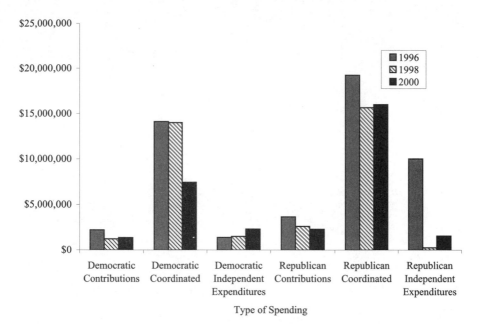

2001). Indeed, some of the national party committees stipulate in their consultant contracts for issue advocacy campaigns that those consultants must not take on clients who are the beneficiaries of the same issue advocacy work. These precautions had some merit. During the 1996 presidential election campaign, the DNC was accused of improperly coordinating its issue advocacy ads with the Clinton campaign organization. Although the FEC dropped its case against the DNC for this coordination, the national parties operated under the assumption that such coordination is not permissible.

Spending Patterns in the Future

Since 1996, when the CCCs began engaging in issue advocacy in earnest, they have altered dramatically how they spend hard money. Where once they tried to maximize the hard money spent directly on candidate races, they decided to transfer hard money to the state committees, where it could be mixed with soft money and spent on issue advocacy ads and voter mobilization. Once the CCCs figured out how best to make use of their soft money, their spending patterns changed to make the most efficient use of these resources.

By 2000, congressional campaign finance was highly centralized at the national level, allowing CCCs to raise the lion's share of both the hard and soft money spent in congressional races. Although much of this money was transferred to the state parties, the CCCs guided, if not dictated, how the state parties spent the money. Consequently, most of this money was spent strategically to serve the interest of the congressional party: It was concentrated on the most competitive races in each election cycle in an effort to maximize the number of seats won (Dwyre and Kolodny 2002).

The situation may change dramatically after the 2002 election if the Bipartisan Campaign Reform Act of 2002 (BCRA) withstands court challenges. Under the new law, the CCCs, the RNC, and the DNC cannot raise soft money, nor can they transfer hard money to be mixed with soft money to buy issue advocacy ads. This loss of soft money, and the restrictions placed on the state parties' use of it, will force the CCCs to find new ways to pursue their unique priorities.

One response would be for the CCCs to urge their big contributors to give to state parties in states with competitive candidates. However, the new law prohibits agents of the national parties from engaging in any soft money fundraising, even at the state level. The new relationships the CCCs have established with the state parties might facilitate communications about how state and local parties might interpret the Levin Amendment, which allows for a very limited soft money role for state and local parties. However, there would be no assurance that this money would be used to help competitive congressional candidates, and no direct assistance from the national party organizations in raising soft money will be allowed.

The issue advocacy provision of the BCRA bars the use of soft money for issue ads that feature the name or likeness of a federal candidate in the weeks before an election. Even if this provision is struck down as unconstitutional, the CCCs will not have access to the soft money critical to running issue ads. But one could imagine the development of allied issue advocacy groups to take the place of party issue ads, perhaps with the encouragement of the CCCs. However, there is no guarantee that such groups will follow the parties' priorities.

Another approach would be for the parties or their fundraisers to bundle contributions from individuals (which have been increased from $1,000 to $2,000 per election under the BCRA) for targeted candidates. This approach would involve a much less direct role for the CCCs, for they would neither raise the money themselves nor decide how it is spent, only suggest which candidates would receive it. However, the CCCs may have a difficult time convincing individual contributors and PACs to abandon their traditional contribution strategies in order to follow the parties' goal of seat maximization.

Yet another alternative is to induce congressional party leaders and well-heeled incumbents to contribute to competitive candidates from their own campaign committees or their leadership PACs. We have known for some time that the CCCs have orchestrated the activities of individual members for the benefit of the common good of the party (Kolodny and Dwyre 1998), and that since 1994 the CCCs have expected members in a position of power to donate extra funds to the party coffers (Kolodny 1998, chapter 7). We can envision a proliferation of member PACs centrally orchestrated by the CCCs. Under all of these scenarios, the CCCs would no longer be the generator of funds, but the coordinator of them.

Under the BCRA, the parties may either make coordinated expenditures on behalf of a congressional candidate or make independent expenditures, but not both, overriding the 1996 *Colorado* decision. Parties may begin to make more extensive use of independent expenditures for their most competitive candidates in the postreform era because independent expenditures will be the only means for the party to spend unlimited amounts in a congressional race. Candidates, of course, prefer coordinated expenditures, for they have some control over how the money is spent. Under the BCRA, the hard money receipts of the CCCs will increase because the limit for contributions to parties has been raised from $20,000 to $25,000, but these new resources are unlikely to replace the huge sums of soft money raised in recent elections.

Clearly, the BCRA will significantly alter the role of the CCCs, the only party committees whose primary task is to maximize seats in Congress. However, if the changing pattern of the CCCs' spending in recent times is any guide, they will not take long to adapt to the new law and find the best way to efficiently pursue majority status in Congress.

Notes

Robin Kolodny wishes to express her appreciation to Temple University for support of this research.

1. The issue of what "coordination" means has been problematic for the parties. In 1996, the NRSC moved a staff dedicated to independent expenditures out of their party headquarters to a separate office to prove the "independence" of the operation (Corrado et al., *Campaigns & Elections* 1998)

2. In all states except Connecticut and Alaska, which ban soft money, party activities that affect both federal and state/local elections and party issue advocacy ads must be paid for with a combination of hard and soft money according to ratios set by the FEC.

3. *Buckley v. Valeo,* 424 U.S. (1976) n. 52. While the Court did not indicate whether this list was exhaustive, most legal, political, and scholarly observers do not regard it as so.

4. The percentages represent the dollar amount of contributions made in a given election cycle divided by the dollar amount of total disbursements for that same election cycle.

5. The senatorial committees may also make contributions to House campaigns of no more than $5,000 per election. This sometimes happens at the suggestion of the head of the House CCC, usually in exchange for some other committee's assistance for Senate candidates.

6. If a party committee were to give its maximum contribution to each of the thirty-three to thirty-four Senate candidates per election cycle, it would spend between $577,500 and $595,000. Likewise, there is an absolute limit of direct contributions for House committees of $5,000 per election (normally two per cycle—primary and general) and a maximum number of races at 435. If a party ran a candidate in each district, it could theoretically contribute $4.3 million in direct contributions. Neither party's CCCs have come close to spending these amounts.

7. The DCCC spent this money solely on phone banks for GOTV (get-out-the-vote) calls in thirty-nine competitive House races one week or less before the elections.

8

State Parties and Soft Money:
How Much Party Building?

Raymond J. La Raja

In March 2002, President Bush reluctantly signed the Bipartisan Campaign Reform Act (BCRA), reforming the campaign finance system that was put in place more than thirty years before. The lack of fanfare surrounding the White House signing underscored the disappointment of many Republicans who disagreed with the reform bill. Among the several arguments they and other opponents made was that the centerpiece of the new legislation—a ban on party soft money—would fundamentally weaken the political parties relative to other political groups. Without access to soft money, they argued, parties would lack critical resources to run their operations and invest in campaigns. Several leaders from both major parties went so far as to say the parties would be "neutered" as political money flowed to less accountable, issue-driven interest groups (Marcus and Eilperin 2001).

One of the main reasons soft money existed was that Congress and the Federal Election Commission (FEC) wanted political parties to have sufficient resources to engage in party-based activities in campaigns across the party ticket. Such concerns about the health of the political parties have received considerable support from political scientists who believe that strong and active party organizations encourage electoral competition, accountability, and participation among citizens. In the ensuing debates over reform, representatives from the political parties argued these points in their efforts to prevent restrictions on using soft money.

According to many reform advocates, however, the use of soft money has been little more than a ruse by the parties to get around federal campaign finance laws that thwarted efforts to get as much money as possible into federal elections. Rather than abide by contribution and expenditure limits imposed by the Federal Election Campaign Act (FECA) of 1971 and its amendments, the national parties exploited loopholes in the law to raise money in unlimited amounts from wealthy contributors and spend it in ways that helped targeted federal candidates. From the perspective of much of the reform community, parties have not used money to build the organization but rather to air "issue advocacy" ads that promote the campaigns of federal candidates without using explicit electioneering words.[1]

In truth, it has been difficult to assess the claims of either side of the reform debate because the data are limited. This study, however, combines party financial records with survey data about party activities to assess what parties achieve with soft money. A central question is whether soft money helped strengthen the party organization in important ways. One alternative is that the parties used soft money for the short-term goal of winning key federal contests, becoming an empty vessel to funnel soft money to their candidates.

The findings of this study suggest that parties have not been merely cash conduits for candidates, even though they have been spending increasing amounts of soft money on candidate-centered issue ads. A considerable portion of soft money has been invested in the party infrastructure in ways that give these organizations greater capacity to perform traditional party functions, such as recruiting candidates, mobilizing voters, and coordinating campaign activity across the party ticket. In short, there appears to be a link between soft money spending and party strength. It also appears that Democratic organizations are not as weak relative to Republican organizations as they have been in the past. The success of Democrats in narrowing this gap may owe much to their ability to raise soft money at equal levels with Republicans. The passage of BCRA raises interesting questions about how the parties will fare under the new campaign finance system.

The Rise of Party Soft Money

In the past decade, political funds controlled by the political parties have surged to unprecedented levels. The national parties, in particular, took advantage of rather loose campaign finance regulations to help their candidates facing increasingly expensive electoral contests.[2] Leaders of the national parties recognized in the 1980s that their organizations could play a vital role in raising funds for campaigns and helping the presidential candidates, in particular, by creating a campaign operation long before the party nominee was selected. That way, the party nominee would lose little time in waging the campaign against the nominee of the opposing party (see chapter 6).

But to achieve this goal, the parties needed money. Under the FECA of 1971 and its amendments, the parties have been allowed to raise "hard" money from individuals and PACs in amounts that do not exceed $20,000 and $15,000, respectively. These funds can be spent in federal campaigns as contributions to candidate committees or coordinated expenditures that benefit the party candidate. But there are strict limits on how much the parties may help their candidates with these funds. House candidates in 2000 elections, for instance, could receive no more than $10,000 in party contributions, and coordinated expenditures were capped at just under $35,000.[3] Such restrictions on fundraising and spending in federal elections created incentives for parties to seek other ways of influencing campaigns.

They found one answer in soft money, a term coined in the 1980s for party money that lacked the "hard" limits of federal laws. According the Federal Election Commission (FEC), the parties can use soft money for generic activities that mobilize voters and defray basic organizational expenses at party headquarters. These party-building activities have been allowed because party representatives convinced regulators at the FEC and members of Congress that such activities were good for democracy (see Corrado 1997b).

Party representatives argued that parties participate in local, state, and federal elections simultaneously and, as a result, federal laws restricting spending would hamper their ability to campaign for candidates up and down the party ticket. They also claimed that federal campaign finance laws violated principles of federalism since state and local parties would be bound by federal laws, even when they engaged in nonfederal campaign work. The compromise, fashioned by the FEC, was to allow parties at all levels to use unrestricted funds for party building, so long as these funds were not invested directly into campaigns for federal office.

Since these decisions in the late 1970s, the parties have exploited ambiguities in the federal laws in order to raise and spend more soft money. In response to FEC regulations that limited the scope of soft money spending by the national parties, the RNC and DNC transferred funds in increasingly large amounts to state parties. At first, these funds were used to expand field operations in the states for the presidential elections, but in 1996 they were also used for producing and airing "issue ads" that were little more than campaign commercials for the presidential candidates (Woodward and Marcus 1997). The congressional campaign committees soon followed the lead of the RNC and DNC and began funneling money to state parties to help congressional candidates (see chapter 7).

As a result of soft money transfers from national to state organizations, party receipts at the state level increased substantially, even though funds raised by the parties themselves have risen only moderately since 1992 (see figure 8.1). The straight lines represent hard and soft receipts in the federal accounts for the one hundred major state party organizations.[4] The dotted lines represent the amount of money transferred from the national committees to the state organizations. The first big increase in state party budgets came in 1996 when the national committees transferred more than $160 million to state parties. In the 2000 elections, they transferred $415 million, pushing up state party budgets even higher.

The trend lines in figure 8.1 show clearly that national party transfers to

Figure 8.1   State Party Money, 1992–2000

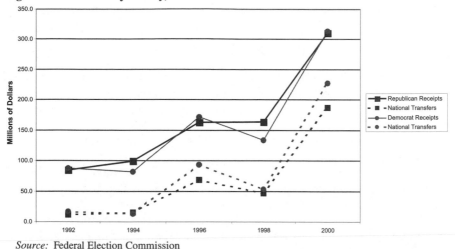

Source: Federal Election Commission

state parties drive much of the increase in state party funds. Over the decade, these transfers comprised an increasing portion of state party money. In 1992, for instance, Republican state parties received 14 percent of their funds from the national organizations. By 2000, this portion had increased to 60 percent. For the Democrats, the change has been more dramatic, rising from just 19 percent to almost three-quarters of state party budgets.[5]

The flow of political funds reflects an extraordinary change for American parties. Only four decades ago, national parties begged state parties to send them money (Heard 1960). The emergence of the national parties as the financial center in American elections corresponds to the shift in focus from local and regional politics to national politics. Today, the national parties stand at the apex of an organizational structure that is no longer "stratarchical," which is a term employed by Eldersveld (1964) to describe the relative autonomy of parties at each level. Instead, lower-level parties appear more integrated into the national organizations whose influence flows, in part, from their capacity to raise money, provide services, and coordinate political activities.

BCRA will stop the flow of soft money from national to state parties, which raises important questions about future intraparty relationships and the capacity of political parties to influence elections. National parties are banned completely from raising soft money, so they will no longer transfer soft money to state parties. State parties, however, may continue to raise soft money, but in amounts that do not exceed $10,000, if they intend to use the funds in federal elections.[6] Without the infusion of soft money from national

parties, will state party activity decline? One way to explore the question is
to understand how state parties have used soft money in the past.

Party Spending Patterns

Prior research on political parties demonstrates that they attempt to target money strategically where it will make the biggest difference in campaigns: in the most competitive races where the outcomes are most uncertain
(see, for example, Jacobson 1985/1986; Herrnson 1989). The federal cap on
political contributions, however, prevents them from investing as much
money as they would like in such races. Parties have learned, however, how
to invest soft money in targeted races throughout the country. The national
parties do this by channeling money to state parties, which in turn mobilize
voters in key areas and air issue ads.

In the above scenario, it would appear that soft money does not
strengthen political parties organizationally. Instead, party leaders and their
staff simply have additional resources to invest in the short-term goal of winning close elections.

Over the long term, however, party soft money spending may have important benefits for the organization itself. With access to soft money, parties
have sufficient funds to invest in personnel and organization building that
will help them win future elections. Indeed, even if soft money is invested
primarily in campaign operations, an ancillary benefit is that state party operatives are more fully engaged in elections at both the federal and state
level. In the process of pulling together integrated voter mobilization campaigns, state party staff interact with national party staff and consultants in
ways that could increase professionalism and improve party operations. The
money that state parties receive through transfers from national committees
may also free up funds that state parties raise on their own. These funds
could be used to develop programs to recruit candidates, improve fundraising, and expand voter mobilization.

Here I explore this notion that soft money strengthens state party organizations. My hypothesis is that parties spending additional increments of soft
money are stronger than those spending less. By stronger, I mean parties that
exceed others in recruiting candidates, providing basic campaign services,
and maintaining substantial headquarter operations even during the nonelection season. Although much work remains to be done, this analysis provides
persuasive evidence that soft money strengthens parties.

Data and Methods

To explore the relationship between soft money and party strength, I
combine data on party finances with new data from a survey about party

activity in the states. Financial data for each of the one hundred state parties were obtained from the FEC, which requires parties at all levels to file reports for any activity related to federal campaigns. In particular, the FEC collects detailed expenditure reports about how the state parties spend soft money. These reports include generic descriptions of self-reported party expenses. I coded these descriptions into six broad categories of party activity: (1) administrative/overhead, (2) media, (3) mobilization, (4) grassroots, (5) fundraising, and (6) unidentified.

Although summary reports indicate how these parties divided their budgets, they provide little information about party organizational capacity because parties, like candidates, hire consultants to perform much of the campaign work (Kolodny 1998). Thus, to determine the intensity and range of party activity, I sent a fifteen-question survey between December 2000 and June 2001 to the executive directors of parties.[7] Fortunately, partisan balance was achieved with thirty-seven responses from Republicans and thirty-seven from Democratic organizations. The regional balance is also good, although states from the Northeast are slightly underrepresented.

The survey asked about party services to candidates, recruitment activities, and basic information about party headquarters. As a framework for analyzing party activity, I draw heavily on the work of Cotter and his colleagues (1984) in the Party Transformation Study (PTS). The PTS surveyed party chairs of fifty-four state parties between 1960 and 1980, and developed three dimensions of party organizational strength:

1. Programmatic: breadth of services to candidates
2. Recruitment: breadth of candidate recruitment activity
3. Bureaucratic: organizational complexity (staff, budgets, headquarters)[8]

The tables for party activity that follow are organized along these three dimensions of party organizational strength to assess the degree to which parties invest in programs, recruitment, or their bureaucracy. Using these three dimensions, it is also possible to compare data collected in 2000 with the PTS data from 1964–1980 to judge whether parties are stronger or weaker than in the past (see this chapter's appendix for the 2000 results).[9]

There are a few caveats about the 2000 data. First, because it was considered important to achieve a high response rate, the 2000 survey asked only fifteen questions, and therefore tapped fewer measures of party activity than those explored by the Party Transformation Study. These measures, then, provide a rougher approximation of party strength than the index compiled by the PTS. One indication that the 2000 measures are valid, however, is that they are highly correlated (about 0.5) with the party organizational strength scores reported by the PTS in 1980. Apparently, the stronger parties in the past persist as the stronger parties of today. There is also the potential problem of response bias. The parties most likely to return surveys are those that are organized and capable of responding to questions from the public. As a result, the strongest organizations may be overrepresented in this sample.[10]

Patterns of Spending

Table 8.1 categorizes state party spending from 1992 through 2000, not including party contributions and coordinated expenditures for federal candidates. According to federal guidelines, these funds should be used for party-building activities that do not directly aid individual federal candidates. Starting in 1996, parties spent increasing money on media. Close observers of campaigns believe that this spending reflects payments for issue ads in support of presidential or congressional candidates, rather than party-based themes (Magleby 2000a, 1998; Krasno and Seltz 2000). By the 2000 elections, state parties spent $236 million on media, or 43 percent of total outlays. In absolute terms, parties more than doubled the amount they spent on media since 1996. Approximately 65 percent of this activity was funded with soft money.

Media spending can hardly be qualified as party building if the intent is to promote the election of a candidate rather than emphasize party themes or generate long-term partisan loyalty among voters. Most of these ads focus on swing voters—partisan leaners and independents—in highly competitive contests. Furthermore, media expenditures reflect the cost of producing and placing ads in media markets rather than investments in the party's organizational infrastructure. Therefore, it is reasonable to assume that soft money spending on media does not, in fact, build the party organization.

The balance of expenditures, however, shows that parties invest considerable resources in activities that are likely to be related to party building. These include efforts by party personnel to run campaigns, mobilize voters, and manage day-to-day party affairs. In the 2000 elections, about 30 percent of party outlays ($159 million) went toward basic overhead and administrative chores at party headquarters. Another 12 percent ($67 million) went toward mobilizing voters, a significant increase from 1996, when the parties spent $25 million (or 9 percent of spending). Party spending on grassroots activity (putting up lawn signs, distributing bumper stickers, and sponsoring volunteer campaign events) is a small portion of party investments, though this has risen during the decade from just $2 million in 1992 (2 percent of spending) to $18 million in the 2000 elections (3 percent of spending).

These spending figures suggest that parties are more active and engaged in campaigns than previously. The numbers, however, tell us little about whether party organizations perform the work or whether they hire consul-

Table 8.1 Party-Building Expenditures by State Parties, 1992–2000 Elections (in millions of dollars)

	1992	%	1994	%	1996	%	1998	%	2000	%
Administrative and Overhead	71	67%	83	63%	112	39%	139	55%	159	29%
Media	3	3%	5	4%	101	35%	42	17%	236	43%
Mobilization	15	14%	20	15%	25	9%	30	12%	67	12%
Party Hoopla (banners, stickers, etc.)	2	2%	5	3%	13	5%	9	3%	18	3%
Fundraising	10	10%	12	9%	22	8%	23	9%	26	5%
Unidentified	5	4%	7	5%	11	4%	11	4%	38	7%
TOTAL										
N	106	100	130	100	284	100	253	100	544	100

Source: Federal Elections Commission

Note: Administrative/Overhead = office-related expenses such as rent, salaries, computers, travel, and utilities.
Media = communication expenditures for television, radio and newspaper, and production and purchase costs.
Mobilization = costs of registering and contacting voters through direct mail, telephone banks, canvassing, and voter files.
Grassroots = includes traditional party "hoopla" such as yard signs, bumper stickers, banners, pins, rallies, fairs, and volunteer work.
Fundraising = costs associated with joint fundraising for federal, state, and local campaigns.
Unidentified = expenditures that could not be determined from FEC reports.

tants to do it. Parties may be akin to financial holding companies, distributing money to satellite groups that carry out the work. Or parties may be "fronts" for candidates, purchasing services that individual candidates request, rather than investing strategically for collective party goals.

Survey responses from party executive directors, however, suggest that parties are more active today than they have been since the 1960s. Table 8.2 shows survey responses by party leaders for 2000 elections compared to similar responses collected for the years between 1964 and 1980 by the PTS.

Given the brevity of the 2000 survey, there are only a few measures to make these comparisons. However, across a range of pursuits, both Republican and Democratic organizations appear more active today than in the past four decades. Republican parties, in particular, demonstrate remarkably steady progress through the decades on most measures of party strength. In the programmatic area, for example, 88 percent of Republican organizations in 2000 designed and conducted polls, showing a steady increase from 33 percent in 1964.[11] The number of organizations providing campaign research increased from 29 percent in 1964 to 84 percent in 2000. Every Republican organization in the sample claims to train campaign staff, a dramatic increase from the 63 percent of organizations doing so in 1964. Similarly, the proportion of organizations that recruit candidates rose steadily from 83 percent in 1964 to nearly 100 percent in 2000.

In terms of bureaucratic capacity, Republican budgets during nonelection years expanded significantly by 2000, although average staff size did not. The only measure of strength for which the Republican organizations decline in 2000 is whether they pay their party chair a salary. More GOP party chairs appear to serve as volunteers or simply receive a stipend than in the past. The decline in salaried chairpersons is unexpected, given that the size of the party staff remained the same between 1980 and 2000. Executive directors, who serve party chairs, may have assumed a more significant role in party management than in the past, which would allow the chairperson to perform honorific duties and fundraising part-time.

The development of Democratic organizations is more uneven but still demonstrates maximum activity in 2000. Organizational growth appears to increase until 1980 when it declines across several areas. In 2000, activity increases to levels that mostly exceed or equal the prior peaks achieved in 1974. The reasons for the dip in 1980 are unclear, particularly since there is no similar drop-off for Republicans. One possible explanation is that Democrats felt triumphant during the post-Watergate period, just before the Reagan presidential victory. They controlled both houses of Congress, as well as most state legislatures and governorships. Democrats may have seen little need to rebuild state organizations, particularly during an era when candidates seemed in control of their campaigns. Democratic incumbents in the majority party could control resources to wage their own reelection cam-

Table 8.2 State Party Activity, 1964–2000

	Republicans					Democrats				
	1964	1969	1974	1980	2000	1964	1969	1974	1980	2000
Programmatic										
Conduct polls (%)	33	59	63	62	88	12	48	52	19	41
Provide campaign training (%)	63	82	92	93	100	47	80	67	82	76
Perform campaign research (%)	29	53	60	78	84	24	52	41	37	77
Recruitment										
Recruit candidates (%)	83	88	90	89	97	82	72	78	44	88
Make contributions to U.S. House candidates (%)	63	65	70	64	71	47	48	56	35	55
Bureaucratic										
Size of staff in off-year	2.1	5.6	5.2	9.0	8.5	2.5	4.2	8.7	5.5	6.6
Size of operating budget in off-year ($ thousands)	185	144	192	492	1,002	49	83	121	182	622
Chair receives salary (%)	29	32	35	37	19	6	44	26	39	28
Permanent headquarters (%)	83	94	98	96	100	77	84	96	85	97
N	24	34	48	27	37	17	25	27	27	37

Source: Data for 1964–1980 is from Cotter et al., 1984. The number of observations for 1960–1974 includes interviews of past party chairs in twenty-seven sample states with oversampling in some states. Data for 2000 is from author's survey.

paigns, and saw little reason to nurture the next crop of candidates. By this logic, Republicans, as the minority party, had a stronger incentive to build a collective enterprise for gathering resources and recruiting candidates.

The discrepancy between Republican and Democratic party building in the 1980s may also reflect the remarkable partisan changes that took place in the South. In the 1960s, Republicans began party building at a time when conservative Democrats controlled almost all public offices. Although Democrats dominated politics, party structures were weak because there was little genuine partisan competition to spur party organizing (Key 1956). Sensing an opportunity, Republicans began their organizational insurgence in the 1960s. Democrats may not have reacted by building their own organizations until the 1990s.

Notably, Democrats are more involved in recruiting than before, rising from 44 percent of organizations that reported doing this regularly in 1980 to 88 percent in 2000. These changes may have been spurred by the competitive threat of Republican successes in statehouses across the country. It is also apparent that Democratic organizations are better-staffed and control larger budgets even in the nonelection years.

Additional measures of party activity gathered through the 2000 survey provide further details about party differences. Table 8.3 shows that Democrats are closing the gap in organizational strength, even though Republican parties are clearly stronger overall. Party scores on each activity are generated from survey responses based on a 0–3 scale (0 = never perform activity, 1 = rarely, 2 = sometimes, 3 = often). On a few variables, as noted, the measures are scored between 0 and 1 (no or yes responses) or based on average staff size and budget figures. The scores illustrate Republican dominance in programmatic, recruitment, and bureaucratic dimensions of party organizational strength, but reveal a few areas where Democrats are more active than Republicans.

In the program area, Republicans have more organizations that conduct campaign events, polls, and research. Democratic organizations, however, participate in and manage coordinated campaigns more frequently. Inaugurated in the 1980s by the national parties, coordinated campaigns integrate local, state, and national efforts to mobilize partisan voters.[12] It is not surprising that Democrats apparently put greater efforts in get-out-the-vote campaigns, given that registered Democrats are less reliable voters than Republicans.

Democratic reliance on coordinated campaigns may reflect a short-term solution to the problem of having weaker state parties. The longitudinal data in table 8.2 revealed that Democrats did not pursue the long-term Republican strategy of building up state and local organizations. The coordinated campaigns could be a "quick fix" substitute that allows national committees to directly influence and monitor campaigns in the states. Republican state parties, which are stronger, do not need as much oversight and additional money from the national parties.

It is also true that the Democrats suffer a hard money disadvantage relative to the Republicans, but equaled their rivals with soft money fundraising in the 2000 elections. The more intense use of coordinated campaigns by Democrats suggests they are trying to use as much soft money as possible in political campaigns to even the playing field.

For recruitment activities, Republicans outpace Democrats in most categories. In 2000, more Republican organizations engaged in recruiting candidates, training campaign staff, and recommending consultants to candidates. Republicans also made more contributions to U.S. House challengers. These findings are not surprising, because Republicans have been the minority party in many states through much of the last fifty years, giving them an incentive to find candidates. Moreover, as the party of small government, Republicans may have to work harder to draw out candidates willing to serve in government.

Democratic organizations, however, appear more active than Republicans in the primary selection process, although these differences are not large. For example, they are more likely than Republicans to make prepri-

Table 8.3   Party Activity in the States, Republicans versus Democrats

	Republicans	*N*	*Democrats*	*N*
Programmatic Activities				
Organize campaign e(scale 0-3)	2.56	36	2.38	37
Design and conduct polls (0-3)	1.86	36	1.30	37
Conduct campaign research on opposition (0-3)	2.36	36	2.08	37
Participate in coordinated campaign (0-3)	2.09	35	2.68	37
Manage coordinated campaign (0-3)	0.48	31	0.71	35
Recruitment Activities				
Recruit candidates (0-3)	2.68	37	2.30	37
Provide campaign training (0-3)	2.46	37	2.14	36
Match professionals/activists with candidates (0-3)	2.35	37	2.19	36
Made contributions to U.S. House challenger(s) in				
2000 election (0-1)	0.51	37	0.43	37
Make pre-primary endorsements (0-3)	0.43	32	0.57	32
Give pre-primary services to favored candidate (0-3)	0.51	37	0.68	37
Bureaucratic Indicators				
Chair receives salary (0-1)	0.19	36	0.28	36
Permanent headquarters (0-1)	1.00	37	0.97	37
Size of staff off-year (number of full-time				
equivalent)	8.5	37	6.6	37
Size of operating budget in thousands, off-year 1999	$1,002	37	$622	37

Source: Author's survey of state parties.
Code for 0-3 scale: Never = 0, Rarely = 1, Sometimes = 2, Often = 3

mary endorsements in states where this is permitted, and help preferred candidates with party resources during the primary. These partisan differences may be rooted in party traditions or the social bases of their respective constituencies. The Democratic Party reflects a more heterogeneous coalition, and its primaries are likely to be more adversarial than those of Republicans (Polsby 1983). Democratic leaders may choose to take sides in primaries more frequently than Republicans to ensure that a viable candidate emerges for the general election. Republicans may sidestep the problem of choosing candidates in the primary because they recruit more heavily. For Republicans, the selection process, in which they encourage favorites to run for office and discourage others, precedes the primary.

Budget and staff levels suggest that Republicans possess greater organizational capacity than Democrats. Republican parties, on average, operate with budgets that exceed $1 million during the nonelection years, while Democrats make do with approximately $600,000.[13] The average Republican committee has an 8.5-person staff, compared with 6.6 people for Democrats. Almost all parties have permanent headquarters, so there is little to say here except that both parties have a local presence between elections.[14] The only other measure for which Democrats outdistance Republicans is their tendency to pay a salary to the party chair. This finding may reflect the different social bases of the party, with Republicans tending to attract chairs from the business elite, and Democrats relying more on people who do not have alternative sources of income when they become party chair.

The findings in table 8.3 should not be surprising to those who study American party organizations. Republican success in organization building corroborates several prior assessments of each party's organizational culture and strategies. It has been shown, for instance, that the Republicans stress organization building more than the Democrats (e.g., Green 1994; Kayden and Mahe 1985). While the differences between parties are not large, they are significant and consistent across several measures. The few measures for which Democratic activity exceeds Republican activity—exploiting the use of coordinated campaigns, making preprimary endorsements, and providing primary services to favored candidates—might be described as short-term strategies to overcome Republican strength.

Soft Money and Strong Parties

These survey data demonstrate that state party organizations are as active as they have been in several decades. They also, incidentally, reveal interesting differences between the two major parties. Since party fundraising has increased significantly during the same time, it is reasonable to speculate whether parties made investments that actually strengthened the organization. One alternative is that parties simply used the money for short-term electoral goals by spending on campaign consultants and television advertisements for candidates.

In this section, I examine whether there is a link between the rise in party activity and the surge in soft money spending in the 1990s. If soft money has been invested only in short-term efforts to elect federal candidates, then there should be little or no relationship between the sums that parties spend and their organizational strength. But if party spending and strength are related, then it is plausible that parties have been making long-term investments in organization building.

Let me be clear, however, that I am not testing whether party soft money spending strengthens organizations. This analysis is more modest than that. I observe only the degree of association between party spending and party strength. The causal mechanism relating money and organizational strength is difficult to untangle: money may strengthen an organization, or strong organizations may simply be good at raising money. In truth, the influence is probably in both directions. At the very least, however, if a relationship exists this much can be said: parties that spend additional increments of soft money behave like stronger parties. I will say more about the implications of this basic relationship later.

To make general statements about the link between soft money spending and organizational vitality, it is helpful to have an overall measure of party organizational strength. To do this, I combine activity scores from survey data and measures of bureaucratic capacity into an index of party strength, with some minor adjustments to account for nonresponse for particular survey questions.[15] The index ranges from weak to strong parties, with a minimum score of .24 for the Mississippi Democratic Party and maximum score of .77 for the Minnesota Republican Party (see the appendix for the list of state parties and their scores). Based on these scores the parties are separated into quartiles of organizational strength: weak, moderately weak, moderately strong, and strong (see figure 8.2). Then, I estimate an average expenditure per voter (to adjust for population in state) for parties in each quartile. The soft money data are combined for election years 1992–2000 and do not include funds spent on media.

The results display a remarkably linear relationship between party soft money spending and party strength. Figure 8.2 illustrates the average expenditure per voter across the party strength quartiles. Strong parties spend, on average, 2.3 soft dollars per voter. Weak parties, in contrast, spend a little more than $1.5 per voter. An additional 20 cents per voter separates weak parties from moderately weak parties, and an additional 30 cents per voter separates moderately weak from moderately strong parties.

The data support the conclusion that money matters for party organiza-

Figure 8.2   Soft Money Spending per Voter and Party Organizational Strength

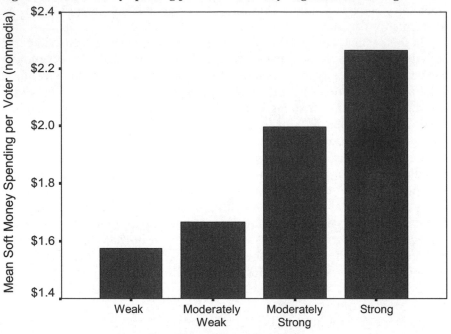

Source: Spending data tabulated from records provided by the FEC and party strength quartiles developed from author's survey data on state party activity during the 2000 election cycle.

tions. Parties that spend additional amounts of soft money tend to be stronger parties. This finding suggests that parties are not simply soft money conduits for candidates, as some campaign observers argue. Instead, parties appear to use soft money for organizational activity and party building.

Conclusion

During the 1990s, party financial activity increased to unprecedented levels, in large part because parties exploited campaign finance laws to raise and spend soft money. Although much of additional party spending was devoted to issue ads, a substantial portion was invested in traditional party work that included voter mobilization, grassroots, and general organizational maintenance. While issue ads have attracted the most attention from political reformers concerned about the potential for corruption, it should not be overlooked that soft money has been used in ways intended by Congress when it enacted provisions to encourage party building. Compared with levels of activity in the 1960s, 1970s, and 1980s, party organizations appear as strong today as in the recent past, and it is conceivable that soft money contributed to party development. Now that soft money is banned from the national parties and limited for state parties, it is realistic to expect party activity to decline.

While this analysis does not unravel the causal mechanism underlying renewed party strength, the findings demonstrate a strong relationship between the amount of soft money a state party spends and its overall strength. Parties that spend additional increments of soft money recruit and train candidates more regularly, provide services more frequently, and have larger budgets and staff size in the off-season than lower-spending parties. It seems clear, then, that soft money helps maintain robust party activity.

There are at least three important implications from this analysis. First, it makes plain that parties are not simply soft money conduits for candidate committees. State organizations use party money for their own collective purposes, even though they continue to concentrate funds in the most critical races. So while soft money has been used like hard money to help specific candidates, it has also been used for organization building.

It is particularly impressive that so many organizations claim to be actively recruiting candidates, as well as helping them run campaigns by referring consultants and training campaign staff. Recruitment has always been a vital party function that benefits the electoral system. By identifying candidates to run against the opposition, the parties encourage greater electoral competition. Further research may investigate whether party money gives them additional leverage to persuade quality candidates to run. The results here suggest that it might.

A second implication is that a reduction of party money may decrease the levels of state party activity and weaken them. BCRA prohibits the national parties from raising soft money. Since the state parties received much of their soft money in the 1990s through transfers from the national party, they will lose a valuable source of funds. State parties will also be restricted from raising soft money for federal elections in increments greater than $10,000. How state parties will reconcile conflicting federal and state laws on party fundraising remains to be seen. Parties and candidates will also be competing more intensely for small donors, which will further constrain their ability to make up for the soft money losses. Given these uncertainties, it is likely that state party coffers will diminish, at least in the short term.

Viewed simply as a budgetary problem, it stands to reason that with less money, an organization will perform less work. Therefore, a ban on soft money will probably reduce the presence of party organizations in elections unless parties can make up for the financial shortfall in soft money by other means. It is fair to assume that party-based activity will go down in the short run until parties develop larger lists of small contributors to raise amounts they accumulated through soft money.

A third implication of this research is that party differences in organizational strength may widen. The findings here suggested that differences in strength between Republican and Democratic organizations appeared to diminish in the 1990s. Whether Democrats at the national level will continue to support their state organizations now that they must use only hard money (albeit with higher contribution limits) remains an important question. They will probably rely even more on labor organizations and other allied groups, as they have in the past, to mobilize voters on behalf of party candidates.

In contrast, Republicans may continue to invest more in their organizations than Democrats, as they have in the past. Only this time, they are constrained by tighter regulations on party fundraising. Even though Republicans are better at raising hard money, it is understandable they are concerned about the organizational support Democrats receive from labor unions, which may give their rivals an advantage in a campaign finance regime that limits party fundraising and spending.

But assuming that a ban on soft money causes party strength to wane, should we care? Indeed, this analysis does not address a more fundamental question about whether party organizations matter. It has been properly noted that the research on party organizations usually fails to link organizational activity with other aspects of the party system (see Coleman 1996b). Do strong party organizations influence the partisan loyalty of voters, develop coherent public policies, and encourage unity in government? Using the survey data collected here, a next step is to observe whether stronger organizations really affect important political outcomes.

Notes

1. By avoiding the electioneering words, parties could spend soft money rather than only hard money, because the parties argued the political advertisements promoted party-based themes, not particular federal candidates.

2. Since 1974, federal candidates are not allowed to raise money from individuals in sums greater than $1,000 per election. They also rely on political action committees, which cannot contribute more than $5,000 per election. These contribution limits have not been adjusted for inflation, yet the cost of campaigns continues to rise because of the intensive use of sophisticated media and direct mail technology.

3. The national committees of each political party have a set amount they may spend on behalf of each U.S. House and Senate candidate. State party committees may spend equal amounts or may transfer their limits to the national committees, effectively doubling the national committees' expenditure limits in those states or districts. The party coordinated expenditure limits were indexed to inflation starting in 1974 with a base of $10,000.

4. The state parties are required to keep a separate federal account for all activities that might, in any way, affect a federal election. For example, this account includes expenditures

for get-out-the-vote drives that benefit local, state, and federal candidates simultaneously. If the state party spends money on activities related solely to local and state elections, they are not required to report expenditures in the federal account; the party is usually required to report these nonfederal transactions to a state agency that enforces state campaign finance laws.

5. These data refer to the state party budgets that apply to federal and state elections. State parties also keep a separate budget account for activities that concern state and local campaigns exclusively.

6. The state parties may raise soft money only if state laws allow such fund-raising.

7. The survey was kept short and delivered by e-mail or fax to maximize the response rate. Half of the parties responded to the e-mail, and another 15 state parties responded to a fax, bringing the total to 65. Follow-up phone calls raised this total to 74.

8. The PTS sent questionnaires to former Republican and Democratic State Party Chairmen (1960–1978) in 27 sample states. They also sent questionnaires to state party chairmen (1978–80) in 54 states of which 27 were part of the original sample for 1960–1978.

9. The PTS data for 1964–1974 is based on recollections of past party chairs when the survey was done in 1978–1980, so these data must be viewed with some caution. Nonetheless, these data provide a rare empirical baseline for judging the health of parties over time.

10. The PTS researchers (Cotter et al., 1984) acknowledge the same response problem for their data, particularly the data from the 1960s. They suggest a higher response rate for stronger parties means that the "base point" (the early 1960s) provides a conservative standard against which change is assessed.

11. In response to queries about whether the party organization participated in a particular activity, the researchers in the PTS counted a response as "yes" if the party chair simply "checked off" in the survey that the party engaged in the activity. In my survey I counted a "yes" response if the executive director responded "sometimes" or "often" to a question about performing an activity.

12. Candidates up and down the ticket are asked to contribute campaign money to the party's efforts to register and mobilize targeted voters. Through pooled resources, the coordinated campaign targets partisan voters and avoids wasteful overlap when various party candidates contact individually the same voters over and over again.

13. These figures do not include funds used exclusively for state and local elections.

14. This was not always true. The PTS reports that in the 1950s through 1960s, party affairs were sometimes conducted from temporary office space or from the homes of party chairs.

15. I created the index by testing bivariate relationships among all of the variables. Within each dimension of party organizational strength (as developed by Cotter et al., 1984), I included correlated variables into an overall measure of party organizational strength. I transformed each variable to a range of 0–1, and took the average of all the scores as a way of minimizing the effect of a nonresponse to a particular question by a party.

Appendix: Party Organizational Strength Scores

	Republicans				Democrats		
Rank	*State Party*	*Score*	*Quartile*	*Rank*	*State Party*	*Score*	*Quartile*
1	Minnesota	0.77	4	1	Kentucky	0.76	4
2	Florida	0.76	4	2	Indiana	0.73	4
3	Indiana	0.74	4	3	Washington	0.73	4
4	North Dakota	0.71	4	4	Georgia	0.72	4
5	Michigan	0.70	4	5	California	0.71	4
6	Ohio	0.69	4	6	Pennsylvania	0.68	4
7	Delaware	0.69	4	7	North Dakota	0.67	4
8	Tennessee	0.68	4	8	Michigan	0.67	4
9	California	0.66	4	9	Ohio	0.66	4
10	Wisconsin	0.65	3	10	Louisiana	0.65	3
11	New Mexico	0.64	3	11	New Mexico	0.62	3
12	Hawaii	0.64	3	12	North Carolina	0.62	3
13	Connecticut	0.64	3	13	Maine	0.61	3
14	Massachusetts	0.62	3	14	New Jersey	0.59	3
15	Oregon	0.62	3	15	Wisconsin	0.57	3
16	Alabama	0.61	3	16	Oregon	0.56	2
17	Utah	0.61	3	17	Texas	0.56	3
18	Nevada	0.60	3	18	Montana	0.55	2
19	South Carolina	0.59	3	19	New York	0.54	2
20	Alaska	0.59	3	20	Delaware	0.53	2
21	New Jersey	0.59	3	21	Oklahoma	0.51	2
22	Oklahoma	0.56	2	22	Missouri	0.51	2
23	Idaho	0.55	2	23	Colorado	0.50	2
24	South Dakota	0.54	2	24	Wyoming	0.48	1
25	Rhode Island	0.53	2	25	West Virginia	0.47	1
26	New Hampshire	0.53	2	26	Florida	0.46	1
27	Mississippi	0.52	2	27	Virginia	0.45	1
28	North Carolina	0.52	2	28	Alaska	0.45	1
29	Virginia	0.52	2	29	Idaho	0.44	1
30	Illinois	0.51	2	30	Connecticut	0.40	1
31	Colorado	0.51	2	31	Tennessee	0.40	1
32	Kentucky	0.50	2	32	Nebraska	0.40	1
33	Arizona	0.48	2	33	Arizona	0.38	1
34	Arkansas	0.48	1	34	Arkansas	0.33	1
35	Maine	0.45	1	35	Nevada	0.32	1
36	Louisiana	0.37	1	36	Hawaii	0.27	1
37	Montana	0.31	1	37	Mississippi	0.24	1

Quartiles: 4 = Strong, 3 = Moderately Strong, 2 = Moderately Weak, 1 = Weak

9

State Parties: Independent Partners in the Money Relationship

Sarah M. Morehouse and Malcolm E. Jewell

Most state parties are multimillion-dollar organizations with experienced executive directors and knowledgeable staffs. Fierce electoral competition has driven these state parties into raising and spending millions on their own or in partnership with the national parties. They now provide sophisticated services to candidates, including training, issue development, polling, media consulting, and coordination of campaign assistance. With their greatly increased role in statewide, congressional, and state legislative campaigns, they supplement the candidates' own campaign organizations and resources. As the executive director of the Kansas Republicans said: "We are necessary but not sufficient."[1]

Fifty years ago, most state parties were poor and weak. The Progressive reformers of the early decades of the twentieth century emasculated the nineteenth-century state party machines, which controlled nominations, monopolized campaign resources, and dominated the mobilization of voters (Mayhew 1986, 212–237). Because state political parties had been primarily labor-intensive organizations, dependent upon patronage for party workers and funds, they were slow to adapt to technologically based campaigning. At first, they could not provide the services to candidates that have become standard in contemporary campaigns. Candidates had to buy these services elsewhere, and thus they became expert at raising money, organizing their candidacies, and running for office independently of the party.

Since that time, increased party competition and large-scale fundraising combined to strengthen party organizations (Bibby 1998; Patterson 1993). This trend appeared first at the national level and then spread to the states. It has produced an often uneasy partnership between the national and state party committees. The national committees are widely perceived as dominating their weaker partners in exchange for the money to function as effective organizations.

This chapter is concerned with the money relationship between the state parties and their national partners. What impact does money coming from the national parties have on the organization and operation of state parties? Do the national parties contribute a controlling proportion of the state party financial resources, or are state parties substantially autonomous?

In order to investigate these questions, party executive directors in thirty political parties in fifteen states (including nine of the largest states, with over 50 percent of the American population) were sent a questionnaire asking about the impact of national party money on their activities and autonomy, among other things.[2] After two waves, the response rate was 63 percent; follow-up telephone interviews were also conducted.

A second line of inquiry consisted of examining the financial reports of the thirty state parties for the 1995–1996, 1997–1998, and 1999–2000 election cycles. The Federal Election Commission (FEC) reports for presidential and midterm elections were consulted as well as the relevant reports filed with the state election agencies. All fifteen of the sample states elected governors in the 1997–1998 cycle. Therefore, state fundraising in presidential and gubernatorial election years could be compared. This inquiry, then, tests the monetary relationship between the state and national parties during presidential elections when the national party would be expected to dominate, and in a midterm election when gubernatorial elections would be expected to claim primary importance.

The following questions were asked: 1) What percent of federal ("hard") money was raised by the state parties? 2) What percent of nonfederal ("soft") money was raised by the state parties? 3) What criteria do national parties use to give money to state parties? 4) What percent of state party funds ("state money") are used only in state-level elections? and 5) How dependent are state parties on money coming from their national partners?

The Rules: Hard, Soft, and State Money

The financial rules that apply to congressional and presidential candidates are not the same as those in effect for state legislative and gubernatorial elections, and likewise, national and state parties face different financial restrictions. Taken together, these rules define three kinds of money for state parties: federal "hard money," nonfederal "soft money," and "state money." We will review each in turn.

Federal "Hard" Money. The FEC describes money raised under the Federal Election Campaign Act (FECA) as "federal" money because it is the only money that can be used to directly support federal candidates; it is also called "hard" money.

FECA prohibits direct contributions from corporations and labor unions to political parties in connection with a federal election. Corporations, unions, and other groups may form political action committees (PACs) and give up to $15,000 a year to a national party and $5,000 per year to a state or local party. In addition, individuals may give up to $25,000 a year to a national party and $10,000 to state or local parties to use for federal candidates.[3] National parties are limited to a $5,000 contribution per election to U.S. House candidates, and $17,500 to U.S. Senate candidates. They are also allowed to make coordinated expenditures on behalf of candidates (these are adjusted for inflation and in 2000 totaled $33,780 for the House; for the Senate the sum varied with state population). State parties are limited to a $5,000 contribution to candidates, and are also allowed to make coordinated expenditures (with the same limits as the national parties). As the result of recent litigation, national and state parties may engage in independent expenditures on behalf of candidates (see chapter 5); these expenditures are unlimited, but must be paid with hard dollars, and not be coordinated with the candidate. FECA allows for unlimited transfers between party committees, including from national to state parties.

Nonfederal "Soft" Money. The FEC describes funds raised and spent under state rules and via state parties that indirectly assist federal candidates as "nonfederal"; it is also known as "soft" money. Many soft money donations and expenditures would otherwise be illegal under FECA. However, federal rules recognized that the activities of parties in a federal system of elections would have an indirect impact on federal candidates.[4]

In the 1990s, soft money could be used for party overhead expenses as well as shared activities that benefit the whole party ticket, including national, state, and local candidates. These activities include voter registration and identification, certain types of campaign material (slate cards), voter turnout programs, and generic party advertising. These activities were paid for with a combination of hard and soft money according to the FEC formula.

The size and sources of soft money were subject only to the laws of the state where it was raised and spent. Thus, if a state allows unlimited corporate and union contributions to state parties, then the nonfederal portion of any "generic" party activity in that state can be paid for with unlimited corporate or union funds. However, if a state imposed contribution limits on parties that were at least as strict as the federal law, there would be no soft money "loophole" in that state. Twenty-four states place limits on contributions to state parties, but some of these allow very generous contributions.

Beginning in 1980, the national parties became deeply involved in raising and disbursing soft money in cooperation with the state parties. In 1996 and 2000, both national parties spent a significant amount of soft money for the first time on "issue advocacy" ads. These ads were run in states and congressional districts as candidate-specific broadcast advertising with the obvious purpose of helping the presidential or congressional candidate. Technically distinct from "express advocacy," federal law and the FEC treated such ads as a form of generic party advertising (see chapter 8). By 2000, the national parties transferred significant sums of hard and soft money to the state parties to purchase issue advocacy ads (see chapter 7).

Federal court rulings in the late 1980s required the FEC to allocate the costs of state party administrative expenses, grassroots activities, and issue advertising that indirectly affect all candidates in ways that reflected the proportion of federal and nonfederal candidates on the ballot. For example, in the presidential election year of 1996, Minnesota parties paid out 60 percent in federal money and 40 percent in nonfederal money for expenses for the above activities. In the gubernatorial election year of 1998, the allocation formula was 17 percent federal and 83 percent nonfederal, and in 2000, the formula was 43 percent federal and 57 percent nonfederal. Another example comes from Connecticut in 1996: the Democratic National Committee (DNC) transferred $1 million in soft money to the Connecticut state party but it had to be raised according to Connecticut law and be matched by the FEC formula.

State Money. Many state party executive directors speak of money that is raised and spent according to state laws as "state money," and we will use the term to distinguish it from nonfederal soft money. There are twenty-four states where contributions by individuals and PACs to political parties are limited, and thirteen of these states have stricter limits than the federal ones (thus in these states, there is no advantage to raising soft money). Table 9.1 shows what these contribution limits were for 2000. In these states, the parties have to raise the money to pay for the nonfederal share of administrative and generic activities according to the dictates of state law. Furthermore, they may not accept transfers of soft money from the national party unless it has been raised according to state law.

In addition, there are twenty-two states (including twelve of the above) where the parties are limited in what they may contribute to statewide candidates. Ten of the states without contribution limits to parties have limits on party spending for candidates. Since they cannot spend much money on their candidates, this situation offers an unusual opportunity for the national parties to send soft money funds to these states, which, for example, could be used for issue advocacy. For instance, one night in 2000 the DNC wired $150,000 to the Minnesota Democratic Party account with the instructions that it be transferred the next morning to a New York advertising agency for issue ads. This transaction appears to make the Minnesota Democrats into a conduit for the DNC's purposes, but it must be remembered that the issue ads had to be paid for according to the FEC formula for Minnesota (40 percent soft money and 60 percent federal money).

In total, thirty-five states have some limitations on contributions to and/

or spending by state parties. Here, too, the state parties may not accept or spend national party soft money unless it is in conformity with state law. For instance, New York parties can receive soft money from the national committees if it is raised in amounts of $76,500 or smaller from individuals and PACs. There are six states that limit the total amount of soft money coming to the state party from the national party. New Jersey has passed a law that limits the amount of soft money from the national committees to a total of $59,000 per year; Hawaii limits soft money to $50,000 and Kansas limits soft money to $25,000 per year. Two states that place much stricter limits of $5,000 or under are Vermont and West Virginia.

Connecticut passed a law in 1998 that banned the receipt of soft money from the national committees. The Republican executive director said: "We would prefer not to have soft money exist as an option. We have been forced to beg national officials for some funds simply to compete with the opposition. Our position is that soft money takes the power away from our local base." The governor said proudly that Connecticut was the first state in the nation to explicitly ban soft money from state politics.

National committees often raise soft money in the states as a joint fundraiser with the state parties, who have insisted that they are entitled to a negotiated share of the receipts. According to the Texas Democrats, they are financing a lot of the DNC budget. Texas donors give at huge fundraisers and the Texas party asks for its share, with the threat that its donors may not be as generous the next time if the share is not forthcoming.

This discussion was intended to emphasize the fact that the rules under which each state party operates are sovereign with respect to what the party may raise and spend for state candidates. The national committees may not give money to a state party unless it conforms to rules in that state. Likewise, federal rules are sovereign with respect to federal candidates. State parties may not support their congressional candidates with state money unless it is raised according to federal rules. Areas of overlap are the administrative and generic expenses to benefit the whole ticket, which are paid out of both federal and nonfederal (or state) money accounts according to a formula set by the FEC for each election cycle.

National Parties and State Parties: Financial Partners

Tables 9.2 and 9.3 report the percentage of hard and soft money raised for the thirty state parties under study for the 1996 presidential year, 1998 midterm (gubernatorial) year, and 2000 presidential year. The funds represent the total hard and soft money raised by state party committees, national party committees, and senatorial and congressional committees. In Table 9.2, the three columns give the total hard money funds raised in 1996, 1998, and

Table 9.1   Contribution Limits to State Parties and from State Parties

State Parties	Annual Individual Contributions to State Parties	Annual PAC Contributions to State Parties	Contributions from State Parties to Candidates for Governor
Alaska	$5,000	$1,000	$100,000
California	25,000[b] (as of 11/6/02)	25,000[b] (as of 11/6/02)	Unlimited
Colorado	25,000	25,000	Unlimited
Connecticut	5,000	5,000	Unlimited
Delaware	20,000[a]	20,000[a]	Limited by office
Hawaii	50,000	50,000	50,000
Kansas	15,000	5,000	Unlimited in general election
Kentucky	2,500	2,500	1,000 per slate
Louisiana	100,000[a]	100,000[a]	Unlimited
Maryland	4,000[b]	6,000[b]	Unlimited
Massachusetts	5,000	5,000	3,000; in kind unlimited[c]
New Hampshire	5,000	Unlimited	1,000; unlimited for public funding
New Jersey	30,000	30,000	2,100 per primary and general elect.
New York	76,500[b]	76,500[b]	Primary prohibited; general election unlimited
Ohio	16,000	16,000	523,000 per primary or general election
Oklahoma	5,000	5,000	5,000
Rhode Island	1,000 (limit 10,000)	1,000 (limit 10,000)	25,000; in kind unlimited[c]
South Carolina	3,500[b]	3,500[b]	50,000
South Dakota	3,000	Unlimited	Unlimited
Vermont	2,000[a]	2,000[a]	400
Washington	Unlimited	3,000[b]	0.60 per voter
West Virginia	1,000	1,000	1,000 per primary or general election
Wisconsin	10,000 (Limit 10,000)	6,000	Unlimited
Wyoming	25,000[a] (Limit 25,000)	Unlimited	Primary prohibited: general election unlimited

2000 by both state and national parties and the percent of these funds raised by the state parties. The three columns in table 9.3 give the total soft money funds raised in 1996, 1998, and 2000 by both state and national parties and the percent of these funds raised by the state parties. In both tables, the states are arranged by population size.

Hard Money Raised. "State party organizations must raise at least enough funds under federal rules to pay the federal portion of their general overhead expenses" (Biersack 1996, 111). Apparently, this requirement is not a great problem for the thirty state parties under study, since the average state share contributed toward their federal money total in 1996 was 69 percent (table 9.2). This figure dropped to 62 percent in the 2000 presidential elections, however, raising the question of whether there is some limitation on the state parties' ability or willingness to raise hard money. Hard money contributions from the national party committees to all fifty states increased from a total of $29 million for the Democrats and $18.4 million for the Re-

Table 9.1 (cont.)

Arizona	None	None	75,610[d]
Arkansas	None	None	2,500
Florida	None	None	50,000 for publicly funded; in-kind unlimited[c]
Georgia	None	None	5,000 election year; 1,000 nonelection year
Idaho	None	None	10,000 per primary or general election
Maine	None	None	5,000
Michigan	None	None	68,000
Minnesota	None	None	20,000 election year: 5,000 nonelection year
Montana	None	None	15,000
Nebraska	None	None	750,000 for publicly funded[d]
Nevada	None	None	5,000 per primary or general election

Source: U.S. Federal Election Commission. 2000. *Campaign Finance Law 2000: A Summary of State Campaign Finance Laws with Quick Reference Charts.* Washington, D.C.: FEC.

Note: Corporations and labor unions are prohibited from contributing in: AK, AZ, CO, CT, MI, MN, NC, ND, NH, OH, PA, RI, SD, WI, and WY. Corporations only are prohibited from contributing in: IA, KY, MA, MT, OK, TN, and WV. Corporations and labor unions are limited the same as PACs in: CA, DE, HI, LA, NJ, SC, VT, and WA. OK and WV: Labor unions only. In KA corporations and unions are limited the same as individuals. In KY labor is limited like individuals. In AL, IN, MS, NY, and TX there are varying limits on corporate and labor contributing. There are fifteen states that do not limit individual or PAC contributions to, or contributions from, the parties: AL, IL, IN, IA, MO, MS, NC, ND, NM, OR, PA, TN, TX, UT, and VA.

[a]In DE, VT, and WY contributions are for a two-year cycle, and in LA and MD contributions are for a four-year cycle.

[b]CA, MD, NY, SC, and WA limit monetary contributions for election purposes, but not contributions to overhead expenses, therefore allowing unlimited contributions to the party administrative and house-keeping account.

[c]In FL, MA, and RI, cash contributions are limited but in-kind contributions are not. Therefore, they are treated as if they permit unlimited party contributions.

[d]In AZ and NE, total is from political party and all political organizations combined.

publicans in 1996 to $77.8 million for the Democrats and $57.5 million for the Republicans in 2000.

In the 1997–1998 cycle, the state parties contributed an average 82 percent of the total raised in hard money funds. Raising hard money is not as difficult in midterm (gubernatorial) election years because less federal money needs to be matched with soft money in the FEC formula (based on the ratio of federal to nonfederal candidates on the ballot).[5] Hard money funds from the national party committees to the fifty states dropped dramatically from the presidential year of 1996, in which they contributed a total of $47.5 million to state parties, to 1998 when the combined total was $31.5 million. In the midterm election years, the state parties must raise most of the needed hard money. Apparently, state parties are able to achieve this goal.

Table 9.2   State Party Percentage of Hard Money Raised, 1995–1996, 1997–1998, 1999–2000 (in thousands of dollars)

State Party	Hard Money Raised for Federal Account 1995–96		Hard Money Raised for Federal Account 1997–98		Hard Money Raised for Federal Account 1999–2000	
	Total	% State Party	Total	% State Party	Total	% State Party
California						
Dem	7,774	87	8,160	53	10,742	44
Rep	8,677	74	7,345	65	18,480	68
Texas						
Dem	3,427	53	1,722	66	2,423	47
Rep	5,093	90	4,163	98	5,578	99
New York						
Dem	1,837	86	4,275	34	11,455	33
Rep	2,328	98	5,027	56	6,132	55
Florida						
Dem	3,148	34	1,075	87	8,515	13
Rep	5,756	85	4,874	96	14,718	56
Pennsylvania						
Dem	2,381	34	730	71	10,656	39
Rep	3,774	79	2,297	91	8,369	54
Illinois						
Dem	2,811	56	1,756	75	5,046	53
Rep	3,265	68	2,084	90	3,978	55
Ohio						
Dem	3,155	49	2,153	87	5,858	33
Rep	6,357	77	4,529	99	9,050	66
New Jersey						
Dem	1,874	77	1,085	90	2,754	84
Rep	3,193	87	1,730	97	3,769	82
Georgia						
Dem	3,114	83	1,076	86	2,550	52
Rep	2,497	73	1,752	98	3,317	· 92
Tennessee						
Dem	1,330	18	654	72	1,401	0
Rep	3,534	79	2,593	100	3,750	86
Minnesota						
Dem	4,019	66	2,296	98	4,023	58
Rep	3,069	95	3,203	100	6,009	76
Colorado						
Dem	2,047	45	704	94	1,104	92
Rep	2,192	72	541	89	1,144	98
Connecticut						
Dem	1,329	74	975	89	1,470	96
Rep	1,134	93	423	55	1,633	78
Oregon						
Dem	2,274	62	652	69	2,225	25
Rep	1,624	71	605	80	1,813	49
Kansas						
Dem	1,038	47	435	83	520	90
Rep	684	68	509	84	751	80
	Avg. = 69		Avg. = 82		Avg. = 62	

Table 9.3   State Party Percentage of Soft Money Raised, 1995–1996, 1997–1998, 1999–2000 (in thousands of dollars)

State Party	Soft Money Raised for Federal Account 1995–96		Soft Money Raised for Federal Account 1997–98		Soft Money Raised for Federal Account 1999–2000	
	Total	% State Party	Total	% State Party	Total	% State Party
California						
Dem	11,078	31	9,410	68	9,641	14
Rep	7,465	0	5,893	74	14,152	49
Texas						
Dem	3,730	38	4,371	39	3,824	17
Rep	3,236	35	2,543	79	3,110	11
New York						
Dem	1,472	96	6,259	31	10,728	0
Rep	3,720	77	13,082	84	4,948	63
Florida						
Dem	5,372	28	2,176	68	16,624	14
Rep	6,441	79	7,244	73	23,823	44
Pennsylvania						
Dem	4,776	0	612	8	13,678	2
Rep	2,631	0	616	63	11,652	17
Illinois						
Dem	2,835	13	3,075	1	7,065	3
Rep	1,882	6	1,879	51	10,256	48
Ohio						
Dem	5,363	25	2,864	30	7,143	2
Rep	4,448	27	2,706	52	7,627	7
New Jersey						
Dem	1,727	89	1,152	90	1,654	88
Rep	4,308	96	3,906	86	2,985	90
Georgia						
Dem	2,785	48	1,575	68	2,737	61
Rep	2,445	0	1,649	49	2,494	17
Tennessee						
Dem	1,511	0	744	65	2,141	5
Rep	1,478	0	758	11	2,791	28
Minnesota						
Dem	2,676	41	2,379	65	4,079	29
Rep	1,664	71	4,474	73	5,168	52
Colorado						
Dem	2,434	21	66	100	634	56
Rep	1,263	7	751	98	1,215	18
Connecticut						
Dem	1,059	7	1,273	38	578	100
Rep	558	100	814	50	524	100
Oregon						
Dem	1,785	4	741	51	4,575	1
Rep	334	25	106	29	3,609	6
Kansas						
Dem	811	86	388	87	551	89
Rep	79	70	230	78	387	89
	Avg. = 37		Avg. = 59		Avg. = 37	

Soft Money Raised. National party soft money increased dramatically from 1992 until the 2000 presidential cycle. Understandably, the 1998 cycle showed a decrease of 14 percent over the 1996 presidential cycle. In spite of this, the amount of soft money more than doubled since the last midterm election of 1994.[6] Not surprisingly, the national party transfers sent soft money to the state parties under study, which reflected this increase in soft money raising (table 9.3). The Democrats increased their soft money from $64,500 million in 1996 to $149,841 million, a 132 percent increase, and the Republicans raised their soft money from $50.2 million to $129.9 million, an increase of 159 percent.

The dramatic increase in soft money at the national level caused the national parties to run short of the federal funds needed to activate soft money at the state level. Meanwhile, some state parties raise money in smaller amounts that conform to state and federal law. This led some state parties, such as the Connecticut and Ohio Democrats, to "sell" federal money to their national parties in return for soft money. They made a "profit" by doing so—a 10 to 15 percent commission according to Common Cause (1998).

Most state party executive directors claim that they are not dependent upon soft money, even in a presidential election year. According to the executive director of the Georgia Republicans: "We are not addicted, but we take what we can get." Other executive directors claimed soft money was helpful, but that they could get by without it if it were cut off for some reason. The Pennsylvania Republican Party executive director said soft money was valuable for voter contact, but that they were not very dependent upon soft money.

State parties do not raise soft money as avidly as hard money. For the state parties under study, the average percent contributed by the state parties to the soft money account in 1996 and 2000 was about 37 percent, and in 1998 the average was about 59 percent. There is a great diversity among the states with regard to soft money. This raised the question of which states are most likely to receive this federal largesse. La Raja and Pogoda (2000; see chapter 8) tested the impact of transfers of national party soft money on the organizational strength of state parties. While party-sponsored issue ads increased dramatically in the 1996 and 1998 elections, they also found that spending on grassroots and voter mobilization efforts also increased. The increased use of soft money was associated with greater spending on political rallies, bumper stickers, and yard signs, as well as voter identification and get-out-the-vote programs.

According to the Illinois Republican executive director, national parties use several criteria in deciding how to bestow nonfederal money upon a state party, but the principal one is closeness of the race for president and members of Congress. If the presidential race is close, then soft money is usually forthcoming in large amounts. In 1996 and 2000, California was a targeted state because of the closeness of the presidential race (13 percent margin of victory for President Clinton and 11 percent margin for Al Gore). In 1996, New York, with a 28 percent margin in the presidential contest, was not targeted and had to raise most of the modest amount of soft money itself. In 2000, however, while the presidential race also strongly favored the Democrats, the U.S. Senate race featuring Hillary Clinton was close, and the DNC provided $11 million.

Of course, Florida parties were the recipients of huge quantities of soft money as the 2000 presidential race progressed. It was incumbent upon Governor Jeb Bush to deliver the state and its twenty-five electoral votes to his brother. The closeness of the Florida contest is reflected in the soft money accounts. Al Gore targeted it early and visited it often and George W. Bush ended up devoting time and money in the state as well.

A regression analysis performed on all one hundred state parties in 2000, using the state presidential election margin as the independent variable and national party soft money funding as the dependent variable, revealed differences in party contribution strategies.[7] The Republicans did not base their funding strategy on close elections as much as the Democrats. La Raja and Pogoda (2000, 22–24) report that Democrats transferred soft money to state parties for issue ads more than Republicans. They explain this difference is due to the fact that the Democrats are the poorer party and attempt to exploit the favorable soft money to hard money ratios at the state level, meaning that the state parties can use more soft money than the national parties to pay for the same activity. In 1996, the states with the highest media spending were highly competitive, and it was mostly the Democratic parties who were doing the high media spending.

The midterm election year of 1998 did not produce as much soft money from the national committees (table 9.3). This change is particularly noticeable in soft money transfers to all fifty states. The Democrats, whose total soft money fundraising dropped from $124 million to $93 million, dropped transfers from its three national committees from $65 million to $35 million. The Republicans, whose national soft money account dropped from $138 million to $132 million, went from $50 million to $34 million in state transfers.

The national congressional parties focus on races for the U.S. Senate and House in midterm election years, and gave much more generously to the state parties in the 1998 cycle than they had in 1996. The Democratic Senatorial Campaign Committee increased its federal and nonfederal transfers from $10.5 million to $28.5 million in the effort. The Senate Republicans increased their money on behalf of their senators from $2 million to $15 million. The Democratic and Republican Congressional Committees also increased their totals, from $9 million to $10 million for the Democrats and from $400 thousand to $5 million for the Republicans.

In midterm elections, the closeness of the Senate and House races may determine the amount of nonfederal money transferred to the state parties. Glasgow (2000b) tested the impact of election margins on the allocation of national and state party money to congressional races and found that the Democrats and more recently the Republicans have distributed their resources strategically.

Overall, it appears that state parties are not the financially dependent partners that many observers predicted. The state parties raised over 60 percent of the hard money and 37 percent of the soft money in presidential election years. When the noise of the presidential election subsides and the midterm election cycles begin, the parties forage for an average 82 percent of the hard money and 59 percent of the soft money to keep the office open, pay for utilities, and pay for national party issue advertising. Also on their minds at this time are a gubernatorial campaign with an underticket and state legislators to keep or challenge and the need to raise state money to pay for it all.

State Parties and State Money

Table 9.4 reports the state money raised by the state parties under study in 1996, 1998, and 2000. What portion of the total receipts in a presidential election year is state money to be spent on state activities? Overall, just about one-half of the total funds came from state money. For the Republicans, the percent of the total raised for state activities was 51 percent in the presidential cycle of 1996 and 49 percent for the presidential cycle of 2000. For the Democrats, the corresponding percentages were 47 percent for 1996 and 53 percent for 2000.

In midterm election years, the percentage of the state share of the total budget is larger, as one might expect given the gubernatorial races. In 1998, the Republican state accounts claimed 55 percent of the total state and federal accounts and for the Democrats the percentage was sixty-three. In summary, state party accounts amount to 50 to 60 percent of the total spending, indicating robust state fundraising.

We speculated that the closeness of the gubernatorial race could have an impact on state party fundraising, and chose 1998 as the year to test this hypothesis since all of our sample states had gubernatorial elections. In order to control for state size, we divided state party money by the state's voting-age population, producing money spent per voter by the state parties. Seven of the fifteen states had close elections for governor and there was a tendency for state parties to spend more to convince the voters in those states. For instance, in Florida, where Jeb Bush won by a margin of 10 percent, both parties spent well over $1.00 per voter to contest the election (and the Republicans spent $2.40 per voter.) In Georgia, both parties spent significantly to

Table 9.4 Funds Raised by State Party Organizations and Legislative Party Campaign Committees, 1995–1996, 1997–1998, and 1999–2000 (in thousands of dollars)

State	1995–96 State Party	1995–96 Legislative Committees	1997–98 State Party	1997–98 Legislative Committees	1999–2000 State Party	1999–2000 Legislative Committees
Democratic State Parties and Committees						
California	12,878	—	18,294	—	22,291	—
Texas	4,683	—	6,174	—	8,479	312
New York	4,219	7,908	2,681	7,862	13,827	7,587
Florida	14,473	—	13,264	—	34,128	—
Pennsylvania	6,686	1,919	2,059	2,162	16,980	5,416
Illinois	3,303	6,645	9,354	5,044	14,271	5,295
Ohio	6,844	1,811	4,843	1,907	10,802	1,008
New Jersey	3,574	2,603	6,514	3,980	8,660	3,056
Georgia	6,411	195	14,183	1,118	10,154	1,669
Tennessee	1,495	656	1,083	1,634	1,281	1,882
Minnesota	3,332	1,533	9,047	1,761	5,122	3,307
Colorado	2,894	355	417	61	756	33
Connecticut	1,012	327	1,696	456	755	567
Oregon	212	22	746	850	5,117	1,854
Kansas	359	302	554	434	1,012	549
Republican State Parties and Committees						
California	9,145	—	11,062	—	18,158	—
Texas	1,109	—	3,615	—	3,470	192
New York	10,900	10,193	22,477	8,881	12,204	8,554
Florida	19,724	—	29,579	—	39,454	—
Pennsylvania	5,936	3,703	5,258	4,490	15,135	7,284
Illinois	3,506	8,569	1,914	8,829	5,755	14,933
Ohio	6,556	7,045	3,280	6,758	11,887	10,115
New Jersey	9,328	4,754	9,114	4,855	6,319	4,562
Georgia	25,747	214	5,418	82	7,318	143
Tennessee	3,394	178	2,213	503	575	749
Minnesota	4,713	2,139	7,231	1,739	9,421	3,006
Colorado	2,391	465	511	13	1,969	—
Connecticut	908	525	2,482	245	1,833	319
Oregon	73	69	168	995	4,215	1,551
Kansas	179	256	190	248	699	311

Source: Campaign finance reports filed with the Secretaries of State, Elections Division

get their candidate elected and the $2.36 per voter spent by the Democrats paid off since Democrat Roy Barnes was victorious. In Illinois, Republican George Ryan won by 4 percent, while the Democrats spent over a dollar per voter. In Minnesota, both parties spent $2.00 or more per voter, but Jesse Ventura, the Reform Party candidate, won the election.

Both parties in New Jersey raised large amounts of money in 1997. Governor Christine Todd Whitman's job rating hovered at no more than 50 percent in a state that had voted strongly for President Clinton the year before. The Democrats sensed that they could win and built up a campaign chest. The Republican National Committee paid $760,000 for an issue advocacy ad urging voters to remember the past record of Democratic governors. Whitman's victory margin was less than 1 percent. Clearly, the closeness of the governor's race influenced money raising in New Jersey.

Contrary to the dire predictions that infusions of soft money to the state parties would render them dependent on their national party, they appear to have a life of their own. The state parties are service agencies for state candidates from the state legislator to the governor.

In many states, state legislative campaign committees (LCCs) play a major role in raising funds for state legislative candidates. Legislative party leaders are expected to assume much of the responsibility for raising these funds, largely because they are better able to extract funding from interest groups than rank-and-file legislators can. Table 9.4 also compares the funds raised by the state party to those raised by LCCs in each party for the 1996, 1998, and 2000 cycles. (Campaign committees have not functioned in California and Florida, because they are banned by law; and in Texas, because the legislative parties have been relatively weak.)

These data reveal that most state party organizations have consistently raised more than the LCCs. Where have LCCs been more active than the state party? In Illinois, the Republican LCC was more active than the state party in all the election cycles, as were the Democratic legislative committees in the 1996 cycle. Presumably, this occurs because these were years when the partisan balance in the legislature was very close. In Ohio, the Republican LCCs were very active during these years, a period when the Republicans were enlarging and protecting their majority in the statehouse after twenty-two years of Democratic control of that body.

In several of the smaller states, LCC funding has been at a relatively low level, partly because legislative campaigns in smaller districts are less costly. In the Southern states, there have been fewer LCCs and lower levels of spending for those that exist. However, there were signs of considerably more Republican activity during the 1998 and 2000 election cycles in a few Southern states. Where Southern LCCs have remained weak, some state party organizations have filled the gap.

State Parties: Independent Partners

Table 9.5 summarizes the state party finances for the states under study and the proportion of total funds from all sources raised within state from all sources in 1996, 1998, and 2000. How much of the total funds did the state parties raise themselves? The short answer is: a very high proportion.

Table 9.5   Party Funds from All Sources and Percentage Raised from State Party (in thousands of dollars)

State Party	Raised in 1995–96 Total	Raised in 1995–96 % from State Party	Raised in 1997–98 Total	Raised in 1997–98 % from State Party	Raised in 1999–2000 Total	Raised in 1999–2000 % from State Party
California						
Dem	31,730	73	35,864	81	42,674	66
Rep	25,386	62	24,300	83	50,790	74
Texas						
Dem	11,840	67	12,267	73	14,999	70
Rep	9,438	72	10,321	94	12,350	77
New York						
Dem	15,435	98	21,077	66	43,597	58
Rep	27,141	97	49,467	91	31,358	86
Florida						
Dem	22,993	74	16,515	95	59,267	63
Rep	31,920	93	41,697	95	77,995	75
Pennsylvania						
Dem	15,762	60	5,563	86	46,730	57
Rep	16,044	79	12,661	97	42,438	68
Illinois						
Dem	15,593	76	19,231	82	31,677	71
Rep	17,222	84	14,706	92	34,291	80
Ohio						
Dem	17,173	67	11,749	81	24,811	56
Rep	24,405	81	17,273	92	38,678	74
New Jersey						
Dem	9,788	94	12,730	98	16,124	96
Rep	21,582	97	19,605	97	17,635	94
Georgia						
Dem	12,505	84	17,952	96	17,110	87
Rep	30,876	90	8,901	90	13,272	82
Tennessee						
Dem	4,992	48	4,115	89	6,705	49
Rep	8,583	74	6,267	86	7,865	68
Minnesota						
Dem	11,560	75	15,483	94	16,530	72
Rep	11,585	95	16,647	93	23,603	83
Colorado						
Dem	7,729	61	1,248	96	2,527	85
Rep	6,312	72	1,816	96	4,328	77
Connecticut						
Dem	3,727	64	4,400	80	3,369	98
Rep	3,124	97	3,964	85	4,308	92
Oregon						
Dem	4,293	40	2,988	81	13,770	55
Rep	2,100	66	1,874	90	11,187	62
Kansas						
Dem	2,510	73	1,811	93	2,631	96
Rep	1,198	80	1,177	89	2,148	91
	Avg. = 76		Avg. = 89		Avg. = 76	

In the presidential years of 1996 and 2000, the state parties provided an average of 76 percent of the total funds raised from all sources. In the gubernatorial year of 1998, the state contribution of the total funds raised averaged 89 percent. Overall, in 1998, the state parties contributed 82 percent of the hard money, 60 percent of all soft money, and of course, 100 percent of the state money. This picture is hardly one of state party dependency on national party largess.

In view of this evidence, it is clear that state parties have maintained their autonomy and will not be seriously impacted by the Bipartisan Campaign Reform Act of 2002 and its ban on soft money. Of more interest is the likely impact of the Levin Amendment, which allows soft money to be raised in amounts of up to $10,000. In thirty-five states where state law allows Levin Amendment money to be raised, state parties will have varying degrees of difficulty (see table 9.1). Six of the largest states have no limits on the amounts which donors may contribute to state parties (Texas, Florida, Pennsylvania, Illinois, Georgia, and Michigan). These states will have to appeal to hundreds of additional donors at $10,000 apiece to reap the same amount of soft money they raised in 2000 (see table 9.3). In general, state parties will have to work harder to raise the party-building money and there will be less of it to spend. They will have to raise their own matching hard money, but they have proved they are capable of doing so, having raised well over 60 percent of it in presidential election years and 82 percent in midterm years.

The fact that there will be less soft money to spend will mean that state parties can better control their operations. They can devote more attention to "ground war" operations: voter registration and GOTV. There is disagreement over the percentage of soft money that was actually spent on issue ads, but researchers agree that issue ads have been problematic for both candidates and state parties. In some cases the ads, generally produced by national consulting firms, have backfired on the candidates; in others they have been inefficient and marginally effective. Hence soft money did not build party strength. The state parties built their strength in the gubernatorial election years. The Minnesota (DFL), Connecticut (R), Georgia (R), and Pennsylvania (R) party executive directors said that they were not dependent upon soft money.

Conclusion

Many state party organizations are becoming stronger, not weaker. The old-style patronage-driven, labor-intensive operation has disappeared and has been replaced by sophisticated service parties (Aldrich 1995). For those who bemoan its demise, the executive director of the Minnesota DFL said:

"Even my church uses caterers for funerals." They began this process of adaptation well before the infusion of money from their national committees. In fact, party development within state parties paralleled the resurgence of national party organizations. As the national parties became stronger and richer, they needed strong state partners because of the increasing competition in every state. This remedy was suggested fifty years ago by the APSA Committee on Political Parties in "Toward a More Responsible Two-Party System" (Committee on Political Parties 1950).

The relationship between the state and national parties has never been closer than it is today. In addition, the state parties have developed mutually beneficial relationships with candidate-centered campaigns and LCCs. In our sample of thirty state parties, they contributed the bulk of the hard, soft, and state money raised within their borders in presidential and midterm election years.

In view of this evidence, it is clear that state parties are not decomposing, as some academics and journalists have been predicting, nor have they become dependent on the national parties. Instead, they have been adapting to technologically driven politics, providing crucial services and financial resources to candidates. They have maintained their autonomy as they have become more sophisticated and professionalized.

Notes

We owe a great debt to Robert Biersack of the Federal Election Commission who provided many tables for our use and patiently explained the intricacies of the financial relationship between the state parties and the national parties.

1. We would like to thank the following executive directors for completing the questionnaires we sent them. Many of them gave the answers over the phone and thus spent much more time on explanations and anecdotes. Unless otherwise noted, quotes from state party officials come from interviews with the following individuals: AZ-D, Melodee Jackson; CO-D, Darryl Eskin; CT-D, Robert Ives; CT-R, George Gallo; FL-R, Randy Enwright; GA-D, Steve Anthony; GA-R, Joe King; IL-R, Chris Dudley; KA-D, Brett Cott; KA-R, John Potter; KY-R, Cathy Bell; MN-DFL, Kathy Czar; MN-R, Tony Sutton; NJ-D, Richard Thigpen; NV-R, Charles Muth; NY-D, David Cohen; OH-D, Amy Young; OH-R, Thom Whatman; OK-D, Pat Hall; OK-R, Quineta Wylie; OR-D, Robert Sacks; PA-R, Hank Hallowell; SC-R, Trey Walker; SD-R, Patrick Davis; TX-D, Jorge A. Ramirez; TX-R, Barbara Jackson; VT-D, Tom Hughes.

2. Other questions included campaign finance reform and relationship with legislative campaign committees (LCCs).

3. The Bipartisan Campaign Reform Act passed in 2002 increased the aggregate limit on individual contributions to national parties from $25,000 per year to $57,500 per two-year cycle ($37,500 of this may be given to PACs and state and local parties thus reducing the amount to national parties).

4. The Bipartisan Campaign Reform Act of 2002 bans soft money raised by the national parties after November 6, 2002. Campaign finance experts believe this soft money ban will be upheld by the Supreme Court (Mann and Ornstein 2002). Therefore, after November 2002,

national parties may not have soft money to bestow on their state partners. The Levin Amendment to the act provides a limited state and local party infusion of soft money to be used for generic voter registration and get-out-the-vote (GOTV) efforts that may be funded by $10,000 per source, if permissible under state law. Contributors may include corporations and labor unions, if state law permits. These funds must not be used for federal candidate-specific or generic advertising. The voter registration and vote activities must be funded consistent with FEC hard money or soft money allocation rules (see the Minnesota example in the text).

5. Midterm election years, as they are termed in FEC language, are actually important gubernatorial election years in most (thirty-six) states. To be sure, U.S. Senators are elected in some, and U.S. representatives in all, but the gubernatorial race claims major importance for state parties.

6. National party soft money reached a high of $245 million for Democrats and $250 million for Republicans in 2000. It made up 47 percent of total receipts for national Democrats and 35 percent for national Republicans. This represents an increase of 98 percent over 1996 for the Democrats (when they raised $124 million), and an increase of 81 percent for the Republicans (when they raised $138 million). In 1998, the national Republicans raised $131.6 million, a 151 percent increase over 1993–1994, and the national Democrats collected $92.8 million, an 89 percent increase. State parties received generous increases as well, with the Republican state affiliates receiving $34.3 million and the Democratic state parties receiving $34.8 million.

7. The regression yielded an adjusted R square of .40 for the Democrats and an adjusted R square of .31 for Republicans. The analysis controlled for the six states that limit the national party's soft money contributions.

Part Three

Party Services in the States

10

The Battle for the Legislature: Party Campaigning in State House and State Senate Elections

Peter L. Francia, Paul S. Herrnson, John P. Frendreis, and Alan R. Gitelson

Political parties were once the central organizers of almost all campaigns for public office. Party machines had power over the nomination process and controlled the content of political information through partisan newspapers, party-produced pamphlets, rallies, and other grassroots activities (Sorauf 1980, 447). However, the rise of electronic media made it easier for candidates to communicate directly with voters, and reforms, such as the direct primary, took away from parties' control over nominations. Declining immigration, a loss of patronage, and a better-educated, increasingly suburban, and more independent electorate reduced the number and significance of inner-city dwellers whose votes party machines had once commanded. Other legal, political, technological, and socioeconomic changes further added to the decline of parties in elections. Several observers of politics concluded from these developments that parties were in a state of decline (Broder 1971; Ranney 1975; Crotty 1984). Others argued that parties were capable of adapting to changing circumstances and continued to play an important role in providing campaign services and assistance to candidates (Cotter et al. 1984; Herrnson 1988; Frendreis and Gitelson 1993; Kayden and Mahe 1993). Most of the evidence marshalled to support this latter argument focused on the role of party organizations in congressional elections during the 1980s.

This chapter examines party campaigning in state legislative races during the 1990s. We focus on state legislative elections because they have undergone significant change in recent years. State politics have become increasingly important in the wake of "devolution" of policy-making powers from the federal government to state governments. As the power of the state legislature has grown, so has the flow of money in state legislative elections (Gierzynski and Breaux 1998). State house and state senate elections have become increasingly expensive, and some candidates for the state legislature now assemble candidate-centered, professional campaign organizations similar to those assembled by U.S. congressional candidates (Frendreis and Gitelson 1993; Salmore and Salmore 1996; Herrnson 2000b).

If state legislative campaigns have become "congressionalized," then what impact has this change had on the role of political parties in state legislative elections? Our expectation is that while state legislative campaigns are still not as professional as campaign organizations for Congress, party organizations have adapted to the new political environment in a similar manner as they adapted to changes in congressional elections. To test this proposition, we rely on data from the Campaign Assessment and Candidate Outreach Project (Herrnson 2000a) and the Election Dynamics Project (Frendreis and Gitelson 1993). Both studies used mail questionnaires to collect information from state legislative candidates about their campaign organizations and the roles of parties in their campaigns.

This chapter has three main sections. First, we review the changes in state legislative elections and the parties' responses to such changes. Next we discuss the campaign activities of contemporary state party organizations, focusing on how they allocate their resources to state legislative candidates. Finally, we assess the impact of the parties' campaign efforts on state legislative elections. We find that party campaigning in state legislative elections during the 1990s underwent changes similar to those that occurred in congressional elections during the 1980s. Party organizations have adapted to the development of candidate-centered state legislative campaigns, and the assistance they provide to candidates can have a significant impact on state legislative elections.

The Changing Nature of State Legislative Campaigns

By the 1970s, legal reforms, new campaign technologies, and other changes in the political environment encouraged national party organizations to adapt and adjust to new circumstances. The parties' congressional and senatorial campaign committees responded by becoming intermediaries between candidates and voters, and among candidates, wealthy donors, political consultants, and others in possession of the resources needed to mount a viable congressional campaign. National party committees began providing House and Senate candidates with assistance in campaign management, fundraising, gauging public opinion, issue development, campaign communications, legal compliance, and voter mobilization (Herrnson 1988, 121–122). More recently, these party committees financed "issue advocacy" advertisements that are very similar to candidate ads, except they tend to be more negative (Herrnson and Dwyre 1999; Magleby 2000b).

State legislative campaigns have experienced similar changes in the election environment in recent years. Average inflation-adjusted expenditures for state legislative campaigns increased about 70 percent from the mid-1980s to the mid-1990s (Moncrief 1998, 47). The rise in campaign expenditures is largely attributable to the increased professionalization of state legislative campaigns. State legislative candidates became more dependent on professionals for strategic assistance, polling, and campaign communications (Moncrief 1998, 38–39).

There also has been a significant increase in the level of party competition in state legislative elections. The Republicans have weakened the Democrats' grip on power in state legislatures across the nation. In 1975, there were 37 states in which Democrats controlled both the upper and lower chambers of the state legislature, seven states where there was split control, and just five states where Republicans controlled both chambers. By 1985, Democrats still had unified control in 27 states, but Republicans increased their number to 11. By 1995, Republicans shot past the Democrats, holding power in both the upper and lower chambers of 19 states, compared to 18 for the Democrats. After the 2000 election, Republicans maintained an 18-17 advantage.

The rising costs of elections, increased reliance on campaign professionals, and the heightened competition in state legislative elections placed state party organizations in a situation similar to the one faced by national party committees in congressional elections during the 1970s and 1980s (Salmore and Salmore 1996, 70). To remain competitive in elections and maintain political power in state legislatures, party leaders strengthened, or in some cases created, state campaign committees (SCCs) and legislative campaign committees (LCCs). The SCCs are primarily concerned with electing candidates to statewide office. The SCCs assist candidates with fundraising activities, running telephone banks, and voter mobilization programs (Shea 1995, 119). The LCCs are party committees that work with the parties' legislative caucuses to help meet the growing demand for money and campaign services in state legislative elections (Gierzynski 1992; Shea 1995). As Shea (1995, 39) explains:

> Because state legislative elections are now exceedingly expensive and because legislators can no longer count on partisan electorates, it makes sense that LCCs have developed as a byproduct. This might help explain why these new units have been created in both strong and weak party states. It would also explain why they are least pronounced in the South—the region where legislative competition has been low until quite recently.

State legislative leaders control the LCCs. Most raise money from individuals, political action committees (PACs), corporations, trade associations, and unions (in states where this is legal), and redistribute these funds to state legislative candidates. Some focus their efforts on helping candidates solicit funds from individuals and groups that routinely contribute to political causes. Many LCCs also recruit candidates and mobilize voters (Gierzynski 1992; Shea 1995). The degree to which each LCC is helpful varies by party and from state to state. Typically, LCCs that are the oldest tend to be the most sophisticated (Gierzynski 1992, 118).

It is uncommon for LCCs to be under the direct control of the SCCs. In fact, most LCCs are autonomous, similar to the congressional and senatorial campaign committees at the federal level. One study found that 56 percent of state party committee leaders reported no legal relationship with the LCC. Roughly 66 percent felt that the LCCs were not part of the party organization. The LCCs that have a formal relationship with the SCCs are typically found in states with laws that are supportive of parties. Although the SCCs do not directly control most LCCs, some of these organizations do have financial ties. About 40 percent of the SCCs provide money and financial assistance to the LCCs, and half of the state party leaders report that the LCCs fund party activities (Shea 1995, 116–119).

Strong state and local parties provide significant financial assistance to state legislative candidates (Frendreis and Gitelson 1995). This is particularly true of state party organizations, which give roughly $7 of every $10 that parties contribute to state legislative candidates (Gierzynski and Breaux 1998, 192). State party organizations also have become increasingly professional in their operations, which has improved the state and local parties' capacity to provide candidates, particularly those running for the state legislature, with campaign services.

National parties also cooperate with the state party committees in legislative elections. National party committees transfer money to state and local party committees to build "farm teams of prospective federal candidates." Local and state party committees often play an important role in recruiting local talent to run for the state legislature, and they can make a difference in drawing candidates into races (Gibson et al. 1983; Frendreis, Gibson, and Vertz 1990, 225). Successful recruitment at the local level deepens the candidate pool and can strengthen party prospects for higher office. The strongest congressional candidates are typically those who have previously held elected office. Furthermore, the parties' national and congressional campaign committees have an interest in building state parties because state legislatures control the redistricting of U.S. House seats. This combination of factors encourages national parties to invest in state and local party-building activities (Bibby 1998).

Indeed, national party assistance has become one of most important factors in strengthening local party organizations (Frendreis, Gibson, and Vertz 1990). In the 1970s and 1980s, the Republican National Committee (RNC), led by Chairman William Brock, developed successful direct-mail and telephone fundraising programs. The RNC directed funds to state Republican parties to help recruit, train, and assist candidates for the state legislature (Bibby 1981). The Democratic National Committee responded by increasing its assistance to state parties in the mid-1980s and 1990s under Chairmen Paul Kirk and Ron Brown (Bibby 1998, 41).

National party organizations continued to assist state and local party organizations in the 1990s. The Democratic committees transferred roughly $15.5 million to state and local party committees in 1994 (figures are in constant 2000 dollars; see figure 10.1). Their transfers rose to $102.4 million in 1996. Likewise, Republican committees distributed substantially more money to their state and local party organizations from 1994 to 1996. Both national parties' transfers to state and local party organizations declined from 1996 to 1998 before dramatically increasing to $231.2 million for Democrats and $190.6 million for Republicans in 2000. This evidence shows both overall increases in national party transfers and the impact that presidential elections have on national party fundraising and transfers. The large increase in party transfers during the 2000 elections is also a function of redistricting. Because many state legislatures control the redistricting process, the national party committees recognized that control of the state legislature had significant implications for partisan control of the U.S. Congress.

Figure 10.1   Congressional Campaign Committee Transfers to State and Local Party Committees

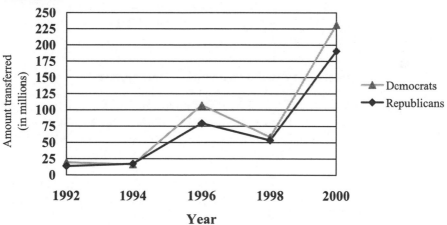

Source: The Federal Election Commission.

Notes: The amounts are based on the sum of federal and nonfederal transfers, and contributions to local and state candidates from national party campaign committees as reported by the FEC. Dollar amounts are adjusted for inflation to reflect 2000 dollars.

Data

We rely on two surveys of state legislative candidates for our analysis. The first survey, the Campaign Assessment and Candidate Outreach Project, includes information collected from a nationwide sample of 1,020 major party state legislative candidates from forty-four states who competed in the 1996 or 1998 general election. The survey yielded a representative and un-biased sample of respondents that closely approximated the underlying population on candidates' party affiliation, region, and incumbency (for more information about the survey, see Herrnson 2000a).

Our second source of information comes from the Election Dynamics Project. This data set includes responses from 2,757 major party statehouse candidates who competed in the 1992, 1994, and 1996 general elections. The survey covered nine states—Arizona, Colorado, Florida, Illinois, Missouri, Ohio, South Carolina, Washington, and Wisconsin—that vary by region, party organizational strength, and party competition. The respondents were near-evenly distributed between Democrats and Republicans, and closely approximated the population of candidates on variables such as incumbency and election outcome (for more information about the survey, see Frendreis and Gitelson 1993).

We use the surveys to compare the percentages over time of state legislative candidates who relied mostly on party staff for campaign management, fundraising, legal compliance, polling, communications, and voter registration activities. We use the more recent data from the Campaign Assessment and Candidate Outreach Project to analyze the targeting of party resources and the impact of party campaign assistance in state legislative elections. Our analysis includes only major party candidates who ran in contested general elections.

Party Services to Legislative Candidates

National party assistance has strengthened state and local campaign committees and led to the increased integration of party organizations. It has also helped state and local party organizations respond to the changes taking place in state legislative elections. Several state parties now provide state legislative candidates with legal advice and assistance with polling, campaign management, fundraising, media communications, and get-out-the-vote operations (Cotter et al. 1984; Frendreis, Gibson, and Vertz 1990; Gibson and Scarrow 1993, 237).

Campaign Management

Campaign management has become a more difficult task in recent years. Campaign techniques have become more advanced and sophisticated, and targeting political resources has become more challenging, as traditional party identification has declined among voters (Wattenberg 1984). Party committees assist some candidates and their campaign organizations with the hiring and training of campaign staff, and in making strategic and tactical decisions. Parties can further draw on experiences from previous elections to offer advice to candidates on potential problems they might encounter in their campaign (Herrnson 2000b).

Few parties have the resources to provide campaign management services, and the rise of the political consulting industry has shifted management responsibility largely to professional advisors (Thurber 2000). The data collected in the Election Dynamics Project and the Campaign Assessment and Candidate Outreach Project indicate that a very small percentage of state legislative candidates rely primarily on party organizations to manage their campaigns (see table 10.1). About 8 percent of all Democratic candidates in 1992 reported that party aides managed their campaigns. Between then and 1998 that percentage declined to less than 5 percent. Between 4 percent and 5 percent of all Republican 1992, 1994, and 1996 candidates reported that party staff managed their campaigns. By 1998 that percentage fell to less than 2 percent.

Table 10.1   State Legislative Candidates' Reliance on Parties to Conduct Major Campaign Activities

	1992	1994	1996	1998
Democrats				
Campaign management	7.8	4.9	4.4	4.6***
Fundraising	10.3	11.8	4.5	2.8***
Legal compliance	7.2	5.4	7.9	9.4*
Polling	10.5	8.9	12.4	16.0***
Communications	6.6	5.1	4.1	3.8***
Voter registration	n/a	22.7	23.3	17.8***
(N)	(454)	(433)	(429)	(107)
Republicans				
Campaign management	4.6	5.3	4.2	1.6***
Fundraising	6.0	10.5	4.5	4.0***
Legal compliance	5.3	7.6	5.9	10.5***
Polling	10.2	14.3	16.7	11.3***
Communications	3.9	5.3	5.7	4.0**
Voter registration	n/a	23.7	18.6	14.3***
(N)	(437)	(449)	(409)	(126)

Sources: The Election Dynamics Project and Campaign Assessment and Candidate Outreach Project.
Notes: Cells represent the percentage of candidates who relied mostly on party staff for the above campaign functions. Respondents include 1992, 1994, 1996, and 1998 major party general election candidates only, from Arizona, Colorado, Florida, Illinois, Missouri, Ohio, South Carolina, Washington, and Wisconsin. There were no data available for voter registration activities in 1992. Chi-square significance tests are based differences over time: * p<.10, **p<.05, ***p<.01.

Despite the small fraction of candidates who rely on parties to manage their campaigns, parties can play a supporting role by recommending particular consultants to state legislative candidates. A recent survey of state party chairmen found that 95 percent advised candidates to hire a professional consultant (Kolodny 2000, 118). Parties may no longer handle the actual responsibilities of campaign management, but they have entered into relationships with the consulting industry that complement their goals of contesting and winning elections. This development offers a striking parallel to how national party committees served as intermediaries between candidates and consultants during the 1980s (Herrnson 1988, 59).

Fundraising

The rising costs of state legislative campaigns have prompted some local, state, and national party committees to organize fundraising events and develop sophisticated direct-mail programs for some candidates (Gibson and Scarrow 1993). However, most candidates are responsible for their own fundraising, and parties have played only a minor role in assisting them (Gibson et al. 1983, 204). An increasing number of state legislative candidates now hire their own professional fundraising specialists.

Party organizations have steadily declined as fundraisers for state legislative candidates. More than 10 percent of the Democrats who ran for state legislatures in 1992 or 1994 reported that they relied on a party official to do their fundraising. By 1996 that percentage dropped to less than 5 percent and by 1998, the number was under 3 percent. The number of Republican candidates who reported that a party operative carried out their fundraising increased from 1992 to 1994, but then declined below 1992 levels in 1996 and 1998.

A decreasing percentage of state legislative candidates rely on party organizations to carry out their fundraising, because of the increased importance of money in state legislative elections. When candidates need to raise large sums, they are best served by hiring fundraising professionals. In congressional elections, for example, campaigns that hire fundraising professionals raise significantly more money than campaigns that rely on amateurs (Herrnson 1992a, 2000b, 75–76). As the costs of state legislative campaigns have increased over time, candidates have moved away from party and volunteer efforts to raise money.

One reason for Republican candidates' diminishing reliance on party organizations is their remarkable electoral success in 1994. The GOP had few incumbents and controlled both chambers of only eight state legislatures before the 1994 elections. After the 1994 Republican victories, the number of GOP legislators skyrocketed and the party held control of both chambers in nineteen state legislatures. Political financiers, including interest groups, are often inclined to contribute to incumbents in order to gain access, especially to incumbents who belong to the majority party in the chamber (Langbein 1986; Austen-Smith 1995; Rudolph 1999). The GOP's ascension to power in many states made it easy for Republican candidates to raise money and reduced their dependence on party organizations. Indeed, the results show that Republican candidates turned increasingly to hired staff and to themselves to raise money for their campaigns. Roughly three of five Republican candidates reported that they were the primary source of fundraising in 1996 and 1998 compared to just two of five in 1992 and 1994.

The evidence demonstrates that fundraising has become more a candidate-centered activity in state legislative elections. This development is consistent with changes in congressional elections. Parties play a supporting, but not a primary, role in the fundraising efforts of both state and national legislative candidates.

Legal Compliance

Political reform has made it more difficult for candidates to stay within the parameters of the law when raising and spending campaign money. Violations of state election and campaign laws can result in bad publicity and fines levied against a candidate's campaign organization. Party organizations have begun to play a more significant role in providing both Democrats and Republicans with legal services. Roughly 9.4 percent and 10.5 percent of Democrats and Republicans, respectively, reported party organizations as their primary source of legal advice in 1998, representing a steady increase since 1992. Some state party organizations now have lawyers on retainer. The intricacies of campaign and election laws have increased the importance of legal services in state legislative elections, and party organizations have moved to assist candidates with this need.

Polling

State legislative candidates have come to increasingly rely on polls over the past several years (Gierzynski and Breaux 1991; Moncrief 1998). Polls provide candidates with an indication of their level of support and of public opinion on major issues. Parties often assist candidates with public opinion data by commissioning surveys. Parties, particularly the legislative campaign committees, purchase polls at discount rates because they contract for multiple candidates. Some party committees can use their contacts with polling firms to arrange to "piggyback" questions on to polls taken for other clients (Gierzynski 1992). This development is similar to changes that occurred at the national level in the 1970s and 1980s (Herrnson 1988).

Democratic party organizations increased the polling services they provided to state legislative candidates between 1992 and 1998. The advantages parties have in commissioning and purchasing polls are one of the reasons that they have increasingly become a primary source of polling data for Democratic state legislative candidates. Republicans' reliance on party organizations for polling services increased steadily from 1992 to 1996, but then declined in 1998. The cause of this drop is not entirely clear. One possible explanation has to do with the context of the 1998 elections, which were overshadowed by the Monica Lewinsky scandal. Republican party organizations conducted several polls on the scandal, which helped them target $10 million in scandal-related advertisements in the final week of the 1998 election (Berke 1998b). The national Republican party's obsession with the Lewinsky scandal may have encouraged a number of state legislative candidates to independently obtain polling information that was more directly relevant to local concerns. Indeed, many Republican state legislative candidates hired their own professional consultants for polling in 1998. Nearly one-quarter of Republicans reported consultants as their primary source for polling in 1998 compared to 18 percent in 1996, 13 percent in 1994, and 17 percent in 1992.

Communications

Unlike the media spectacle that often accompanies presidential, statewide, and some congressional campaigns, state legislative races rarely receive significant media coverage. Unable to obtain substantial free (or "earned") media, state legislative candidates need to disseminate their messages through campaign activities. Television and radio advertising are typically the most effective method for presidential, statewide, and some congressional candidates to build name recognition and make their ideas known. However, television and radio stations almost always cover many state legislative districts, making the electronic media an inefficient means of communication for state legislative candidates. Instead, most state legislative candidates communicate with voters through campaign literature and direct mail. Some state and local party organizations own printing presses, write direct mail copy, print direct mail letters, and mail them to voters. Nevertheless, few party organizations take responsibility for candidates' campaign communications. Roughly 4 percent of all Democrats and 4 percent of all Republicans report that party organizations were responsible for their communications efforts in 1998.

Voter Registration and Volunteers

Party organizations have long played an active role in grassroots campaign efforts. Parties, particularly local party committees, have traditionally organized voter registration drives, distributed posters and lawn signs, and encouraged prospective voters to support party candidates on Election Day. These tasks are important because they target actual and potential party supporters (Frendreis and Gitelson 1999).

Voter registration is the most commonly cited activity that state legislative candidates turn to party organizations to perform. Local party organizations, for example, have traditionally had detailed knowledge of neighborhoods that comprise each district. More important, most local and state parties have volunteers and field organizations to carry out effective grassroots activities. While the percentage of candidates who relied on party organizations for voter registration dropped slightly in 1998, a higher percentage of candidates—nearly 18 percent of all Democrats and 14 percent of all Republicans—continue to rely on the parties for this activity than for fundraising, legal, management, media, and polling. Parties continue to be an important provider of grassroots services for state legislative candidates.

Categorizing Party Services

Party services to state legislative candidates can be classified into two general types: specialized campaign services, and assistance with voter mobilization. Factor analysis demonstrates that party assistance in gauging public opinion, researching policy issues, and providing advice on campaign techniques and management load heavily on one factor, and that local, state, and national party assistance with get-out-the-vote drives load heavily on another (see table 10.2).[2] State party organizations handle most specialized services and can distribute assistance to the candidates throughout the state who are involved in the most competitive contests. Local party organiza-

Table 10.2 Factor Analysis of Party Assistance Variables

	Specialized Services Factor 1	Voter Mobilization Factor 2
Public opinion	.844	.391
Policy issues	.879	.312
Campaign techniques and management	.785	.328
Local party get-out-the-vote	.373	.778
State party get-out-the-vote	.426	.860
National party get-out-the-vote	.223	.768
Eigenvalue	2.9	1.1
% Variance explained	48.4	19.3
(N)	(856)	(856)

Source: The Campaign Assessment and Candidate Outreach Project.

tions, on the other hand, are the primary source of voter mobilization assistance. Local parties tend to support their own local candidates, and do not always place a high priority on targeting close races (Gierzynski and Breaux 1998).

Party Activity in Contemporary State Legislative Elections

During the days of the old-fashioned political machines, parties directly carried out most major campaign activities. As the preceding section demonstrated, this pattern does not hold in contemporary state legislative campaigns. Nevertheless, party organizations have not completely abandoned state legislative candidates. State-level party committees, especially the LCCs, seek to provide candidates with campaign contributions and assistance in many areas of campaigning.

During the 1998 elections, Democratic candidates who competed in a contested general election raised an average of $.10 per voter from political parties, whereas Republican candidates received an average of $.11 per voter (see table 10.3). This accounted for roughly 10 percent of Democrats' and 12 percent of Republicans' total campaign receipts, which averaged $.97 and $.89 per voter respectively. Democratic and Republican candidates also gave virtually identical evaluations of the help they received from their respective party committees. Substantial numbers of state legislative candidates report that parties were "moderately, very, or extremely helpful" in campaign management, assessing public opinion, researching policy issues, and carrying out get-out-the-vote drives. A majority received substantial assistance in

Table 10.3   Party Assistance in State Legislative Campaigns

	Democrats	Republicans
Avg. contributions per voter	$0.10	$0.11
Campaign Assistance		
Campaign management	74.7%	78.1%
Policy research	71.4	71.9
Public opinion	63.9	63.9
Local party get-out-the vote	61.9	62.1
State party get-out-the-vote	52.0	54.9
National party get-out-the-vote	15.3	15.9
(N)	(443)	(474)

Source: The Campaign Assessment and Candidate Outreach Project.
Notes: Figures for campaign services are the percentage of candidates who reported that state parties were moderately, very, or extremely helpful in each aspect of campaigning. Respondents include major party general election candidates who ran in contested elections in 1998. Chi-square tests revealed no significant differences between Democrats and Republicans at the .10 level.

getting out the vote from state and local party committees, although only a small number of state legislative candidates assessed national party get-out-the-vote efforts to have been at least moderately helpful.

Party Targeting in State Legislative Elections

We systematically test whether parties distribute their campaign contributions and services strategically to state legislative candidates using ordinary least squares (OLS) regression. The dependent variable in the first model is party spending in dollars per voter. We use this standardized measure because the population of state legislative districts varies tremendously. State legislative districts in North Dakota, for example, represent less than 5,000 eligible voters, whereas state legislative districts in California can include upwards of 200,000 eligible voters. The dependent variable in the second model is a factor score of party specialized assistance with public opinion and policy research, and campaign management. The dependent variable in the third model is a factor score of party assistance with voter mobilization activities.

The main explanatory variable for each equation is the competitiveness of the election. The measure for competitiveness is the vote margin that separates the top two finishers.[1] We expect candidates to receive less party money and fewer services if they competed in races in which the margin of victory was largest. Parties can better maximize their resources in close, competitive contests.

We also control for campaign professionalism, incumbency, chamber competition, party affiliation, and office level. These variables are measured as follows.

Campaign professionalism is a dummy variable that reflects whether the candidate hired at least one political consultant or paid campaign aide. Candidates who assemble professional campaigns are more likely to mount a serious bid for office, and should receive the most party contributions and services. Challengers and open-seat candidates are dummy coded in separate measures. We created an interaction between our measures for candidate status and campaign professionalism because parties typically provide increased support to the most viable nonincumbents (Herrnson 2000b, 92). To control for chamber competition we record the difference in the percentage of seats each party controls in the chamber. The larger the percentage, the less competitive is the chamber. Candidates in states where control over the legislature is uncompetitive are less likely to receive party support because party organizations are most active in close elections (Gierzynski and Breaux 1998, 196). The model includes a dummy variable for Democratic candidates to examine if partisan differences exist in how the parties distribute their campaign resources. It also includes a dummy measure for candidates who ran for the state senate to examine if there are differences in how party organizations target their resources to candidates for upper and lower chambers. The results show that parties do indeed target their contributions to candidates in the most competitive elections, reflecting the parties' goal of winning as many seats as possible (see table 10.4). State legislative candidates in contests decided by a 55-45 margin (which demarcates the margin for the top quartile) received roughly \$.10 more per voter than those in a contest decided by a margin of 72-28 (which demarcates the margin for the bottom quartile). The median population size of a district in our sample is 27,000, meaning that parties gave roughly \$2,700 more per candidate to contestants in competitive races than they did to candidates in uncompetitive elections.

The results further suggest that challengers who assemble a professional

Table 10.4   The Targeting of Party Contributions and Party Services

	Contributions (per voter)	Specialized Services	Voter Mobilization
Vote margin	−.003***	−.006***	−.004**
	(.001)	(.002)	(.002)
Campaign professionalism	.036	−.300***	.096
	(.033)	(.110)	(.111)
Challenger	−.033	.022	−.100
	(.033)	(.111)	(.111)
Open seat	.059*	.176*	.008
	(.041)	(.135)	(.136)
Campaign professionalism X challenger	.109*	.240*	−.189
	(.051)	(.172)	(.172)
Campaign professionalism X open seat	−.013	.088	−.196
	(.055)	(.185)	(.186)
Less chamber competition	−.002***	−.001	.003*
	(.001)	(.002)	(.002)
Democrat	−.009	.069	−.109*
	(.022)	(.073)	(.073)
Upper chamber	−.031	.015	.270***
	(.027)	(.091)	(.092)
Constant	.224***	.313***	.092
Adjusted R²	.08	.03	.02
(N)	(762)	(738)	(738)

Source: The Campaign Assessment and Candidate Outreach Project.

Notes: Coefficients are based on OLS regression estimates. Standard errors are in parentheses. Campaign professionalism indicates a campaign that hired a paid professional to carry out at least one of the following services: campaign management, media advertising, press relations, issue research, polling, fundraising, direct mail, mass telephone calling, voter mobilization activities, legal advice, or accounting. Respondents include major-party general election candidates who ran in contested races in 1998. Some cases were dropped because of incomplete or missing data. * p<.10, **p<.05, ***p<.01.

campaign organization receive more money from party organizations. Challengers who hire specialists to handle advertising, polls, or media relations demonstrate that their campaigns are a good investment (Herrnson 1992a, 865). Parties also target their money to open-seat candidates, regardless of whether they hire a campaign professional. Parties give more money in open-seat elections because they are usually the most competitive and can often serve as the battleground for control of the legislature.

The competitiveness of the chamber is another significant factor related to how parties target campaign contributions. Parties provide the least money to candidates when one party holds a large majority in the legislature. Parties give the most money when they have a legitimate chance to win control of the legislature. National parties often assist in these races because partisan control of the state legislature affects congressional redistricting.

The results also indicate that party organizations make similar considerations when distributing their campaign services to state legislative candidates. Candidates in competitive elections report receiving the most party assistance in specialized areas of campaigning. State parties have developed stronger campaign management expertise, and more sophisticated policy and public opinion research capacities. They distribute these services to candidates with the best opportunity to win, reflecting their seat maximization goals. Parties provide fewer of their specialized services to incumbents who run professional campaigns. Incumbents who have their own campaign experts on staff do not need the parties to carry out management, policy research, and public opinion services. Parties, however, provide more specialized assistance to challengers who hire professionals and to open-seat candidates, regardless of whether they hire professionals. For similar reasons mentioned earlier, parties assist these candidates because they present a valuable opportunity for parties to gain seats in the legislature.

Parties also distribute most of their voter mobilization services to candidates involved in the most competitive elections. The variable for less chamber competition, however, is positive, indicating that party get-out-the-vote efforts are strongest when there is less competition for control of the legislature. This result is probably a function of party strength. A political party that dominates a particular state is likely to have more supporters, making it easier to recruit and mobilize grassroots volunteers. Republican Party organizations were slightly more helpful with voter mobilization assistance than Democrats. Many Democrats who run for the state legislature can depend on strong grassroots support from other organizations, such as labor unions, whereas Republicans have fewer alternatives outside of the assistance they receive from party organizations (Francia et al. 1999). The results also indicate that parties provide more voter mobilization assistance to state Senate candidates. Higher office elections draw more public attention and interest, which allow party organizations to more easily energize voters in those contests.

The Impact of Party Activity in State Legislative Elections

We assess the impact of party campaign efforts on state legislative candidates' electoral performances in the 1998 elections also using OLS regression. The dependent variable in this equation is the percentage of the vote each candidate received in the general election. We hypothesize that candidates who report receiving substantial party money, support in specialized services, or voter mobilization assistance win a greater percentage of the vote than do others. We expect party services to be particularly important when candidates receive significant help with both specialized assistance and voter mobilization. To test that expectation, we create an interaction term between the measure for specialized services and voter mobilization.

We also test whether party voter mobilization efforts have unequal effects on districts with different demographics. The model includes a measure for party affiliation and the percentage of minority (nonwhite) citizens in the district. We use an interaction term for Democratic candidates and the percentage of minorities in the district. Democrats attract disproportionate support from nonwhite voters and should perform better in heavily populated minority districts. We use another interaction term for Democratic candidates and party voter mobilization efforts because Democrats often are the primary beneficiaries of high voter turnout, and party support in this aspect of campaigning should benefit Democratic candidates more than Republicans. We also use an interaction term for Democrats, party voter mobilization efforts, and the percentage of minorities because Democrats who run in districts with minority constituents often do particularly well when there is a high turnout among minority voters. Hence, these candidates stand to benefit the most from party voter mobilization services.

The model controls for campaign professionalism, district partisanship, and chamber and fundraising advantage. The coding for party affiliation, professionalism, and chamber are the same as in the previous model. Fundraising advantage is the candidate's campaign expenditures per voter minus the opponent's campaign expenditures per voter. District partisanship is the percentage of voters in the district who share the same party affiliation as the candidate. Candidates who wage professional campaigns, raise more money, or run in districts with the highest percentage of citizens in the district who share the same party affiliation should perform best in their election.

For nonincumbents, we include two additional controls for political experience and open-seat elections. Elected officials is a dummy variable for candidates who previously held elective office. Candidates with political experience typically wage stronger campaigns. Open-seat elections are operationalized with a dummy variable. Open-seat elections attract stronger nonincumbent candidates than those that involve an incumbent. The effects of party and candidate campaign efforts on incumbent and nonincumbent candidates are assessed using separate equations because of differences in the dynamics of these campaigns.

The results show that party expenditures and voter mobilization services have no statistically significant impact on the percentage of the vote received on Election Day (see table 10.5). Party expenditures and voter mobilization services generally do little to increase incumbents' vote margins, because these candidates are relatively well-known and have the ability to wage well-financed, professional campaigns. Incumbents usually raise more resources than they need, overwhelming any benefits they might derive from party services. Party specialized services are significant, but in a negative direction. Incumbents who need this type of assistance likely face a difficult reelection battle, and the fact they receive party services is a sign of weakness that is associated with an unusually competitive election. The findings also show that incumbents' spending advantages have a positive effect on the percentage of the votes they receive. Not surprisingly, incumbents perform better in districts that are dominated by their fellow partisans. These findings parallel those for congressional elections (Herrnson 2000b, 227–238). The results also show that Republican incumbents are more vulnerable in districts with large percentages of minority voters, while Democratic incumbents earn a higher percentage of the vote (Lublin 1997).

Challengers and open-seat candidates, on the other hand, do significantly better in elections when they receive generous party contributions. Nonincumbent state legislative candidates, like their congressional counterparts, benefit from party contributions (Herrnson 2000b). Interestingly, while neither specialized services nor voter mobilization are statistically significant alone, their interaction is, suggesting party assistance matters the most when candidates receive wideranging support. These findings suggest that parties provide nonincumbents with critical tools to campaign effectively.

Perhaps the most interesting finding is that party voter mobilization activities have a significant impact on nonincumbents' vote shares, particularly when Democratic Party organizations target their voter mobilization activities in districts with the highest concentration of minority citizens. Democratic party organizations that effectively mobilize voters in districts with large percentages of minority voters can make a critical difference in helping Democratic nonincumbents wage stronger and more competitive campaigns. Not surprisingly, nonincumbents also perform best when they raise more money than incumbents, run in districts that have the highest percentage of

Table 10.5   The Effects of Party Contributions, Party Services, and Other Factors on Candidates' Vote Shares

	Incumbents	*Nonincumbents*
Party contributions (per voter)	−3.44	2.18*
	(3.78)	(1.64)
Specialized services	−1.42**	.53
	(.84)	(.69)
Voter mobilization	−1.08	.38
	(1.04)	(.88)
Specialized services X voter mobilization	.18	.98*
	(.79)	(.68)
Democrat	−1.94	−1.24
	(.19)	(1.54)
Percentage of minorities in district	−.25***	−.20***
	(.10)	(.05)
Democrat X percentage of minorities in district	.24**	.26***
	(.11)	(.09)
Democrat X voter mobilization	.60	−2.71**
	(1.66)	(1.33)
Democrat X voter mobilization X percentage of minorities in district	.06	.08*
	(.05)	(.06)
Campaign professionalism	−3.57**	.98
	(1.56)	(1.24)
Fundraising advantage ($ per voter)	2.36***	1.65***
	(.93)	(.54)
District partisanship (in favor of candidate)	.34***	.32***
	(.06)	(.05)
Upper chamber	1.44	2.54**
	(1.90)	(1.41)
Elected experience	—	2.36**
		(1.21)
Open seat	—	10.30***
		(1.27)
Constant	52.89***	28.52***
Adjusted R²	.15	.40
N	(328)	(411)

Source: The Campaign Assessment and Candidate Outreach Project.

Notes: Coefficients are based on OLS regression estimates. Standard errors are in parentheses. Campaign professionalism indicates a campaign hired a paid professional to carry out at least one of the following services: campaign management, media advertising, press relations, issue research, polling, fundraising, direct mail, mass telephone calling, voter mobilization activities, legal advice, or accounting. Respondents include major party general election candidates who ran in contested elections in 1998. Some cases were dropped because of incomplete or missing data. *p<.10, **p<.05, ***p<.01.

registered voters who belong to their party, run for higher office, have previously held elective office, or run in an open-seat election.

Conclusion

Party organizations have adapted to a number of changes in the political environment. The days when parties played the defining role in state legislative campaigns have been replaced by a new era in which parties assist candidates who employ their own campaign professionals. In many respects, party campaigning in state legislative elections has become congressionalized. Parties at the state legislative level offer sophisticated campaign services that complement the efforts of the candidate's own professionally managed campaign organization, as the national party committees began to do in the 1970s and early 1980s.

Parties also target their resources to state legislative candidates in competitive elections. This fact is important because effectively targeted party expenditures can significantly help challengers wage more competitive campaigns. It is particularly true for Democrats, who benefit when parties provide support with voter mobilization in minority-populated districts. The parties' ability to influence state legislative elections makes them important players in the battle for the statehouse, despite the development of candidate-centered state legislative campaigns. Evidence from our research suggests party organizations are likely to continue to adapt to changing circumstances and to have a significant role in state legislative elections.

Notes

We wish to thank The Pew Charitable Trusts for a grant that funded some of the research included in this chapter. The opinions expressed in this chapter are those of the authors and do not reflect the views of The Pew Charitable Trusts. We thank Loyola University at Chicago and the Ray C. Bliss Institute of Applied Politics at the University of Akron for funding support for our data collection. We thank Jennifer Lucas and Dave Clifford for their assistance.

1. This is mathematically expressed as the absolute value of the winner's vote share minus the second-place candidate's vote share.

2. For the factor analysis, the method of extraction was Principal Component Analysis with oblique rotation.

11

Casting a Weak Net: Political Party Web Sites in 2000

Rick Farmer and Rich Fender

The Internet presents new opportunities and new challenges to political parties. Organizations who master this new medium will find many opportunities to communicate directly with activists and voters. Those who fail to develop this line of communication may soon find themselves at a competitive disadvantage. Since politics is "Darwinism in action" (Ansolabehere, Behr, and Iyengar 1993, 3), those who adapt will thrive and those who stagnate will struggle to remain relevant.

Although the Internet and its graphical offspring, the World Wide Web, are in their infancy, they have already become an important communications medium. This research examines and documents the form and content of state party web sites during the 2000 election cycle. An aggregate measure, the Party Web Quotient, is developed for comparing state party sites. The findings indicate that while state party web sites attempted many essential party functions, they lacked technical sophistication. Parties were particularly good at providing services directly related to campaigns (such as networking and recruiting volunteers). They were less adept at fulfilling their broader duties to democracy (such as informing citizens or encouraging general participation). On the technical side, parties generally offered the basics (such as graphics), but few took advantage of the Web's broader opportunities. In 2000, state parties demonstrated that important party functions could be conducted through the Web. However, much of the potential found in the Web remains unexploited by parties.

Party Adaptation

Political parties are essential to democratic government (Schattschneider 1942). When parties function well, leaders gain the tools they need to lead, and voters' choices are simplified (Committee on Political Parties 1950). A variety of scholars (Reichley 1992; Goldman 1994; Bibby 2000) list the essential functions parties should perform in a well-developed democratic system. Democracy can't survive without someone performing these functions, and if parties do not engage in these activities, other political actors will (see Selnow 1998). Generally, it is better if institutions like parties, whose leaders are elected by citizens, perform the work of democracy, rather than institutions whose leaders are often self-appointed, like corporations, consultants, and news media.

Strong state organizations are essential to the success of both major parties' candidates and agendas. State party organizations have become important components of party service delivery, and the 2002 Bipartisan Campaign Reform Act (BCRA) may enhance their role (see chapter 9). The 2000 presidential contest highlighted the fact that presidential elections are state contests. In addition, in each election cycle 33 U.S. senators, 435 U.S. representatives, thousands of state legislators, and other state and local officials are elected in the fifty states.

By the late 1800s, parties controlled every aspect of politics from ballot access to political patronage. Parties were the primary means of communication between political candidates and their voters. This "golden age" of political parties ended with the Progressive reforms and the advent of electronic communication. The Progressive reforms of the early 1900s significantly reduced the parties' control over political life, including patronage and ballot access. Freed from the party machines, candidates and voters were open to a new communications medium. First radio, and then television filled the gap. By the end of World War II, TV was bringing politicians directly into people's living rooms. Public officials and candidates were able to communicate directly with the voters and a very personal, candidate-centered politics was developing. Virtually abandoned by aspiring politicians and voters (see chapter 19), parties adapted to the electronic candidate-centered environment, discovering new roles and organizational opportunities. As ongoing organizations, parties realized they had significant campaign expertise and fundraising prowess and they could provide many of the services candidates needed. Service-oriented parties soon emerged as a powerful force (Shea 1999).

The Digital Challenge

Once again the parties' power is threatened by a new electronic medium. The Internet provides candidates with another opportunity to take their message directly to the people. At low cost, they can build candidate-centered organizations without the assistance of a party. To remain relevant, service-oriented parties must adapt to this new digital environment.

Because the Internet is in its infancy, its full potential for reaching voters is still unknown. In the 2000 election, the Internet was an excellent tool for communicating with a select group of activists and supporters, but not very useful for communicating with voters. Two major obstacles remain: not all citizens have Internet access in their homes, and those who do are unlikely to use it to seek political information. Advancing technology will soon relieve both of these problems, creating a new communications environment for parties.

While many voters may have access to the Web at home, work, or school, many do not (*Falling through the Net* 2000). The lack of Internet access is likely only a temporary circumstance. In April 2002, 55 percent of American homes had Internet access (Taylor 2002). The Internet is penetrating living rooms much more quickly than did radio in the 1920s or television in the 1950s (Meeker and DePuy 1996). Before the first decade of the twenty-first century is complete, Internet penetration will likely be equivalent with telephone penetration. The Web is quickly becoming a universal platform for political news, information, organization, and advertising.

Even if every voter had access to the Internet, most would not use it to seek political information. In the early days of electronic media there were very few channels, and listeners' or viewers' attention was readily available to politicians who needed to broadcast a message. With the deployment of cable and satellite TV the audience became much more fragmented. Broadcasting to large audiences became very difficult, and narrowcasting to targeted audiences became easier (Ranney 1990). Candidates and parties adapted by advertising to targeted cable audiences (Friedenberg 1997). Web-based communication can be described as "hyper-narrowcasting." Millions of viewing options exist on the Web (from nakednews.com to bmwfilms.com) and the audience is fragmented into very narrow groups. Given a wide range of entertainment options, political news will rarely be viewers' first choice (Margolis and Resnick 2000).

New technologies like Web-based interactive television may assure universal access to the Internet and hold audiences together in traditional viewing patterns, easily within the advertising reach of campaigns. The forthcoming Moxi Media Center will simply and affordably merge high-speed Internet, cable TV, and digital video recording into a single device to be shared wirelessly by video screens throughout the home. The result will be something approximating interactive television (iTV). Already, London-based Two Way TV produces interactive shows for its eight million subscribers (Moran 2002). Devices like TiVo currently offer interactive advertising in conjunction with a viewer's favorite TV shows. The thirty-second spot ad may not change significantly, but to take full advantage of the new medium candidates and parties will want an extensive Web presence.

Television is a passive medium. Entertainment or information is received with little action required of the viewer. It can be enjoyed "leaning back."

The Web is an active medium in which viewers must search out the information or entertainment they desire. It requires "leaning forward" (Schenker 1999). The coming convergence of the Internet and cable TV creates a "lean back" medium with "lean forward" options. When cable and satellite TV companies deploy iTV set-top boxes more widely than the current Explorer series, consumers will have live, interactive, and on-demand entertainment in their living rooms (Baumgartner 2002). Advertisers will find their target audience congregated around popular shows as before. The challenge will be to entice viewers, through "lean back" messages, to pause their entertainment and seek additional information using seamless "lean forward" options. Preparing for and adapting to this new Web-based, video-driven, interactive medium will determine the survivors in the next evolution in communications technology. As Jim Nicholson, chairman of the Republican National Committee from 1997 to 2001, said, "it's a new world, where you are digital or die" (Van Natta 2000).

Campaigning on the Web

In keeping with America's candidate-centered politics, most of the research on political web sites deals with candidates and not parties. Myers (1993) noted the use of electronic mail in the 1992 presidential campaign. The 1996 Republican presidential candidate sites varied greatly, but still contained basic information on how to make a contribution and how to get on a candidate's mailing list (Helpren 1996). Sullivan (1995) observed that every U.S. senator and most U.S. House members either had or were rapidly creating their own web sites. Minor party candidates made less use of the Web than Republicans and Democrats in both 1998 and 2000 (Kamarck 2002). Republicans running for U.S. Senate in 2000 tended to be more "Web savvy," including more features on their web sites than their Democratic counterparts (Puopolos 2001). Generally, campaign sites provided little interactivity and little information that was not available in other campaign media (Greer and LaPoine 1999). It is for this reason that critics such as Stone (1996) claim that political web sites are nothing more then virtual brochures.

Some observers, like Skiba (1995) and Tackett (1995), have been concerned about the amount of negative advertising on the Internet. However, James and Sadow (1997) have found relatively low rates of negative campaigning on candidate web sites. However, Koltz (2001) worried that negativity on campaign web sites may be growing.

Mundy (1995) noted that although the Internet is an unfiltered source of information, official political web sites are filtered by those who post the information. Diamond and Geller (1995) noted the existence of two "online" worlds. One online world includes bulletin boards and chat rooms where anyone can post anything, without regard to bias or truthfulness. The other online world is made up of official web sites and has real information and hard data. Mundy (1995) noted that candidate web sites are a combination of both worlds. In other words, candidate web sites can be both biased and factual. The same thing could be said about many political party web sites.

Looking specifically at parties, some contend that the Web can level the playing field for minor parties and underfinanced challengers (Stone 1996; Peniston 1996). However, Margolis, Resnick, and Wolfe (1999) found that the two major parties had more extensive web sites and received more attention on the Web than minor parties. Similarly, Kamarck (2002) found that minor party candidates did not use the Web as much as their opponents.

Despite the Web's growing importance, little research has been conducted on the form and content of political web sites. The criteria for comparing web sites are still under discussion. Those studies that have been published suggest that both candidate and party web sites generally remain below their full potential. Researchers will want to observe, document, and analyze web site development over the next several election cycles. This comprehensive study of state party web sites in 2000 seeks to contribute to the measurement criteria discussion and provide a benchmark for future studies.

Data and Methods

This analysis was limited to the two major parties. Creating a complete list of minor parties working in each state would have been a major undertaking in itself. (See Margolis and Resnick 2001 for a discussion of minor party web sites.) The list of state major party URLs was compiled from the Republican National Committee and Democratic National Committee web sites. Web sites were archived during the week of October 29–November 4, 2000. In four instances the archive failed. In those cases (MT-D, PA-D, MA-R, and ND-R) the live sites were collected in August 2001. Three state parties did not have a web site in November 2000 or August 2001 (MS-D, RI-D, and RI-R).

Two professional coders independently completed a content questionnaire for each web site. The results were compared and discrepancies were resolved by jointly reexamining the site. Two teams completed fifty-six sites each. Overlapping sites were compared for intercoder reliability between the teams. Simple agreement across all questions was 88 percent between teams.

A variety of communications scholars (such as Democracy Online Project 2000, Margolis, Resnick, and Wolfe 1999) and media experts (Ireland

and Nash 1999, Boerner et al. 2000) have suggested criteria for judging the quality of a web site. The criteria generally focus on substantive content, interesting visuals, ease of navigation, and technical aspects. Weare and Lin (2000) suggested that web site studies focus too much on presentation and should pay more attention to content. Gibson and Ward (2000) propose that studies consider the purpose of web site content and the technical delivery of that content. This study examines both the content and form of state party web sites.

In the twenty-first century many party functions are likely to be performed via the World Wide Web, and parties will want to master this new medium and take advantage of its opportunities. Of course, not every function can be transferred to the Web. Gibson and Ward (2000) describe five essential party tasks that can be Web-enabled: information provision, campaigning, resource generation, networking, and promoting participation. In discussing potential research methodologies, they propose a complex coding system that includes word counts of various documents and web pages.

This chapter operationalizes Gibson and Ward's (2000) five party tasks using specific content indicators. Those tasks are briefly defined in table 11.1. The process is simplified to identify the presence or absence of each indicator. Scores for each task are calculated by dividing the number of indicators present by the total number of indicators of that task. Task scores are then averaged to create a Party Functions Score.

Content must be delivered to viewers in an interesting and accessible fashion. Examining the multiple lists of Web techniques coded by previous researchers and discussed above, five technical tasks were identified: special effects, use of symbols, navigation, ethics, and marketing. These tasks are also briefly defined in table 11.1. They are operationalized using the presence or absence of specific indicators. Task scores, as described above, are averaged into a Technical Functions Score.

In all cases in which the minimum score was zero, at least one state party included none of the relevant indicators in its web site. Where the maximum score was one, at least one state party included all of the relevant indicators (see table 11.3).

An overall Party Web Quotient is calculated by averaging the Party Functions Score and the Technical Functions Score. A reasonable criticism of any scoring scheme like the one proposed here is that the selection of indicators is arbitrary. While these selections were based on earlier work, the scoring system reduces the impact of any one indicator, making it possible to add or delete specific indicators without significantly affecting the overall score. This method of aggregation also makes the measure capable of being adjusted as the technology evolves. Thus, future research can use the same scoring system while employing updated indicators.

Table 11.1   Measured Tasks Defined

Party Functions	
Informing	Provide general political education and socialization information
Campaigning	Overt solicitation of voters on behalf of candidates
Recruiting	Develop human capital and financial resources for party activities
Networking	Build relationships with other entities pursuing similar goals
Participation	Encourage citizen participation in the political process
Technical Functions	
Special Effects	Use of various graphical formats
Symbolism	Use of symbols to create a sense of pride or identity
Navigation	Use of techniques that make it easier to find desired content
Ethics	Provide appropriate disclaimers and options
Marketing	Use of common web advertising techniques within the site

Content and Form

Table 11.2 lists 47 content and form indicators in descending order of usage by parties. The three most common elements were clip art, contact information, and links back to the state party's home page from other pages on the site. However, these were the only items that came close to universal acceptance, with 90 or more cases including them. The ten most common items were contained in as few as 73 sites. One-half of state party sites failed to include more than 22 of the observed indicators.

This result indicates two things. First, it shows the appropriateness of the indicators for the 2000 election cycle. Roughly one-quarter of the parties included 25 percent of the elements, and 50 percent of the parties included 50 percent of the elements. Second, the list of basic elements absent from a large number of web sites suggests that state parties were not very sophisticated Web producers in 2000.

Some of the ten least-used elements required substantial technical sophistication, such as streaming media, merchandise order forms, and search engines. However, others used very common and easily implemented items, including site maps, privacy statements, and a "frequently asked questions" page. Indeed, many state party web sites were missing basic elements such as headquarters' telephone numbers, navigation bars, simple photographs, and their parties' street address. The lack of these easily produced elements shows how little effort parties directed at their web site in 2000.

The growing Hispanic population suggests that many state parties might offer their content in more than one language. Only four sites (TX-D, CA-R, OR-R, and TX-R) presented a Spanish alternative. No other languages or help for people with special needs were provided.

Table 11.2 Web Site Content and Form Indicators by Usage, Function, and Task

Count	Party Functions	Task	Count	Web Functions	Task
93	contact information	Networking	96	clip art	Special Effects
87	national party link	Networking	90	home page link	Navigation
85	candidate links	Campaigning	85	icons for links	Special Effects
82	directory of personnel	Networking	80	site feedback	Ethics
79	events calendar	Campaigning	73	photos	Special Effects
70	party affiliate links	Networking	68	party symbols	Symbolism
65	contribution form	Recruiting	57	state symbols	Symbolism
63	slate card	Campaigning	46	national colors	Symbolism
62	volunteer form	Recruiting	46	animation	Special Effects
58	county party links	Networking	39	U.S. flag	Symbolism
56	voter registration info.	Participation	24	link to plug-ins	Ethics
54	party platform	Informing	21	pop-ups	Marketing
52	volunteer alerts	Campaigning	18	what's new	Navigation
51	party press releases	Campaigning	15	site search	Navigation
50	official president or Congress links	Participation	14	other American symbols	Symbolism
46	party news	Informing	11	streaming	Special Effects
43	volunteer duties	Recruiting	10	cookies enabled	Marketing
43	advocacy groups links	Networking	8	FAQs	Marketing
41	official gubernatorial or leg. links	Participation	7	site map	Navigation
41	media web sites links	Participation	7	send e-mail postcards	Marketing
25	current news headlines	Informing	5	privacy statement	Ethics
18	recent quotes or photos	Informing	4	Spanish	Ethics
17	talking points	Informing	1	text form only	Ethics
14	party store	Campaigning			

Better at Politics than Technology

Statistics for the Party Web Quotient and its component functions and tasks are reported in table 11.3. The mean score for the Party Web Quotient was .453. This low mean reveals that parties have done a poor job developing their web sites.

The specific party and technical functions offer greater insight into parties' strengths and weaknesses on the Web. The Web offers parties a unique means of interactive communication with activists, supporters, and voters. Parties used this medium best for networking. Visitors to the parties' sites could generally find ways to contact the party, its affiliates, and allied groups. Also, parties were reasonably good at campaigning and recruiting activists on their web sites. Tasks less related to campaign organization did not receive as much attention. Parties have a role in stimulating voter participation and informing citizens about the political system, but these mean scores lagged well behind the other party function tasks. Overall, the mean score for party functions was .547.

To compete with other sources of news and entertainment, parties must develop web sites that are visually interesting and sensorially stimulating. Most parties made good use of special effects, like clip art, photos, and icons. However, more sophisticated effects like streaming media were used less often. Mean scores for other technical function tasks were very low, suggesting that parties put very little effort into developing technically sophisticated sites. Overall, the mean score for Technical Functions was .358.

The Party Functions Scores and the Technical Functions Scores indicate that parties made a greater effort at substantive content than they did at Web delivery. State parties should be commended for pursuing the opportunities

Table 11.3   Descriptives of Party Web Quotient and Its Component Functions and Tasks

	Mean	*Minimum*	*Maximum*	*Std. Dev.*
Party Web Quotient	.453	.127	.792	.116
Party Functions	.547	.133	.933	.182
Networking	.744	.167	1.000	.200
Campaigning	.591	.000	1.000	.231
Recruiting	.584	.000	1.000	.340
Participation	.485	.000	1.000	.348
Informing	.330	.000	1.000	.260
Technical Functions	.358	.120	.670	.096
Special Effects	.641	.200	1.000	.180
Symbolism	.462	.000	1.000	.230
Navigation	.335	.000	1.000	.191
Ethics	.235	.000	.600	.129
Marketing	.119	.000	.750	.177

for networking, campaigning, and recruiting that the Web affords. However, they need to improve their technical delivery if they hope to compete for viewers' attention.

Correlates of Web Site Quality

The range of Party Web Quotient scores is wide. Finding predictors of this measure may indicate which state parties are likely to adapt most easily to the Web. There are many potential predictors of state party web site development. Three are examined here.[1] Overall, these predictors provided little indication as to why some state parties have more highly developed web sites than others. More research is needed in this area.

Obviously, if one of the major parties was adapting to the Web faster than the other, then party label may be a predictor of the Party Web Quotient. Table 11.4 shows each state party's score and rank. Republican state parties produced seven of the top ten web sites. However, the correlation between Republicanism and the State Party Web Quotient is only .107. Such a weak correlation leaves little room for a substantive claim that Republicans generally produced better web sites. Thus, the conclusion must be that there is little overall difference in the quality of web sites between the two major parties.

Similarly, no correlation was found between substantive content and party label. The correlation coefficient between Republicanism and the Party Functions Score was −.020. The scores indicate that both parties did a similar job of providing important substantive content on their web sites.

Republicans did score better on technical delivery of their content. The Technical Functions Score was correlated with Republicanism at .296. The scores suggest that Republicans tended to do a better job of delivering the content to the viewer. The sites were more visually interesting and offered more features than Democratic sites. However, this was not enough of an advantage to make the Republican sites better overall, as seen in the previous correlations.

Another potential predictor is the strength of the state party organization. Stronger parties may have greater resources for developing useful and interesting web sites. However, a party organizational strength score (reported in chapter 8) was not related strongly to any of the three web site scores.[2] The Party Web Quotient and party organizational strength scores were correlated at .063. The Party Functions Score was correlated to party strength at −.002. The Technical Functions Score was correlated at .158, showing a very modest impact of organizational strength. Overall, well-developed web sites do not appear to be related to party organizational strength.

Finally, the population of the state may be related to state party web site

Table 11.4   State Party Web Quotient by Rank

Rank	Party	State	PWQ	Rank	Party	State	PWQ
1	R	HI	0.7917	50	R	CO	0.4517
2	R	OR	0.7417	51	R	VT	0.4517
3	R	IA	0.6450	52	D	ND	0.4500
4	D	OR	0.6367	53	D	NV	0.4483
5	R	CA	0.6300	54	R	MA	0.4433
6	R	FL	0.6117	55	R	SC	0.4433
7	D	TX	0.6067	56	D	TN	0.4433
8	R	ME	0.6017	57	D	NM	0.4417
9	R	IL	0.5917	58	D	CO	0.4400
10	D	MO	0.5883	59	D	PA	0.4400
11	D	OH	0.5883	60	R	AZ	0.4367
12	R	VA	0.5883	61	D	FL	0.4367
13	R	MN	0.5800	62	R	WY	0.4350
14	R	TN	0.5767	63	D	AR	0.4333
15	R	KY	0.5683	64	R	OH	0.4317
16	R	GA	0.5650	65	R	DE	0.4267
17	R	NC	0.5650	66	D	VT	0.4233
18	D	VA	0.5617	67	R	WA	0.4217
19	D	NY	0.5583	68	R	CT	0.4150
20	R	WI	0.5583	69	D	CT	0.3933
21	R	TX	0.5483	70	D	IA	0.3883
22	R	NM	0.5467	71	R	AL	0.3750
23	D	MI	0.5417	72	D	WY	0.3750
24	D	WI	0.5383	73	D	IN	0.3700
25	R	PA	0.5333	74	D	KS	0.3650
26	D	CA	0.5267	75	R	MS	0.3633
27	R	LA	0.5250	76	R	AR	0.3550
28	D	AL	0.5167	77	D	IL	0.3483
29	D	MT	0.5100	78	D	MD	0.3467
30	D	AK	0.5017	79	R	MI	0.3400
31	D	NE	0.5017	80	R	MT	0.3367
32	D	NC	0.5000	81	R	NY	0.3300
33	R	UT	0.4983	82	D	LA	0.3233
34	D	MN	0.4967	83	R	WV	0.3233
35	D	NH	0.4933	84	D	ID	0.3033
36	D	SC	0.4883	85	D	NJ	0.2983
37	R	SD	0.4867	86	R	OK	0.2983
38	D	MA	0.4833	87	R	MO	0.2967
39	D	KY	0.4800	88	R	NE	0.2950
40	D	DE	0.4767	89	D	ME	0.2917
41	D	OK	0.4767	90	D	UT	0.2917
42	D	WA	0.4717	91	R	AK	0.2883
43	R	NH	0.4650	92	R	KS	0.2850
44	R	MD	0.4600	93	R	ND	0.2567
45	R	NJ	0.4583	94	D	WV	0.2533
46	D	AZ	0.4550	95	D	GA	0.2417
47	R	ID	0.4550	96	R	NV	0.2267
48	D	HI	0.4533	97	D	SD	0.1267
49	R	IN	0.4533				

development. Parties in larger states have more activists, more resources, and larger potential audiences. Thus, making the transition to the Web may be easier to justify and finance. The Party Web Quotient was correlated with state population at .276. Similarly, the correlation with the Party Functions Score was .228 and the correlation with the Technical Functions Score was .236. These correlations are modest but substantive. Parties in larger states do tend to produce better web sites than those in smaller states. Since new technologies are generally deployed in high-population areas, parties in larger states may have had more time to develop their web sites. As the Web develops, it will be important for these state parties to continue to innovate.

Conclusion

This study proposed and developed a measure for comparing state party web sites, examining the substantive content and technical delivery of each site in 2000. The Party Web Quotient was an aggregation of a Party Functions Score and a Technical Functions Score. Several conclusions can be drawn from this effort.

First, parties are not taking full advantage of the World Wide Web's capabilities, either substantively or technically. Party web sites need improvement for the parties to compete effectively with other kinds of organizations. The Web is an exceptional organizational and communications tool. Parties must learn to use it, as they learned to use newspapers, radio, and television.

Second, parties are doing a better job providing substantive content than presenting the content technically. The substantive effort is a hopeful sign for parties. They are executing some basic functions on the Web. Parties are networking with activists, campaigning for candidates, and recruiting volunteers reasonably well. Functions that support broader democratic responsibilities need more attention.

Third, parties have a long way to go in developing technically powerful web sites. Few parties offer major technical services like streaming media and many failed to make use of simple concepts like the photographs. If state parties want voters or activists to visit their sites to view the substantive content, then they must produce more interesting and stimulating sites. The competition for the Web viewer is sites such as MSNBC.com and Broadcast .com. The parties can't afford to lag behind.

Fourth, state parties in larger states tend to have stronger web sites both in terms of party functions and technical functions. As the Web develops, parties in larger states may very well lead the way.

Much more research is needed to understand the development of state party web sites. Most of the research to date has focused on candidates. State parties are key players in the political process, yet their use of this new medium has been largely ignored. Measures for comparing web sites need to be refined and correlates need to be found.

Parties adapted in the twentieth century by recognizing their role as campaign service providers. They will thrive in the next era when they develop the expertise necessary to help candidates take their message directly to the voters via the World Wide Web. It is "digital or die" in the twenty-first century, and state parties are behind at the first checkpoint.

Notes

1. Because the entire population of major state parties is reported, no inferential statistics are associated with the correlation coefficients.

2. In chapter 8, Raymond La Raja calculates party organizational strength scores for 72 of the 97 state parties studied.

12

No Mo[mentum] in Ohio: Local Parties and the 2000 Presidential Campaign

Melanie J. Blumberg, William Binning,
and John C. Green

Losing a close election breeds endless recriminations and explanations, especially if the defeated candidate was expected to win handily. Thus, it is hardly surprising that Al Gore's loss in the election "tie" of 2000 has produced a bumper crop of such commentary, from the failure to carry his home state of Tennessee to the Florida ballot fiasco.[1] In the spirit of the times, we would like to add another explanation: Gore's loss of Ohio.

A win in the Buckeye State would have sent Gore to the White House, regardless of the realigning forces in Dixie and ballot disputes in the Sunshine State. After all, the Clinton/Gore ticket carried Ohio in 1992 and 1996, and in 2000, Gore won the rest of the industrial megastates of Illinois, Michigan, and Pennsylvania. In fact, Ohio was absolutely critical to the Republican strategy, as it had been in previous elections. This missed opportunity was especially galling to Ohio Democrats because Gore abandoned Ohio in early October, moving his campaign money and operatives elsewhere. Despite these decisions, the results were very close, with Bush winning by less than four percentage points. With 20/20 hindsight, it is widely believed that Gore would have carried the Buckeye State if he had stayed the course.[2]

In Gore's defense, most (but not all) public and private opinion polls gave Bush a double-digit lead in the state by early October, while Gore was running even or ahead in Florida.[3] Gore had no momentum in the Buckeye State and the Ohio Democratic Coordinated Campaign was in disarray, down to the county level. The Democratic effort suffered from problems typical of local party organizations and contemporary presidential campaigns (Blumberg, Binning, and Green 1997, 1999; Heldman 1996). What makes these typical problems noteworthy is the sharp contrast between the weaknesses of the 2000 Gore campaign and the strengths of the 1996 Clinton/Gore campaign, which easily carried Ohio. The experience of Mahoning County in both elections helps explain the complex factors that translate into winning or losing. It also reveals much about the mercurial nature of contemporary local parties. Simply put, the grassroots matter even in media-driven national campaigns, and their weakness can be felt on Election Day.

Mahoning County: A Mother Lode of Democratic Votes

Carrying Mahoning County by a wide margin is critical for any Democratic statewide candidate in Ohio because, as one wag puts it, it contains a "mother lode of Democratic votes." Best known as the home of James Traficant, it is essentially a one-party area, with Democrats outnumbering Republicans nearly five-to-one. Although the choice of local voters is rarely in doubt, turnout often is: High turnout bolsters Democratic hopes statewide, while a sluggish performance benefits the Republicans. Thus, Democratic candidates ignore the area at their own peril.

In 1992, when Clinton and Gore first won Ohio, Mahoning County had the remnants of a traditional party machine, led by long-time "boss" Don Hanni. The Hanni machine used labor-intensive, street-level politics to get out the vote, a style of politics whose effectiveness was in decline. Hanni refused to adapt to modern campaign technology, and partly for this reason, he was ousted in 1994 by a group of media-savvy reformers, "Democrats for Change," led by Michael Morley (Blumberg, Binning, and Green 1997).

Morley and his associates were closely aligned with the "New Democrats" Clinton and Gore, both in terms of substance and style. They enjoyed considerable local success. One of the high points came when Morley coaxed a multimillion-dollar federal airport grant from the Clinton White House just days before the 1996 election. And in that election, the Mahoning County party was a vital cog in the 1996 Democratic Coordinated Campaign, which combined a sophisticated grassroots strategy with the national media campaign. An unusual degree of integration among the national, state, and local party organizations produced impressive results: Mahoning County gave the Clinton/Gore ticket its largest margin in Ohio, accounting for one-third of the Democratic plurality statewide (Niquette 1996).

But by 2000, the reformers were themselves in disarray. Morley had resigned as party chair and the reformers chose David Ditzler, a township trustee, to lead the party. Unlike Morley or Hanni, who could afford to be full-time chairs, Ditzler had work obligations that periodically took him overseas. He also had few connections to state and national party leaders and lacked Morley's personal and political skills. Funds dried up and the party lost its staff and facilities. The local party activists were exhausted from the political infighting and disillusioned by extensive federal investigations into corruption. These investigations eventually led to the conviction of over seventy elected officials and attorneys, including then-congressman Traficant (who was eventually expelled from the House of Representatives and sent to federal prison). The Mahoning County Democrats were in a poor position to play a major role in the 2000 Democratic Coordinated Campaign. These weaknesses were exacerbated by other political problems.

The 2000 Ohio Democratic Coordinated Campaign

Ohio Democratic Party chair David Leland delivered successive victories to the Clinton/Gore ticket in 1992 and 1996, and, by most accounts, was confident that he could put Gore over the top in 2000. In 1996, trusted state party chairs, like Leland, had been given a great deal of autonomy by the national campaign. Leland had, in turn, given greater autonomy to local party chairs whom he trusted, like Michael Morley. However, the 2000 Democratic campaign returned to a more centralized operation, with all of its typical problems. For example, Leland was underutilized by the Gore/Lieberman campaign and not given credit for his understanding of presidential politics in the Buckeye State. National campaign operatives, "outsiders" to Ohio, thought they knew better than the "locals." In addition, Ditzler lacked the credibility and experience of Morley, so Leland granted him less autonomy as well. This lack of autonomy hindered the effective integration of local, state, and national efforts. These difficulties can be seen in the organizations, activities, and finances of the state Coordinated Campaign, and its local expression in Mahoning County.

Organization

In 2000, the Ohio Democratic Coordinated Campaign headquarters was staffed with eleven individuals, one-half the number assigned in 1996. Rather than relying on predominately Ohio natives as in 1996, nearly 50 percent of the team was from out of state, which caused tension between the state party and campaign staff. Caroline E. Heldman (1996) suggests this pattern is not unusual, and Barbara Trish (1994) argues that it may rupture party integration, as outsiders tend not to be trusted by local party activists and vice versa.

A partial exception to this rule was the hiring of Danny Thomas as a regional director to run the effort in Mahoning County. A veteran of presidential and gubernatorial campaigns, and an ally of state chair Leland, Thomas is a savvy political operative known for finding creative ways to overcome obstacles. He has a reputation for understanding local politics and delivering the vote.

But despite these credentials and connections, Thomas had difficulty working with his state and national counterparts, describing the outsiders as "anal-retentive" people who "micro-managed everything." When Thomas called Ohio Democratic Party Executive Director Bill DeMora to voice his dismay, he learned that others were lodging similar complaints across the state.

In contrast to 1996, there was a constant struggle to get anything accomplished. For example, in 1996, regional issues were discussed in breakout sessions at state campaign headquarters in an effort to customize campaign messages such as those used in phone scripts. The regional director also researched local hot-button issues prior to the vice president's campaign swing through the state so he would not be caught off guard. Thomas tried to discuss local issues with the Midwestern regional director prior to Gore's visit to the Mahoning Valley in 2000, but he was not very receptive. The campaign, according to Thomas, seemed to "lack organizational capacity," and there was no "long-range planning."

Thomas was virtually a one-man operation in the Democratic stronghold of Mahoning County, having assistance from just two volunteers and the Ohio Legislative Black Caucus (OLBC) point person. This was a dramatic change from 1996, when each regional office had three full-time administrative staffers. The staffing problems were compounded further by the absence of three full-time workers from the local party and an intern who had supplemented the work of the regional staff in the previous presidential election. Although no paid operatives were sent to work with the smaller counties in 2000, during Clinton's reelection bid three "volunteers" from the administration—political appointees who took vacation time to work on the campaign—arrived shortly before Election Day to assist in getting out the vote. The "volunteers" were in addition to paid "auxiliary staff" sent to work with smaller county parties in each region (Blumberg, Binning, and Green 1999).

Local volunteers were scarce in 2000. Thomas had difficulty convincing precinct committeepeople to work the telephone banks and do literature drops. Volunteers became scarcer after the Gore campaign pulled its ads from Ohio in October. Party regulars asked Thomas whether the Democrats were conceding Ohio. "After all," he noted, "no one wants to be on a losing team."

Grassroots Activities

Grassroots activities played an essential role in 1996, helping to increase voter turnout and support for the entire slate of Democratic candidates. The 2000 effort paled by comparison.

Ongoing Activities. In 1996, the regional office carried out a complex grassroots strategy throughout the campaign, including telephone banking, voter registration drives, literature drops, party mailings, news monitoring, surrogate speakers, debate parties, and letter-writing programs (Blumberg, Binning, and Green 1997, 1999).

The 1996 telephone banking had two purposes: First, undecided voters were mailed three separate pieces of literature in the hope of convincing them to vote for the Democratic ticket. Second, self-identified supporters were contacted during the final days of the campaign in a massive get-out-the-vote (GOTV) push. The Mahoning County operation made nearly 23,000 calls with the help of volunteers called into action by Chairman Morley. Volunteers from local campaigns also worked the telephone banks with the promise that their particular candidate would have his or her name included on the telephone script.

In 2000, Thomas had difficulties from the start. Ten phone lines were installed at headquarters, but no telephones were provided. The state Coordinated Campaign did not make telephone lists available until well after Thomas began to use the ones left from the 1998 gubernatorial campaign. When he finally received a current list on CD-ROM, the party lacked the computer capacity to open and print the files. Once the campaign paid for someone to print the database, Thomas had to work from the two different paper lists. Whereas the previous campaign narrowed the telephone list to include only those precincts with a Democratic Performance Index (DPI) of 65 percent or better, the 2000 database included all registered voters in the county, making it difficult to target likely Gore supporters.

Thomas had moderate success convincing local precinct committeepeople and campaign workers to staff the telephone banks, but there was a general lack of enthusiasm. Gore did not have the "charisma" necessary to mobilize the party faithful into action, and Chairman Ditzler lacked Morley's organizational skills, political connections, and personal warmth.

The political environment also was less conducive to a strong local party effort. In 1996, there were seven high-profile local races, which generated intense interest in party work. But in 2000, only five local races were undecided. One race that did energize partisans was an especially bitter campaign for the Ohio Supreme Court that pitted business against labor. Nominally nonpartisan, this race assumed an unexpectedly high profile, but only in the waning days of the campaign.

In 2000, there were no organized voter registration drives except for one mounted by the OLBC, a phenomenon that Thomas attributes to the passage of the National Voter Registration Act of 1993 (Motor Voter). Various minority groups also registered voters, but chose not to dovetail their efforts with the OLBC. State Representative Sylvester Patton Jr., who served as the OLBC campaign representative locally, criticized the other efforts for lacking follow-through. He kept meticulous records for GOTV purposes, something the other groups failed to do.

There was only one literature drop, which was done in conjunction with organized labor. The Coordinated Campaign did help to pay for absentee ballots mailed to voters sixty-two years of age and older and for Democratic slate cards used for literature drops.

Other labor-intensive activities were generally ignored. Thomas clipped newspaper articles about the campaign and faxed them to Columbus on a daily basis, but news program and talk show monitoring was abandoned due to lack of volunteers. There were no local surrogate speakers to fill the local requests that were received, although a few national figures visited the area.[4] There was little in the way of organized letter-writing to the local newspaper, and what was done rarely got printed. The only successful holdover from 1996 was presidential debate parties, which created media coverage on the late local news.

Outreach Programs. Some of the outreach programs that were instituted to increase voter mobilization in 1996 were missing in 2000. The OLBC mounted the most extensive effort, exceeded only by the unions. Patton was "discouraged" by the poor communications between the state Coordinated Campaign and the OLBC: The "outsiders thought they knew everything," a point echoed by Thomas. The OLBC stood its ground, arguing that its staff in urban areas knew how to energize African-Americans better than the Gore campaign. In this regard, the Coordinated Campaign made some major mistakes. For instance, it sent its own operative to Youngstown to meet with black ministers. The campaign wanted the black clergy to urge parishioners to vote for Gore, not realizing that many refrain from telling their congregations how to vote. The operative had no area contact, and after making several telephone calls was put in touch with Patton. Not knowing how to proceed, he returned to Washington the next day, mission unaccomplished.

The Coordinated Campaign did have an "ethnic identification" outreach, but according to Thomas, the program was ineffective. For example, he worked to get a high-level Hispanic in the administration as a guest at the *Organizacion Civica y Cultural Hispana Americana* annual dinner, but the staff director was not interested in sending another surrogate to the area.

Unions were paid more attention, but Thomas sensed that the trade unions received preferential treatment over the industrial unions. A good example was a local Gore rally where the United Auto Workers Local 112 President was slighted because he was relegated to watching the door rather than being on stage with the candidate. There was no women's vote director at the state level, which is curious given that tracking polls indicated that Gore was not doing as well as Clinton had among women. No specific program targeted gay voters, although there had been one in 1996, complete with local coordinators.

GOTV. GOTV was made more difficult once the news leaked that Gore was pulling his resources from Ohio. Most of the state staff was sent to other battleground states shortly before the election, which left the regional directors to rely on their own resources. With a small volunteer base, Thomas could not work the entire county as had been done in 1996. The telephone banking began in select precincts ten days prior to the election. However, he could not convince local businesses to rent their telephones to the campaign for the final push. Thomas combed the lists of telephone providers from 1996, but none of the principals were willing to have their operations disrupted when there was "no earthshaking reason" to do so. In contrast, the 1996 effort obtained the use of more than one hundred telephones with relative ease: Business owners and professionals with ties to Chairman Morley were quick to oblige his requests.

The field office did not have enough workers to cover all polling places, let alone have enough people to check voter turnout in bellwether precincts. Thomas was unable to rely on local candidates to supplement the workers he did find, as there were few hotly contested local races. The OLBC arranged to provide rides to the polls on Election Day, but the effort did not match 1996, when there were six church vans, six private vehicles, and a handicapped-accessible van to take people to vote.

Finances

In 1996, the Coordinated Campaign to the Mahoning County effort committed a total of $71,867, of which $49,843 came from state and national sources (Blumberg, Binning, and Green 1999, 164). This money covered absentee ballots and slate cards mailed to everyone sixty-two years old or older, sample ballots to nearly 72,000 households in the county, telephone banking equipment, and the three pieces of mail to undecided voters. In 2000, the Coordinated Campaign had approximately $15,000 in state and national funds. Much of this money went for Thomas's salary, and the rest for installing telephone lines, printing and mailing absentee ballots, and printing slate cards. The Mahoning County Democratic Committee spent approximately $10,000 on the Coordinated Campaign, less than one-half of the $21,000 the local party spent in 1996.

Thomas received no other financial assistance during the campaign, including nothing for supplies and refreshments. He spent approximately $400 of his own funds for parking and pizza for volunteers. He used supplies, such as copy paper and toner, that were surplus from the previous presidential election. The Coordinated Campaign refused to pay for a new fax machine, and the one at headquarters could only send faxes but not receive them. Thomas also had no way to send or receive e-mail, so he would wait until he got home in the evening to read the latest communiqués from the state headquarters.

The Ohio Democratic Coordinated Campaign normally contracts for field office space when the local party headquarters does not have adequate facilities. In 1996, the Mahoning County Democratic Party had a street-level office in downtown Youngstown, which was staffed with a full-time director of operations, a field coordinator, and a general office person. In 2000, the local Coordinated Campaign was only an answering machine on the upper floor of a bank building.

"No wonder we were in neutral here," Thomas said. "Mahoning County was taken for granted the entire election."

The OLBC made a significant difference by providing a paid "volunteer" corps. It committed $36,000 to cover the cost of voter registration, advertising, and "street" money, an increase of $19,000 from four years earlier. The three hundred "volunteers" participated in literature drops and worked the polls, in addition to helping staff the phone bank at campaign headquarters.

The level of local campaign expenditures also differed from 1996, when there were seven high-profile local races. Democratic candidates spent more than $318,000 on television and newspaper advertising, various program advertising, and friend-to-friend cards.[5] In 2002, local Democratic candidates spent approximately $84,000 on television and radio spots, with nearly $53,000 of it spent by the Democratic candidate who ran for the Ohio General Assembly, whose district included only a small portion of the county.

Political Mistakes in Mahoning County

The problems in Mahoning County were not entirely the fault of a mismanaged Coordinated Campaign or local party weakness. The Gore campaign made a fair number of its own mistakes, many of which may have ultimately contributed to the decision to abandon the Ohio campaign in October.

During the fall, Gore tried to avoid coming to Youngstown because of his poor relationship with Congressman Traficant and Youngstown Mayor George McKelvey. Gore's irritation with Traficant can be traced to errant votes on Clinton administration priorities. Gore, however, did not have to worry about keeping his distance from Traficant: The local folk hero stayed in Washington rather than be snubbed by the vice president. Meanwhile, Mayor McKelvey was demanding that Gore promise Youngstown an empowerment zone to compensate for its application being denied one year earlier. Gore did not feel overly pressured because the Democratic mayor had never been an enthusiastic supporter. In fact, McKelvey had met with George W.

Bush when he made a brief stop in the area immediately following the Republican National Convention.

Gore finally agreed to appear at a rally in the nearby city of Warren. Although it was the largest rally to that point in the presidential campaign, it "left bad feelings in its wake," according to Thomas. The campaign ignored local officeholders at the rally, angered labor leaders, and then made things worse by arranging an "impromptu" meeting with Mayor McKelvey—at the bookstore of the local state university. This "secret" meeting hurt Gore's image with local Democrats. A more serious mistake, according to Thomas and Patton, was the national campaign's decision not to use President Clinton. Clinton remained very popular in the area, despite his personal problems, and his active campaigning could have helped increase turnout.

These sorts of mistakes are common in presidential campaigns, of course. But the lack of integration of the local, state, and national campaigns deprived Gore of good intelligence on how to campaign in a crucial state and its important localities. Indeed, according to local party officials, Gore "just couldn't get it right" in Mahoning County, and probably in other parts of the state as well.

Election Day 2000

In 2000, Gore carried Mahoning County with slightly more than 63 percent of the two-party vote, almost seven percentage points less than Clinton/Gore did in 1996. Gore received 3,500 fewer votes than Clinton/Gore in 1996. Some of the Democratic defections may have gone to Ralph Nader when it appeared that Bush would win in Ohio: Nader garnered 3,322 votes in the county, almost enough to compensate for the Gore deficit over 1996. Interestingly, Bush gained 9,000 voters over Dole's 1996 performance, largely drawn from Ross Perot's large following in the county (more than 13,000 votes).

Voter turnout declined more than 3 percent between 1996 and 2000. Gore gained in only 23 of 125 urban precincts, with declines in the 2 predominately black wards: Support for Gore was down by more than 4 percent in the First Ward and almost 8 percent in the Second Ward. Turnout decreased in nearly 82 percent of all precincts.

Looked at another way, Gore lost Ohio to Bush by 173,974 votes, or 1,977 votes per each of Ohio's 88 counties. Thus, the decline of 3,500 votes in Mahoning County was 1.77 times the average vote deficit per county. No wonder Bill De Mora observed: "Mahoning County under-performed."

Despite these declines, Gore did much better than expected in Ohio on Election Day. Some local parties were far better organized than in Mahoning County, and African-American groups, such as the OLBC, and the labor unions had effective GOTV programs. The bitter race for the Ohio Supreme Court also may have bolstered turnout unexpectedly. If the Gore campaign had remained active in Ohio, it might have built upon these strengths for victory. However, the weakness in the state Coordinated Campaign, and in places like Mahoning County, may still have proven fatal. In fact, under this scenario, Ohio might have been as close as Florida, and since the urban counties in Ohio also used punch cards, and in many cases butterfly ballots, something like the Florida debacle might have occurred anyway.[6]

The Grassroots Matter

Recent presidential elections in Mahoning County reveal that the grassroots matter even in media-driven national campaigns (Binning, Blumberg, and Green 1995, 1996; Blumberg, Binning, and Green 1997, 1999). In 1996, an excellent local effort paid big dividends by generating high turnout, and in 2000, a weak local effort cost in terms of lower turnout.

The 2000 Coordinated Campaign and Gore made numerous mistakes, but if even there had been fewer, the campaign would have had difficulty integrating its efforts with the local party because there was only a shell of an organization. Party organizations have their own dynamics, and often this produces weak leaders and poor organizations, as was the case with the Mahoning County Democratic Party. When this cycle occurs at both the local and national levels, serious trouble ensues. The skills of party leaders are crucial. The Morley era demonstrates that local parties can be vital, integrated, and effective organizations; the Ditzler era shows that local parties can be hollow, disconnected, and ineffective. Thus, the health of local parties can have national consequences.

Notes

The authors wish to express their appreciation to Danny Thomas Jr., Sylvester Patton Jr., Derrick Clay, Bill De Mora, and Tad Devine, who shared their experience and insights about the Coordinated Campaign in Ohio.

1. See, for example, Ceaser and Busch (2001), Dionne and Kristol (2001), Simon (2001), and the *Washington Post* staff (2001).

2. These assessments are based on interviews with Derrick Clay, who managed the Coordinated Campaign, and Bill De Mora, the executive director of the Ohio Democratic Party.

3. This information comes from an interview with Tad Devine, the Gore campaign official responsible for pulling out of Ohio.

4. Geraldine Ferraro came to rally women, but drew a relatively small crowd; Senator Tom Harkin met with local union leaders at the United Auto Workers hall, but few rank-and-file members were invited; and Al Franken arrived for a rally the Thursday before Election Day.

5. Campaign finance reports for Philip Chance, Democratic candidate for county sheriff, are unavailable. The Federal Bureau of Investigation is holding the records pending further legal action against him. His independent opponent, however, spent more than $37,000 on television and radio advertising. The figures also exclude the media expenditures made by Representative James A. Traficant Jr.

6. According to Ohio Secretary of State Kenneth Blackwell, many of the same problems that plagued the Florida vote occurred in Ohio. However, in no cases was the raw vote close enough for these problems to have made a difference in the final outcome. Other differences between Ohio and Florida are clearer ballot standards and legal mechanisms for resolving ballot disputes. Such a close election might have produced a similar dispute in Ohio, but in all likelihood it would have been resolved more quickly.

13

The Symbiotic Relationship between Political Parties and Political Consultants: Partners Past, Present, and Future

David A. Dulio and James A. Thurber

Political parties and consultants are often seen as competitors in a zero-sum electoral game, with consultants having made most of the gains in recent times. Indeed, to many scholars, parties and consultants are enemies. For instance, Sabato (1981, 286) argues that professional consultants have been one of the contributing factors to the so-called decline of parties:

> In fact, [consultants] themselves, along with their electoral wares have played a moderate part in . . . the continuing decline of party organizations . . . [and have] abetted the slide, sometimes with malice aforethought. . . . The services provided by consultants, their new campaign technologies, have undoubtedly supplanted party activists and influences.

Others have criticized consultants for hurting parties by taking over many of their functions, such as voter contact and communication, usurping the connection between candidates and voters, and acting as the strategic brains behind candidates' campaign organizations (Sabato 1988; Petracca 1989; Agranoff 1972; Kelley 1956; Crotty 1984).

We believe this assessment is an inaccurate description of the relationship between political parties and consultants. Consultants did not drive parties further into decline; rather, both actors developed *together* within a changing electoral landscape. Perhaps one reason for these negative conclusions is that research on parties and consultants has tended to occur separately, rather than together. In this chapter, we use surveys of both actors to develop a more complete view of their relationship.

We argue that parties and consultants have enjoyed a symbiotic and mutually beneficial relationship since consultants appeared on the electoral scene, and that this alliance sets the stage for a future in which parties are even better equipped to meet the demands of candidates. We demonstrate that parties and consultants have been long-term partners and that this partnership has evolved into a modern-day division of labor, with both sets of professionals sharing the responsibilities of providing the electioneering services to candidates. We conclude that the future relationship between political parties and consultants will be healthy and helpful to parties' success in meeting many of their electoral goals.

Parties, Consultants, and Their Cooperative Past

The history of parties and consultants is deeply intertwined. Prior to 1900, parties were the only source of assistance to candidates, as they controlled nearly every aspect of the election cycle from the recruitment of candidates, to candidates' platforms, to voter contact and mobilization. In effect, "the political organizations that existed during the golden age of political parties had a virtual monopoly over the tools needed for campaigning" (Herrnson 1988, 9; Sorauf 1980).

However, the exclusivity with which parties controlled electioneering was diminished by reforms initiated during the Progressive Era, when changes to government and elections altered the electoral playing field for parties, candidates, and voters. Changes such as the abolition of patronage, the institution of the direct primary, and the introduction of nonpartisan elections all reduced the degree of control political parties could exert over election campaigns. Instead of looking to the party organization for electioneering assistance, candidates were encouraged, and to some extent forced, "to develop their own campaign organization," which included a greater presence of nonparty fundraising and other campaigners not directly associated with the party apparatus (Herrnson 1998, 26).

Thus, consultants did not arrive on the campaign scene when parties were at their strongest and push them to the side of electioneering, but rather appeared to meet a need that both candidates and parties faced. This trend would continue as new campaign technologies developed—for example, the use of television to advertise and computers for voter identification and targeting—and as the number of individuals eligible to vote continued to grow (Salmore and Salmore 1985). Candidates needed help in their campaigns and consultants were there to provide it.

During the late 1970s and early 1980s, the role of parties in elections again changed significantly, and they recovered some of their previous influence. A large part of this renewed influence was due to organizational modernization and innovations in fundraising. Both of the major parties acquired permanent national headquarters, larger professional staffs, and the ability to offer sophisticated campaign services to candidates (Herrnson 1988). For example, both major parties built state-of-the-art media production facilities in their respective headquarters located near Capitol Hill, in which candidates could develop their own television and radio advertisements.

However, much of the parties' "revitalization" would not have been possible without the help of professional consultants who were not formally part of the party structure. In some situations, the parties hired consultants to supplement their staffs and to provide services for the benefit of the party (Menefee-Libey 2000; Kolodny 1998), and both parties recommended outside consultants who were loyal to the party and to their candidates (a practice that still exists today).[1] Both parties employed the services of outside consulting firms to do a large share of the work on their fundraising campaigns. Charles Manatt and William Brock, the national chairs of Democratic and Republican parties respectively, instituted large-scale direct mail campaigns to attract donors, and both parties looked to consultants for help in building these donor bases. Manatt hired Craver Matthews Smith and Company, a leading Democratic mail firm at the time. Brock was able to do much of the work in-house because of the staff advantages Republicans enjoyed, but still looked to consultant Richard Viguerie for critical help.

The fact that parties cultivated relationships with consultants is also evident in that they looked to outside professionals to help with their public opinion polling. Even though both parties expanded their professional staffs, they found that they needed more technical expertise to fully conduct survey research. Democrats hired pollsters such as Peter Hart and Matt Reese to collect and analyze public opinion data, and Republicans looked to prominent pollsters such as Richard Wirthlin and Robert Teeter to assist with their survey research. The polling conducted by professional consultants became an essential tool for both the parties' own needs and for individual candidates.

The most telling example that the parties needed consultants to provide the full range of services to their candidates is the use of the parties' new media production centers. If not for the presence of consultants, the parties' media centers would have been of little use to candidates. Candidates were able to take advantage of the sophisticated facilities—cameras, lighting, sound, filming, and editing—as well as the technical knowledge of the party staff. However, candidates needed to bring in their own consultants to produce the ads and develop the message that would be communicated to potential voters (Herrnson 1988).

Another aspect of the party-consultant relationship that is often overlooked is that the parties are training grounds for political consultants (Kolodny and Logan 1998; Thurber, Nelson, and Dulio 2000). Roughly one-half of all current professional consultants worked for a party organization at some level before joining a consulting firm or starting their own business.[2] Indeed, there is a "revolving door" between consultants and parties. Many consultants first spend a few election cycles with a party organization, and then move to the "private" side of the revolving door, working for a consulting firm. They may then return to the party as a senior staff member, only to again return to the world of consulting.

This brief history of the symbiotic relationship between consultants and parties illustrates three important points. First, consultants did not cause parties to decline—the catalysts for "decline" were already in place in the form of electoral reforms and contextual changes. Second, consultants and parties have been working *together*, as parties turned to consultants to aid in their own work and to help their candidates. Third, many campaign consultants start their career within the party organization and spend their careers in the context of the party. We show below how this relationship has blossomed into a true partnership between parties and consultants, with a clear division of labor in which each kind of actor specializes in certain electioneering activities.

The Current Joint Venture of Parties and Consultants

The debate over the party-consultant relationship can be simplified by answering this question: Are parties and consultants allies or adversaries (Kolodny and Logan 1998; Magleby, Patterson, and Thurber 2002; Dulio 2001)? On the one hand, critics tend to see them as adversaries that cannot work in tandem. Or as Kolodny and Logan put it "According to the adversarial view, consultants do not complement parties and act as little more than advertising agencies" (1998, 155). Many critics believe the profit motive leads consultants to want to drive parties from campaigns. On the other hand, those who view consultants and parties as allies see each bringing special talents and resources to electioneering (Dulio 2001). As Kolodny and Logan describe it: "consultants do for candidates what political parties simply cannot" and consultants are part of a party "network" (1998, 155). Along these lines, Kolodny and Dulio note "consultants are necessary for parties to compete in the digital/telecommunications or post-modern campaign age" (2001, 10).

To more fully understand the relationship between parties and consultants, we compare the results of two unique surveys. The first is a national survey of senior-level professional political consultants conducted in the spring of 1999. Data were collected with thirty-minute in-depth telephone interviews with 505 consultants who were either principals or presidents in their firms. The second is a national survey of state party executive directors (or their equivalents) conducted in the spring of 2002.[3]

Interestingly, consultants tend to agree with scholars who see a decline in importance of political parties in American elections. Consultants see the influence of parties, at all levels of elections—local, state, and national—as having decreased in recent times. Nearly one-half of all consultants (46.5 percent) said that they believe political parties' influence at the state level has decreased since they became involved in politics (55 percent and 39 percent reported a decrease at the state and national levels, respectively). At the same time, they see the influence of consultants as having increased (see table 13.1).

Not surprisingly, state party executive directors have a different view: They see state parties (and parties at all levels) as having *increased* in influence. Nearly 70 percent reported seeing an increase since they became involved in party politics in a professional capacity. One reason for this discrepancy may be that nearly 71 percent of party officials around the nation came to their jobs in 2000 or later, while most consultants had been active for many years (data not shown). Thus, the party leaders and consultants may be evaluating very different spans of political history.

Table 13.1   Political Consultants' and State Party Elites' Assessment of the Role of Parties and Consultants over Time

	Consultants' Mean Ranking*	Party Elites' Mean Ranking*
Do you think the role of *parties* in electing candidates at the *local* level has . . .	2.38	3.53
Do you think the role of *parties* in electing candidates at the *state* level has . . .	2.71	3.89
Do you think the role of *parties* in electing candidates at the *national* level has . . .	2.90	3.83
Do you think the role of *consultants* in electing candidates at the *local* level has . . .	4.40	3.70
Do you think the role of *consultants* in electing candidates at the *state* level has . . .	4.44	3.95
Do you think the role of *consultants* in electing candidates at the *national* level has . . .	4.37	4.04

* Mean ranking is based on a scale where 1 = decreased very much, 2 = decreased somewhat, 3 = stayed the same, 4 = increased somewhat, and 5 = increased very much.

Complete question wording for consultants: Thinking back to when you first began working as a campaign consultant—and comparing that to now—do you think the role of [political parties; political consultants] in electing candidates at the [local; state; national] levels has increased, stayed about the same, or decreased? Please use the same 5-point scale where "5" means increased very much, "4" means increased somewhat, "3" means stayed the same, "2" means decreased somewhat, and "1" means decreased a lot.

Complete question wording for party elites: Thinking back to when you first began working in party politics in a professional capacity—and comparing that to now—do you think the role of [political parties; political consultants] in electing candidates at the [local; state; national] level has increased, stayed about the same, or decreased? Please use a 5-point scale where "5" means increased very much, "4" means increased somewhat, "3" means stayed the same, "2" means decreased somewhat, and "1" means decreased a lot.

The consultants see a clear division of labor between their activities and the parties in modern political campaigns (see table 13.2). This division is based on the degree of technically sophisticated knowledge and expertise required to provide the services, roughly between "message creation and delivery" techniques and those services that require extensive time and staff resources (Dulio 2001, 206; Kolodny and Logan 1998).

The consultants are clearest in saying that political parties are no longer the best source of strategic advice when it comes to a candidate's campaign; instead, it is the paid professional who is in a better position to offer this kind of advice. Advising candidates on their strategy, theme, and message is one of the most important services that professional consultants provide to candidates (Dulio 2001). It is difficult to imagine that parties could provide race-specific advice to all their candidates, even if they wanted to. There are simply too many candidates with too many specific needs during this era of candidate-centered elections when local issues can be so important.[4] In addition, consultants claim to have become the main service providers for media or campaign advertising, survey research, and direct mail.

For the most part, state party leaders concur with this assessment. A full 71 percent of party staffers in the 2002 survey report that consultants furnish services to campaigns that the parties are incapable of providing. In addition, the party leaders report that consultants have taken over providing the same services that the consultants reported in our survey in 1999, with one exception—strategic advice and campaign management. As seen in table 13.2, management and advice falls far down state party executive directors' rankings of services they believe consultants have taken over for parties. These party officials undoubtedly see a place for their advice at the electioneering

Table 13.2   Have Consultants Taken over for Political Parties in Providing Electioneering Services?

Service	Consultants' Mean Ranking*	State Party Elites' Mean Ranking*
Management or strategic advice	3.51	2.46
Media or campaign advertising	3.49	3.04
Polling	3.42	3.14
Direct mail	3.31	2.85
Opposition research	3.07	2.48
Campaign finance or fundraising	2.91	2.41
GOTV or field operations	2.65	1.78

* The mean ranking is based on a 4-point scale where 1 = strongly disagree, 2 = somewhat disagree, 3 = somewhat agree, and 4 = strongly agree.

Complete question wording for both consultants and party elites: Thinking specifically now, please tell me whether you strongly agree, somewhat agree, somewhat disagree, or strongly disagree that political consultants have taken the place of political parties in providing each of these services . . .

table, and believe that they have some valuable strategic advice to offer. However, they also agree that polling, media production, and direct mail are the services best provided by consultants.

What services do consultants think are currently provided by the parties? They report that parties are bett r able to provide opposition research, fund-raising, and get-out-the-vote (GOTV)/field services, areas in which consultants admit they are less active. And on this matter, the state party leaders tended to agree.

Table 13.3 reveals the other side of the coin, reporting the relative values of party-provided services. Consultants reported a very clear ordering of services that they found helpful when coming from the party: assistance with campaign funds, opposition research, polling, direct mail, GOTV efforts, coordinated television advertisements, and management/strategic advice. This ordering illustrates the division of labor in campaigns. State party leaders agree with part of this assessment. They give a similar ranking to campaign funds, opposition research, and polling, but are more likely to give parties a more positive assessment than the consultants with regard to direct mail, GOTV/field operations, coordinated television ads, and management/strategic advice. Perhaps it is not surprising that party leaders see a larger role for their own efforts, but they do not denigrate the assistance of consultants.

These and other data (Kolodny and Dulio 2001; Dulio and Kolodny 2001) strongly suggest that political consultants and political parties are not so much adversaries as allies. Further evidence of these tendencies is the report by party leaders that their own organization had hired, or would soon

Table 13.3   What Party-Provided Services Do Consultants and State Party Elites Find Helpful in Competitive Campaigns?

Service	Consultants' Mean Ranking*	State Party Elites' Mean Ranking*
Campaign funds	1.63	1.53
Opposition research	1.86	1.84
Polling	1.99	1.71
Direct mail	2.18	1.85
GOTV or field operations	2.19	1.89
Coordinated television ads	2.33	1.90
Management or strategic advice	2.79	1.84

* The mean ranking is based on a 4-point scale where 1 = very helpful, 2 = somewhat helpful, 3 = not very helpful, and 4 = not helpful at all.

Complete question wording for both consultants and party elites: I am going to read you a list of services that are sometimes provided to candidates by the national party organization or Congressional Campaign Committees. Thinking about *competitive* races, please tell me whether, in your experience, each service has been very helpful, somewhat helpful, not very helpful or not helpful at all to the success of your campaign or campaigns . . .

likely hire, consultants for use in the upcoming election cycle: 87.9 percent said they would hire a pollster, 83.3 percent a direct mail specialist, and 68.2 percent a media consultant (data not shown). The reason the party operatives gave for such hiring, in the vast majority of cases, was that their own organization does not provide the service. Does delivery of services by consultants weaken parties? We think not, and party elites tend to agree: If consultants help candidates win and capture government offices, they have helped the parties meet one of their main objectives.

The Future of the Consultant-Party Relationship

Prognostications about any aspect of the U.S. electoral landscape are difficult at best, and can even be dangerous—as those who predicted a landslide victory by Vice President Al Gore in the 2000 presidential election discovered. We cannot know for sure what the future holds for the relationship between consultants and parties, but one thing is certain—professional political consultants will be an important part of the electoral equation. Additionally, we can surmise from the evidence presented here that parties and consultants will continue to have a close and symbiotic relationship. Political parties are not likely to reverse the trend of the past twenty years and return to providing specialized services to their candidates when they can hire outside professionals to do the job more efficiently and possibly more effectively. But parties will continue to be important electoral actors for candidates because they offer their party label, as well as assistance with campaign necessities requiring more organizational stability than consultants can provide. Individual candidates will continue to develop their messages through survey research and disseminate those messages through mass-media communications strategies including radio, television, and direct mail, all of which require the help of the consultants they hire.

However, the shape of this alliance will largely depend on regulations governing how money can be spent in campaigns. A good example is the disposition of *McConnell v. Federal Election Commission,* centering on the constitutionality of the recently enacted Bipartisan Campaign Reform Act (BCRA) of 2002. The specifics of both the reform legislation and the court cases are beyond the scope of this discussion. However, suffice it to say that whether or not national party organizations are banned from raising and spending soft money will have a tremendous effect on state parties' level of influence. If soft money remains outlawed at the federal level, but state parties are permitted to raise and spend it (if only in $10,000 increments, as allowed by BCRA), state parties will likely become much bigger players in the party-consultant relationship because they will control the resources to hire consultants.

If the Courts uphold BCRA, the influence of private political consultants is likely to increase relative to other political actors. Some have argued that consultants opposed BCRA because of provisions that restrict parties, interest groups, and other political organizations from airing issue advocacy advertising. After all, this provision would cut into their business. This assumption may be valid in the case of media consultants in the short run, but candidates (as well as parties, interest groups, and other organizations interested in the election outcome) will continue to face the need to develop and disseminate their campaign messages, and the expertise of consultants will be especially critical if party resources are cut back.

The issue advocacy ban in BCRA has implications for parties, who will be restricted in their ability to put together a media campaign to spread their message about issues they feel are important to the campaign. The area most likely to see an increase is direct mail, one of the few areas of electioneering not affected by the new regulations. In this case, the media consultant's loss is the direct mail consultant's gain; or, as one Democratic direct mail consultant put it, "What you used to do in TV, you'll do in mail only" (quoted in Keller 2002, 18). As noted above, campaign messages must still be spread to all potential voters and constituencies that are important to candidates and parties, and the reform legislation "will drive a lot of [candidates, parties, and interest groups] to expand their direct-mail campaigns," says GOP mail consultant Dan Hazelwood (quoted in Keller 2002, 18). The consultant's influence here is that mail is most successful when it is strategically targeted. Television ads are broadcast to millions of viewers at the same time, but direct mail specialists can carefully target the pieces they create to specific constituencies.

Furthermore, political parties may look to outside mail consultants to assist them in their fundraising activities, as they did during the early 1980s. If soft money is indeed outlawed, parties will have to raise more hard money, which must be gathered in smaller increments, limited to $2,000 per individual per election, rather than the current limit of $1,000. With this change, "national party committees will have to work harder than ever to pull in greater numbers of limited donations from their donor bases," and direct mail will likely be the method they employ (Keller 2002, 18). In sum, the new electoral context created by the campaign finance reform law only serves to strengthen the symbiotic relationship between parties and consultants. Both kinds of actors will continue to develop their partnership, strengthening their division of labor to meet the goal of electing candidates to office.

Notes

1. See Herrnson 1988 on party recommendations in the 1980s and Dulio 2001 for a discussion of the current context.

2. Exact estimates of the numbers of consultants who have a party background vary from study to study. For example, Kolodny and Logan (1998) report that about 41 percent of the consultants in their survey ("general consultants" only) worked for the party before they became consultants. Thurber, Nelson, and Dulio reported that 62 percent of the consultants in their study have "worked for a national, state, or local political party committee" (2000, 194). However, this figure also includes those who may have been part of the "revolving door" between consultants and parties where party staffers become consultants who then go back to the party. The survey evidence reported below from a more recent survey of campaign consultants estimates that 44 percent of consultants worked for a party organization prior to becoming a consultant.

3. Both surveys were designed by The Center for Congressional and Presidential Studies (CCPS) as part of the "Improving Campaign Conduct" project, funded by a grant from The Pew Charitable Trusts. Yankelovich Partners, Inc. (currently Harris Interactive) administered the surveys with their "Executive Council" of interviewers who are specially trained to conduct high-level interviews. More information on the surveys, including sampling procedures and a copy of the questionnaire, can be obtained from the authors or by visiting the center's web site, www.american.edu/academic.depts/spa/ccps (accessed December 2002).

4. For examples of how consultants help develop candidates' strategies, themes, and messages, and the importance of local issues in congressional campaigns, see the case studies in Thurber (2001).

Part Four

Party in Government

14

A Double-Edged Sword: Party Dilemmas in Mobilizing Electoral Bases in U.S. House Elections

Jeffrey M. Stonecash

Congressional party leaders engage in an endless process of assessing their present and the future political situation. They must respond to their current electoral base, but also look for ways to develop support beyond their base. They must try to anticipate the future and how it might affect their future political fortunes. Social change is relentless, creating new issues and new groups. If a party miscalculates how social change will affect them, they could lose out to their opponents. The political situation in the House of Representatives after the 2000 election exemplifies these uncertainties.

The Republicans and Democrats each assess present trends and see a favorable future. Yet each party also faces the danger of focusing primarily on their voter base, and ignoring important social changes. Republicans derive a favorable interpretation of their future from the electoral trends of the last several decades. The party has mobilized conservative voters with an argument for less government, lower taxes, and more emphasis on personal morality. The electoral trends of the last thirty-five years reveal a steady, if fitful, increase in support for the party in response to these themes. In contrast, Democrats see a bright future for themselves based on future demographic trends. The continued growth of economic inequality and less-affluent nonwhites may allow the party's message of equality of opportunity and government services as a way to provide more opportunity to triumph at the polls. This chapter offers an analysis of the trends affecting each party and the risks these trends pose. Although it is difficult to predict which scenario will prove to be correct, some limited evidence about what may occur in the near future will be reviewed.

The Republican Tide

While it took some time to develop, Kevin Phillips' prediction of an "emerging Republican majority" (1970) has proved to be right: beginning in the mid-1960s, the electorate began moving in a Republican direction. His argument was deceptively simple. The political culture of the Northeast and large cities was liberal and supportive of an active role for the national government, while the rest of the nation was more conservative and less supportive of national government activity. With most population growth occurring outside the Northeast, the dominance of liberalism in the nation's political culture would fade. In addition, the movement of people into suburbs, where national government programs were less popular, would add to this liberal decline. Associated with these trends were a decline in class conflict and the rise of new social issues. While this Republican tide arrived slowly, it followed these demographic trends, aided and abetted by a presumed decline in class conflict and the rise of social issues.

While Phillips argued that Republican electoral fortunes were improving in the 1960s, the trend was difficult to see in the 1970s, given controversies such as the Watergate scandal and the GOP debacle in 1974. But overall, Republicans began making gains in House elections in 1966 and continued to 2000. Table 14.1 summarizes data on incumbent electoral success by party. From 1946 to 1964, 56.1 percent of Republicans won with less than 60 percent of the vote, and from 1966 to 2000, only 29.9 percent won with less than 60 percent. Meanwhile, there was virtually no change among Democrats. For all Republican winners, their average vote percentage also improved, rising from 59.6 to 66.3, and the Democrats experienced a drop from 74.5 to 70.4. Clearly, the fortunes of Republicans slowly improved (Stonecash 2001).

Geographic Shifts. The South and Western states stretching from Texas to California constitute the Sunbelt (Bernard and Rice 1985, 7), and they are often regarded as more conservative than the North (Erikson, Wright, and McIver 1993, 18). Greater population growth in the Sunbelt has made that region a larger proportion of the nation. As a result, the North now elects fewer members of the House of Representatives: in 1940, the North contained 53 percent of the nation's congressional districts, and in 2002 this proportion is 40.[1] A similar pattern was obtained with the move to the suburbs across the country. The proportion of the population living in the sub-

Table 14.1　Republican Electoral Fortunes before and after 1966

	Incumbents <60% of Vote		*Winners Average Percent*	
	Republicans	*Democrats*	*Republicans*	*Democrats*
1946–1964	56.1	29.8	59.6	74.5
1966–2000	29.9	27.6	66.3	70.4
Change	− 26.2	− 2.2	6.7	− 4.1

urbs has grown from 23 percent in the 1950s to roughly 50 percent now (*New York Times* 1990, A20; Lemann 1991, 42).[2]

The regional base of the Republicans also shifted. In the 1940s, the party did well in the North and the West, but did poorly in the South. Since then, its success has steadily increased in the South, along with the party's reliance on Southern seats. Figure 14.1 presents the percentage of Republican House seats from each region since 1946. The North, the most liberal region of the nation, has decreased from being 71 percent of all Republican seats to 36 percent, while the South, the most conservative region of the nation, has steadily grown to 35 percent of all Republican House seats.

Decline in Support for Government. Republicans successfully appealed to the conservatism of these new Sunbelt-suburban populations, arguing that expansion of the national government results in too much intrusion into private life and reduces personal freedom. As Ronald Reagan stated in his 1981 presidential inaugural address, "Government is not the solution to our problems; government is the problem." The prominence of this argument was accompanied by a steady decline in trust of the national government (Flanigan and Zingale 1998, 13; Craig 1996, 46–55).[3] Support for "big government" also appears to have declined in a parallel fashion. Since 1984 several polling organizations have asked the public whether they favor "smaller government with fewer services or larger government with many services" (Ladd 1998, 10–11). While the electorate was divided almost evenly on this issue in the mid-1980s, by the 1990s support had clearly shifted toward a preference for smaller government.

Diminishing Class Conflict and the Rise of Social Issues. The growth of

Figure 14.1   Proportion of Republican Seats for Each Region, U.S. House, 1946–2000

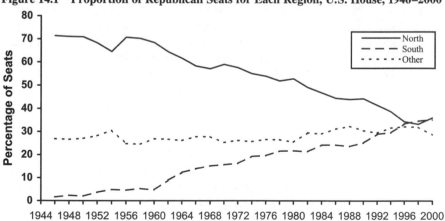

Sunbelt/suburban populations coincided with a widely accepted presumption that class conflicts were declining in American politics. About the time Phillips was developing his analysis, others argued that sustained increases in real income levels had reduced concerns about economic scarcity (Nisbet 1959; Bell 1962; Wilensky 1966; Bell 1973; Lipset 1981, 253). The conclusion was that "blue collar workers have moved into the same middle-class bracket as white collar workers" (Bonafede 1981, 317), and were less interested in government playing a redistributive role. Material issues were seen as secondary to quality-of-life concerns (Inglehart 1971; Ladd and Hadley 1975, 195–200; Ladd 1984; Rae 1989, 641; Clark, Lipset, and Rempel 1993, 298).

Class issues were thought to have been displaced by the emergence of an array of disturbing social trends. Violent crimes per 100,000 population increased (Wattenberg 1996, 143–146); the birth of illegitimate children and welfare spending expanded (169–170); the divorce rate grew, and educational success declined (187). Republicans seized on these trends to stress the importance of the "social issues" of families, morality, and an orderly society (Scammon and Wattenberg 1970, 40–43), accusing the Democrats of being overly compassionate and "permissive" (Magnet 1993; Murray 1984). Working-class whites were seen as angry over the demise of their traditional values, and they fled the Democratic Party. Long-simmering racial divisions also played a part in these developments (Edsall and Edsall 1991, 77–80; Kazin 1995, 221–242; Carter 1995, 324–370) Affluent whites in the Sunbelt and suburbs, in particular, objected to these developments, wanting more emphasis on "values" to arrest "social decay" (Schneider 1987, 42–48).

Table 14.2 documents the growth of conservatives in American society and among those voting for House candidates, success with conservatives for Republican House candidates, and their reliance on conservative voters. In the 1970s, 29.2 percent of the nation identified itself as conservative; by the 1990s, 34.6 percent did so. Conservatives as a percentage of all voters increased from 35.2 to 40.5 over this period. From the 1970s to the 1990s, the percentage of conservatives that voted for Republican presidential candidates increased from 58 to 69, and the percentage voting for Republican House candidates increased from 45.9 to 58.7. Gallup polls indicate that in the last decade conservatives have constituted 65 percent of the Republican Party.[4]

These electoral, geographic, and attitudinal shifts in favor of the Republicans appear to fulfill Phillips's prediction of an "emerging Republican majority," the final culmination of which was the GOP takeover of the House in 1994 and its retention from 1996 to 2000. It is clear why Republicans would see the country moving steadily in their favor.

Indeed, some recent events suggest just how strong the Republican tide might be. The Republicans have been able to take actions seemingly against

Table 14.2   The Increasing Presence and Role of Conservatives for Republicans: Percent Identifying as Conservative, Voting for House Republicans, and Reliance of House Republican Candidates on Conservatives

| | *Conservatives as %:* | | *% Voting Republican:* | | | *% of Republican Vote from:* | | |
	Nation	*All Voters*	*Lib.*	*Mod.*	*Con.*	*Lib.*	*Mod.*	*Con.*
1970s	29.2	35.2	28.5	44.7	59.9	11.1	26.5	45.9
1980s	31.9	37.9	25.5	42.7	63.6	10.3	23.0	48.5
1990s	34.6	40.5	23.4	47.9	75.6	9.1	22.2	58.7
Change	5.1	5.3	−5.1	3.2	15.7	−2.0	−4.3	12.8

Source: The data are taken from the National Election Studies files for 1952–2000. The National Election Studies, American National Election Studies Cumulative Data File, 1948–2000 [computer file]. 11th ICPSR version. Ann Arbor, Mich.: University of Michigan, Center for Political Studies [producer], 2001. Ann Arbor, Mich.: Inter-university Consortium for Political and Social Research [distributor], 2002.

Results are grouped as: 1970s: 1972–1980, 1980s: 1982–1990, 1990s: 1992–2000. Yearly responses are averaged within each decade. The table presents the percentage of those with the conservative position, their percentage of voters in House elections, how many identify with the Republican party, and the percentage of Republican voters who are conservative. The question: "We hear a lot of talk these days about liberals and conservatives. Here is a 7-point scale on which the political views that people might hold are arranged from extremely liberal to extremely conservative. Where would you place yourself on this scale, or haven't you though much about this?" 1–3 are then collapsed into liberal, 5–7 into conservative.

the majority of public opinion and survive with minimal, if any, damage. In 1997 and 1998, the House Republicans intensely pursued impeachment proceedings against President Clinton, and even though their public ratings dropped significantly as the process unfolded, they still won the 1998 and 2000 elections.[5] In 2000, George W. Bush proposed a large income tax cut, with most of the benefits flowing to the more affluent.[6] Although public opinion polls revealed only modest support, President Bush and the congressional Republicans went forward with their proposal and enacted a large tax cut during 2001. While seemingly defying public opinion, George Bush's ratings did not decline.[7] There are potential risks on the horizon for Republicans, but before reviewing the dilemma the party faces, we need to consider the Democrats' interpretation of the future.

The Democratic Hope

Despite the Republican gains of the last several decades, there are reasons for Democrats to be optimistic about their future (Judis 2000). Three trends inform the Democratic hope. First, voter identification with the Democratic Party is relatively stable and still greater than that for the Republican Party. More importantly, two changes in American society are creating a growing proportion of the electorate that may be receptive to the Democratic message of equality of opportunity: increases in economic inequality and ethnic diversity.

The Persistence of Democratic Partisanship. Despite the political set-backs the Democrats have encountered since the 1960s, still more than 50 percent of the citizenry identify themselves with the party and less than 40 percent see themselves as Republicans (figure 14.2). The data indicate that the position of the Democratic Party has been relatively stable in recent decades (see chapter 3). By the late 1990s, party voting was also higher than it has been in the last thirty years thirty years (Bartels 2000), indicating that the electorate is not deserting the party in large numbers. As we have seen, this level of party affiliation has not always translated into Democratic electoral victories, but party affiliation gives the Democrats the opportunity to recover this support.

Rising Economic Inequality. Economic conditions are evolving in a way that may create renewed interest in the Democrats' core messages. Table 14.3 presents data on changes in real income by quintiles since 1979. As other studies have shown, economic growth over the last several decades has mostly benefited the relatively affluent (Danziger and Gottschalk 1995). Citizens in the lower income groups are experiencing real economic decline, resulting in greater inequality in the distribution of income (Weinberg 1996). Median family income, adjusted for inflation, has grown modestly, even as more and more families have two income earners.

Further, access to the widely presumed route to greater income—higher education—is also becoming more unequal. Over the last thirty years a much

Figure 14.2   Party Identification, 1952–2000

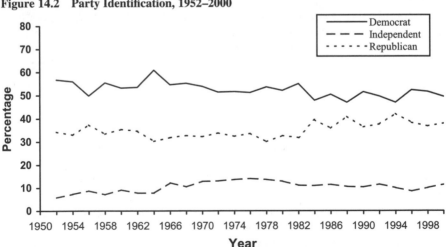

Table 14.3   Average Pretax Income by Income Group (1997 dollars)

	1979	1989	1997	% Δ 79–97	$ Δ 79–97
Lowest fifth	$11,800	$11,700	$11,400	− 3.4	− $400
Second fifth	27,100	27,300	28,600	5.5	1,500
Middle fifth	41,400	42,700	45,100	8.9	3,700
Fourth fifth	56,800	61,900	65,600	15.5	8,800
Highest fifth	109,500	138,000	167,500	53.0	58,800

Source: Isaac Shapiro, Robert Greenstein, and Wendell Primus. "Pathbreaking CBO Study Shows Dramatic Increases in Income Disparities in 1980s and 1990s." Center on Budget and Policy Priorities, Washington, D.C., May 31, 2001, 10.

higher percentage of students from more affluent families are attending college, while there has been only a marginal increase for those from families in the bottom half of the income distribution (Mortenson 1995, 1). For those who do go to college, there is now more emphasis on federal loans (Hearn 1998), and the average total student loan has increased (Fossey 1998, 11).

When combined, these trends may be creating a population that is more receptive to political appeals based on equality of opportunity and expanded government than in past decades. For example, polls from 1988 to 2001 asked, "Are we a have/have-not society?" The percentage responding "yes" has risen from 26 in 1988, to 39 in 1999, to 44 in 2001 (Pew Research Center 2001).

These trends have political consequences that appear to benefit the Democrats. While many concluded that Democrats were alienating less affluent whites, the opposite has happened. Table 14.4 first presents the extent to which whites in the bottom and top thirds of the income distribution have supported the Democratic Party since the 1950s. Support for Democrats among the less affluent has increased, and beginning in the 1970s and 1980s, differences in support between the two income groups increased steadily. Similarly, the percentage of liberals voting for, and identifying with, the Democrats has steadily increased since the 1970s. It is quite plausible for Democrats to conclude that their messages regarding inequality and opportunity are connecting with the less affluent.

Increasing Ethnic Diversity. The ethnic composition of the nation is shifting in ways that are likely to benefit the Democrats. The nonwhite population is growing steadily and becoming a larger part of the U.S. population. Because of immigration, the percentage of the U.S. population that is foreign-born is now 10.4 percent, higher than it has been since the 1930s.[8] The Hispanic population has grown tremendously in the last two decades (Gimpel 1999, 332; Suro 1998, 299–301), increasing from 3.5 million in 1960 and 9.1 million in 1970 to 24.1 million in 2000.[9] The percentage of the population that is Hispanic has increased from 8 in 1990 to 12 in 2000.[10]

Table 14.4 Income and Ideological Divisions: Percent Voting and Identifying with Democrats, by Income and Ideological Groups, by Decade, 1950s–1990s, Whites Only

	House Election Voting			Party Identification		
Income	*Low*	*High*	*Diff.*	*Low*	*High*	*Diff.*
Decade						
1950s	56	48	8	55	51	4
1960s	56	52	4	54	51	3
1970s	61	49	12	53	45	8
1980s	62	48	14	53	40	13
1990s	56	39	17	53	38	15
Change	0	−9	9	−2	−13	11
Ideology	*Lib.*	*Cons.*	*Diff.*	*Lib.*	*Cons.*	*Diff.*
Decade						
1970s	75	43	32	73	32	41
1980s	78	39	38	75	30	45
1990s	79	31	48	80	19	61
Change	4	−12	16	7	−13	20

Numbers are the percent indicating they either voted for Democrats in House elections, or identified with the Democratic party. Results are averages of yearly percentages within a decade. To derive the groupings of low and high (bottom and top third) of income groupings, the groupings of family income for each year were recoded so that those in the 0–33 percentile were in the bottom third, and those in the 66–100 percentile were coded as top third. Only whites are included because for the last several decades this has been the conventional approach. Ideology is coded as in table 14.2.

Source: National Election Studies 1952–2000.

These ethnic changes favor Democrats because of the political inclinations of nonwhites. The CNN exit poll from the 2000 elections indicates that a majority of whites voted for Republican House candidates (55-43) and George Bush (54-42) at nearly identical rates.[11] African Americans voted 88-11 for Democratic House candidates and 90-9 for Al Gore. Hispanics voted 64-35 for Democratic House candidates and 62-35 for Al Gore. To the extent that the U.S. population becomes more African American and Hispanic, the Democrats anticipate a growing electoral base.

Table 14.5 indicates the changes in the presence of nonwhites in House districts since the 1960s. The results are grouped by the percentage of the district that is nonwhite. The top category of 20 percent or more is particularly important, since districts with this percentage or more are likely to be won by Democrats. The changes in the distribution of districts since the 1960s are remarkable. In the 1960s, 65 percent of districts had a composition that was 90 percent or more white and only 22 percent had 20 percent or more nonwhites. The Census Bureau reported the 2000 population composition using district boundaries drawn after the 1990 census. Those data indi-

Table 14.5 **Distribution of House Districts by the Percentage Nonwhite, 1960s–1990s, and Districts Using 2000 Census for Existing Districts**

% Nonwhite, Nationwide	*Decade of Apportionment and % Distribution*				2000 Data	2000 Voting % Democrat
	1960s	*1970s*	*1980s*	*1990s*		
0–9	64.8	61.6	44.8	40.6	22.5	36.8
10–19	13.1	18.5	24.9	24.6	26.7	33.6
20 plus	22.1	19.9	30.3	34.9	50.8	63.8

By State	*Decade of Apportionment and Number of Districts*				2000 Data	Change
	1960s	*1970s*	*1980s*	*1990s*		
New York						
0–9	30	25	15	11	5	−25
10–19	6	7	8	11	8	2
20 plus	5	7	11	9	18	13
Total	41	39	34	31	31	
Florida						
0–9	1	2	5	12	1	0
10–19	7	11	9	6	15	8
20 plus	4	2	5	5	7	3
Total	12	15	19	23	23	
Texas						
0–9	9	10	3	2	0	−9
10–19	8	9	11	8	6	−2
20 plus	6	5	13	20	24	18
Total	23	24	27	30	30	
California						
0–9	33	32	5	2	0	−33
10–19	1	7	15	15	3	2
20 plus	4	5	25	35	49	45
Total	38	44	45	52	52	

cate the 1960s distribution has reversed. Now there are only 22 percent of districts that are 90 percent or more white, and 51 percent of districts are 20 percent or more nonwhite.

These changes are especially dramatic in some important states. New York has increased from 5 to 18 of 31 districts that are 20 percent nonwhite, even as it has lost congressional seats. Texas has changed from 6 of 23 to 24 of 30 districts that are 20 percent nonwhite. California has experienced the greatest change, changing from 4 of 38 in 1960 to 49 of 52 districts in 2000 that are 20 percent nonwhite.

These changes have political consequences. Table 14.5 also presents the percentage of each category of district won by Democrats in 2000. In districts more than 20 percent nonwhite, Democrats won 64 percent of districts. In districts with less than 20 percent nonwhites, Democrats win about one-third of seats. From the Democratic perspective, as the presence of non-whites increases in House districts, the prospects for Democrats to win House seats will also increase (Stonecash, Brewer, and Mariani 2002a, 2002b).

In sum, the Democratic view that stable partisanship combined with increasing economic inequality and ethnic diversity favors them is quite plausible. But as with the Republicans, these opportunities present the Democrats with political risks, a matter to which we now turn.

The Party Dilemmas

The Republican tide and Democratic hope suggest that the political future of each party could be bright. There is also a risk, however, that each party could misjudge the consequences of responding primarily to trends that appear to favor them. The Republicans face the danger that they may be seen as too conservative.[12] A strident message of personal responsibility and less government may be counterproductive at a time of growing inequality and ethnic diversity. If the GOP is perceived as the vehicle for perpetuating inequality and as largely unconcerned about the problems of minorities, the party could find itself in trouble. Perhaps the most significant danger faced by Republicans is that Hispanics, who are less affluent and who do not vote at high levels now, will be mobilized into the political process and vote heavily Democratic (Ponnuru 1998, 2001)

The Democrats face a similar dilemma: they could become too identified with economic redistribution and nonwhites.[13] This posture could cost the Democrats the support of moderate and white voters. Already, an increasing proportion of the Democratic House Party is coming from districts that have higher percentages of nonwhites. In the 1970s, 26.7 percent of all Democratic House members were from districts that were 20 percent or more non-white. During the 1990s that percentage was 50.6. The percentage of Democratic House members from districts that are 90 percent white has declined from 52.6 percent in the 1970s to 29.2 in the 1990s. Too strident a message of equality and expanded government could cost the Democrats dearly if economic and social trends do not materialize as expected.

Given the uncertainty each party faces, is there any evidence suggesting that one of these scenarios is more likely? For the immediate future there are three relevant and important trends: Republican success in districts with higher percentages of nonwhites, party support among whites, and turnout differences by class and race. Evidence of these trends offers some shaky guesses about the prospect for each party.

A crucial factor for Republicans is how they are faring in districts with higher percentages of nonwhites, the number of which will increase in the near future. If Republicans are steadily losing these districts, they will likely face a limited future. Table 14.6 summarizes Republican success by the composition of House districts from the 1960s to 2000. Interestingly, the Republicans have steadily done well in districts with modest *and* high percentages of nonwhites. It is plausible for Republicans to conclude that their message of individualism has universal appeal, and an increasingly nonwhite population is not a threat to their success.

Survey data suggests that there has been a recent shift to Republican voting among whites. Figure 14.3 indicates the percentage of whites voting for Democratic House candidates over time. Beginning in 1994, white support for the Democratic Party dropped below 50 percent. Not only are Republicans improving their fortunes in districts with a substantial percentage of nonwhites, they are doing better among whites. They could easily conclude that Democrats are alienating whites with their historic messages, and the GOP can count on continued high levels of white support.

With less-affluent and nonwhite voters becoming a larger portion of American society, and given their tendency to vote Democratic, the crucial matter is whether they actually turn out to vote. Table 14.7 presents voting rates, of all those eligible, for the last several decades. Voting rates among the less affluent are consistently twenty percentage points below those for the more affluent. Hispanics and blacks also vote at much lower rates than whites. All of these differences are stable over time. The combination of lower participation rates among the less-affluent and nonwhite voters makes these voters much less relevant than their numbers in census counts might suggest. This trend is also encouraging to Republicans.

These factors all work together in House elections. Low turnout by these Democratic-leaning groups allows Republicans to win even in economically and ethnically diverse districts by mobilizing their base of conservative, white, and affluent voters. Indeed, there are numerous cases in California where a district has 30 percent or more nonwhites, but Republican candidates win, even while having very low Americans for Democratic Action scores.

Table 14.6   Republican Success by District Composition, 1960s–1990s, and 2000 Elections

% nonwhite	1960s	1970s	1980s	1990s	2000
0–9	54.2	47.7	53.8	62.7	64.0
10–19	24.5	30.8	43.2	58.5	58.9
20 plus	13.7	16.8	17.0	27.4	28.1

Figure 14.3   Percentage of Whites Voting for Democrats, House of Representatives, 1952–2000

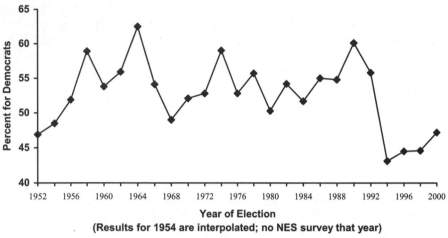

Year of Election
(Results for 1954 are interpolated; no NES survey that year)

The dilemma for Republicans is that these lower turnout levels may not persist. Indeed, if the party continues on a conservative path, its very actions may antagonize nonwhites and the less affluent, and prompt them to vote in higher numbers. The dilemma for Democrats is no simpler. In some ways, their situation is similar to the late 1920s. The distribution of income is becoming more unequal and the ethnic composition of the nation is changing, but the citizens critical to Democratic success register and vote at low levels (Ponnuru 2001). The Democrats could change the outcome by attempting to get these voters to the polls. However, such efforts may not succeed: disadvantaged groups are difficult to mobilize in any event, and strident appeals concerning inequality and expanded government may drive more affluent and white voters to be Republican in even larger numbers.

Table 14.7   Voting Rates by Relative Income and Racial Identity

| | Income Group[a] | | | Racial Identity[b] | | |
Decade	Bottom	Middle	Top	Hispanic	Black	White
1970s	38.6	46.2	59.1	28.9	46.1	54.0
1980s	38.7	54.2	61.8	28.2	50.8	55.7
1990s	38.6	51.5	61.7	23.4	44.1	51.4

[a]The data are from the NES cumulative file, 1948–2000.

[b]The data for 1970 through 1996 are from an October 17, 1997, release from the Bureau of the Census. Available from www.census.gov/population/socdemo/voting/history/vot01.txt (accessed December 2002).

There is no way to anticipate how these trends will evolve, and there is no simple answer as to which path each party should pursue. For this reason, congressional party leaders are engaged in a contentious debate on how to proceed. Each party has a plausible scenario for success and each faces serious risks. Watching how each party manages these tensions will be of great interest.

Notes

1. Karen M. Mills, "Congressional Apportionment," July 2001, U.S. Department of Commerce, Economics and Statistics Administration, U.S. Census Bureau, C2KBR/01-7, Washington, D.C., p. 2. The North includes Connecticut, Delaware, Illinois, Indiana, Maine, Maryland, Massachusetts, Michigan, Minnesota, New Hampshire, New Jersey, New York, Ohio, Pennsylvania, Rhode Island, Vermont, West Virginia, and Wisconsin. The South includes Alabama, Florida, Georgia, Kentucky, Louisiana, Mississippi, North Carolina, South Carolina, Tennessee, Texas, and Virginia. All others are in the "Other" category.

2. While the proportion of the population living in suburbs is widely discussed, there is not a simple process for calculating that proportion. The Bureau of the Census has no definition, and it does not provide a summary time series on the number of suburban residents. One approach is to take the Standard Metropolitan Statistical Area population and subtract the central city population; what remains should be the suburban population. The difficulty is whether to use one central city, or include as central cities all of the older municipalities. In addition, over time the definition of a metro area by the census has changed. Good discussions of this are contained in Drier, Mollenkopf, and Swanstrom 2001 and Gainsborough 2000.

3. The question is: "How much of the time do you think you can trust the government in Washington to do what is right—just about always, most of the time, or only some of the time?" This is defined as the percentage of people who chose "just about always" or "most of the time."

4. David W. Moore, "Little Change in Philosophy Among Rank-and-File Republicans in Past Eight Years," June 1 2000, www.gallup.com/poll/results (accessed December 2002).

5. Beginning in 1984 CBS, *New York Times* polls asked respondents of this survey if they had a favorable or unfavorable opinion of each party. From 1984 through 1991 the Republican Party generally received a 60 percent favorable and a 40 percent unfavorable rating. Beginning in 1992 their favorable rating dropped to around 50 and the unfavorable rating rose to 50 percent. By the 1996–1998 time period, when the federal government was shut down by a dispute over the budget and the Republicans voted to impeach President Clinton, their ratings had dropped to 40 percent favorable, and their unfavorable rating dropped to 50 percent.

6. As an example, see the Special Reports 92, 101, and 102 released by the Tax Foundation. See "Newest Data Show High-Income Taxpayers Earning and Paying More," at www.taxfoundation.org/prtopincome.html (accessed December 2002). This organization is conservative, but other studies confirm that most taxes are paid by the affluent. The difference is that liberals emphasize the distribution of income and the changes in burdens across time.

7. Wendy W. Simmons, "Majority of Americans Continue to Support Bush's Tax Cut Plan." Release of March 9, 2001, at www.gallup.com/poll/releases/pr010309.asp (accessed December 2002). David W. Moore, "No Change in Public Opinion on Desirability of Tax Cuts." Release of May 1, 2001, at www.gallup.com/poll/releases/pr010501.asp (accessed De-

cember 2002). Jeffrey M. Jones, "Americans Generally Satisfied with Tax Cut." Release of August 22, 2001, at www.gallup.com/poll/releases/pr010822.asp (accessed December 2002).

8. Data on current situation taken from Lisa Lollock, "The Foreign Born Population of the United States," March 2000, Current Population Reports, P20-534, U.S. Census Bureau, Washington, D.C., p. 1. Historical data are taken from information provided by the Immigration and Naturalization Service, "Total and Foreign-Born U.S. Population: 1900–1990," at www.ins.usdoj.gov (accessed December 2002).

9. Data taken from "We the American . . . Hispanics." U.S. Department of Commerce, Economics and Statistics Administration, Bureau of the Census, Washington, D.C. Issued September 1993, p. 4. The classification of an individual as nonwhite is based on his or her self-reported category. Since many Hispanics report themselves as white, reliance on the percentage of nonwhites understates the existence of blacks plus Hispanics in the population. If Hispanics who identify as white are added to nonwhites, and the total is classified as minority, the distribution for 2000 is 0–9 percent minority: 17.8 percent; 10–19 percent minority: 23.8 percent; 20–29 percent minority: 17.8 percent; and 30 percent minority or greater: 40.7 percent. This results in 58 percent of districts with 20 percent or more "minorities."

10. Current information from Melissa Therrien and Roberto R. Ramirez, "The Hispanic Population in the United States," March 2000, Current Population Reports, P20-535, U.S. Census Bureau, Washington, D.C., p. 1.

11. CNN Exit Poll, available at www.cnn.com/election/2000/results/index.epolls.html (accessed December 2002).

12. At the same time, there are conservatives who think their party is too moderate and that it needs to define itself as a serious conservative alternative, and that the greatest danger is that the party will become moderate and not mobilize conservatives. For example, see Crane 1999.

13. At the same time there are those who argue that the party is squandering its potential by being too moderate to appeal to and mobilize the less-affluent and nonwhite population of the society or becoming too clearly identified as a party of nonwhites. Liberals argue that the party has been too eager to moderate its positions and has lost its identity and ability to attract this new constituency (Kinsley 1981; Conniff 2000; Levison 2001).

15

The Unprecedented Senate: Political Parties in the Senate after the 2000 Election

Larry Schwab

In one of the most amazing elections in American history, the Republicans and Democrats tied with fifty seats apiece in the 2000 Senate race. After the election, the members of the Senate faced the difficult and historic challenge of performing their legislative functions in a chamber evenly divided between the two parties. Since the vice president may vote in the Senate on tie votes, the vote of Vice President Al Gore allowed the Democrats to control the Senate for a few days in January with Senator Tom Daschle (D-SD) as the Majority Leader. On January 20, Vice President Dick Cheney took office, and his vote shifted control of the Senate to the Republicans. They organized the chamber as the majority party with Senator Trent Lott (R-MS) reclaiming his position of Majority Leader. The Democrats, however, negotiated a deal with the Republicans that gave them more power than the minority party traditionally has in the Senate. This arrangement lasted until early June when Senator James Jeffords left the Republican Party to become an independent. His decision gave the Democrats a 50-49 advantage and control of the chamber. The Democrats organized the Senate as the majority party, with Daschle again taking the office of Majority Leader.

Three major predictions developed on what impact the close party division would have on legislative politics in the Senate. First, the "partisan thesis" suggested that the Senate would continue with little change in 2001 as the party leaders and the majority of each party opposed each other on many key issues. The assumption here is that the party division was already close in the 106th Congress (1999–2000), and thus an even split would not be much different than the previous situation. Also, the close division, according to this view, would put pressure on senators to stick with their party colleagues because of the many close votes along party lines. In addition, a vote of 60 senators for cloture is needed on many bills to stop filibusters. Therefore, if the goal is often 60 votes rather than 51, a shift in the majority party from 54 to 50 or 51 will have a limited impact on the power relationship between the two parties.

Second, the "bipartisan thesis" suggests that the party leaders and many other senators would come to realize that a bipartisan approach is the only way to avoid gridlock in a legislative body with an even or nearly even party split. The prediction was that the party leaders would be forced to seek compromises early on in the consideration of legislation if anything was to be accomplished. Indeed, the enactment of innovative rules suggested the possibility of regular bipartisan consultation.

Finally, several political analysts suggested a "moderate thesis": moderates in both parties would gain power in the Senate in 2001 (e.g., Nather and Bettelheim 2001). It was assumed that they would dominate in a legislative environment with a close party split because they are in the best position to form bipartisan coalitions on bills and are more likely to gain influence by voting, or threatening to vote, with the opposition party.

This chapter examines the impact of the close party division on the Senate political parties during 2001. In sum, the "unprecedented Senate" produced only a few significant and short-lived changes. With just a few exceptions, the partisan thesis best explains the behavior of the Senate. Although the moderates took the lead on a few bills, bipartisanship dominated the Senate for several weeks after the September 11 terrorist attack. Some new rules were adopted for a short period of time, but the Senate continued to reflect the underlying ideological divisions of its members.

Ideology and the Senate Parties

Overall, the 2000 election moved the Senate a little to the left, with the Democrats gaining four seats in the election. This small shift made little difference in the ideological balance between the Senate parties and the ideological factions within the parties. In this regard, the 2000 Senate was starkly different from the Senate of the 1950s and 1960s, but remarkably like the Senate of the 1980s and 1990s. (On ideology and the Senate political parties, see Smith 1993; Rae and Campbell 2001.)

In the 1950s and 1960s, Democratic senators were divided about evenly into liberals, moderates, and conservatives. In 1968, for example, there were 19 Democratic senators who rated as liberals on the Americans for Democratic Action (ADA) 100-point liberalism scale (between 76 and 100); 26 moderates (between 25 and 75), and 19 conservatives (0 to 24). During this period, the main ideological debate among Senate Democrats, as among Democratic leaders in general, was the debate between the conservative and liberal wings of the party on issues such as black civil rights and social welfare legislation. Most of the conservative Senate Democrats were Southerners.

By the 1980s and 1990s, the major ideological debate among Senate Democrats shifted to the differences between moderates and liberals as the conservative Southern wing disappeared. The South changed from electing mostly conservative and moderate Democrats to electing Republicans and moderate-to-liberal Democrats. Now, Senate Democrats rarely have ADA ratings below 50 (see table 15.1). For example, John Breaux (D-LA), one of the most conservative Senate Democrats, had only two ADA scores below 50 from 1991 to 2000.

During the 1950s and 1960s, the Senate Republicans were mainly conservatives, with a small minority of moderates and a few liberals. In 1968, for instance, 23 Senate Republicans had rated as conservatives on the ADA scales (0 to 24), 10 as moderates (25 to 75), and 3 as liberals (76 to 100). As of the 1980s and 1990s, Senate Republicans were even more dominated by conservatives. There were only a few moderates and no liberals. The shift toward more conservatives occurred primarily because of the increase in Southern Republicans.

The 2000 election produced a small increase in Senate liberals and moderates, and a small decline in conservatives.[1] In a shift to the left, five liberal Democrats (Nelson D-FL, Stabenow D-MI, Dayton D-MN, Carnahan D-MO, and Cantwell D-WA) replaced five conservative Republicans (Mack R-FL, Abraham R-MI, Grams R-MN, Ashcroft R-MO, and Gorton R-WA), respectively. Also, a moderate Democrat (Carper D-DE) replaced a moderate Republican (Roth R-DE). In a shift to the right, a liberal Democrat (Kerrey D-NE) was replaced by a moderate Democrat (Ben Nelson D-NE), and two liberal Democrats (Bryan D-NV and Robb D-VA) were replaced by two conservative Republicans (Ensign R-NV and Allen R-VA). So overall, the Senate gained a net of two liberal and two moderate Democrats.[2]

Tables 15.1 and 15.2 show that no Senate Democrat could be classified as a conservative. Most Senate Democrats had ADA scores in the 80s and 90s. The 2001 data indicates a slight shift in the moderate direction among Senate Democrats. The number of moderates increased from 6 to 10. The small moderate gains came from two sources. First, moderate senators Thomas Carper (D-DE) and Ben Nelson (D-NE) were elected in the 2000 election, and Zell Miller (D-GA) was reelected. Miller was appointed to the Senate in July of 2000 and thus was essentially a freshman in 2001. Second, several veteran Democratic senators (e.g., Baucus D-MT) had more moderate voting records in 2001 as compared to the previous year. Part of the reason for the more moderate Democratic voting was the votes on the tax cuts and the budget resolution. (On moderate Democratic senators, see Berke 2001b and Victor 2001b.)

The Senate Republicans had few changes. They remained an over-

Table 15.1 Senators' ADA Ratings in 2000 and 2001

		2000 ADA Score	2001 ADA Score			2000 ADA Score	2001 ADA Score
Alabama	Shelby (R)	0	5	Mississippi	Cochran (R)	0	15
	Sessions (R)	0	5		Lott (R)	5	0
Alaska	Stevens (R)	5	21	Missouri	Bond (R)	0	11
	Murkowski (R)	0	0		Ashcroft (R)	5	—
Arizona	McCain (R)	6	40		Carnahan (D)	—	85
	Kyl (R)	0	5	Montana	Baucus (D)	85	80
Arkansas	Hutchinson (R)	5	10		Burns (R)	5	10
	Lincoln (D)	70	85	Nebraska	Kerrey (D)	85	—
California	Feinstein (D)	74	85		Nelson (D)	—	70
	Boxer (D)	85	95		Hagel (R)	0	25
Colorado	Campbell (R)	0	16	Nevada	Reid (D)	90	100
	Allard (R)	0	5		Bryan (D)	90	—
Connecticut	Dodd (D)	95	95		Ensign (R)	—	20
	Lieberman (D)	83	95	New Hampshire	Smith (R)	10	5
Delaware	Roth (R)	20	—		Gregg (R)	0	0
	Carper (D)	—	90	New Jersey	Lautenberg (D)	90	—
	Biden (D)	80	100		Corzine (D)	—	100
Florida	Graham (D)	80	100		Torricelli (D)	75	90
	Mack (R)	5	—	New Mexico	Domenici (R)	0	11
	Nelson (D)	—	95		Bingaman (D)	85	95
Georgia	Coverdell (R)	0	—	New York	Moynihan (D)	85	—
	Miller (D)	—	35		Clinton (D)	—	95
	Cleland (D)	70	85		Schumer (D)	95	95
Hawaii	Inouye (D)	80	95	North Carolina	Helms (R)	5	0
	Akaka (D)	85	95		Edwards (D)	85	95
Idaho	Craig (R)	0	0	North Dakota	Conrad (D)	85	85
	Crapo (R)	0	10		Dorgan (D)	90	85
Illinois	Durbin (D)	95	95	Ohio	DeWine (R)	10	25
	Fitzgerald (R)	26	15		Voinovich (R)	10	15
Indiana	Lugar (R)	10	15	Oklahoma	Nickles (R)	0	10
	Bayh (D)	80	100		Inhofe (R)	5	10
Iowa	Grassley (R)	0	5	Oregon	Wyden (D)	90	95
	Harkin (D)	95	100		Smith (R)	10	25
Kansas	Brownback (R)	0	0	Pennsylvania	Specter (R)	40	40
	Roberts (R)	0	0		Santorum (R)	0	10
Kentucky	McConnell (R)	5	5	Rhode Island	Reed (D)	95	100
	Bunning (R)	5	0		Chafee (R)	70	65
Louisiana	Breaux (D)	50	55	South Carolina	Thurmond (R)	0	5
	Landrieu (D)	80	85		Hollings (D)	85	90
Maine	Snowe (R)	30	35	South Dakota	Daschle (D)	85	100
	Collins (R)	25	40		Johnson (D)	80	85
Maryland	Sarbanes (D)	95	95	Tennessee	Thompson (R)	0	20
	Mikulski (D)	95	95		Frist (R)	0	10
Massachusetts	Kennedy (D)	90	100	Texas	Gramm (R)	0	5
	Kerry (D)	90	95		Hutchison (R)	0	10
Michigan	Levin (D)	90	100	Utah	Hatch (R)	0	5
	Abraham (R)	5	—		Bennett (R)	5	5
	Stabenow (D)	—	100	Vermont	Leahy (D)	85	100
Minnesota	Wellstone (D)	100	100		Jeffords (R&I)	55	40
	Grams (R)	0	—	Virginia	Warner (R)	0	20
	Dayton (D)	—	100		Robb (D)	80	—
					Allen (R)	—	15

Table 15.1 (cont.)

Washington	Gorton (R)	5	—	Wisconsin	Kohl (D)	85	95
	Cantwell (D)	—	100		Feingold (D)	100	95
	Murray (D)	90	89	Wyoming	Thomas (R)	0	5
West Virginia	Byrd (D)	75	85		Enzi (R)	9	11
	Rockefeller (D)	85	100				

Source: Americans for Democratic Action.
Note: The ADA ratings were recalculated to take into account the times that senators did not vote.

whelmingly conservative group. The number of moderates remained the same, at eight, from 2000 to 2001. James Jeffords' departure from the party, however, reduced the total to seven. Olympia Snowe (ME), one of the Senate Republican moderates, said in a TV interview that being a Republican moderate is like being on the TV show *Survivor*. The other Republican moderates in 2001 were John McCain (AZ), Peter Fitzgerald (IL), Susan Collins (ME), Gordon Smith (OR), Arlen Specter (PA), and Lincoln Chafee (RI). Senator McCain was the only Senate Republican who substantially changed his/her voting pattern from 2000 to 2001. Although many reporters during the 2000 presidential nomination race portrayed McCain as a moderate, his voting record was generally conservative until 2001. His average ADA score during the 1991–2000 period was only 9. In 2001 he worked with Democrats on several high-profile issues and had an ADA score of 40. (On Senator McCain's ideological change, see Victor 2001c.)

Patterns of Legislative Politics

Under these conditions, what happened to legislative politics in the Senate? Table 15.3 presents data on Senate party unity votes as a percentage of the total votes from 1968 to 2001. Overall, partisan voting remained high in 2001, and especially before September 11 (for the year 55 percent of roll-call votes were party unity votes—64 percent before 9/11, 34 percent after 9/11). The percentage of party unity votes before the terrorist attack indicates that this period was one of the most partisan in the Senate during the past thirty years. This provides strong support for the partisan thesis. If the bipartisan or moderate thesis had prevailed in the Senate in 2001, the proportion of party-line votes would have declined considerably.

Table 15.4 reports the number of bipartisan roll-call votes (i.e., the majority of each party votes on the same side). If the bipartisan thesis holds, then the number of bipartisan floor votes should increase substantially. However, a comparison of the Senate votes in 1999 and 2001 (the first year of the 106th Congress compared to the first year of the 107th Congress) indicates that this did not occur. While the percentage of bipartisan votes was a

Table 15.2 Senators' Party Support Scores in 2000 and 2001

		2000	2001			2000	2001
Alabama	Shelby (R)	97	88	Mississippi	Cochran (R)	98	84
	Sessions (R)	97	95		Lott (R)	98	98
Alaska	Stevens (R)	92	88	Missouri	Bond (R)	96	94
	Murkowski (R)	99	94		Ashcroft (R)	94	—
Arizona	McCain (R)	83	67		Carnahan (D)	—	85
	Kyl (R)	99	98	Montana	Baucus (D)	88	67
Arkansas	Hutchinson (R)	95	88		Burns (R)	90	96
	Lincoln (D)	80	79	Nebraska	Kerrey (D)	83	—
California	Feinstein (D)	88	85		Nelson (D)	—	58
	Boxer (D)	100	98		Hagel (R)	94	92
Colorado	Campbell (R)	97	89	Nevada	Reid (D)	94	96
	Allard (R)	98	98		Bryan (D)	94	—
Connecticut	Dodd (D)	95	98		Ensign (R)	—	88
	Lieberman (D)	88	93	New Hampshire	Smith (R)	97	96
Delaware	Roth (R)	78	—		Gregg (R)	98	96
	Carper (D)	—	80	New Jersey	Lautenberg (D)	98	—
	Biden (D)	88	94		Corzine (D)	—	96
Florida	Graham (D)	91	94		Torricelli (D)	81	78
	Mack (R)	94	—	New Mexico	Domenici (R)	94	89
	Nelson (D)	—	92		Bingaman (D)	87	91
Georgia	Coverdell (R)	98	—	New York	Moynihan (D)	92	—
	Miller (D)	—	42		Clinton (D)	—	97
	Cleland (D)	84	78		Schumer (D)	97	94
Hawaii	Inouye (D)	91	98	North Carolina	Helms (R)	98	98
	Akaka (D)	98	98		Edwards (D)	94	91
Idaho	Craig (R)	100	96	North Dakota	Conrad (D)	87	90
	Crapo (R)	100	94		Dorgan (D)	98	91
Illinois	Durbin (D)	99	95	Ohio	DeWine (R)	86	83
	Fitzgerald (R)	81	79		Voinovich (R)	78	92
Indiana	Lugar (R)	86	92	Oklahoma	Nickles (R)	97	96
	Bayh (D)	92	82		Inhofe (R)	100	96
Iowa	Grassley (R)	94	93	Oregon	Wyden (D)	97	90
	Harkin (D)	97	97		Smith (R)	89	82
Kansas	Brownback (R)	98	94	Pennsylvania	Specter (R)	67	60
	Roberts (R)	97	95		Santorum (R)	96	95
Kentucky	McConnell (R)	99	98	Rhode Island	Reed (D)	97	99
	Bunning (R)	98	97		Chafee (R)	37	50
Louisiana	Breaux (D)	73	59	South Carolina	Thurmond (R)	98	98
	Landrieu (D)	88	81		Hollings (D)	90	95
Maine	Snowe (R)	71	64	South Dakota	Daschle (D)	93	98
	Collins (R)	74	67		Johnson (D)	91	87
Maryland	Sarbanes (D)	99	99	Tennessee	Thompson (R)	93	91
	Mikulski (D)	97	98		Frist (R)	95	97
Massachusetts	Kennedy (D)	98	97	Texas	Gramm (R)	97	96
	Kerry (D)	96	98		Hutchison (R)	96	90
Michigan	Levin (D)	97	98	Utah	Hatch (R)	94	95
	Abraham (R)	86	—		Bennett (R)	92	96
	Stabenow (D)	—	96	Vermont	Leahy (D)	94	98
Minnesota	Wellstone (D)	97	99		Jeffords (R)	55	61
	Grams (R)	96	—	Virginia	Warner (R)	92	85
	Dayton (D)	—	99		Robb (D)	93	—
					Allen (R)	—	93

Table 15.2   (cont.)

Washington	Gorton (R)	93	—	Wisconsin	Kohl (D)	87	89
	Cantwell (D)	—	98		Feingold (D)	92	89
	Murray (D)	94	96	Wyoming	Thomas (R)	97	97
West Virginia	Byrd (D)	72	86		Enzi (R)	97	95
	Rockefeller (D)	96	97				

Source: CQ Weekly, January 6, 2001 and January 12, 2002.

Note: The party support score of Senator James Jeffords is based on the votes he cast as a Republican. See endnote 1 for an explanation of numbers in this table.

little higher in 2001 than in 1999, the percentage before September 11 (36 percent) was the same as in 1999.

One way to test the moderate thesis is to examine the impact of moderates on the outcome of Senate floor votes. If the influence of Senate moderates expanded in 2001, there should have been a significant increase in the number of roll calls in which the winning party needed the votes of the other party's moderates to form a majority. For the analysis, the number of roll calls where the votes of moderates were needed was counted, and reported in table 15.4.[3]

Table 15.4 also provides very little support for the moderate thesis. The number of votes in which the winning party needed the votes of the other party's moderates increased from 14 to 43. This increase, however, represents a change of just 4 to 12 percent of the total vote. So while the moder-

Table 15.3   Senate Party Unity Votes as a Percentage of Total Votes, 1968–2001

Year	% of Party Unity Votes	Year	% of Party Unity Votes
1968	32	1985	50
1969	36	1986	52
1970	35	1987	41
1971	42	1988	42
1972	36	1989	35
1973	40	1990	54
1974	44	1991	49
1975	48	1992	53
1976	37	1993	67
1977	42	1994	52
1978	45	1995	69
1979	47	1996	62
1980	46	1997	50
1981	48	1998	56
1982	43	1999	63
1983	44	2000	49
1984	40	2001	55

Source: January 6, 2001, *CQ Weekly* for 1968–2000. January 12, 2002, *CQ Weekly* for 2001.

Table 15.4   1999 and 2001 Senate Bipartisan Roll-Call Votes and Roll-Call Votes in Which the Winning Party Needed the Votes of the Other Party's Moderates

	1999		2001	
	N	%	N	%
Bipartisan Votes	136	36	168	44
Winning Party Needed Votes from the Other Party's Moderates				
Democrat	3	1	21	6
Republican	11	3	22	6
Other Votes	224	60	169	45
Total	374	100	380	101

ates' influence did expand, the number of times the winning party needed the opposition party's moderates to win remained small in comparison to the total number of votes. Thus, in almost 90 percent of the Senate votes in 2001, the votes of the opposition party's moderates were not needed in the winning party's majority coalition.

Finally, it is useful to examine the Senate debate and votes in specific policy areas during 2001. Similar to the previous analysis, the results here support the partisan thesis on most of the issues, and coalitions of moderates rarely had a major impact. While bipartisanship developed in a few policy debates, it occurred mainly in areas that usually have been bipartisan in the past (e.g., presidential nominees and crisis management).

Most of the Senate roll-call votes before September 11 were on executive branch nominations, bankruptcy, tax cuts, campaign finance, education, patients' rights, and the budget. The votes after September 11 were primarily on antiterrorism, defense, farm programs, appropriations, and economic stimulus.

Moderate Republicans stayed with their party on President Bush's nominees. Republicans voted unanimously on most of the nominations. Also, many of these roll calls were bipartisan votes. In most cases, therefore, the support of moderate Democrats was not essential for the Republicans to win on these votes.

Voting patterns varied significantly on the votes on the bankruptcy bill. There were bipartisan votes, closely divided votes, votes with one party united and the other badly split, and votes with both parties badly split. Moderates did not play a major role in determining the outcome of the votes. In only one roll-call vote were the votes of the moderates of one party essential for the other party to form a majority.

Although all of the moderate Democrats voted for the budget resolution on the final vote for passage, the Republicans' 50-0 margin meant that they could have passed it without the Democrats' support. The Republicans also won several other key budget roll calls with unanimous party votes. There were only four votes on the budget resolution for which the winning party needed the votes of the opposition moderates.

Moderates influenced the outcome of the tax cut more than any other area of legislation. The opposition of Chafee and Jeffords prevented the Republicans from passing President Bush's $1.6 trillion tax cut package (Parks 2001a; Rosenbaum 2001). Then Republican and Democratic moderates, lead by Baucus and Breaux, played a big part in the negotiations that produced the final $1.35 trillion tax cut plan. Senate Republicans won some of the key tax cut roll calls with a 50-0 vote, but they needed the votes of moderate Democrats on several others.

However, even though moderate senators modified the Bush tax plan, it would be difficult to conclude that the moderates won out over the conservative Republicans. Most citizens and political commentators refer to the 2001 tax cut as the Bush tax cut or the Republican tax cut. They do not refer to it as the moderate Republican and Democratic tax cut. While President Bush and conservative congressional Republicans failed to achieve all they sought, they still passed a huge tax cut that contained many of the provisions in the original proposal. So while the Senate moderates had an important impact on the tax bill, their influence, if considered in this broad context, was limited.

The McCain-Feingold bill continued as the main focus of the campaign finance debate in the Senate. The coalition behind the bill had previously consisted of most of the Democrats and a few, mostly moderate, Republicans. In 2001, however, McCain and Feingold received additional support from several conservative Republican senators. The parties split 12-38 Republican and 47-3 Democratic on the final passage of the bill. For the Republicans, five conservatives (Stevens-AK, Cochran-MS, Thompson-TN, Lugar-IN, and Domenici-NM) joined the seven moderates. A wide variation in voting patterns occurred on the votes before the final passage of the campaign finance bill. The Democrats won three votes with the help of the moderate Republicans, while the Republicans won on two votes with the aid of the moderate Democrats. Several votes were bipartisan, and a few others followed the pattern similar to the final vote.

The Democrats had a high degree of unity on the patients' rights legislation and won all of the roll-call votes. On most of the roll calls, the Democrats had unanimous votes or only one or two defections. Because of their high unity and the consistent support of Senator Jeffords, who had become an independent by the time of the patients' rights debate, the Democrats needed the support of moderate Republicans on only four votes. Jeffords joined all of the Democrats (50-0) and nine Republicans in the final vote to pass the bill.

The patterns varied considerably on the education roll calls. These patterns included the parties voting together, one party united against the other

badly split, and the parties united against each other. With this wide variation, the winning party needed the support of the opposition party's moderates on only seven (four for the Republicans and three for the Democrats) of
the forty-five education votes.

The terrorist attack of September 11 produced a period of bipartisan policy making. While there was some disagreement on a few of the antiterrorism measures, most Republicans and Democrats agreed on the various bills.
Several of the key votes on terrorism and homeland security were unanimous.

Then several weeks after the September 11 terrorist attacks, the Senate
gradually shifted back to partisan politics. The debate on an economic stimulus package was one of the main factors in this change. Republicans and
Democrats strongly disagreed on proposals to help the economy recover
from the recession. Senators voted along party lines on the economic stimulus votes. The differences between the plans were so large that the congressional leaders and the White House were unable to come to a compromise
by the end of the year.

The Senate also took up the reauthorization of the farm program in the
last part of the 2001 session. There is much dissatisfaction with farm policy
but little agreement on what to do about it. This was reflected in the Senate
debate and the variety of voting patterns on the bill. The Democrats won
most of the votes because the Republicans were often badly split. However,
the Senate Republicans were able to extend the debate into 2002 by filibus-
tering the bill. The Democrats could not come up with the sixty votes for
cloture.

Finally, the Senate spent part of the last few weeks of the 2001 session
voting on appropriations bills and their conference reports. And as is often
the case on the final votes on appropriations, most of the votes were bipartisan.

Party Leaders

Except for the bipartisan approach on antiterrorism legislation, Senator
Daschle and Senator Lott maintained the leadership style and strategies they
had employed in the past. They continued to focus on developing a policy
agenda for their party and building majorities on bills by encouraging high
levels of unity among their party colleagues; this pattern supports the partisan thesis. They did not, as some political analysts predicted, focus on a
strategy of either courting the moderates (i.e., the moderate thesis) or seeking a bipartisan compromise at the beginning of the debate on an issue (i.e.,
the bipartisan thesis). This continuation of the partisan leadership strategy

can be seen in the following discussion about the leadership activities of Lott and Daschle in 2001.

Senator Lott had to develop a strategy for the negotiations on the rules for the 50-50 split and then a strategy on how to lead the Senate and his party colleagues during this period. Then, with the shift in party control in June, Lott had to plan for new negotiations on the rules relating the majority and minority and for his new role as leader of the minority. Senator Daschle, of course, had to decide on tactics for the same situations, except that he was working from the minority perspective in the first period and the majority in the second. (For background on the Senate leadership, see Matthews 1960, Peabody 1976, Loomis 2001, and Sinclair 2001.)

Daschle's strategy during the negotiation on the rules was to aim high by demanding a nearly equal share of power (e.g., cochairs on committees) and then compromising to possibly attain powers for the Democrats well beyond the usual minority position. He was in a strong bargaining position because some of the resolutions that are necessary to organize the Senate are subject to a filibuster. So Daschle threatened to hold up President Bush's appointees and the Republican agenda unless Lott met the Democrats' demands.

Lott's goals were to keep the Democrats' power under the organizational rules close to the usual minority situation and to get off to a quick start on the Republican appointments and agenda. In the end, he decided that it was more important to allow the Bush administration and the congressional Republicans to begin working on their policies as soon as possible rather than keeping the Senate Democrats from acquiring new powers. Although several Senate Republicans criticized Lott for giving away too much to the Democrats, none of them organized a challenge against the Lott-Daschle agreement (Taylor 2001a).

After the Democrats became the majority party, the two leaders had to decide how to approach the new situation. In a memo sent to Republicans on June 2, Senator Lott reacted angrily to Senator Jeffords' decision to leave the Republican Party and threatened to hold out for special considerations for the Republicans in the reorganization negotiations. However, within a few days he became much more conciliatory (Shenon 2001). Also, he did not attempt to tie up the Senate for a long period of time to gain extra concessions from the Democrats on the reorganization plan.

On strategy, he planned to use all of the powers available to the minority by utilizing many of the same tactics (e.g., loading the other party's bills with his party's amendments) the Democrats had used against the Republicans. He claimed, however, the Republicans would not be as obstructionist as the Democrats were in using these tactics (Kane 2001).

Senator Daschle promised that he would follow a bipartisan approach in leading the Senate by working closely with President Bush and the Senate

Republicans. He also claimed that he would allow more open and fair floor debates than the Republicans had provided the Democrats. The most important power he acquired as Majority Leader was the ability to control the Senate's floor agenda. This has allowed the Senate Democrats to shift the focus from the agendas of President Bush and the Senate Republicans to their agenda. For example, the passage of a patients' rights bill was one of the Democrats' main policy goals. So, soon after the change in party control in June, Daschle brought the patients' rights bill to the floor, and the Democrats passed it. (On Senator Daschle and the Senate Democratic takeover, see Clymer 2001; Lancaster 2001; Mitchell 2001; and Parks 2001b.)

Daschle's focus on the Democratic agenda abruptly ended on September 11. He shifted to a bipartisan approach as he worked closely with Senator Lott, President Bush, and the House leadership on terrorism and security issues. Then, toward the end of the year, Daschle gradually changed back to more Democratic issues by promoting policies such as the Democrats' economic stimulus package.

New Rules for the Majority and Minority

One of the few aspects of the Senate that significantly changed in 2001 was the new rules adopted during the 50-50 split to regulate the relationship between the majority and minority. However, when the Democrats took control in June, most of the rules changed back to what had been in place before the 50-50 split. The Senate Republicans and Democrats faced a rare situation in organizing the chamber after the 2000 election. Instead of one party clearly in the majority and the other the minority, both parties held an equal number of seats. Consequently, there was the question of whether the old rules would still be used, with key positions and powers given to the majority (i.e., the Republicans with the vice president's tie-breaking vote), or new rules more favorable to the minority would be developed. The agreement that was worked out gave the Democrats more power than usual for a minority party.

Before, the majority party members held the positions of majority leader, assistant majority leader (majority whip), committee chair, subcommittee chair, and the presiding senator during floor proceedings. Also, the majority party controlled the floor agenda, held the majority of seats on the committees, subcommittees, and conference committees, and had the larger share of committee staffs, committee budgets, and office space. Under the new plan, the Republicans retained all of the majority positions except the presiding senator during floor debate. The parties agreed to share that position. Each party received an equal number of seats on the standing committees. If committee members split evenly on a bill or nomination, the full Senate could vote to send it to the floor. The parties were also given equal staff and office space. In addition, limits were placed on the ability of senators to block amendments on the floor (Taylor 2001a).

With the shift to Democratic control and the 50-49-1 split, most of the rules changed back to the usual situation of a majority party in charge. The Democrats took over all of the top positions, and they were given a one-seat advantage on each committee. (On the shift in power to the Senate Democrats, see Allen and Marcus 2001; Alvarez 2001; Bettelheim 2001; Goldstein and Milbank 2001; Seelye 2001; Taylor 2001b; and Victor 2001b.)

Conclusion

In sum, the "unprecedented Senate" produced only a few significant and short-lived changes. The overall policy making process in the Senate generally remained the same. Contrary to the predictions of some analysts, neither the moderate nor bipartisan thesis was especially prominent. Thus, the partisan thesis best explains the behavior of the 107th Senate, which continued to operate as in the recent past with regard to roll-call votes, agenda setting, and coalition building. There were no significant changes in the party leaders' legislative strategies. However, new rules adopted during the period of Republican control did give the Democrats unprecedented power as the minority party. Also, the even party division created the opportunity for Senator Jeffords to shift party control by leaving his party. But besides these two developments, the close party split did not substantially change the Senate in 2001.

Notes

1. This analysis uses ADA ratings and party support scores to identify ideological factions among senators. The ADA rating is based on a few major votes, while the party support scores are computed from all of the votes during a year. Party support scores are based on the percentage of times members of Congress vote with their party in party unity (the majority of each party voting against each other) votes. Using the two indexes together provides a good measure of ideology. Liberal Democrats have high ADA ratings and high party support scores, and conservative Republicans have low ADA ratings and high party support scores. Moderate Republicans and Democrats have more moderate ADA ratings and party support scores.

2. Two other liberal Democrats (Corzine D-NJ and Clinton D-NY) replaced liberals in their party (Lautenberg D-NJ and Moynihan D-NY).

3. A "moderate needed" roll-call vote is one in which the winning party needs the votes of the opposition party's moderates to form a majority. Thus, the majority coalition consists of one party and the moderates of the other party. A comparison is made of the roll-call votes in 1999 and 2001. Senators are classified as moderates based on their ADA ratings and party support scores for 2001. The moderates in 2001 who were also in the Senate in 1999 are considered to be the moderates in 1999.

16

Taking Responsibility Seriously: Assessing Party Strength in the House of Representatives

R. Lawrence Butler

"I suggest that the United States is moving toward a system of parliamentary government, a fundamental change in our constitutional regime," asserts Gerald Pomper (1999, 251) in a recent essay that catalogues moves toward responsible party government in the United States. This bold argument is simultaneously provocative and plausible. Although Pomper's essay covers a wide range of topics, this chapter will investigate what is perhaps the least controversial aspect of this assertion—the claim that the legislative parties, particularly in the House of Representatives, are beginning to resemble those in parliamentary systems.

There is no doubt that the Republican and Democratic caucuses in the House have become more ideologically polarized and cohesive than in the past (Rohde 1991; Aldrich, Berger, and Rohde 1999). However, is that the same thing as saying that the parties are acting like parliamentary parties? The standard tools scholars use to discuss party strength give us evidence of the former, but cannot speak to the latter. To answer that question, we need to reexamine the critical elements of parliamentary parties and how such elements translate into the American system of separation of powers and checks and balances. Only then can we examine whether the legislative parties have been moving toward a parliamentary system, and whether such a trend is likely to continue.

A Model of Party Government in Legislatures

When we look for a model of the prototypical strong-party parliament, we naturally turn to the British House of Commons. This chamber meets all of the criteria mentioned by the advocates of "responsible party government" over the years (for example, Wilson 1885; Schattschneider 1942; Ranney 1954; Chambers and Burnham 1975). All members of parliament from a given party run on a unified platform that serves as the governing agenda for the Commons if that party achieves a majority. Majority party members agree to vote together as a bloc to ensure passage of the items in the platform, typically over the unified opposition of the minority party. As a result, voters get clearer information about the policy consequences of their vote choice and they know whom they should hold accountable for the result. Furthermore, policy making is more efficient because the Parliament will be enacting a coordinated agenda that does not lose its coherence in the give and take of legislative bargaining.

Pomper is not the only scholar to detect a movement toward stronger parties in the House over the past several decades. Rohde (1991) develops a model called "conditional party government" to explain this trend. He argues that conditional party government resulted from a change in the institutional relationship between the party leadership and followers in the U.S. Congress. The changes instituted in 1975 weakened the committee chairs by dispersing some of their powers to the subcommittees and giving the caucus a greater say in their selection. Party leaders were granted more responsibility for setting the party policy agenda, but mechanisms were created to require more consultation with the caucus in performing this duty. Thus, party government in the House under strong party leaders is conditioned on institutionalized consultation processes for the caucus. The party sticks together if all members have had a say in policy development.

With these as models for a strong party legislature, the current measures of party strength are understandable. The traditional method of "Party Voting Scores" (PVS) described by Brady, Cooper, and Hurley (1979) was the starting point for these endeavors. Other approaches focus more directly on voting unity among party members. The "Rice Index" calculates the average percentage of party members that vote together on roll-call votes (Rice 1928). A similar measure, the "Party Unity Score" (PUS), is published by *Congressional Quarterly.* Unlike the Rice Index, the PUS restricts the universe of votes for its tally to those defined as party votes (as is the case with the PVS). Pomper uses the PUS to demonstrate increased party cohesion in the Congress (1999, 260–263).

Each of these measures assesses the extent to which the House of Representatives resembles some aspect of the House of Commons. The PVS measures how frequently the parties disagree. The Rice Index and the PUS assess the extent of party unity on roll-call votes, which is the hallmark of parliamentary legislatures. Yet they all make the mistake of assessing how much the Congress exhibits the outward manifestations of parliamentary legislatures, rather than examining whether it displays the essential qualities of responsible party government.

What must the majority party in the House accomplish in order to achieve the accountability and coherence of responsible party government?

It does not need perfect unity or unwavering opposition as is frequently found in the House of Commons. Rather, these qualities exist when the majority is certain to win roll-call votes no matter what choices minority party members make. In short, the opposition party must be made *irrelevant* in responsible party government. We refer to this condition as "outcome certainty." Under outcome certainty, majority parties are strong not because they are *highly unified*, but because they are *unified enough* to ensure victory on a regular basis.

This insight suggests that threshold level should be applied to measures of party unity. Applying the threshold concept of outcome significantly changes the way we assess party strength. Instead of examining the amount of unity on the typical vote or the frequency of party conflict, we ask how often the majority party succeeds at making the opposition party irrelevant. Therefore, we can define majority party strength in the House of Representatives as the ability to achieve outcome certainty. When the majority party achieves this result, we say that it is engaging in "single party legislating." It is as if the majority party has caucused, agreed on a policy stance with enough internal support to guarantee its passage, and then marched out onto the floor to pass the party position.

To develop a measure of this phenomenon, we need to specify the conditions under which the roll call votes are consistent with a strategy of single party legislating. This situation occurs when the net majority party vote for its preferred outcome is greater than the total number of opposition party members casting votes on a given roll call (see the appendix of this chapter for details). Such a condition ensures that the majority party position will prevail no matter what the opposition party decides to do.

Applying this procedure to each roll-call vote forms the basis for a new measure of party strength—the Majority Party Strength (MPS) index. The MPS index is the ratio of the number of roll-call votes in a given Congress consistent with single party legislating the total number of roll-call votes. It thus calculates the ratio of votes for which the majority party has succeeded at guaranteeing the approval of its preferred outcome.

Majority Party Strength and the House

What does the MPS index tell us about the current state of the House of Representatives? Does the House resemble a parliamentary government, as Pomper suggests? Does Pomper's conclusion hold up if we use the MPS index as a measure of party strength? If not, what has caused party unity and party strength to diverge?

To answer these questions, we begin by comparing the value of the MPS index to the PVS and Rice Index. This comparison begins in 1887, the first year for which PVS was calculated (Brady, Cooper, and Hurley 1979), and continues to the present. We then take a closer look at the period since 1969 emphasized by Pomper. These comparisons will tell us if the MPS index suggests a different conclusion about parliamentary government in the modern House. To the extent that the measures do vary, we will use Butler's (2001) analysis of the causes of party strength to figure out why.

Figure 16.1 compares the MPS index with the Brady, Cooper, and Hurley's Party Strength (BCH) for Congresses since 1887.[1] If we look at the broad trends of the two indices, they run parallel to each other over most of the period covered. Both are high at the turn of the twentieth century when Speakers Reed and Cannon exercised czar-like control over the House, although the MPS index is more consistently high during that era. The indices then decline gradually before rising again toward the end of the century. There are two noteworthy differences between the indices. First, with the exception of the Reed/Cannon years, the MPS index shows much greater variation between Congresses. The BCH appears to reflect broad historical trends, whereas the MPS index shows large short-term fluctuations around the trend line. The second noteworthy difference occurs in the period from the late 1950s to the mid-1970s, in which the MPS index has turned upward while the BCH continues its decline.

Figure 16.1   Majority Party Strength Index and Brady, Cooper, and Hurley Party Strength Index, 1887–2001

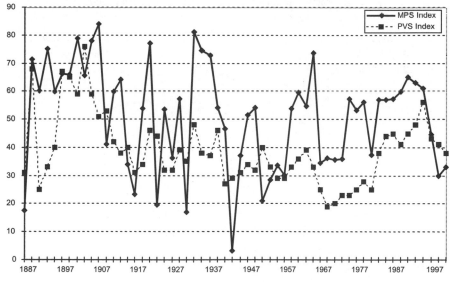

Congress (Year Beginning)

Figure 16.2 compares the MPS index with the Rice Index for the period after 1968 examined by Pomper (1999). The MPS index suggests that party strength declined slightly between 1993 and 1996, and then plummeted thereafter. By contrast, the Rice Index (which is a modest variation of the PUS used by Pomper) continues moving upward. Thus, the MPS index is consistent with Pomper's conclusion of growing parliamentary government from 1969 to 1992, but contradicts it thereafter.

What could have caused these changes and deviations? Butler (2001) develops a model to explain the level of the MPS for all Congresses since 1789. It finds that six independent variables explain 73 percent of the variation of the index from its mean. These six variables are 1) the extent of ideological polarization in the House, 2) the size of the majority party coalition, 3) the institution of the Reed Rules in 1890, 4) the recent election of a new president of the same party as the House majority, 5) a dummy variable representing Democratic Congresses after 1958, and 6) which party has the House majority.[2]

Do these variables explain the large drop in party strength that began in 1993? Figure 16.3 presents the MPS index and its value as predicted by the model above for Congresses beginning in 1969. The predicted and actual MPS values are very close for most Congresses. Unfortunately, that has seldom been the case since the 1994 election. The switch in party control in

Figure 16.2   Majority Party Strength Index and Rice Index, 1969–2001

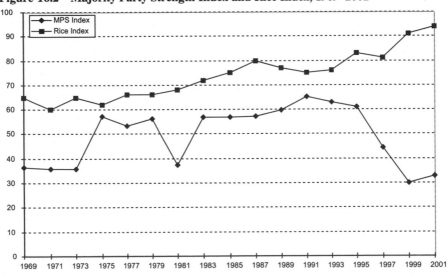

Congress (Year Beginning)

Figure 16.3   Actual and Predicted Majority Party Strength Index, 1969–2001

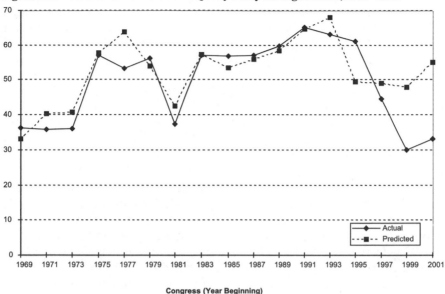

Congress (Year Beginning)

1995 from Democrat to Republican, along with the substantially smaller size of the majority party caucus, leads the model to predict a dramatic drop in the MPS index. The model predicts small declines between 1997 and 2000, resulting from the shrinking majority size and the increased ideological polarization of the House. The election of George W. Bush in 2000 causes a slight uptick in the predicted level for 2001. But instead, the actual MPS index values showed a very modest decline in 1995 before falling sharply in the two following Congresses, which, combined, yield a larger than expected drop. And the rise in 2001 after President Bush took office is smaller than predicted. Consequently, the model dramatically underestimates the value of the MPS index for the 104th Congress, and dramatically overestimates it for the 106th and 107th Congresses. The model does not, therefore, fully explain why party strength has fallen so sharply since 1996.

Party Government at the Turn of a New Century

Why did the MPS index in the House drop so dramatically during the 1990s? Our model can provide part of the answer. Large Democratic Party majorities transformed into narrow Republican ones. Because of the narrow majorities, the Republicans needed extremely high unity in order to engage in single-party legislating. Thus, even though the Rice Index has risen to a level of 94 percent, Republicans have not been consistently unified enough to obtain a high value of the MPS index. Most of the time, Speaker Hastert has had to rely on the support of Democratic members of Congress in order to win roll-call votes. Thus, we conclude that the level of party strength has declined dramatically in the 1990s.

However, these factors are not sufficient to explain the decline. The MPS index remained unexpectedly high in the first Republican-controlled Congress (the 104th), but fell to the predicted level for the second (105th). Yet, the steep decline continued once Speaker Hastert took the gavel, reaching levels more than twenty points below expectations. What other factors could have caused such a decline?

One possible hypothesis is that the unique events surrounding the passing of the torch from Speaker Newt Gingrich (R-GA) to Dennis Hastert (R-IL) has temporarily sidetracked the movement toward parliamentary government in the House. By the time of Gingrich's departure from the House after the 1998 elections, he had lost the confidence of his caucus. Many members felt that they had set aside their own beliefs and followed his lead for "the good of the party" and all they had gotten for it was a smaller majority. It is likely that, had Gingrich not resigned, the caucus would have voted him out of the Speaker's chair. Thus, despite institutional changes that empowered party leaders at the expense of the backbenchers, the rank and file demonstrated that they had retained the ultimate power to select their leaders.

Speaker Hastert brought an abrupt change in leadership style after the 1998 election. He focused more on building bipartisan coalitions to pass legislation than have his recent predecessors. In his floor speech upon receiving the Speaker's gavel, Hastert pledged, "I'm going to meet the Democratic leadership and the Democratic Caucus halfway, and I expect them to come halfway to meet me" (Eilperin 1999). If one looks at the House agenda in 2001, it becomes apparent that Hastert has generally proceeded without a fully unified caucus. Tax cuts and the president's Faith-Based Initiative were about the only major pieces of legislation in that year on which the Republican caucus was virtually unanimous. On issues like education reform, the energy bill, the farm bill, and the annual appropriations, Democratic votes were required for passage. Moreover, 2001 showed a marked increase in the percentage of votes taken under Suspension of the Rules. In previous Congresses, fewer than 20 percent of votes required a supermajority for passage. In 2001, 28 percent did. Together, these suggest that Hastert has relied much less on single party legislating than have his recent predecessors.

It is possible, therefore, that the last few Congresses have been an historical anomaly. The Republican caucus felt betrayed by its leadership and was unwilling to entrust it with that much power. Consequently, it elected a Speaker that was more of a consensus builder. Moreover, the size of the majority shrank so much that Single Party Legislating became much more difficult. If so, we can expect Pomper's march toward parliamentary government in the House to resume once confidence in the leadership and larger majorities is restored.

Nonetheless, we must consider the possibility that the era of conditional party government is over. If so, it is also likely that we are no longer headed toward parliamentary government. For this pattern to be the case, we must be at the beginning of institutional changes that have undone or superseded those that launched conditional party government. Let us examine the changes in how the House operates that were brought about in the 1990s to see if any fit this description.

When Gingrich became Speaker, he instituted several changes that affected the power relationship between legislators, committee chairs, and party leaders. These measures enhanced the power of the committee chairs and the party leaders at the expense of the backbenchers. First of all, Gingrich sidestepped the seniority system for selecting committee chairs by reaching down the roster to pick leaders who he thought would be more aggressive in advancing the party agenda. The most notable such selection was his choice of Bob Livingston (R-LA), the fourth-most senior member of the Appropriations Committee, to be its new chair. He also gave the committee chairs greater control over their committees by abolishing the Subcommittee Bill of Rights.[3] However, the caucus also imposed six-year term limits on committee chairs to keep individuals from amassing too much legislative power. Moreover, Gingrich frequently bypassed the committee chairs by creating task forces to develop legislation on issues of great political importance to the party. These changes clearly weakened the caucus and strengthened the party leaders, but their impact on committee chairs was mixed.

Hastert undid some of the structural reforms but kept most of them. Gone were the multiple task forces to prepare legislation. Nonetheless, Hastert enforced term limits on committee chairs and continued the practice of sometimes ignoring seniority in their selection. If we look at the Gingrich/Hastert institutional changes in the aggregate, they represent a partial rollback of conditional party government. Power has shifted back from the rank and file to the committee chairs, but the chairs have to exercise that power under closer scrutiny of the party leaders. These changes have strengthened party leaders while loosening the strings of accountability. This could have led to the unwillingness of the backbenchers to follow their leaders after a series of mishaps and electoral defeats. By removing the institutional structures that constituted the "conditions" of conditional party government, Gingrich and Hastert may have inadvertently precluded party leaders from being able to gain the confidence of the caucus required for parliamentary government.

If this hypothesis turns out to be true, it would cause major problems for

Pomper's claim about the shift toward parliamentary government. Pomper would have drawn accurate conclusions from the data available at the time. However, he would have reached his conclusion and projected its future development just as the strong-party era was drawing to a close. If, on the other hand, the Democrats restore conditional party government when they next take power and the MPS index rises accordingly, we may find that the trend toward parliamentary government has returned to the House of Representatives.

Conclusion

Pomper (1999) asks precisely the right question. To what extent is the House of Representatives acting like a parliament? If we are to understand party strength in the House, this is exactly how we need to think about it. Despite the fact that the United States has a system of separated powers with checks and balances, it is possible for its institutions of government to act like those in a parliamentary government by exhibiting responsible party government.

Unfortunately, the most common measures of party strength do not speak to Pomper's question. Rather, they measure partisanship in the chamber or the unity of the majority party. These are not the same concepts. Party strength is not the same thing as partisanship or party unity. In contrast, the MPS index, with its focus on outcome certainty and single party legislating, can tell us how frequently the majority party in the House acts like the majority party in a parliamentary system.

The MPS index leads to somewhat different conclusions: through 1996, the MPS index is largely consistent with Pomper's (1999) conclusion that the House was acting increasingly like a parliamentary government. However, the following years show a dramatically different trend. The MPS index drops rapidly after 1996 to levels not seen in decades. Are we therefore to conclude that Pomper discovered a trend toward party governance just as it was drawing to a close? At this point, we cannot be sure. Perhaps we are seeing a minor detour caused by the unusual circumstances surrounding the fall of Speaker Gingrich and the rise of Speaker Hastert. Perhaps the House will return shortly to its path toward parliamentary government. But it is possible that the move toward stronger congressional parties, and responsible party government, has run its course and we have entered a new weak party era.

Notes

The Dirksen Congressional Center and the Caterpillar Foundation provided some of the funding for this project.

1. Data for the 107th Congress represent only those votes cast during the first session—calendar year 2001. BCH equals the product of PVS and the Rice Index.

2. The last two variables result from an adjustment of the date for the onset of conditional party government, from 1975 to 1959, and suggest that it was purely a Democratic Party phenomenon. For a full discussion and justification, see Butler 2001.

3. The Subcommittee Bill of Rights, enacted in 1975, expanded the number of subcommittees and enhanced the autonomy of the subcommittee chairs by, among other things, allowing them to choose their own staff. In 1995, Gingrich reduced the number of subcommittees and gave full committee chairs the option of hiring all subcommittee staff.

Appendix

The Majority Party Strength (MPS) index equals the percentage of votes on which the majority party acts as if it is engaging in single party legislating. Single party legislating—the act of making opposition party members irrelevant to the outcome of the vote—occurs on any roll call that meets the following conditions:

$$\text{For } M_Y > M_N: \qquad M_Y - M_N > O_v \qquad\qquad (1)$$
$$\text{For } M_N \geq M_Y: \qquad M_N - M_Y \geq O_v \qquad\qquad (1')$$

where M_Y is the number of majority party members voting yes, M_N is the number of majority party members voting no, and O_v is the number of members in the opposition party or parties voting on a given roll call. In this model, we consider independents and members of third parties to be part of the opposition even if they are ideologically compatible with the majority party. The fact that such members are unwilling to formally side with the majority party suggests that the party leadership does not have complete leverage over them.

For roll-call votes taken under suspension of the rules or other procedures requiring a two-thirds margin for passage, the equations would be:

$$\text{For } M_Y > M_N: \qquad M_Y - 2{*}M_N > 2{*}O_v \qquad\qquad (2)$$
$$\text{For } M_N \geq M_Y: \qquad 2{*}M_N - M_Y \geq O_v \qquad\qquad (2')$$

On any roll-call vote that meets these conditions, the majority party is acting as if it were engaging in single party legislating.

Part Five

Party Responsibility

17

Parliamentary Government in the United States: A New Regime for a New Century?

Gerald M. Pomper

American life has been transformed by the terrorist attacks of September 11, 2001. As of this writing, the nation is at war, and has rallied behind the administration of George W. Bush. In this time of crisis, the most remarkable feature of domestic political life may be the persistence of trends in the party system. Note the following developments in the first year of the new century.

Despite his controversial selection with a minority of the popular vote, the new president attempted to implement his campaign program and platform as if he had an electoral mandate. His greatest domestic success came on his tax program. His proposal for large cuts tilted toward high-income groups followed his party platform and his own campaign promises. Although it never gained majority support in opinion polls, it was passed with relatively little change by cohesive Republican roll calls in Congress. The president had less success in another area, environmental policy. The Bush program generally supported the interests of energy producers, consistent with previous positions. It drew its strongest criticism, however, when it abandoned a different promise, which called for restriction of emissions of carbon dioxide, the most evident source of global warning (Jehl 2001).

The greatest political failure of Bush was the defection of Republican Senator James Jeffords, which shifted control of the Senate to the Democrats. Citing a series of policy disagreements with Bush and the Republican Party to justify his move, Jeffords declared, "It is only natural to expect that people like myself, who have been honored with positions of leadership, will largely support the president's agenda. And yet, more and more, I find I cannot" (Alvarez 2001a).

These incidents alert us to a major shift in the character of American politics. In pushing his program, without benefit of a popular majority, Bush has acted like a parliamentary leader. In criticizing Bush for abandoning his promise on global warning, critics are relying on the standards of policy commitment expected of parliamentary leaders. In defecting from the Republicans on grounds of policy disagreement, Jeffords casts parties as policy-oriented parliamentary parties.

These events reflect the argument of this chapter. To baldly summarize its thesis, I contend that the United States is moving toward a system of parliamentary government, a fundamental change in our constitutional regime. This change is not a total revolution in our institutions, and it will remain incomplete, given the drag of historical tradition. Still, it is my forecast of our future politics in the new century.

Institutional change is not necessarily reflected by formal change in the written (capital letter "C") Constitution. For example, in formal terms, the president is not chosen until the Electoral College meets in December, although—with rare exceptions like the 2000 election—we know the outcome within hours of the closing of the polls in early November. In parliamentary governments as well, reality may be different from formal appearance. In Great Britain, it is still formally true that the Queen has the final say on legislation, although in fact no law has been vetoed by a British monarch in three hundred years.

The British example leads us to examine the meaning of parliamentary government. The parliamentary model is evident in both empirical and normative political science. Anthony Downs begins his classic work by defining a political party virtually as a parliamentary coalition, "a team of men seeking to control the governing apparatus by gaining office in a duly constituted election" (Downs 1957, 25). Normatively, for decades some political scientists have sought to create a "responsible party system" (Committee on Political Parties 1950), resembling such parliamentary features as binding party programs and legislative cohesion.

The United States, I believe, is moving in this direction, toward a more parliamentary system. This trend can be seen if we look beyond the formal definition of such governments, the union of legislature and executive. Instead, let us go beyond "literary theory" and compare the present reality of United States politics to more general characteristics attributed to parliamentary systems.[1] In the ideal parliamentary model, elections are contests between competitive parties presenting alternative programs, under leaders chosen from and by the parties' legislators or activists. Electoral success is interpreted as a popular mandate in support of these platforms. Using their parliamentary powers, the leaders then enforce party discipline to implement the promised programs.

Significant trends toward parliamentary government can be seen in six aspects of American politics:

- The content of party programs;
- Parallel development of presidential and congressional party programs;

- Enactment of party programs;
- Cohesion within Congress and party elites;
- Strengthening of the national political party organizations; and
- The choice of presidential candidates.[2]

Party Programs

A parliamentary system provides the opportunity to enact party programs. By contrast, in the American system, observers often have doubted that there were party programs, and the multiple checks and balances of American government have made it difficult to enact any coherent policies. To look for evidence, I examine the major party platforms of the party winning the White House from 1992 to 2000, as well as the 1994 Republican "Contract with America" and the 1996 Democratic "Families First Agenda."

In previous research (Pomper and Lederman 1980, chapter 7 and 8), we argued that party platforms were meaningful statements and that they were good forecasts of government policy. We found, contrary to cynical belief, that platforms comprised far more than hot air and empty promises. Rather, a majority of the platforms were relevant defenses and criticisms of the parties' past records and reasonably specific promises of future actions. Moreover, the parties delivered: Close to 70 percent of their many specific pledges were actually fulfilled to some degree.

Furthermore, parties have differed in their programs. Examining party manifestos in the major industrial democracies over forty years, Budge concludes: "American Democrats and Republicans . . . consistently differentiate themselves from each other on such matters as support for welfare, government intervention, foreign aid, and defense, individual initiative and freedom. . . . Indeed, they remain as far apart as many European parties on these points, and more so than many" (Budge 1993, 696).

In recent years, we might expect platforms to be less important. National conventions have become television exercises rather than occasions for party decision making. The expansion of interest groups has made it more difficult to accomplish policy intentions. Candidate-centered campaigning reduces the incentives to achieve collective party goals, and appears to focus more on individual characteristics than on policy issues.

The party platforms of 1992–2000 provide a test.[3] An independent replication confirms our previous research on platform content. Perhaps surprisingly, this new work indicates that the most recent platforms, like those of previous years, provide significant political and policy statements. These manifestos meet one of the tests of a parliamentary system: meaningful party programs.

The platforms can be divided into three overall categories: puff pieces of rhetoric and fact; approval of the policy record and candidates of one's own party; and pledges for future action. The pledges, in turn, can be categorized as being vague rhetorical or general promises, or more useful statements of future intentions, such as promises to continue existing policies, expressions of party goals, pledges of action, or quite detailed proposals.[4]

As seen in figure 17.1, there is much in the platforms that induces yawns and cynicism. Both parties provide examples every year. In 1992, for example, the Democrats were fond of such rhetorical statements as "It is time to listen to the grassroots of America" (actually a difficult task, since most plants are speechless). The Republicans were prone to vague self-congratulation, as when they boasted, "Republicans recognize the importance of having fathers and mothers in the home." (Possibly even more so if these parents are unemployed, and not distracted by jobs?)

Nevertheless, the platforms—while hardly models of rational discussion—do provide useful guides to party positions. They tell voters what the parties like and dislike about the past and present, and what they intend to do in the future. The platforms of 2000, for example, show differences in future intentions between Democrats and Republicans on a vast range of issues, including abortion, taxes, education, health care, social security, and nuclear arms testing. On health insurance, illustratively, Republicans promised to broaden health insurance coverage through individual, tax-favored medical savings accounts. Democrats pledged "efforts to bring the uninsured into coverage step-by-step" and that they would "guarantee access to affordable health care for every child."

Figure 17.1   Content of Winning Party Platforms, 1992–2000

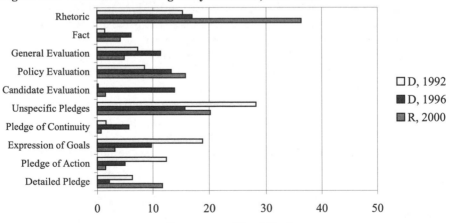

Percentage of Total Platform

These programs show a familiar and continuing difference between the two parties. When Democrats see a social problem, their first instinct is to find a solution through government action. When Republicans see the same problem, their first instinct is to look for some remedy in the private economy. That philosophical difference is evident even in the most intimate matters of sex. When dealing with teenage pregnancy, Republicans would foster private action (or, actually, inaction) by promoting abstinence education, while Democrats were more favorable to government action, such as distribution of condoms in schools.

Overall, from one-third to one-half of each winning party's platform was potentially useful to the voters in learning its intended policies.[5] The 1994 Republican "Contract with America" was even more specific. It consisted entirely of promises for the future, potentially focusing attention on public policy. Pledges of definite action comprised 42 percent of the total document, and detailed pledges another 27 percent. The national Republican platform of 2000 was quite different, with unspecific rhetoric comprising 36 percent of its content. This vacuity was compensated for to some extent by its length, over a hundred pages, and by extensive evaluations of past policies and a reasonable percentage of detailed pledges. There is more than enough specificity in these party manifestos to facilitate party accountability to the electorate.

Party as Programmatic Bridge

The great obstacle to party responsibility in the United States has always been the separation of powers, the constitutional division between the executive and legislative branches. Political parties have sometimes been praised as a bridge across this separation (Ford 1914), and party reformers have often sought to build stronger institutional ties, even seeking radical constitutional revision to further the goal (Ranney 1954). Despite these hopes and plans, however, the separation has remained. Presidential parties make promises, but Congress has no institutional responsibility to act on these pledges.

In a parliamentary system, current research argues—contrary to Downs—"that office is used as a basis for attaining policy goals, rather than that policy is subordinated to office" (Budge and Keman 1990, 31, chapter 2). In the United States as well, party program rather than institutional discipline may provide the bridge between the legislature and its executive. In previous years, however, we lacked a ready means to compare presidential and congressional programs.

That separation was closed, at least for a time, during the first Clinton administration. For this period, although not later, we had authoritative statements from both institutionalized wings of the parties. In Congress, both parties issued detailed programmatic statements, which we can compare to the national platforms of the presidential candidates.

The Republican "Contract with America" in 1994 marked a major first step toward coherent interinstitutional programs. The Contract with America was far more than a campaign gimmick or an aberrational invention of Newt Gingrich. It was actually a terse condensation of continuing Republican party doctrine, as can be seen in the left-hand columns of table 17.1, a comparison of its specific pledges with the 1992 and 1996 Republican platforms. A majority of these promises had already been anticipated in 1992, and the party endorsed five-sixths of its provisions in 1996.

For example, the 1992 national platform criticized the Democratic Congress for its refusal "to give the President a line-item veto to curb their self-serving pork-barrel projects" and promised adoption of the procedure in a Republican Congress. The 1994 Contract with America reiterated the pledge of a "line-item veto to restore fiscal responsibility to an out-of-control Congress," while the 1996 platform reiterated that "A Republican president will fight wasteful spending with the line-item veto which was finally enacted by congressional Republicans this year over bitter Democrat opposition."[6] Republicans built on traditional party doctrine, specified the current party program, and then affirmed accountability for their actions.

The Democrats imitatively developed a congressional program, the Families First Agenda, for the 1996 election. Intended primarily as a campaign document by the minority party, it was less specific than the Republican Contract with America. Still, 90 of its 204 statements were reasonably precise promises. The legislative Democrats also showed significant and increasing agreement with their presidential wing and platform. By 1996, as detailed in the right-hand columns of table 17.1, three-fourths of the congressional Families First Agenda was also incorporated into the Clinton platform, which also specifically praised the congressional program. Its three sections—"security," "opportunity," and "responsibility"—paralleled

Table 17.1   Inclusion of Congressional Pledges in National Party Platforms

	Republican "Contract" (N=42) Party Platform of		Democratic "Agenda" (N=90) Party Platform of	
	1992	1996	1992	1996
Mentioned only	5 (12%)	3 (7%)	5 (6%)	1 (1%)
Took credit	2 (5%)	16 (38%)	0 (0%)	16 (18%)
Future promise	16 (38%)	16 (38%)	36 (40%)	48 (53%)
No mention	19 (45%)	7 (17%)	49 (54%)	25 (28%)

those of the national platform (which added "freedom," "peace," and "community," values presumably shared by congressional Democrats), and many provisions are replicated from one document to another.

The Republican Contract with America and the Democratic Families First Agenda, then, can be seen as emblems of party responsibility and likely precedents for further development toward parliamentary practice in American politics. Institutional cooperation has also been furthered by shared electoral constituencies: in 2000, the number of congressional districts (86) that "split the ticket" in the presidential and House races was at the lowest point in nearly fifty years. Party doctrine and partisan voting have built bridges across the separation of powers.

Program Fulfillment

Both Democrats and Republicans, as they held power, followed through on their election promises, as expected in a parliamentary model. With remarkable consistency in the results, about 70 percent of policy promises have been fulfilled in one manner or another. Both Democrats and Republicans have achieved this level of fidelity throughout the period from 1992 to the present, as illustrated in figures 17.2, 17.3, and 17.4.

The record begins with the 1992 Democratic platform. Despite the clumsiness of the first Clinton administration, and despite the Democrats' loss of their long-term control of Congress in their catastrophic election defeat in 1994, they actually fulfilled most of the 167 reasonably specific pledges in their manifesto.

A few examples illustrate the point. The Democrats promised negative action, in opposing major change in the Clean Air Act—and they delivered. In their 1993 economic program, the Democrats won action similar to their platform pledge to "make the rich pay their fair share in taxes." Through

Figure 17.2   Platform Fulfillment in First Clinton Administration

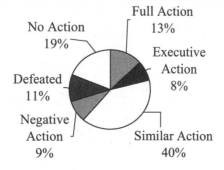

Figure 17.3   Platform Fulfillment in Second Clinton Administration

executive action, the Clinton administration redeemed its promise to reduce U.S. military forces in Europe. The Democrats achieved full action on their platform promise of "a reasonable waiting period to permit background checks for purchases of handguns."

To be sure, the Democrats did not become latter-day George Washingtons, unable to tell an untruth. There was no action on the pledge to "limit overall campaign spending and . . . the disproportionate and excessive role of PACs." In other cases, the Democrats did try, but were defeated, most notably in their platform promise of "reform of the health-care system to control costs and make health care affordable."

Most impressive are not the failures, but the achievements, illustrated in figure 17.2. Altogether, Democrats did accomplish something on nearly 70 percent of their 1992 promises, in contrast to inaction on only 19 percent. In a completely independent analysis, another researcher came to remarkably similar conclusions, calculating Clinton's fulfillment of his campaign prom-

Figure 17.4   Platform Fulfillment in G. W. Bush Administration

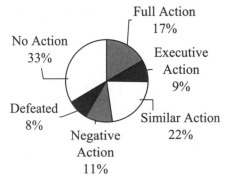

ises at the same level, 69 percent (Shaw 1996).[7] I do not believe this record is the result of the virtues of the Democratic Party, nor can this record be explained by Bill Clinton's personal qualities of steadfast commitment to principle. The cause is that we now have a system in which parties, whatever their names or leaders, make and keep promises.

This conclusion is strengthened if we examine the Republicans. While the GOP of course did not hold the presidency at the time, it did win control of Congress in 1994. In keeping with the model of parliamentary government, Republicans interpreted their impressive victory as an endorsement of their Contract with America, and then attempted to implement the program. We must remember that the 1994 election cannot be seen as a popular mandate for the Republican manifesto: two-thirds of the public had not even heard of it in November, and only 19 percent expressed support. The Contract with America expressed party ideology, not voter demands.

Despite its extravagant tone and ideological character, the Republicans delivered on their Contract with America, just as Democrats fulfilled much of their 1992 platform. Of the more specific pledges, 69 percent were accomplished in large measure (coincidentally, perhaps, the same success rate as the Democrats). On the general range of American government, as encapsulated in their advocacy of a balanced budget, they won the greatest victory of all: They set the agenda for the United States, and the Democratic president eventually followed their lead. Such initiative is what we would expect in a parliamentary system.

Platform fulfillment continued in the second Clinton administration. Despite Republican control of Congress, and even in the face of the Lewinsky scandal and Clinton's impeachment, some action was taken in the first two years of Clinton's second term on about 70 percent of the party pledges, as seen in figure 17.3. This measure of achievement was similar to the fulfillment record of previous years. However, the achievements tended to be only partial successes: not full action on platform pledges, but more of the character of executive actions, compromises, and fulfillment of negative pledges.

At this writing, the second Bush administration has had only a year in office since its controversial selection. Nevertheless, it has already achieved a large measure of platform fulfillment, as seen in figure 17.4. Using somewhat different standards to adjust for the short tenure of the Republican return to power, we see a similar degree of achievement, much of it even before the terrorist attacks.[8] Nearly three-fifths of the party's specific pledges of 2000 have been accomplished, including an unusually strong performance in legislative achievement. Illustratively, the Bush administration fully achieved its promise to cut the highest income tax rates, took executive action to reduce Occupational Safety and Health Administration (OSHA) regulations, and opposed national registration of firearms.[9] There surely will be further fulfillment in the coming years, particularly on issues related to national defense.

The parties' performance on their various sets of pledges also carries significant implications for the theory of political parties. Overall, the implementation of party programs lends support to a "cleavage" model developed by Page (1978), in which the parties "offer ideologically distinct positions . . . on those issues which have historically divided the parties and are related to support from voting blocs and interest groups" (Monroe and Bernardoni 1995, 2). This model fits well with that developed through the Manifestos Research Project, comparing party programs across Western democracies. In this model, "what parties offer electors thus seems to be a choice between selective policy agendas, not between specific alternative policies addressed to items on a universal agenda" (Klingemann, Hofferbert, and Budge 1994, 25).

Party Cohesion

Program fulfillment results from party unity. The overall trend in Congress, as expected in a parliamentary system, is toward more party differentiation.[10] One indicator is the proportion of legislative votes in which a majority of one party is opposed to a majority of the other—that is, "party unity" votes. Not too long ago, in 1969, such party conflict was evident only on about over one-third of all roll calls. By 1995, nearly three-fourths of House votes, and over two-thirds of Senate roll calls, showed these clear party differences. Partisan division declined somewhat after this high water mark, but was still evident on nearly one-half of the roll calls during the second Clinton term, and has continued into the Bush administration.

Figure 17.5 shows the increasing commitment of representatives and senators to their parties. The average legislator showed party loyalty (expressed as a "party unity score") of less than 60 percent in 1970. By 1996, the degree of loyalty had climbed to 80 percent for Democrats, and to an astounding 87 percent for Republicans. Party discipline in Congress continued through the first year of the current Bush presidency. On the first nine critical votes in the House, an average of only two Republicans dissented on each roll call. This unity, in circumstances of close party division, brought Bush victory on such issues as health care, energy, and taxes. Neither the British House of Commons nor the erstwhile Supreme Soviet could rival this record of party unity.

The congressional parties now are ideologically cohesive bodies, even with the occasional split among Democrats on such issues as trade or Republicans on environmental issues. We need to revise our political language to take account of this ideological cohesion. There are no more "Dixiecrats"

Figure 17.5 Partisan Unity in Congress

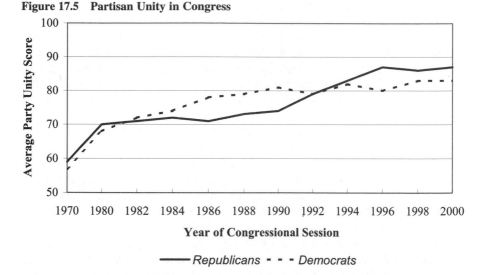

or Southern conservative Democrats, and therefore there is no meaningful "conservative coalition" in Congress. It also seems likely that "liberal Republican" will soon be an oxymoron restricted to that patronized minority holding a pro-choice attitude on abortion, confined to the back of the platform or, so to speak, to the back of the party bus.

Republicans have been acting like a parliamentary party beyond their ideological unity on a party program. The "central leaders' efforts during the Contract period were attempts to *impose* a form of 'party government'" that succeeded in winning cooperation from committee chairmen and changed roll-call behavior as "many Republicans modified their previous preferences in order to accommodate their party colleagues" (Owens 1997, 259, 265). Beyond programmatic goals, the Republicans have created strong party institutions in Congress, building on previous Democratic reforms (Rohde 1991).

In their first days in power after 1994, as they organized the House, the Republicans centralized power in the hands of the Speaker, abolished institutionalized caucuses of constituency interests, distributed chairmanships on the basis of loyalty to the party program and in disregard of seniority, and changed the ratios of party memberships on committees to foster passage of the party program. Instruments of discipline have become more prevalent and more exercised, including caucus resolutions, committee assignments, aid in securing campaign contributions, and disposition of individual members' bills.

The building of parliamentary party institutions continues. Some of the structural changes in the House were adopted by both the Senate and the Democrats, perhaps most significantly the rotation of committee chairmanships, curbing the antiparty influence of seniority. That rotation also has spurred greater turnover in Congress, as chairmen at the end of their term, such as Jesse Helms, choose to go home rather than accept a back seat in Washington. The Republicans insisted that committees report party bills, even when opposed by the chairman, as in the case of the "patients' bill of rights."

The party differences and cohesion in Congress partially reflect the enhanced power of legislative leaders. The more fundamental reason for congressional party unity—as in parliamentary systems—is not discipline as much as agreement. Party members vote together because they think the same way. Republicans act as conservatives because they *are* conservatives; Democrats act like liberals or, as they now prefer to be called, progressives, because they believe in these programs.

Supportive evidence on the ideological consistency of party elites can be found in studies of other partisans. In research conducted nearly forty years ago, Herbert McClosky and his students (1960, 406–427) demonstrated the large ideological differences among the two major parties' national convention delegates. Continuing party differences are also shown in more recent studies of convention delegates. John Kessel and his students (Bruce, Clark, and Kessel 1991, 1089–1106) have drawn the ideological structures of these party representatives. Though not monolithic, they are sharply distinct between the parties. These divisions persist among broader layers of party activists, such as contributors and campaign workers (Bruzios 1990, 581–601; Green, Jackson, and Clayton 1999). Similarly, extensive surveys of state party convention delegates show consistent ideological differences, independent of state cultures (Abramowitz, McGlennon, and Rapoport 1986, chapter 3). There is a difference, consistent with the expectations of a parliamentary system.

The most recent nominating conventions provide further support for the ideological cohesion of the national parties. The *CBS News Poll* in 2000 found massive differences between Republican and Democratic delegates on questions involving the scope of government, social issues, and economic policy (see table 17.2 and chapter 4). The party elites were sharply different—and more different than their mass supporters—on each of fifteen measures, including self-identified ideology, social issues, and economic policy. The median difference was a chasmlike divide of 53 percentage points.

Party Organization

Party unity has another source, related to the recruitment of individual candidates with a common ideology. Unity is also fostered by the develop-

Table 17.2   Convention Delegates' Issue Attitudes in 2000 (in percentages)

	Democratic Delegates	Democratic Voters	GOP Voters	GOP Delegates
Scope of Government				
Self-identified as conservative	4	16	49	57
Self-identified as liberal	34	34	11	1
Government should do more to solve				
the nation's problems	73	44	21	4
protect the environment even if				
community jobs are lost	63	72	57	32
promote traditional values	20	36	55	44
Social Issues				
Abortion should be permitted in all				
cases	63	34	16	10
Favor required child safety locks on				
guns	94	91	76	48
Favor special efforts to help				
minorities get ahead	83	59	44	29
Allow children of illegal immigrants				
to attend public school	86	67	46	28
Favor death penalty for murder	20	46	55	60
Paid vouchers for private schools	10	41	53	71
Economic Issues				
Free trade desirable even with harm				
to domestic industries	37	31	30	67
Private investment for social security	23	44	61	89
Favor prescription drugs in Medicare	58	59	36	34
Large tax cut good for economy	7	9	25	76

Source: CBS News Poll, July 30, 2000 (Republicans), August 13, 2000 (Democrats).

ment of strong national party organizations, precisely measured by the dollars of election finance. Amid all of the proper concern over the problems of campaign contributions and spending, we have understated the increasing importance of the parties in providing money, "the mother's milk of politics."

There are two large sources of party money: the direct subsidies provided by the federal election law, and the "soft money" contributions provided for the parties' organizational work. Together, even in 1992, these funds totaled $213 million for the major candidates and their parties. Underlining the impact of this party spending, the Republican and Democratic presidential campaigns in 1992 each spent twice as much money as billionaire Ross Perot, whose candidacy is often seen as demonstrating the decline of the parties.

The party role expanded hugely in 1996 and 2000, bolstered by the Supreme Court in its 1996 *Colorado* decisions. The Court approved unlimited "independent" spending by political parties on behalf of its candidates. Four justices explicitly indicated that they were prepared to approve even direct unlimited expenditures by parties, but the Court rejected that view, 5-4, in the second *Colorado* case in 2001 (see chapters 5 and 6).[11] Given the likelihood of both more litigation and newer justices, the way remains open for a further expansion of the parties' campaign spending.

The parties have taken great advantage of the Court's opening. Together, the six Republican and Democratic national party groups spent $1.2 billion in the 2000 election, nearly $700 million in "hard money" funds spent directly on behalf of candidates, and a shade under $500 million in "soft money" funds used for general electoral activities, without even counting the $160 million in federal subsidies for the parties' national conventions and presidential campaigns. Altogether, party money accounted for over 40 percent of the total election spending, the largest of all sources (Corrado 2001; *Capital Eye* 2001).

Despite the commonplace emphasis on "candidate-centered" campaigns, the parties' expenditures were greater than that of all individual congressional candidates for *both* parties and *both* the House and Senate. In discussions of election finance, political action committees (PACs) receive most of the attention, and condemnation, but the reality is that PACs are of decreasing importance, having barely increased since 1988. Even if independent spending is added to PAC money, interest groups were outspent by the parties in 2000 by a ratio of at least 2.5:1. Moreover, legislative candidates were closely allied with their parties in the campaign, receiving both direct contributions and the benefits of generic party activity, and in turn contributing to common funds for their party's national campaigns (Herrnson 2001). The parties now have the muscle and cohesion to conduct campaigns and present their programs, to act as we would expect of parliamentary contestants.

Party Leadership

Parties need leaders as much as money. In parliamentary governments, leaders achieve power through their party activity. That has always been the case even in America when we look at congressional leadership: A long apprenticeship in the House and Senate has usually been required before one achieves the positions of Speaker, majority or minority leader, and whip. A strong indication of the development of parliamentary politics in the United States is the unrecognized trend toward party recruitment for the presidency, the allegedly separate institution.

The conventional wisdom is quite different. Particularly since the "reforms" of the parties, beginning with the McGovern-Fraser Commission after 1968, presidential nominations have apparently become contests among self-starting aspirants who succeed by assembling a personal coalition that appeals directly to the voters in a series of uncoordinated state primaries. We have come to assume the disappearance of party influence in presidential nominations.

In reality, however, the parties have become important sources of leadership recruitment. Since 1980, as specified in table 17.3, we have seen twelve presidential nominations, all of them the choice of an established party leader, even in the face of significant insurgencies. These selections include four renominations of the sitting party leader, with only one facing a strong challenge (Carter in 1980); six selections of the leader of the established dominant faction of the party; and two selections of the leader of a major party faction.

Presidential nominations certainly have changed, but the trend is toward different, rather than less, party influence. Look back at the "traditional" convention system, as analyzed by Paul David and associates in 1960 (David, Goldman, and Bain 1960). Historically, some presidents retired voluntarily or involuntarily after one term, but every chief executive since 1972 has been renominated, including Gerald Ford, never elected to national office. When nominations have been open, inheritance and factional victory have become the universal paths to success, as they were historically. In contrast, past patterns of inner-group selection or compromise in stalemate have disappeared.[12]

The selection of presidential nominees still evidences influence by leaders of the organized parties or its factions, even if formal party leadership has not primarily made these choices (such as Democratic "super-delegates" and similar Republican officials). These decisions are quite different from

Table 17.3   Recent Presidential Nominations

Year	Party	Candidate	Type
1980	Democrat	Carter	Renomination of incumbent
1980	Republican	Reagan	Dominant factional victory
1984	Democrat	Mondale	Dominant factional victory
1984	Republican	Reagan	Renomination of incumbent
1988	Democrat	Dukakis	Factional victory
1988	Republican	Bush	Dominant factional victory
1992	Democrat	Clinton	Factional victory
1992	Republican	Bush	Renomination of incumbent
1996	Democrat	Clinton	Renomination of incumbent
1996	Republican	Dole	Dominant factional victory
2000	Democrat	Gore	Dominant factional victory
2000	Republican	Bush	Dominant factional victory

the selection of such insurgents as Goldwater in 1964 or McGovern in 1972, the typical illustrations of the asserted decline of party. While insurgents do now have access to the contest for presidential nominations, the reality is that they fail in that contest. After thirty years of "reform," Mayer concludes appropriately, "the American presidential nomination process has become, if anything, even more hostile toward outsiders and insurgents than the system that preceded it" (Mayer 2001, 12).

The presidential nominations of 1992 through 2000 particularly evidence the party basis of recruitment. There were notable insurgent candidates: Republican Pat Buchanan twice attempted to reincarnate Barry Goldwater, Jerry Brown imitated George McGovern, and John McCain and Bill Bradley eschewed partisanship. In contrast to earlier years, however, all were soundly defeated by established party figures. Each George Bush typified the career of a party politician. The father secured his nomination as the heir of the retiring leader, Ronald Reagan. The son was the choice of the inner party circle. Their endorsements, funding, and campaign support were more than enough to overcome limited personal experience and incomplete command of national issues. By 2000, the dominant faction had the ability to chase most contenders from the race even before the New Hampshire primary, to convince Pat Buchanan that insurgency within the party was now fruitless, and to humiliate McCain, an attractive war hero.

The Democrats have duplicated the pattern. Bill Clinton came to party leadership from the position of Governor, reflecting the variety of career opportunities available in a federal system, but Arkansas was hardly a robust power center. Clinton's real base was the Democratic Leadership Council (Hale 1994), which provided much of his program, his source of contacts and finances, and his opportunity for national exposure. Clinton's 1992 success is a testament to the influence of that faction, far more than evidence of the decline of party and the substitution of unmediated access to the voters. Al Gore won his own nomination as Clinton's heir, certainly not on the basis of his dynamic personality. His support by party leaders including superdelegates, endorsements of critical groups, particularly unions, and relentless fundraising chased all possible opponents from the contest other than the ineffective Bradley.

Contrary to the fears of many observers (Polsby 1983), the new presidential nominating system has developed along with new institutions of party cohesion. Front-runners have great advantages in this new system (Mayer 1995, chapter 2), but that means that prominent party figures—rather than obscure dark horses stabled in smoke-filled rooms—are most likely to win nomination. Contrary to fears of a personalistic presidency, the candidates chosen in the postreform period often deal with tough issues, support their party's program, and agree with their congressional party's leaders on policy positions as much as, or even more than, in the past (Patterson and Bice 1997).

Contemporary presidential nominations have become comparable—although not identical—to the choice of leadership in a hypothetical U.S. parliamentary system. Is the selection of Reagan in 1980 that different from the British Tories' choice of Margaret Thatcher to lead the party's turn toward ideological free-market conservatism? In a parliamentary system, would not the Bushes, Reagan's successors, be the ideal analogues to Britain's John Major? Is the selection of Mondale as the liberal standard-bearer of the liberal Democratic Party that different from the lineage of left-wing leaders in the British Labour party? Is the Democratic turn toward the electoral center with Clinton and Gore not analogous to Labour's replacement of Michael Foot by Neil Kinnock, John Smith, and Tony Blair?

To be sure, American political leadership is still quite open, the parties quite permeable. Presidential nominations do depend greatly on personal coalitions, and popular primaries are the decisive points of decision. Yet it is also true that leadership of the parties is still, and perhaps increasingly, related to prominence within the parties.

Toward Parliamentary Government?

Do these changes amount to parliamentary government in the United States? Certainly not in the most basic definitional sense, since we will surely continue to have separated institutions, in which the president is elected separately from the legislature, and the Senate separately from the House of Representatives. Unlike a formal parliamentary system, the president will hold his office for a fixed term, regardless of the "votes of confidence" he wins or loses in Congress. By using his veto and the bully pulpit of the White House, Bill Clinton proved that the president is independent and still "relevant." By presenting a focused agenda, George W. Bush proved that even a president without clear legitimacy can accomplish many of his goals.

It is also true that we will never have a system in which a single political party can both promise and deliver a complete and coherent ideological program. As Charles Jones (1996, 19) correctly maintains, American government remains a "separated system," in which "serious and continuous in-party and cross-party coalition building typifies policy making." These continuing features were strikingly evident by actions from the adoption of welfare reform in the 104th Congress to the rapid mobilization of the American government after the terrorist attacks on September 11.

But parliaments also evidence coalition building, particularly in multiparty systems. British parliamentarians can be as stalemated by factional and party differences on issues such as Northern Ireland as the Democrats and Republicans have been on health care from 1993 to the present. Achieving a consensual policy on the peace process in Israel's multiparty system is as difficult as achieving a consensual policy on abortion between America's two parties.

After the ideological conflicts of the 104th Congress, we have seen more open coalition building. With a close division among the parties in the House, changes in party control and more frequent use of filibusters in the Senate, and each president's veto threats, the necessities of politics and government have forced compromise, most notably in fiscal policies. Nevertheless, the party basis of parliamentary government will continue, because the ideological basis of intraparty coherence and interparty difference will continue, and even be increased with the ongoing departure of moderate legislators of both parties and the possibility of split-party control of government (Owens 1997, 269–272).

The status of the presidency is uncertain. In some recent years, it came close to being superfluous, or at least outside of party politics. President Clinton fostered his reelection by removing himself from partisan leadership, "triangulating" the White House between congressional Democrats and Republicans. Cramped by the Lewinsky and the impeachment scandals, he became less involved in controversial issues, while appealing to consensual attitudes such as "family values" and school achievement. He governed by following the model of the patriotic chief of state created by George Washington and prescribed in *The Federalist:* "to guard the community against the effects of faction, precipitancy, or of any impulse unfriendly to the public good" (Madison [1787] 1941, 477).

The terrorist attacks of September 11 changed American politics dramatically. Budget constraints, worsened by the Bush tax cut and the declining economy, were eliminated. In a single week, Congress passed the president's program for new spending of $55 billion; past pieties of the social security "lock box" and the sanctity of balanced budgets are totally forgotten. Foreign policy, the domain of the chief executive, has again become central. The president has been given the public support, the broad powers, and the reputational transformation that comes to a wartime leader.

Party politics was temporarily forgotten and some observers even hoped that the crisis would lead "to a softer partisanship—and debates that are more meaningful," tackling "matters of consequence, gravity and complexity."[13] Although partisan rancor did diminish, basic party differences soon reemerged, in keeping with their consistent philosophies. Democrats favored and Republicans opposed the federalization of airport security workers. Republicans sought new tax cuts to stimulate the flagging economy and Democrats urged increased unemployment benefits.

America needs help and it cannot come from a disengaged president on the Clinton model. Nor can our democracy survive through crisis government, which suspends politics in the interests of national unity, granting the presidency excessive and unchecked power. It may be time to end the fruitless quest for a presidential savior, even in times of conflict, and instead turn our attention, and our support, to the continuing and emerging strengths of our political parties. We are developing, almost unnoticed, institutions of semi-parliamentary, semi-responsible government. Perhaps this new form of American government is both inevitable and necessary.

Notes

1. The phrase "literary theory" is from Walter Bagehot's classic analysis ([1867] 1928, 1) of the realities of British politics.

2. Two excellent undergraduate students at Rutgers performed the analysis of party programs—Andrea Lubin for the 1992 and 1996 platforms, and Avram Fechter for 2000.

3. The 1992 texts are found in *The Vision Shared* (Republican National Committee 1992) and, for the less loquacious Democrats, *Congressional Quarterly Weekly Report* 50 (July 18, 1992), 2107–2113. The 1996 Democratic platform was distributed as www.dncc96 .org/platform (accessed September 2002.) The Republican platform was printed as *Renewing America's Purpose Together* (Republican National Convention 2000).

4. Each sentence, or distinct clause within these sentences, constituted the unit of analysis. Because of its great length, only alternate sentences in the Republican platform were included. No selection bias is evident or, given the repetitive character of platforms, likely. For further details on the techniques used, see Pomper and Lederman 1980, 235–248. To avoid contamination or wishful thinking on my part, the students did the analysis independently.

5. The "useful" categories, graphed in figure 17.1, are: policy evaluations, candidate evaluations, and future policy promises classified as pledges of continuity, expressions of goals, pledges of action, and detailed pledges.

6. *The Vision Shared* (1992 Republican Platform), 46; "Contract with America," in Wilcox (1995, 70); *Restoring the American Dream* (1996 Republican Platform), 25.

7. Using the same content categories, Carolyn Shaw (1996) of the University of Texas lists one hundred fifty presidential campaign promises of 1992 in the more specific categories. In regard to fulfillment, she finds that there was "fully comparable" or "partially comparable" action on 69 percent of Clinton's proposals. This record is higher than that found by Fishel (1985) for any president from Kennedy through Reagan.

8. In "full action," we include proposals that are still in congressional conference committees, while "similar action" includes proposals advanced through administrative actions or included in the Bush budget, even if these measures have not yet been enacted into law. Bills that have passed only one house of Congress are considered "defeated."

9. A Knight Ridder newspaper analysis also finds considerable fulfillment. See Ron Hutcheson, "Bush Meets 40% of Campaign Goals," *Akron Beacon Journal* (January 20, 2002), A1.

10. These data are drawn from *CQ Weekly* 59 (January 6, 2001), 67, and similar reports in annual reports of *Congressional Quarterly*.

11. *Colorado Republican Federal Campaign Committee v. Federal Election Commission* (No. 95-489, 518 U.S. 604 [1996]).

12. The only exception to the trend away from inner-party selection or compromise since 1924 is Alf Landon's designation at the Republican candidate in 1936. The last president to "voluntarily" decline a second term was Lyndon Johnson in 1968.

13. Douglas Sosnik, adviser to President Clinton, in Richard L. Berke, "It's Not a Time for Party, But for How Long?" *New York Times* (September 23, 2001).

18

Schattschneider's Dismay:
Strong Parties and Alienated Voters

Daniel M. Shea

The state of parties in America is as uncertain as it is fascinating. The transformation we are now witnessing in party politics is rivaled only by the sweeping changes of the Progressive Era. Given the economic and cultural adjustments during the industrial revolution, and their reverberations in the political realm, it makes perfect sense that our own information-age upheaval would yield a similar disequilibrium.

There are two principal trends in the current transformation of party politics. The first trend is growth and revitalization. Party organizations have reemerged from the depths of candidate-centered/interest group politics of the 1970s. The national party organizations, in particular, have more resources and a higher level of technological prowess, and are able to give candidates more help than at any point in history. Perhaps much related, the growing potency of in-government party structures has taken many scholars by surprise. For example, in the 1970s, the "average" Democrat and "average" Republican member of Congress voted with their party about 60 percent of the time. More recently, this figure has risen to over 80 percent (Davidson and Oleszek 2000, 268).

The second trend is voter withdrawal. The movement away from partisanship among voters began in earnest in the 1970s and continues into the twenty-first century. While *some* indicators of partisanship, in *some* regions of the country offer reasons for optimism, most suggest that a shrinking number of voters feel a connection to the party system. Perhaps more troubling, a host of other indicators suggest citizens are less interested, trustful, efficacious, and supportive of the political system than they were prior to the recent resurgence of party organizations.

Most observers agree that simplistic notions of party "decline" and "revival" no longer work—if they ever did. Unidimensional perspectives rarely describe the nature of party politics. Moreover, one could reasonably argue that the scholarship on parties is muddled due to the diversity of analytic battlegrounds (see Green and Shea 1996). Sorauf's (1964) call for the greater use of concepts, models, and theories, echoed by Crotty (1969) has, for the most part, gone unheeded.

The foremost battleground in the studies of parties has been the fit between party activities and popular sovereignty. It is only honest to admit that our interest in the "so what question" waned a bit during the behavioral revolution and as organizational studies grabbed the scholarly headlines in the 1980s and 1990s. The real excitement during the first State of the Parties conference in 1993, for instance, stemmed from criticism of organizational studies for not paying enough attention to normative issues. John Coleman's "dissent from the new orthodoxy" (1994) was all the buzz during the event. Due to the fiftieth anniversary of the 1950 American Political Science Report, "Toward a More Responsible Two-Party System" (Committee on Political Parties 1950), the precise link between parties and democracy is drawing renewed interest.

This chapter follows that path. The first section explores how E. E. Schattschneider, one of the better-known advocates of responsible party government, saw the impact of parties on voters. In particular, he argued that strong party organizations would cause "ripples" in the citizenry, encouraging greater involvement, trust, efficacy, and support for the party system. Next, I look for evidence of such ripples among citizens, using data from the 1960–2000 National Elections Studies. I find some evidence of Schattschneider's "ripples," but not nearly as much as one would assume given the recent revitalization of party organizations. In the final section, I suggest how the revitalized party organizations might actually be contributing to voter alienation.

Parties and Popular Sovereignty

One could argue that the "great debate" in the party's literature has been over the precise means by which parties enhance or detract from popular sovereignty.[1] To many scholars, parties are the linchpins of the democratic system, helping to articulate the demands of average citizens, and minimizing the importance of affluence and standing. For others, parties serve to structure and promote competitive elections, yielding a democratic system as a by-product. Either way, attention to parties has been a staple of political science.

During the nineteenth century, political parties did not receive close scholarly attention. This appears rather odd, given that nearly every aspect of political life during much of this period was dominated by partisan activities (White and Shea 2000, chapter 2; Silbey 1991, 9–13). Perhaps, as suggested by Epstein (1986, 13), scholars stayed away from this subject because they shared the negative view of earlier thinkers. Madison's hostility to factions was well understood and rarely challenged. John Burgess, for example, made no mention of parties in his two-volume study of political science, first published in 1890 (see Epstein 1986, 10–12). The few works of this period were more likely to highlight the shortcomings of party activities than note their potential benefits. Believing parties inevitable in democratic systems, Bryce (1891), for example, was highly critical of their excessive power.

One exception to this early skepticism was the work of Francis Lieber (1938), who argued parties are indeed desirable because they produce steadfast opposition to the government-of-the-day and without such structures government takes on the form of a secret conspiracy. He argued that parties promote accountability and help translate the public will into appropriate government action. As such, Lieber was the first to see parties as linkage institutions—an idea that seemed to challenge notions of direct popular government by Ostrogorski (1964), echoing Rousseau, who proclaimed serious deficiencies in any intermediary organization between the people and the government.

It is ironic that near the turn of the twentieth century, precisely when government officials were moving to curb the excessiveness of party machines, a recognition of party benefits began to appear in scholarly circles. There was an interest in eliminating the spoils system and corrupt machine politics, to be sure, but many scholars held that parties were the only instruments of genuine popular sovereignty in a modern society. Town meeting–style democracy was fitting for small communities, but impractical in a large-scale polity. Even Michels' acclaimed work (1962), often cited as a forceful attack against parties, can be read to imply parties are the best possibility for democracy—that is, given the "iron law of oligarchy."

Party advocacy had reached its full form by the 1940s, with Herring (1940), Schattschneider (1942), and Key (1942) leading the way. This view gained further legitimacy, of course, with the report of the Committee on Political Parties of the American Political Science Association (1950). The celebration of American-style democracy following World War II led scholars to search for the true underpinnings of the American system, and parties were found to be a core ingredient.

Schattschneider's Ripple Effects

Schattschneider's theories are worth exploring for a number of reasons. For one thing, his clear articulation of the potential of parties to connect voters to the government and, in addition, his responsible party model has become the default argument for a generation of normative party scholars. Indeed, few works on parties fail to quote the third sentence of Schattschneider's *Party Government* (1942): "Modern democracy is unthinkable save in terms of political parties." When combined with his leadership of the 1950 Committee on Political Parties (1950), and, of course, his *Semisovereign People* (1960), his work represents perhaps the strongest pro-party discourse in the field.

Schattschneider's theory centers on viable partisan in-government structures and accompanying robust external organizations. By adhering to a set of principles and policies, legislative parties simplify alternatives and offer voters a coherent choice. "The people are a sovereign whose vocabulary is limited to two words, 'Yes' and 'No'" (1942, 52). This coherence makes holding the government accountable easier for the electorate. This insight is especially true as the size of the electorate increases. Through their drive to mobilize voters, win elections, and build coalitions, parties make modern, diverse governments democratic. Schattschneider calls for a party-dominated legislative decision making, programmatic parties, strong leaders, and engaged followers.

Schattschneider's works shed additional light on the connection between party organizations and the electorate. Parties work to acquire power, but as they do so, the electorate is pulled into the process in a more meaningful way. A few points are illustrative:

- On low turnout during elections, he writes: "More significant operation of the party system would create greater interest in voting." (Committee on Political Parties 1950, 76)
- Parties expand the size of the participating electorate: "Once party organizations become active in the electorate, a vast field of extension and intensification of effort is opened up, the extension of the franchise to new social classes, for example." (1942, 47)
- He spends a good bit of time outlining his notion of American-style partisanship. He admits that partisans are not members of a party in a traditional sense, in that they do not control—nor do they wish to control—the workings of the organization. They are, he suggests, similar to fans loyal to a ball club. He notes that a "good will" relationship must develop between the organization and the partisan—much like a merchant and his customers. (1942, 60)
- Elections are made more meaningful because of parties: "[They] have given elections a meaning and importance never before thought possible." (1942, 208)
- A viable party system pulls individuals into the local party organization, and failure to do so undermines the democratic character of the system: "Widespread political participation thus fosters responsibility as well as democratic control in the conduct of party affairs and the pursuit of party policies. A more responsible party system is inti-

mately linked with the general level as well as the forms of political participation." (1950, 65)
- He suggests that the national party system must be nourished from the local structures: "To this end, local party groups are needed that meet frequently to discuss and initiate policy." (1950, 67)

These examples are hardly exhaustive, but the logic is clear: Strong political parties, comprised of coherent in-government structures and active external organizations, enhance the role of the citizen in the democratic process.

Given that Schattschneider's theory gained broad support during the 1950s, it should come as no surprise that many political scientists took the shift away from party politics in the 1970s as an ominous turn. But the party organizations, struggling to remain players, took a dramatic turn of their own, adopting a "service-oriented" position. By the early 1980s, it was clear that American parties were "resilient creatures" (Bibby 1990, 27). Both major parties had developed campaign-centered branch organizations, revamped their internal operations, and devised innovative ways to raise huge sums of cash. As one observer remarked, "the growth chart for this political 'industry' exhibits an ebullience more familiar in Silicon Valley" (Putnam 2000, 37).

This organizational transformation brought with it a sigh of relief for party advocates because it was assumed the new resources would "ripple" through the electorate. The new, institutionalized party system would surely foster a stronger sense of party identification, improve levels of political participation, build trust in the system, and afford average citizens a greater sense of empowerment.

Measuring the Ripples

Two propositions, therefore, seem clear from the foregoing discussion. First, a vital party system should engage the electorate. Citizens should understand the differences between the two parties and these differences should enhance public accountability of the government. Citizens should be engaged in political activity and have a greater sense of their potential in the political process. Second, there has been a dramatic upsurge in party activity in the past three decades, especially the revitalization of party organizations and increased coherence of in-government party structures. The straightforward logic, then, is that the current period of party growth should carry with it positive changes with regard to voters—that is, if the current system is similar to what Schattschneider envisioned some fifty years ago.

Party Distinctiveness. Schattschneider and recent organizational scholars speculated that strong parties lead to distinctive policy positions—a difference that will be noticed by voters. This pattern is the core of the responsible model. Figure 18.1 charts National Election Study (NES) voter perceptions of differences between the Democrats and Republicans from 1960, just before the organizational resurgence movement, until 2000. Two points emerge from the figure.[2] First, Americans, as a whole, find it difficult to sort through the differences between the parties. During most of the last four decades, roughly four in ten citizens did not believe there were important distinctions between them. Second, the trend since the 1960s has been upward slightly. In the 1970s, less than 50 percent of the public saw important differences; more recently that number is roughly 60 percent. While this change might not represent the distinctiveness that Schattschneider hoped for, responsible party advocates can take heart that things may be improving.

Mobilization of the Electorate. Strong parties get more voters to the polls. The story here is, of course, a bit different. The decline in voting rates since the 1960s is well documented: Whereas in the 1960 presidential contest over 60 percent of the electorate turned out, in 2000 slightly over 50 percent came to the polls. There have been a few upturns, such as in 1992 (55.1 percent), but for the most part the decline has been steady. As for nonpresidential election years, the decline has been similar. Moreover, turnout in primary elections has declined at even a faster rate. The strong parties/ mobilization nexus envisioned by Schattschneider does not seem to be occurring.

Shattschneider also speculates that vibrant organizations will mobilize

Figure 18.1   Important Difference in What Democratic and Republican Parties Stand for, 1960–2000

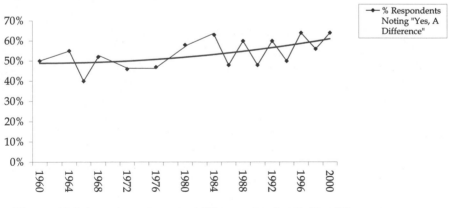

"Do you think there are any important differences in what the Republicans and Democrats stand for?"

Source: Natural Election Studies

voters at all social/economic levels. The theory that competition will compel parties to "enlarge the scope of conflict," thereby drawing in an ever-wider circle of citizens, is the heart of *The Semisovereign People* (1960). Figure 18.2 notes self-reported turnout among all respondents, and among respondents at the bottom of the economic ladder (the lowest 16 percent). The rates are clearly inflated due to a social desirability effect, but the trend is downward for both. More importantly, the decline is steeper for the low-income voters.

Other Measures of Political Participation. If party organizations are more active than in the past, we might speculate that citizens would be more involved in a range of civic activities. It has become a near truism in scholarly works that active parties help engage citizens. Yet, there are many indicators of a dramatic decline in civic-oriented activities. Putnam (2000, 45), for example, refers to Roper Center surveys from 1973 (roughly just before the resurgence period) to 1994 (well into the period) to suggest staggering declines. These are nationwide figures and we may find activism higher in specific communities that boast aggressive party organizations. These data do not suggest very much "bang for the party buck"—at least when it comes to civic involvement.

Returning to NES data, there are a number of questions dealing with political participation, broadly defined. Whereas about 9 percent attended meetings in the 1960s and the 1970s, more recently that number has shrunk to about 5 percent. Figure 18.3 explores the number of Americans who worked for a party or candidate during this same period. This figure has

Figure 18.2   Voter Turnout: Overall and Low-Income, 1960–2000

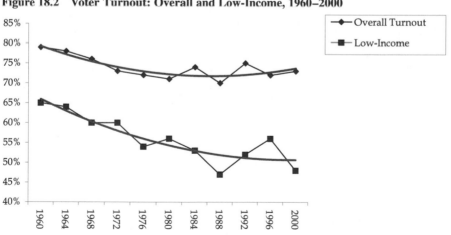

Source: Natural Election Studies

never been especially high—a phenomenon discussed at length by Schattschneider (1942, chapter 3)—but one is hard-pressed to explain how revitalized parties would lead to significantly lower levels.

Interest in the Election Process. One would speculate that, similar to
electoral mobilization and other forms of political participation, stronger
parties would create more interest in the political process. Here again the
trend is downward. Two indicators of involvement are explored. The first is
a question dealing with how much attention the respondent paid to the election that year. There are a few elections that have sparked more public interest, such as 1992 and 2000, but the overall drop is clear. Perhaps a better
indicator is the number of Americans who tuned in to presidential debates.
Figure 18.4 charts the decline in presidential debate viewers from 1980 to
2000. What is most interesting about the data is that the 2000 race was an
open-seat contest and exceedingly close. One might have expected a great
deal of interest in these debates, especially compared to, say, 1984, where
the race was never close and was quite boring to many. These two figures
clearly suggest waning interest in the electoral process.

Perceptions of the Role of Citizens in the Electoral Process. Schattschneider felt that strong parties would give voters a sense of empowerment.
That is, responsible parties lead to policy coherence, which leads to easier
accountability assessments, which leads to notions of empowerment. One
bit of data examines where respondents feel that elections make those in
government pay attention; another looks at whether the respondent feels

Figure 18.3   Worked for a Party or Candidate, 1960–2000

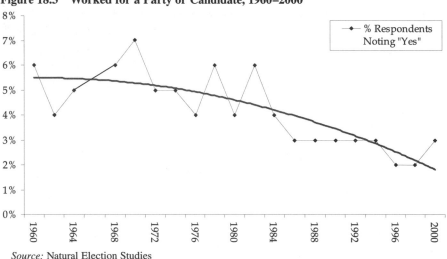

Source: Natural Election Studies

Figure 18.4 Viewership for Presidential Debates since 1980

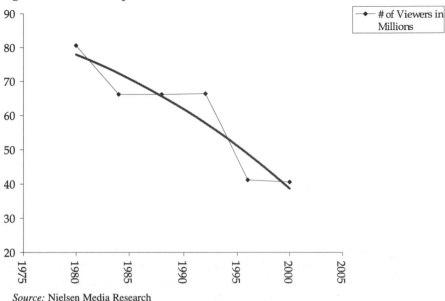

Source: Nielsen Media Research

elected officials care about average folks; and still another queries perceptions of whether government is run for all Americans or for special interests.
Again, for each of these indicators a dramatic decline has occurred at precisely the same time party organizations and in-government structures blossomed. There is a bit of an upturn in the last few elections, but there is no
denying that the public is more cynical about the election process and the
nature of government than before the organizational resurgence period.

The final figure (18.5) is particularly revealing. It is based on the NES
"External Political Efficacy Index." The trend is downward and significant.
Americans feel less empowered in the twenty-first century than they did at
the end of the last century.

Explaining the Paradox

How do we reconcile revitalized party organizations with voter withdrawal from the party system? Schlesinger (1985, 1991) argues that changes
in party-in-the-electorate over the last several decades, exogenous to the
party system itself, help explain the growth of party organizations. "It is the
very weakness of partisan identification among the voters which is a stimulus for the growth of partisan organizations" (Schlesinger 1985, 1167).
Given that split-ticket voting, a good measure of electoral volatility, hit its

Figure 18.5   External Political Efficacy Index, 1960–2000

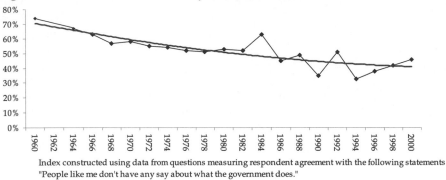

Index constructed using data from questions measuring respondent agreement with the following statements
"People like me don't have any say about what the government does."
"I don't think public officials care much what people like me think."

Source: Natural Election Studies

peak immediately prior to the organizational buildup of the 1980s, this argument is plausible. Putnam (2000, 40) makes the same argument: "Since their
'consumers' are tuning out from politics, parties have to work harder and
spend much more, competing furiously to woo voters, workers, and donations, and to do that they need a (paid) organizational infrastructure." Aldrich (2000) takes a similar tack, by arguing that the growth of electoral competition in the South during the last two decades has led to the creation of
aggressive, vibrant party structures.

But could the problem lie with the revived party system itself? Instead
of the organizational revitalization of parties being caused by voter withdrawal, it could be a cause of voter withdrawal (Shea 1999; White and Shea
2000). The overall reconfiguration of party activities has shifted party concerns away from greater links with the electorate to greater help for candidates, and as a result much of what parties now do turns off voters to the
political process. Although a full development of this thesis is beyond the
scope of this chapter, a few common features of the revitalized parties are
suggestive.

Campaign Finance Shenanigans. Given the public's uneasiness about
campaign fundraising, and also given that money is the jet fuel of the new
parties, we might expect the public to be even more skeptical about "party
politics." Parties bend the limits of finance regulations every election. Few
should be surprised that in a recent poll, 75 percent of the respondents agreed
that "many public officials make or change policy decisions as a direct result
of money received from contributions" (Lehmann 1997). Surely perceptions
of political parties and "partisanship" have been linked to concerns over the
financial corruption of politics.

Going Negative, Often. Negative campaigning may be turning off the electorate, especially those less partisan (Ansolabehere and Iyengar 1995). At the same time, party organizations have shown an increased receptiveness to negative, attack-style electioneering (Ginsberg and Shefter 1990; Shea 1999). During the waning days of the 1998 election, for example, both parties spent record-breaking amounts on "issue advocacy," nearly all of which was negative. This pattern led one observer to call them "issue attacks" (Abramson 1998).

Scandal Politics. Much related, Lowi has argued "party leaders have responded to gridlock not with renewed efforts to mobilize the electorate but with a strategy of scandal" (1996, 47). Indeed, the list of examples of where parties responded to opposition with personal attacks, rather than policy alternatives, seems to grow each year (see also Ginsberg and Shefter 1990).

Depressing Turnout. Given that party operatives are some of the best-trained, new-style campaign consultants, we can imagine that they would pursue new-style tactics and strategies. One such approach that is widely rumored to be in use is to deliberately reduce turnout, a strategy that would benefit some candidates.

Promotion of "Nonpartisan" Candidates. It seems that one of the best ways to win a race in which there is a dealigned electorate is to pitch the candidate as "independent." We can understand that consultants would be anxious to move in this direction, but that party operatives would reject it. This is not the case. For example, the 2000 GOP Nomination Convention not only downplayed George W. Bush's partisan badge, but also accented this nonpartisan approach. Neither presidential candidate mentioned his party very often in 2000, even when it would seem that doing so would give him an edge. Surely voters would have been receptive to the claim that Democrats have a better reputation for environmental concerns, for example. That point was never made by Gore.

The Breakdown in Tickets. Both parties have established election organizations geared to specific offices. These are the "Hill" committees at the national level and legislative campaign committees at the state level. Over the past decade, we have seen a separation of these units to the point where they will refrain from assisting one another and will work toward inconsistent ends at times. In the waning weeks of the 1996 presidential race, for instance, the National Republican Campaign Committee ran a series of television advertisements that suggested to voters they might feel better about supporting Clinton if they also voted for a Republican for the House. Bob Dole was furious about the commercials, but notions of tickets are out of fashion these days—even for party operatives. Two years later, Charles Rengel, chair of the Democratic Congressional Campaign Committee, berated Roy Romer, then the general chair of the DNC, for hoarding money for Al Gore's 2000 race. George W. Bush, the GOP establishment candidate from the beginning, refused to campaign with other members of his ticket in 2000.

Sacrificing Local Party Structures. Finally, the focus of party rejuvena-
tion has been primarily at the national and state levels. As the party system
moves away from the local structures (the mom-and-pop shops of politics,
so to speak), voters find less of a connection to the entire electoral system.
Consider the Connecticut woman in 1996 who sent a check to the DNC. She
then received dozens of additional requests for money, via direct mail and
the telephone, "but the Democratic National Committee could not tell her
where the Democratic Party in her state or community was located" (Miroff,
Seidelman, and Swanstrom 1998, 184). Putnam suggests this shift may have
wide repercussions: "There may be nearly as many fans in the political sta-
dium nowadays, but they are not watching an amateur or even a semipro
match. Whether the slick professional game they have become accustomed
to watching is worth the increasingly high admission is another matter"
(2000, 40).

Conclusion

A conservative estimate is that during the last decade the national party
committees have spent well over $2 billion (White and Shea 2000, 223). In-
deed, party organizations are major players and few candidates head into the
electoral trenches without their aid. What a dramatic turn since the "party-
less" age of the 1970s.

After all of this money is spent and all of these activities undertaken, it
seems logical that we tally the profits and losses. From the perspective of
candidates, the payoff has been immense. National party organizations and
state-level units have become the largest single contributor to candidate coffers, and their services extend far beyond financing. Candidates now *start*
with a trip to the party headquarters—a dramatic change from the 1970s.

But are candidates the *only* consumers in the party system? Historically,
party units first cultivated voter loyalty and then transmitted this base into a
resource for candidates. Build the voter bank, so to speak, and they will
come. This insight seems to be the core logic of Schattschneider's party-
centered democracy, and one might suspect that this was precisely the logic
that compelled revivalist scholars to make such optimistic predictions. Nonetheless, at precisely the same time that party organizations "rose from the
ashes," voters moved away from the political system. Perhaps, as suggested
above, service-oriented organizations grew precisely *because* voters abandoned partisanship. But that was in the beginning. We might expect now,
after some forty years of "nucleus building" (Schlesinger 1985), that party
activity would have spread into higher levels of participation and a greater
sense of external efficacy. Schattschneider would have assumed that the
electorate would have been pulled in by now.

What difference might a nationalized, service-oriented system make? Perhaps, as suggested by some, we are simply entering a new party era with some similarities and some differences from previous ones. The good news is that party organizations are resilient. But there are serious ramifications as well. For one, the nature of our democratic experiment may be shifting toward an elite pole—precisely away from the model that pushed Schattschneider and others to proclaim the virtues of "party government." Schattschneider's model places a premium on civic involvement in the conduct of government. This assumption implies an ongoing, meaningful involvement. When this occurs, citizens develop an affinity for the system because they feel as though they have a stake in the outcome. "[C]itizenship, after all, is an acquired taste or discipline. For the most part, people are drawn to politics by private motives, and only later develop public ones" (McWilliams 2000, 3). The proper party system, then, is one in which citizens connect with local organizations—units that are amateur-based, localized, and ideologically driven.

For Schattschneider, party politics should provide the mechanism for pulling voters into the political process—against their inclinations. In *Party Government* he writes:

> [The Framers] made the very natural mistake of underestimating the difficulties arising from the numbers, preoccupation, immobility, and indifference of the people. Everyone took for granted that the people themselves would assume responsibility for the expression of their own will as a matter of course without so much as dreaming of the intervention of syndicates of self-appointed political managers and manipulators who for reasons of their own might organize the electorate and channelize the expression of popular will. Thus the great omission in the theory of democracy formulated by the classical philosophers who dealt exclusively with imaginary democracies. (1942, 14)

What is telling about this excerpt is that voters today are indeed *not* left to themselves, but are surrounded by "syndicates of self-appointed political managers and manipulators." Schattschneider envisioned that rationality and self-interest would serve the larger good. It seems, however, that party operatives have found a way of remaining relevant—indeed key players—by linking their services to candidates. Today, party scorecards tally only wins and losses after Election Day—rather than any long-term cultivation of voters. Many forces have been at work driving voters from the process, and one would be hard-pressed to suggest that the parties themselves are all to blame. But surely Schattschneider would be dismayed by the current the state of the party system.

Notes

1. Portions of this section are taken from Green and Shea (1996).
2. American National Elections Study, Cumulative Data File, 1952–2000.

19

Responsible, Functional, or Both? American Political Parties and the APSA Report after Fifty Years

John J. Coleman

Over half a century ago, the American Political Science Association (APSA) entered the arena and study of politics in an unusually blunt manner. With the publication of "Toward a More Responsible Two-Party System," the association's Committee on Political Parties (1950) made a strong claim that American political parties—and American politicians—were serving democracy poorly. Stopping short of advocating widespread changes in U.S. constitutional structure, the report's authors called for extensive and far-reaching changes in elite political behavior and the internal operation of political parties.

At the same time that it entered the world of practical politics, the report also embraced a fundamental framework that would animate party scholarship for decades. The report's essence was that American political parties were weak, noncohesive, and insufficiently centralized. Parties were balkanized entities with little central control, vision, or identity. Controlled by local bosses, the parties were opportunistic and unprincipled, denying voters a significant lever on government. These criticisms were not entirely new: Similar arguments had informed Progressive, Mugwump, and even earlier complaints about the parties. Where Progressives saw the solution for decrepit parties as weaker, sanitized institutions, the APSA committee called for stronger, more aggressive organizations (David 1992).

To critics, who soon came out in force, the report was flawed in its empirical analysis of American parties and naive or worse about the normative value of responsible parties (Pennock 1952; Turner 1951). Touting a functionalist alternative, critics argued that American parties were as modern as their European counterparts and served critical systemic needs for the American polity (Epstein 1956, 1967; Herring 1940; Kirkpatrick 1971; Ranney and Kendall 1956; Sorauf 1975). Parties put together what the Constitution sought to separate. Perhaps responsible parties and a parliamentary ethos might reduce friction between the executive and the legislature, but this friction was a central premise of the Founders' vision and implicitly endorsed by the public (Jones 1994; Livingston 1976; Ranney 1951). And in a manner unlike parliamentary systems, critics argued, the political and party system in the United States did hold officials accountable—responsible parties were unnecessary for that task. Parties also performed "constituent" functions critical to the working of democracy: educating citizens, recruiting candidates, mobilizing voters, conducting campaigns, and providing incentives for cooperation across institutional and federal boundaries (Lowi 1975). American parties worked about as well as could be expected given a web of institutional, federal, constitutional, cultural, and pragmatic constraints (Herrnson 1992b).

Critics of the report saw American parties as a force for social cohesion and harmony in a tremendously heterogeneous society (Pomper 1971, 918). Political parties provided essential glue for a society facing any number of potentially debilitating divisions and conflicts.[1] Parties channeled disagreements that might otherwise lead to violence and repression. Fractious parties were the functional equivalent of "the frontier" in Frederick Jackson Turner's famous and influential analysis of American history: They provided an outlet for social stress and helped reduce tension in American society by discouraging and slowing down potentially inflammatory policy. In this interpretation of "indigenous" parties, the United States had precisely the parties it needed. Wistful thinking about responsible parties was impractical and perhaps dangerous.[2]

After fifty years, this debate between "responsibilists" and "functionalists" must be rated a draw. Especially given their inclination to avoid constitutional restructuring, responsibilists were too quick to dismiss the amount of responsibility already present in American parties.[3] Functionalists, on the other hand, wrongly asserted that responsible parties were incompatible with the American system, and they assumed rather than demonstrated that the parties clearly performed social cohesion functions.

More important that these shortcomings, however, the report embraced a false—and influential—dichotomy between responsible and functional parties. Scholars following the report embraced one side of the argument or the other, portraying responsibility and functionality as the flip sides of a single dimension of party politics (Pomper 1971; Kirkpatrick 1971).

A central reason responsibility and functionality were treated as mutually exclusive ends of a single dimension is that the two schools of thought disagreed fundamentally about the nature of parties and their relationship to the rest of the social order. Responsible party proponents typically saw parties as independent variables, as entities that potentially could and probably should shape their political environment. Functionalist analysts tended to take a more constrained view of what parties could accomplish. In this analysis, parties adjusted to fit into their environment and the changes in it. Functional analysis accepted implicitly the idea of a "narrow path of history" on which society and the economy traveled, and to which the parties must adapt. In this perspective, social and economic forces push toward certain types of societal arrangements. Politics reacts to, but does not create, this societal shift.

"Responsible *versus* functional" is a stale debate with diminishing returns; one could assume instead that responsibility and functionalism are separate dimensions of political parties.[4] In this revised framework, parties can be simultaneously responsible and functional or simultaneously neither. It is possible, as in the traditional framework, that parties can be functional without being responsible, but neither characteristic precludes the other. Dropping the presumed pairing of responsible/shaping and functional/reactive opens up the possibility of conceptualizing functionality and responsibility as separate dimensions: It is not necessary that responsible parties be shaping and proactive, and that functional parties be adaptive and reactive.[5] Rather than simply reacting to change in the social and economic environment, parties can be functional for the political system by helping *build* that environment. In this role, functional parties can prevent some of the social tension that functionalist analysis emphasizes. One can certainly make a case, for example, that Roosevelt and the Democrats shaped the American political economy in a manner that smoothed some of the rough edges off corporate market capitalism and aided the stability of the economic and political systems.

Hints about treating responsibility and functionality as potentially compatible dimensions appear in macropolitical accounts such as realignment theory and micropolitical accounts in rational choice. By arguing that critical realignments serve as a "surrogate for revolution," Burnham in effect posits that responsible parties during realignments serve preservation functions for the overall political system (Burnham 1970). Aldrich argues that political parties solve key problems facing politicians and the system at large and that politicians rationally build the party organizations that best further their goals; it is conceivable (but not necessary) that responsible parties might be the organizational choice of particular politicians at particular times (Aldrich 1995). Hints about responsibility as a continuum also abound. Pomper writes about the current party system as being "semi-responsible" (Pomper 1998). Rohde analyzes "conditional" party government (Rohde 1991). Even the authors of the APSA report, if not later responsibilists, wrote about moving "toward" a "more responsible" two-party system.

Placed in this framework of responsibility and functionality continuums, parties historically were neither as irresponsible as the report asserted nor as functional as the report's critics assumed. This observation raises several issues. First, it suggests the authors of the APSA report were wrong in their diagnosis of the American polity, which may bring their prescriptions into question. Second, it rejects the functionalist argument that responsible parties simply do not fit in the American framework. Third, it implies variations over time in the functionality and responsibility of parties in the American political system.

The Reponsibilist Critique

Responsibilists lodged three chief critiques against American parties: they were too decentralized and disorganized, not unified on policy stances, and wedded to meaningless campaign practices. I consider each point in turn.

American parties are insufficiently centralized. The APSA report argued that the parochial interests of local party leaders dominated American parties. Local party chiefs, interested less in the substance of public policy than in the rewards of patronage and pork, dominated the national parties. Policy preferences varied widely within the parties, especially as one moved from state to state. The needs of local parties determined or heavily influenced the selection of party officials and presidential candidates and hamstrung national policy-making efforts. Even the New Deal, a prime period of American state building just prior to the publication of the APSA report, suffered from its obligations to local Democratic parties. Far-reaching measures, especially with regard to labor rights, were thwarted by the economic needs of Southern Democrats. To keep parochial partisans satisfied, programs such as unemployment insurance and Aid to Dependent Children (later renamed Aid to Families with Dependent Children) allowed vast disparities in benefit levels across states despite being "national" social assistance programs.

The report saw these ingredients as a recipe for disaster. In particular, the authors cited the following dangers to democracy (Committee on Political Parties 1950):

- "The inadequacy of the party system in sustaining well-considered programs and providing broad public support for them may lead to grave consequences in an explosive era."
- "The American people may go too far for the safety of constitutional government in compensating for this inadequacy by shifting excessive responsibility to the president."
- "With growing public cynicism and continuing proof of the ineffectiveness of the party system, the nation may eventually witness the disintegration of the two major parties."
- "The incapacity of the two parties for consistent action based on meaningful programs may rally support for extremist parties, poles

apart, each fanatically bent on imposing on the country its particular panacea."

Much in this account rings true. State parties often did have different policy priorities than the national party, and party-building efforts were often based on state or local elite needs rather than promulgation of a national program (Pomper 1971, 927–929; Aldrich 1995; Reynolds 1988). Skowronek (1982) argues that through the late-nineteenth century the American state was a "state of courts and parties." Party, in his view, was exceptionally strong in this era: Parties linked the national government to each locale, linked the discrete governmental units horizontally in a territory, and organized government institutions internally. Parties were notable less for their programs than for the "procedural unity" they lent the state. With most government activity occurring at the local and state level, it was a party structure designed to integrate national government services into local governing centers. This local emphasis weakened the likelihood of, and perhaps the need for, a positive national program (Skowronek 1982, 26). Milkis (1993) argues that Franklin Roosevelt was so convinced that responsible parties were futile that he sought to institutionalize programs in the executive branch to minimize potential future party interference—if parties were unable to coordinate policy control and priorities, the state would do it for them.

But there is another side to the story. The complaints of responsible party proponents that American parties were too decentralized and lacked cohesion sidestepped the point, often noted by functionalists, that the United States is a federal system. As Herrnson (1992b) suggests, surely one has to consider this limitation before pronouncing the party system nonresponsible. Conceptually, this is more difficult than it might seem. Should American parties be declared nonresponsible even though they must deal with federal pressures not faced by parties in most other countries? Or should scholars acknowledge the structural constraints placed on American parties and assess how well they perform within that structure? Ideally, depicting responsibility as a continuum allows analysts to have a firm sense of what "responsible" means but also the flexibility to grant that parties can be at differing, and still effective, levels of responsibility.

In other words, American parties may founder on the shoals of federalism, but this limitation need not mean writing off party responsibility altogether. First, the parties have often overcome these federal barriers. Bridges indicates that nineteenth-century workers, as a minority, found it necessary to work with partisan coalitions at the state and federal level. The tariff, a national-level issue with obvious local implications, was "the policy cement of the view that labor and capital shared the same interest. . . . Workers became Republicans and Democrats . . . in the service of quite objective working-class goals" that stretched beyond local boundaries (Bridges 1986, 187, 192). Erie's stimulating work on party machines also indicates that central party leaders had more authority over state and local parties than the traditional story suggests. Local and state machines, dependent heavily on federal government largesse, accepted that "fiscal federalism" could reshape their priorities (Erie 1988). Finally, Bensel's (1990) depiction of the Civil War and Reconstruction makes clear that the Republican Party was a national party promoting a nationalist agenda; unity in support of this agenda tied the state and national parties together. Republican policies not only offered patronage and pork for the local party, but also defined areas in which the local and state party would be a lesser player.

Second, in the federal system, some issues are simply more relevant at one level of government than another. As dual federalism evolved into cooperative federalism, these distinctions by governmental level became less clear, but for much of American history there was something like a division of labor. Given this division, how important a problem is it for the party system if Democrats in Pennsylvania in 1888 have different ideas about educational policy than Democrats in Rhode Island? This disparity across state lines might become more problematic when education becomes a more truly cooperative venture between levels of government, but even that is not obvious. If Democrats in Pennsylvania and Rhode Island largely agree on the relative roles of the state and national governments, but happen to differ on the best education policy within their state, responsibility need not be absent for voters within each state. If voters have clear choices and parties act in a relatively unified manner to fulfill their pledges, there is a level of responsibility.

American parties are not cohesive. Responsibilists cared about party decentralization because they believed it impaired party unity and cohesion. On national issues, however, this charge is not convincing. Gerring (1998) makes a strong case for American party platforms and major presidential speeches as programmatic throughout American history; other scholars have similarly argued that broad thematic differences have separated the parties over time.[6] Part of the responsible model is indeed that parties compete electorally on broad themes that indicate to the public the general direction it can expect in public policy, so this historical pattern is a sign of responsibility. Are the parties programmatic in the same sense "on the ground," in day-to-day politicking and legislative conflict? Perhaps not, but such a standard overreaches. Even if not programmatic, American parties have been strongly policy-oriented and this policy orientation has mattered to both the mass public and elites (Bridges 1994; James 1992). The policy consistency of American parties is not easily dismissed. If not ideological, one might label the parties "policyist." Silbey (1984) argues that parties verged on the responsible party model at certain times in the nineteenth century, perhaps most prominently in the 1830s and 1840s; Herrnson (1992b) and others point to the great realigning periods of the 1860s, 1890s, and 1930s as other instances.

The late nineteenth century is often seen as a heyday for American political parties: mobilization was high, policy differences were numerous, and parties controlled access to public office and organized the functioning of government at the local, state, and national levels. Late-twentieth-century parties were not mistaken for these heyday parties, but policy differences did appear to be significant. Responsible parties need to offer different visions to the public, and this was indeed the case in these periods. Figure 19.1 presents the distribution of the first dimension of Poole and Rosenthal's D-Nominate scores for the Congresses at the end of the nineteenth and twentieth centuries. The first dimension of the D-Nominate scores, based on roll-call votes, represents a general liberal to conservative ideological scale.[7] Democrats and Republicans in the late nineteenth century offered distinctive choices to voters, with little overlap in the ideological positioning of party members. The range of D-Nominate scores within the parties, though not insignificant, was relatively constrained. In the late twentieth century, there is more overlap between the parties and more dispersion within the parties, especially from 1983 through 1988. After that, the parties begin to separate and move toward the conservative and liberal ends of the scale. The 104th and 105th Congresses, from 1995 to 1998, begin to resemble the pattern from the prior century, suggesting that in roll-call voting contemporary parties are becoming more nearly like the parties of an earlier era. In two different historical periods and under highly contrasting social and economic conditions, American parties can be placed at the higher end of the responsibility continuum when measured by intraparty cohesion and interparty polarization (Rohde 1991; Cox and McCubbins 1993; Coleman 1996a; Krehbiel 2000).

American campaigns are empty rituals. Responsibility involves not only cohesive elite behavior, but also elections that provide potential voters with an accurate sense of what the parties will attempt to accomplish in office. While the militarist campaign style of the nineteenth century—spectacle-driven campaigns designed to mobilize "armies" of voters—thrived on bombast and ritual, the campaigns were at their core driven by substance and content. As noted above, voters were partisan for specific policy reasons, whether these were cultural or economic in nature. McGerr (1986) suggests that the militarist style was broadly informative, particularly on broad matters of philosophy and approach. These militarist campaigns were by no means flawless—McCormick (1986) and Gerring (1999) suggest that national elites concentrated disproportionately more on economic matters in office than on the cultural and moral issues that purportedly drove voters. Overall, however, nineteenth-century campaigns performed well: Voters

Figure 19.1   Distribution of D-Nominate Scores in the U.S. House, 1883–1898 and 1983–1998

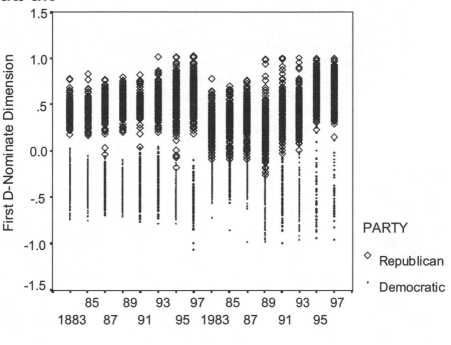

Note: Negative values represent liberal ideology, positive values represent conservative ideology.

were deeply familiar with the key concerns of each party and voted accordingly.

Campaigns in the latter half of the twentieth century have been criticized as candidate-centered affairs that de-emphasize linkages between the candidate and his or her party (Wattenberg 1991). Again, the empirical evidence presented in numerous studies provides substantial support for this view for most of the postwar period. Recent history, however, evidences signs of change: Studies of party platforms show a relationship between platform emphases and subsequent policies; survey respondents recognize that the differences between the parties are growing; and campaigns in the mid-1990s were often ideological in tone. Voters still tie candidates to parties to some degree (Coleman 1999b). Even within a candidate-dominated campaign system, then, there are some ways for responsible party campaign linkages to endure. This fact does not deny that these linkages are less constraining than in the past.

Since the publication of the APSA report, the election system has moved toward greater responsibility as measured by the prescriptions of the report. Baer and Bositis (1993; see also Herrnson 1992b; also see Green and Herrnson 2002) extract all of the reform suggestions from the APSA report. They then determine whether these reforms have been fully implemented, partially implemented, given "some de facto movement," been rejected by movement in the opposite direction, or had no action taken. Performing simple computations on Baer and Bositis's list shows that 83 percent of the suggested reforms in the election system have shown at least some positive movement.

The election system is not alone in this regard, as positive movement has also occurred on the other responsibilist critiques discussed above. On centralization and party organization reforms, the Democrats had at least some movement toward 90 percent of the reforms, while Republicans showed some movement toward 63 percent. On congressional party cohesion and structure, the Democrats showed at least some movement on 82 percent of the recommendations; Republicans tallied 51 percent. Baer and Bositis's report covers developments through 1992; the Republican percentage for congressional party reform would no doubt be higher since Republicans have controlled of one or both houses of Congress since 1995.

I have argued that the historical record casts doubt on the APSA report's arguments. American parties have been more responsible historically than responsibilists have acknowledged. This record, along with the significant movement toward many of the APSA report prescriptions over the past fifty years, is problematic for the functionalist account as well: The claim that these reforms are incompatible with the American political system does not hold.

The Functionalist Analysis

American parties have performed over time the "constituent" tasks delineated by Theodore Lowi (1975). By this term, Lowi means tasks that are constitutive for the political system, functions without which the political system could not operate. These include overcoming the constitutional separation of powers and branches, keeping conflict within boundaries, monitoring the fairness of the rules of the game, integrating new citizens into politics, recruiting and training candidates, running campaigns, and informing voters. The functional aspects of parties most frequently cited fall into two categories. First, parties are said to provide key components for the governing and political process. Second, parties contribute to social stability.

Assisting the governing process. Recruiting candidates, providing linkages across branches, and similar tasks have long been part of the party tool kit, but how vital parties are for each activity ebbs and flows historically. This fluctuation raises difficult questions but does not necessarily negate the functionalist argument. As more candidates are self-starters and not re-cruited by parties, the *necessity* of parties for this function diminishes—candidates can now purchase most campaign tasks in the marketplace. But functional arguments do not merely state that parties perform functions. If that were so, letting the air out of the functionalist argument would be as simple as noting the presence of other entities performing these tasks. One could further deflate functionalism by pointing to the prevalence of nonparti-san—at least in formal terms—campaigning and governing at the local and county levels. Governments throughout the United States manage to govern while prohibiting party politics. It is simple enough, then, to show that American politics and governing can function even in the absence of formal party organization.

To say that parties are functional is therefore not simply to say that par-ties perform tasks, but that party control of certain activities seems on the whole *preferable* for governing in some respects. Two common measuring sticks are productivity and legitimacy. Regarding productivity, despite some questioning earlier in the 1990s, recent research shows that unified party control improves government's legislative productivity and responsiveness (Mayhew 1991; Edwards, Barrett, and Peake 1997; Binder 1999; Coleman 1999a). Regarding legitimacy, nonpartisan elections and elections focusing on candidates much more heavily than parties depress turnout and deprive citizens of useful voting cues (Bridges 1997). These elections also deprive voters of the powerful lever of the party label, a lever that can be employed to wield broad-scale changes to the political system even when, as is typical, voters are not deeply knowledgeable about all of the candidates on the ballot. This magnification of a voter's leverage, I would suggest, is an important legitimating device.

At about the same time as the APSA report, Key (1949; see also Schatt-schneider 1960) highlighted the dangers of personal-based factions, wild electoral swings, and issueless campaigning in the South's one-party states, particularly for the socioeconomic "have-nots." In these ways, parties not only perform functions but also *improve* the operation of the political sys-tem. It is worrisome, from the functionalist perspective, when parties are pushed out from or abdicate particular roles, because parties produce sys-temic advantages when they, rather than some other entity, perform these functions. This fact is one reason why functionalist and responsibilist ana-lysts alike were concerned with the postwar decline of parties. Functionalists feared parties pulling away from roles that enhanced systemic productivity and legitimacy, while responsibilists worried about parties that seemed to become more alike, less internally unified, and less useful for voters.

Survey data provide additional evidence of the legitimating assistance provided by parties. Although functional analysis often focuses on the per-formance of parties in government (e.g., legislative productivity), public attitudes are also relevant. Strong partisans should, in the functionalist view, express more confidence in the political system and have more belief that their involvement makes a difference. Figure 19.2 graphs the External Efficacy and Governmental Responsiveness indexes from the National Election Studies from 1952 to 1998. Each index converts NES items into a 100-point scale and then averages the responses for each survey respondent. Data points in the figure represent the mean score on the index for each year (higher scores indicate higher efficacy and a higher sense of government responsiveness). The figure suggests both the functional strengths and weaknesses of parties. Respondents identified as "strong partisans" score about 20 points higher in efficacy and about 10 points higher in perceived government responsiveness in the early and late years than do "independents." The legitimating salve of partisanship clearly has its limits, however, as independents and partisans jointly exhibit a decline in efficacy and perceived responsiveness over time.[8]

Assisting social stability. Critical to analysts such as Pendleton Herring (1940) was the notion that parties provide a forum for consensus rather than a means to emphasize differences: "The present party system helps to preserve existing social institutions by blurring sharp issues and ignoring others. Party rule discourages the alignment of economic differences through political channels" (131); "Capitalism and the party system grew up together. All went well so long as the economic sphere fulfilled the hopes of the citizens" (125); "our party system is significant not as a way of clarifying differences but as an institution for seeking broad terms of agreement" (168). These

Figure 19.2   "Constituent" Parties in the Public, National Election Studies, 1952–1998

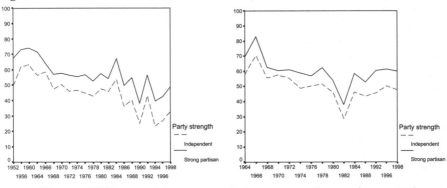

    a. External Efficacy Index   b. Government Responsiveness Index

a. Do public officials care what the respondent thinks? Do people like the respondent have any say in government?

b. How much does government pay attention to the people? Do elections make government pay attention?

remarks concern contests between economic groups, but the functionalist point encompasses other social groups as well.

One need only recall some of the campaign rhetoric of the nineteenth century to recognize that a system of vibrant parties did not deter brutal charges of one group toward another. Indeed, the entire ethnocultural line of analysis in political history stresses the organization of ethnic and religious values, cultures, resentments, and hatreds as a prime ingredient in nineteenth-century politics (Kleppner 1970; Jensen 1971), and the period after Reconstruction was laden with party-based racial appeals. One cannot conveniently overlook the fact that purportedly functional American parties thrived at the same time that blacks, native Americans, and other racial and ethnic groups were deprived, often violently, of basic civil rights and civil liberties by elected officials and their constituents (R. Smith 1993). The functionalist argument works only if we turn a blind eye to history.

Parties did not consistently perform the functionalist role of social integration at the political system level, but did partisanship at least affect the views of individuals? If parties perform the functional work of societal consensus building and group integration, then partisanship should help diminish sharply negative impressions of social groups. Looking at the latter half of the twentieth century, however, partisanship does not matter much in evaluations of social groups. Figure 19.3 presents the NES mean "feeling thermometer" ratings for groups by all respondents identifying themselves as strong partisans or independents (i.e., figure 19.3 looks at overall public attitudes *toward* these groups, not attitudes of the members of these groups). Differences between partisans and independents are minimal. Strong partisanship does not equate to dramatically—or, in most cases, even marginally—more generous or tolerant appraisals of social groups. Differences between strong Democrats and strong Republicans are similarly negligible. Looking at other groups—women, the middle class, welfare recipients, Southerners, the elderly—though not shown in figure 19.3, produces the same results.

A less restrictive functionalist formulation would be that parties do not reduce group antagonisms, but instead bring competing interests and groups into the political arena to settle disputes, rather than resolving conflicts through other means. The "consensus" here is not necessarily about policy but about process—parties provide the organizational mechanism that makes groups willing to accept temporary defeat and compete again another day. Parties are coalitions of social groups that, as Aldrich (1995) suggests, see these organizations as the most reliable way to achieve their ends over the long haul. This formulation also implies greater social peace. Parties have an incentive, in this framework, to find common ground between groups by adjusting and fine-tuning agendas and priorities to maintain majority status. As a general principle, this softer version of functionalism is plausible, but

Figure 19.3   Mean NES Feeling Thermometers for Selected Social Groups

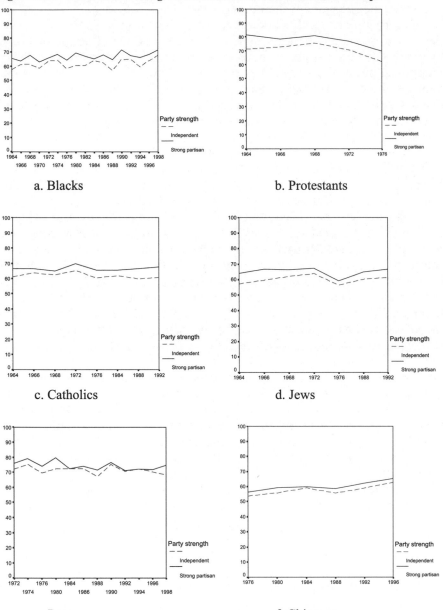

a. Blacks

b. Protestants

c. Catholics

d. Jews

e. Poor

f. Chicanos

the experience of numerous groups in American political history, including women, blacks, and poor whites, suggests that parties often manipulate and accept groups grudgingly rather than actively seeking to incorporate these groups into political life (Frymer 1999; Harvey 1998). Even more problematic for this account, the presence of purportedly functional parties in American history did *not* repel other methods of solving group conflict. American political history has been laden with violence, from the mobs of early American history, to labor uprisings and repression in the late nineteenth century and early twentieth century, to race riots and violent outbursts across the landscape from the earliest times to the 1960s and later. No one making a functionalist argument has shown that the geographical distributions of these outbreaks has been related to the ability of local or state parties to defuse social tensions.

Parties as Functional and Responsible

The "responsible versus functional" debate was common even before the APSA report, perhaps most classically in Schattschneider's (1942) and Herring's (1940) dueling volumes, but the report gave this conception pride of place in the study of American parties. Generations of students and scholars have been influenced by the basic framework that parties were or should be *either* responsible *or* functional. To functionalists, functional parties fit the American constitutional framework and social conditions precisely; the need to build social cohesion, consensus, and compromise argued against responsible party tenets. Responsible parties advanced representation and choice at the expense of stability, social peace, and perhaps even legitimacy if any side perceived itself as permanently subordinate in the governing process. The very conditions that made the United States hospitable to functional parties made it most unlikely that responsible parties would emerge, and particularly unlikely that they would persist. To responsibilists, functional parties were almost guaranteed to be dysfunctional. Voters would lose interest in campaigns that seemed bland and unimportant. Linkage between leader and led would be sketchy and uncertain. Rather than organizing politics by ideas, functional parties would organize politics by social groupings, symbols, or slogans, thereby accentuating rather than diminishing conflict based on culture or social characteristics.

Using the single yardstick of "responsible *or* functional," the party system most always seemed to fall on the functional end. With this standard measure, scholars have identified responsibility in the party system on only limited, highly contingent occasions such as the first years of a realignment. To some scholars, even these moments pale in comparison to responsible party behavior in other political systems. By considering functionality and responsibility as potentially compatible rather than inversely related, however, a broader conceptualization of American parties is possible.

The grid in figure 19.4 presents functionality and responsibility as separate dimensions. By thinking of these characteristics as continuums, one can place any period in party history on the grid. These dimensions are straightforward. For responsibility, to what degree do parties represent the kind of unified, cohesive coalitions depicted in the APSA report? For functionality, to what degree do parties perform the governing (legitimacy) and consensus-building (social stability) functions cited by functionalist accounts? This dimension is not wed to the particular interpretation of functionalist critics of the APSA report. Those critics assumed that responsible parties were likely to increase social division and conflict, and nonresponsible parties would defuse these problems, but those assumptions are absent here. In the grid, responsible parties can coexist with governing legitimacy and social cohesion.

For illustrative purposes, I place several periods of party history on the grid. Others might place these periods differently. My objective is not to argue for a particular placement of a particular period but to suggest that party analysis will improve by taking the steps of conceptualizing responsibility and functionality as, first, continuums, and second, continuums that are not inversely related. These are necessary first steps before scholars can proceed to other tasks such as the quantification of these dimensions (see Katz 1986 for "partyness" as a continuum). They are necessary steps to move beyond the stale debate of functional versus responsible parties.

High Responsibility and High Functionality. I place the late-nineteenth century, for many of the reasons discussed above, as a period relatively high

Figure 19.4   Party Responsibility and Functionality as Separate Dimensions

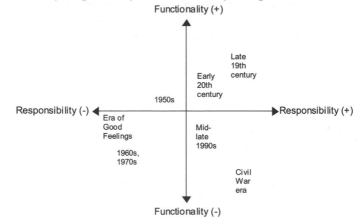

on both functionality and responsibility. The period is not at the extreme end of either dimension, however. Waves of violent responses to labor and incipient socialist uprisings, deep ethnic tensions in the cities, and widespread and often violent removal of blacks from the post-Reconstruction Southern political system suggest serious weakness in the functionality of the dominant parties. On the positive side, parties were keenly important in organizing elections, legislatures, and the public's perception of political reality. During this period, party differences were acute, and parties in Congress were highly cohesive. Speakers, making use of reforms such as Reed's Rules, more effectively pushed party agendas through the House of Representatives. However, the impressive rise of the Populist movement, a result of the two-party system's failure to process some of the key economic issues of the day, suggests serious shortcomings in responsibility (Ritter 1997). In the early twentieth century, functionality and responsibility diminished as party differences began to erode, centralized party power in Congress weakened, and party machinery became less central to candidate nomination and election.

Low Responsibility and High Functionality. By dropping the notion that responsibility or functionality are either present or absent and by dropping the idea that responsibility and functionality must be mutually exclusive, it becomes surprisingly difficult to find the ideal type of the combination that the critics of the APSA report emphasized: low responsibility, high functionality parties. One period that seems to fit this combination is the 1950s. Congressional parties were cohesive and distinctive, though at a diminished level from the 1930s and 1940s. The sectional split in the Democratic Party over racial issues kept possibly divisive issues from the floor. In this manner, party leaders exercised some significant control, but, overall, power in Congress devolved further to committees and subcommittees and away from central party control. These parties are fairly placed at about the midpoint on a responsibility scale. For functionality, the parties of this era are closer to the higher than the lower end. Although their role in organizing government and running campaigns declined from previous levels, these parties retained significant salience with the public. Attitudes toward parties and government were relatively positive, turnout substantial, and the impact of partisanship as a perceptual filter was considerable. By focusing heavily on voting rights, the incipient civil rights movement effectively endorsed the utility of partisan and electoral politics as vital routes toward group empowerment and social integration. In these ways, the parties afforded the political system some measure of legitimacy.

High Responsibility and Low Functionality. High responsibility and low functionality marks the party system in the Civil War era. This system proved unable to process deeply contentious issues and preserve or build consensus or social harmony, thus ranking very low on functionality. One cannot fault the Civil War era parties for lack of responsibility, however—

they were relatively cohesive and distinctive, and carried through with their plans. I also include the most recent period of party history in this quadrant. I discuss this period below.

Low Responsibility and Low Functionality. In the third quadrant, I place two periods in which party functionality and responsibility were both at a low ebb: the Era of Good Feelings and the 1960s and 1970s. Regarding the Era of Good Feelings, clearly responsible parties are absent in a one-party period. Bogue (1994) notes, "By the early 1820s a state of highly factionalized nonpartisanship had been attained" in Congress. I also place this era on the lower half of the functionality scale. This era precedes mass mobilization and modern party organization. Selection of presidential candidates was the province of clubby, personalized caucuses. Sectional pressures displaced the partisan resolution of lingering national strains, notably slavery. In the House, Henry Clay displayed strong control and leadership, but it is arguable whether that leadership is properly considered partisan in the manner of powerful Speakers toward the end of the century.

Parties in the Present Era. The 1960s–1970s and the mid- to late 1990s are located on the bottom half of the functionality dimension, but on opposite sides of the responsibility dimension. The diminution of parties in the American political landscape during the first decades of the postwar period is a frequently told story, as is the recognition that the status of parties improved somewhat in the 1980s and after. The 1990s also culminated in the kind of secular and critical realignment commonly linked to responsible parties (Abramowitz and Saunders 1998; Burnham 1996).

The public did not reject political parties in the 1960s and 1970s, but there was increased skepticism about exactly how the increasingly indistinct parties made much of a difference and, especially among the young, movement toward interest groups as the preferred way to express political preferences (Mayer 1998; Wattenberg 1998). As noted above, partisans along with independents grew decreasingly confident and trusting in government and in their own efficacy. Other signs the two-party system was failing to some degree in providing functional assistance to the broader political system were the widespread protests, demonstrations, and riots of the 1960s, the dysfunctional Democratic Party convention of 1968, the rise of social movements and interest groups to promote the views of people feeling locked out of party power structures, increased third-party activity, and a drop in voter turnout.

For parties to reverse these postwar functionality and responsibility deficits, changes in the parties' role in policy making were necessary (Coleman 1996a). Changes began in the 1970s and accelerated in the 1980s. They show that, contrary to the "responsible versus functional" rubric, parties need not purchase responsibility at the expense of functionality, as some progress was made on both fronts. Most significantly, Congress—and congressional parties in particular—began to take a more aggressive role in fiscal policy formation through the passage of budgetary reforms, and the consensus over Keynesian nostrums broke down with the stagflation of the 1970s. With the old policy formulas no longer working, the arena was open for new ideas about economic management. As Keynesianism faltered, Republican and Democratic visions of government's role in the economy and society, as reflected in congressional voting patterns, began to diverge. These diverging party visions revealed a fundamental struggle underway to define economic policy for perhaps the next two to three decades. Simultaneously, divisions over social and cultural policy hardened and became more politically salient. Given this stimulus, the party organizations became much more adept at raising funds and professionalizing their operations (Cotter et al. 1984; Herrnson 1990). Large pools of individuals and groups feeling threatened by economic, political, social, and cultural disarray were eager to invest their money in the "right" message. By the mid-1990s, the result was stronger, more active party organizations and stronger, more unified congressional parties.

As the public perceived Congress taking a more central role, saw the congressional parties as increasingly critical in the policy-making process, and sensed important differences on policy preferences, party was elevated as a component of citizen decision making. Signs of this rebound are evident in the declining proportion of split-ticket voters and the declining proportion of congressional districts in which voters elect a candidate of one party while supporting the presidential candidate of the other major party. The point, simply, is that the more functionally important parties appear to the governing process on fundamentally important policy domains, and the more parties offer cohesive and distinctive choices, the more seriously citizens take the parties. If parties matter in the political system, they will matter to citizens, particularly if the parties are also behaving as responsible parties.

In other areas, progress toward responsibility and functionality was more modest or nonexistent. In the electorate, turnout and efficacy remained generally low and skepticism high. Except for 1994, when public attitudes turned sharply negative, these and other measures of public dissatisfaction generally leveled off in the 1990s at low rates. The explosion of scholarly interest in "civic engagement" was, in part, a telling sign of the shortcomings of contemporary parties and the fraying linkage between the public and the parties. Accordingly, I place the 1990s on the higher end of the responsibility scale and the lower, but not polar, end of the functionality scale.

Entering into the early years of the twenty-first century, there is little reason to expect much change in the parties' location on the grid. Responsibility should remain on the higher end of the continuum. With the parties' balance of power nearly split down the middle nationally, each party would employ a risky gambit if it moved toward the center or toward the ideological extreme, so staying put will have strong appeal. Nonetheless, individual members of Congress might see a move to the extreme or the center as electorally advantageous, resulting in less party cohesion. If that is so, one might place the parties slightly lower on responsibility than in the 1990s. Functionally, we might also anticipate a slight decline along the continuum as the elimination of soft money eliminates a major source of party financing. All of this projection relies on a rather static vision of party politics. If the arguments of campaign finance reformers are correct, then the elimination of soft money should move parties toward alternative forms of voter mobilization and education and should allow members of Congress to vote their conscience rather than the interests of large contributors. If this view is right, then parties would improve both in functional and responsible terms, compared to the 1990s. The jury is obviously still out on this matter, but the results of previous episodes of campaign finance reform do not suggest that this rosy scenario is a sure thing.

Conclusion

The publication of "Toward a More Responsible Two-Party System" was momentous not only for the American Political Science Association but also for party scholarship. Whether a report proponent or dissenter, one has to admire the association's audacity in staking out these twin turfs of practical politics and party scholarship. The report significantly shaped scholarship on political parties. Whether American parties were responsible or functional, and whether American parties *could* be responsible, became a major theme in scholarship on the historical development of American parties as well as analyses of contemporary parties. The report did not invent this debate, but it solidified "responsible versus functional" parties as the key yardstick by which to measure American parties.

Once analytically enlightening, placing functionality and responsibility on a single yardstick has proven problematic. Over half a century after the APSA report, it is time to reconceptualize this basic framework. Considering responsibility and functionality as potentially complementary rather than contradictory characteristics of parties provides a means to rethink parties throughout American political development. This two-dimensional approach separates the more responsible parties of the 1990s from the parties of the 1950s–1980s without having to say the United States has returned to the party system of the 1890s. This analytical flexibility allows scholars to test empirically whether party periods with varied mixes of functionality and responsibility differentially affect political development. Abandoning the notion that more of one must mean less of the other, analysts can also become more empirically precise about what functionality and responsibility entail.

Looking ahead, such a rubric could assist in informed speculation about the paths party politics might take during an era of historic economic and social transformation—particularly paths that might help reconnect the public and the parties.

Notes

1. Other scholars were more skeptical. To Burnham (1970), a gap developed between the inertial political party system and the dynamic socioeconomic system that could only be solved by periodic electoral earthquakes in the form of realignment. These realignments, not normal party politics, served as a "surrogate for revolution."

2. See Pomper 1971 for an extensive rebuttal of the central points made by the critics.

3. The most significant constitutional changes advocated by the report were a four-year term for members of the House of Representatives (coinciding with the president's term) and abolishment of the Electoral College. As White (1992) notes, later scholars would suggest that constitutional reform was essential for the party system to become responsible.

4. In a similar vein, White (1992) notes, "Far from furthering academic inquiry, the report froze the debate on various points because both supporters and critics accepted the critical assumptions contained in the report."

5. Shaping versus adapting may well be a third dimension on which parties could be characterized, but not one I will pursue here.

6. See John Gerring, *Party Ideologies in America, 1828–1996* (New York: Cambridge University Press, 1998); Ian Budge and Richard I. Hofferbert, "Mandates and Policy Outputs: U.S. Party Platforms and Federal Expenditures," *American Political Science Review* 84 (1990): 111–132; Douglas A. Hibbs Jr., *The American Political Economy: Macroeconomics and Electoral Politics* (Cambridge, Mass.: Harvard University Press, 1987); Richard I. Hofferbert, "Society, Party, and Policy, Party Programs as Mechanisms of Mediation," paper prepared for the Annual Meeting of the American Political Science Association, 1993; Richard Jensen, "Party Coalitions and the Search for Modern Values: 1820–1970," in *Party Coalitions in the 1980s,* ed. Seymour M. Lipset (San Francisco: Institute for Contemporary Studies, 1981); Joel H. Silbey, "'The Salt of the Nation': Political Parties in Ante-bellum America," in *Political Parties and the Modern State,* ed. Richard L. McCormick (New Brunswick, N.J.: Rutgers University Press, 1984).

7. Poole and Rosenthal (1996) exclude only roll-call votes that were nearly unanimous (100 percent of one party voting in a particular direction and at least 97.5 percent of the other party voting in that direction).

8. For all figures comparing strong partisans to independents, I also looked at weak partisans and independents who lean toward a party. In almost all instances, these two groups fall between the strong partisans and independents.

Part Six

Minor Parties

20

Spoiler or Builder? The Effect of Ralph Nader's 2000 Campaign on the U.S. Greens

John C. Berg

In 2000, the Association of State Green Parties (ASGP) and the Greens/ Green Party USA (GGPUSA) both nominated Ralph Nader as their candidate for president of the United States. No one expected Nader to be elected, and many Democrats argued that his campaign might bring about the election of George W. Bush. Nader ran anyway, because he, the two national Green organizations, and those who joined his campaign hoped thereby to achieve a variety of other goals. These goals included developing the Green Party, helping provoke a realignment of the two-party system, inserting issues that would otherwise be suppressed into the public consciousness and debate, changing the national agenda, sending a message to the Democratic Party, and helping the Greens grow into a significant political force. This chapter focuses on the last of these, the effects of the campaign on the development of the Greens as a party.

Many of those who shared the Greens' criticisms of Bill Clinton and Al Gore were nevertheless perplexed by the decision to nominate Nader, and Nader's decision to accept the nomination. To understand why decisions that seemed destructively insane to some could make sense to the Greens, we first need to examine the political context that led to those decisions. We will then proceed to a brief account of the Nader campaign itself, and finish with an assessment of its impact on the state of the Greens and on American politics.

Context of the Campaign

Three factors converged to make a Green presidential campaign seem like a good idea and Nader a good candidate in 2000. First, a successful (in Green terms) campaign would help resolve some internal problems in the Greens and promote their growth as a party. Next, the party system seemed to be as ripe as it ever would be for an outside insurgency to have some impact. Finally, the combination of other candidates (Gore, Bush, and Buchanan), which was already clear by the time of the June 2000 ASGP convention in Denver, promised a window of opportunity for Green intervention. Let us look at each of these in turn.

The State of the Greens

The U.S. Greens trace their existence to 1984, when a group at the first North American Bioregional Congress issued a manifesto as the "Green Movement Committee." Later that summer they organized more formally as the Committees of Correspondence (Tokar 1992, 52–53).[1] Over the next few years, this loose network developed into the Greens, and eventually the GGPUSA. In 1992, eleven Green candidates for the U.S. House received 110,351 votes, while two Green Senate candidates received 69,940. In 1994, the single Senate candidate (in California) received 127,807 votes, while six House candidates received 47,015, and five candidates for governor received 116,944 (Berg 1995).

As the movement grew, internal debate over various political and organizational issues developed, leading eventually to the launching of a competing national Green organization, the ASGP. It is difficult to describe the basis for the split objectively, since its nature is one of the points in contention. The precipitating issues were 1) whether membership should be defined by the payment of dues (GGPUSA) or by party registration in those states where such registration was possible (ASGP); and 2) whether representation in national decision-making bodies should be restricted to locals and at-large members (GGPUSA) or should include direct representation of state parties (ASGP). On a more political level, those who remained with the GGPUSA tended to think of themselves as placing relatively greater emphasis on direct action and consciousness raising than on electoral politics, and more committed to opposing racism and sexism and building an organization with a diverse membership. Those who joined the ASGP, in contrast, tended to think that the GGPUSA structure made it impossibly difficult to comply with state electoral laws and cumbersome to take effective action of any kind (Affigne and Rensenbrink 1994; Rensenbrink 1999; Hawkins 1996).

By early 1996, those who were to later form the ASGP felt that it was time for a Green presidential campaign. If an attractive candidate could be recruited, such a campaign would bring the Greens visibility, membership, and perhaps even money from the Federal Election Commission (FEC). A number of national figures were asked if they might be willing to run, and Ralph Nader responded positively. The future ASGP leaders had grown impatient with the GGPUSA decision-making structure, which allowed their factional opponents to delay action almost indefinitely, and decided to act outside that structure. They proposed that the Green Party of California, which had ballot status, should hold a convention to nominate a candidate to run for president in that state, and then invite other states to join in. This plan was brought to fruition, and Nader's name was placed on the California ballot as the Green Party candidate for president. Despite complaints from GGPUSA members that this procedure was undemocratic, once Nader was nominated they felt considerable pressure to join in the campaign, and most of them did, some reluctantly and others with enthusiasm.

In the fall of 1996, the GGPUSA filed for recognition by the FEC. GGPUSA leaders considered this step a legitimate and natural one for them to take, since theirs was the oldest Green electoral organization in the U.S. Leaders of the ASGP, which established itself formally as a national organization shortly after the election in 1996, regarded the FEC filing as an attempt by the GGPUSA to arrogate to itself any federal matching funds that Nader's campaign, which had been primarily an ASGP effort, might earn. In the event, Nader's vote total fell far short of the 5 percent needed to qualify for FEC matching, and the GGPUSA withdrew its registration in the face of criticism. The dispute left a residue of bad feeling. Bitter polemics were launched from both sides. However, many state and local Green parties expressed the desire for unity of their members by voting to join either both or neither of the feuding national organizations.

The U.S. Party System

The state of the U.S. party system constituted another important context for the Nader campaign. Left electoral activists, who had been growing more and more unhappy with the direction of the Democratic Party since the defeat of George McGovern in 1972, were faced with two strategic choices. They could try to recapture the Democratic Party, or try to displace it.[2] This strategic choice was one factor dividing left minor parties, with the New Party and at least the leadership of the Labor Party more oriented to the former, and the Greens to the latter. Parties devoted to each of these strategies grew through the 1990s, encouraged on the one hand by evidence that the two-party system was ripe for realignment, and on the other hand by their belief that issues important to most people are currently excluded from the major party debate.

Realignment. Without attempting to resolve the many debates about the causes of party realignment, and whether the U.S. party system has just had, is about to have, or will never again have a realignment, I will restrict myself here to a few points on which there is some level of consensus. First, the combination of Duverger's Law and presidential government make the system of two-and-only-two major parties very strong in the United States (Duverger [1951] 1954, 217; Duverger 1986; Riker 1982, 1986). Second, the periodicity of realignment cycles (Aldrich 1999; Reichley 1996; Berg 1999b), indicators of disenchantment with the major parties (Wattenberg 1998), and an upsurge of minor party activity (Berg 1998; Herrnson and Green 1997, 2002) all suggested that realignment was more possible than it would otherwise be. While those two points were encouraging to left minor party activists, the successes of such right-centrist candidates as Ross Perot and Jesse Ventura were frustrating, as they raised the possibility that any realignment would move the country to the right, not the left. The Greens were committed in principle to building an organization from the grassroots up, but they did not wish to see the potential for change seized by the Reform Party.

Suppressed Issues. There is a close association between party-system re-alignment and the appearance of new issues that are important to many voters, but not to either of the dominant parties. The Greens exist because their members feel unrepresented by either the Democratic or the Republican Parties on many issues, such as global trade, ecology, militarism, decentralization, and drugs. (Aldrich 1995; Burnham 1970; Berg 1999b). Thus, one of the objectives of the Nader campaign was to inject Green issues into national electoral politics, and recruit both activists and voters for whom these issues were important to the Greens. After all, Duverger's law does not leave much room for a party of the far left or right; hence a challenging new party will do best if it can define itself along a new ideological dimension, thereby attracting supporters from both parties for whom that ideology is salient.

This pattern occurred with the last successful creation of a new major party in the United States: During the 1840s, first the Liberty and then the Free Soil Party proved that growing numbers of voters found slavery a more salient issue than public improvements or the tariff, while the American Party of the 1850s proved a similar saliency for immigration issues. Ulti-mately, ambitious antislavery politicians chose to abandon both the Whigs and Democrats to launch the Republican Party, which won the presidency the second time it tried (Berg 1999a; Aldrich 1995, 155).

Some Greens would like their party to be seen as a manifestation of post-materialist "new politics," as envisioned in the work of Ronald Inglehart (1977).[3] Others (Nader, perhaps, among them) believe that the Democrats have abandoned their working-class roots by endorsing a pro-corporate, free-trade agenda, thus creating space for a new party that would unite the working class with small business and small-town Americans against global corporate hegemony. In either case, the time was ripe to redefine the political debate by means of a new party.

The Election of 2000

In addition to the general considerations discussed above, two particulars of the 2000 election season made a Green presidential campaign seem more auspicious. First, the anointing of Al Gore promised to continue the identification of the Democratic Party with the North American Free Trade Agreement (NAFTA), the World Trade Organization (WTO), and the rest of the global corporate agenda. Second, it was becoming apparent by the spring of 2000 that Pat Buchanan would win the Reform Party nomination, thereby moving that party from the center to the far right of the political continuum and leaving behind a bloc of voters who had already shown their dissatisfaction with the major parties. The Greens had gained members, local chapters, and new state parties from the 1996 campaign, and Nader, who had waged a minimalist campaign in 1996, was now willing to campaign seriously. The decision was made (by Nader and by ASGP leaders) for Nader to run again.

From the ASGP point of view, the campaign had several goals: to help the Greens grow in membership; to gain ballot access in more states; to prove that the Green agenda had to be taken into account by ambitious politicians; to get 5 percent of the popular vote and thereby qualify for federal funding in 2004; and to establish Green unity under ASGP hegemony. The GGPUSA shared the first four goals, although many of its members worried that Nader's platform would not represent Green principles clearly. As for organizational unity, some GGPUSA leaders recognized that they had no choice, since Nader's name recognition, popularity, and previous campaign identified him with the Greens in the public mind; other GGPUSA activists remain opposed to unity to this day. In the remainder of this chapter we first take a brief look at the progress of the Nader campaign, and then attempt to evaluate the degree to which the Green goals were achieved.

The Campaign and Election of 2000

Three things stand out about the Nader 2000 campaign: the professionalization of the Greens, the strength of grassroots support for Green politics, and the power of Duverger's law. Nader ran a slick, well-organized campaign with limited resources; he drew paying crowds of ten thousand and up in city after city, but voters abandoned him at the last moment as the closeness of the Gore-Bush contest became apparent.

A Professional Campaign

In 1996, Nader and the Greens had been criticized for mounting a non-campaign in which Nader raised and spent no money and seemed reluctant to embrace the Green platform.[4] The 2000 campaign was very different. Nader established a formal campaign committee ("Nader 2000"), raised money energetically—including about $700,000 in FEC "primary-season" matching funds, hired a national staff and a significant number of field organizers, and used a very limited budget for network television to leverage free media by running an ad that parodied a well-known credit card commercial. In comparison with the Bush and Gore campaigns, Nader's was amateurish and improvised (Sifry 2002), but in comparison with the typical left electoral effort, it was a model of professionalism.[5]

The June 2000 ASGP convention in Denver typified the new Green professionalism.[6] Previous national Green meetings, like most large conferences of the left, had consisted mostly of numerous workshops and endless debate, rewarding to the participants but incomprehensible to outside observers. The Denver convention, in contrast, was clearly made for television. Debate on the platform was limited and tightly controlled; there were no workshops or breakout sessions.[7] The other candidates for the nomination, Jello Biafra and Stephen Gaskin, stressed Nader's virtues, as did Joel Kovel, who had withdrawn his candidacy earlier. A series of well-known plenary speakers (Jim Hightower, John Anderson, Ronnie Dugger, and Tony Mazzochi) roused the delegates and gained press coverage for the convention.

The convention set the tone for the campaign. Although state and local Green parties joined in enthusiastically, the campaign was run by the Nader 2000 staff, which raised money, organized rallies, and printed literature. To the extent that funds allowed, state campaign coordinators were on the Nader 2000 payroll. William Hillsman, one of the architects of Jesse Ventura's Reform Party victory in Minnesota (Lentz 2002, 41–52), was retained as a media consultant and made a quick impact with his ad parodying a credit card commercial. Broadcast during the major party conventions, the ad provoked a copyright infringement suit.

Although the campaign budget was far more than Greens were accustomed to, it was far from adequate for a modern national campaign. There was little television advertising, and considerable emphasis on grassroots mobilization and free media. Nader used his unsuccessful demand for participation in the debates to garner press coverage—in Boston, for example, he obtained a ticket to watch the debates, got a television news crew to film him as he traveled to the site on the subway, and then got more press by suing the debate commission after he was excluded from the audience.

Large rallies in major cities were the most important campaign activities. By amassing paying crowds of ten thousand or more, the campaign generated local press and demonstrated that Nader had significant popular support. The campaign also gained visibility from Nader's decision to concentrate his efforts in September and October on states where his presence might affect the outcome. This decision compelled the Gore campaign to respond, both by emphasizing what it claimed to be its affinity to Green positions on various issues, and by arguing publicly that a vote for Nader was, in effect, a vote for Bush. These attacks by Gore may have brought Nader's campaign more press coverage than anything else the campaign did.

The Demise of the Reform Party

While Nader's campaign grew, the collapse of the Reform Party proceeded as expected. The fascinating story of this collapse is tangential to the purposes of this chapter. Suffice it to say that the party's possession of $12 million in FEC funds made it an inviting takeover target, while the unwillingness of H. Ross Perot and Jesse Ventura either to run or to cede influence to others weakened its ability to resist such a takeover. The result was a descent into farce. First Perot sought to use Pat Buchanan as a cat's-paw against Ventura. Ventura, unwilling to run himself because he felt bound by his promise to serve a full term as governor of Minnesota, sought futilely to recruit first Lowell Weicker and then Donald Trump as cat's-paws of his own, and ultimately quit the Reform Party. Finally Perot—whose cat's-paw had now become Frankenstein's monster—turned to John Hagelin, twice candidate of the Natural Law Party (Berg 1998, 221–223; Natural Law Party 1992), in a last-ditch attempt to block Buchanan. The sorry affair ended with a series of court wrangles about which candidate could use the Reform label, and the evaporation of both the Reform Party and Pat Buchanan as political forces.

With Reform effectively out of the picture, the Greens moved up in the political hierarchy. They were now the "Third" Party. While this new status did not get Nader into the debates, or gain national media coverage for his campaign, it did make him the default choice for any voters who might become disenchanted with the two major parties. Most important, it left a void in the center of the political spectrum. The Greens had no wish to become a centrist party, nor would a shift to the center have been credible with the electorate. But the absence of a centrist candidate left more space for the Greens' strategy of realignment along a new ideological dimension.

The Final Weeks

By mid-October polls showed support for Nader at 7 to 8 percent in California, Connecticut, New Jersey, and Rhode Island, 10 percent in Minnesota and Oregon, and 17 percent in Alaska. California and Alaska were not competitive, but in the other states, such as Washington and Wisconsin, the Gore campaign began to worry that Nader might win enough votes to tip the states, and perhaps the election, to Bush (Sifry 2000a). The Gore campaign, which had been trying to ignore Nader, now struck back. Gore proclaimed his commitment to environmentalism while arguing that a vote for Nader would help elect Bush. A group of major environmental organizations repeated the argument. Regular stories about Nader—albeit negative ones—began to appear in the election coverage of the *New York Times* for the first time since the Green convention at the end of June (Nichols 2000).

While Gore was attacking Nader, Nader was targeting Gore, having made the strategic decision to campaign hardest in the swing states, including Florida, during the last few weeks before the election (Nichols 2000). Understandably, this decision was not popular with Democrats, but it helped establish the Green Party as an electoral force to be reckoned with.

The Election Results

On Election Day 2000, Nader received 2,882,782 votes nationwide, 2.74 percent of the total, finishing third—well ahead of Buchanan with 0.43 percent, but far behind the 50 million vote totals of Bush and Gore.[8] Nader also fell far short of the 5 percent cutoff needed to qualify the Greens for FEC general election matching funds in 2004.

There is little room for doubt that Nader's presence in the campaign changed the outcome of the election. Whatever the actual vote in Florida may have been, the official results gave Bush 2,912,790, Gore 2,912,253, and Nader 97,488 in the Sunshine State. Not only Nader, but Reform Party candidate Patrick Buchanan (17,484), Libertarian candidate Harry Browne (16,415), Natural Law candidate John Hagelin (2,281), Workers World candidate Monica Moorehead (1,804), Constitution Party candidate Howard Phillips (1,371), Socialist Party USA candidate David McReynolds (approximately 620 votes), and Socialist Workers candidate James Harris (563) received more votes than the official Bush-Gore margin of 537.

In that sense, any of these candidates' withdrawal would have changed the outcome if all of their votes had gone to Gore instead. However, for Nader at least it is questionable whether all of his votes would have gone to Gore. A national exit poll taken by CNN on Election Day asked voters who they would have supported if the only candidates had been Bush and Gore, and this data is probably the best estimate available. Of those who had reported voting for Nader, 46.3 percent said that they would have voted for Gore, 23.7 percent said that they would have voted for Bush, and 30 percent said that they would not have voted.[9] If we apply these percentages to Nader's Florida vote, we can guess that a little more than 45,000 of those votes would have gone to Gore and a little more than 23,000 to Bush had Nader's name not been on the Florida ballot. This would have given Gore a Florida margin of 21,000, perhaps enough to have moved the election out of disputed territory.

The Nader vote was greater than the Bush-Gore difference in seven other states: Iowa, Maine, Minnesota, New Hampshire, New Mexico, Oregon, and Wisconsin. All of those except New Hampshire were won by Gore, whose margin would have been increased by Nader's absence. In New Hampshire, Bush received 273,559 votes to Gore's 266,348, a margin of 7,211, while Nader received 22,188 votes. As in Florida, if all of the New Hampshire

Nader voters had supported Gore, he would have won the state—and the presidency. However, if we apply the CNN exit poll percentages, we get 10,273 votes for Gore and 5,259 votes for Bush. This would have left Bush still the victor, by 278,818 votes to 276,621. Unfortunately, the CNN poll does not allow us to determine whether New Hampshire Nader voters were more or less pro-Gore than the national average.

Whatever the hypothetical outcome of Nader's absence might have been, the consensus of political insiders is clearly that he must be included among the large number of factors such as Gore's neglect of Tennessee and Arkansas, the Supreme Court, Katherine Harris, and Jeb Bush, any one of which would have changed the outcome. For some, this situation makes the Green Party a force to be reckoned with, as was the Perot organization after the 1992 election. For others, it makes it a pariah to be shunned by all good Democrats.

The Impact of the Campaign

The Nader campaign's impact must be evaluated against its purposes, as discussed above: to develop the Green Party, help provoke a realignment of the two-party system, and insert issues that would otherwise be suppressed into the public consciousness and debate. The focus of this chapter is on the first of these purposes; the others are discussed briefly in the conclusion.

The Greens in 2001

Almost all Greens I have interviewed believe emphatically that their party benefited from the Nader campaign. The Greens grew in membership, office holding, public visibility, and ballot access. They are closer to organizational unity than they have been for a long time, and they have eclipsed the New Party and Labor Party as the voice of the non-Democratic electoral left. However, they failed to qualify for FEC general election funds, and they have incurred the opprobrium of many liberal interest groups. Each of these impacts will be examined in turn.

Green Benefits. Membership in the Greens is difficult to measure, since the definition of "member" is the central legal issue dividing the two national Green organizations. As of September 2001, the former ASGP—now the Green Party of the United States (GPUS)—had thirty-three state party members (including the District of Columbia);[10] seven of those state parties had affiliated during the year 2000. Missouri was in the process of applying for membership, and the remaining seventeen states had GPUS-affiliated local organizations.[11] Green registration reached 193,332 (of which 138,695 were in California) by the 2000 election; this figure was a 63 percent increase over the total of 118,537 (with 98,443 in California) for 1998.[12] The GG-PUSA reported that its dues-paying membership nearly doubled, from 1,200 to 2,350, between July 2000 and January 2001 (Rankin 2001).

Mike Feinstein of the Green Party of California has compiled lists of Green candidates and elected officials since 1986.[13] Most of the candidates and almost all of the elected officials are for municipal offices, many of which are nonpartisan; but all are Green Party members who generally ran as self-proclaimed "Green" candidates.[14] Feinstein's data for the first few years are spotty; data for even-numbered years from 1990–2000 are given in table 20.1. The increase in both candidates and victories from 1998–2000 is by far the largest since 1992 (when large percentage increases were added to low starting points). The time series is not long enough to support a firm conclusion or to separate the impact of the Nader campaign from the ongoing upward trend, but it seems reasonable to think that Nader's presence on the ballot may have encouraged more and better candidates to run.

The increase continued into 2001. As of September 25, the Green Party of the United States reported that 244 Greens had run or were running for mostly local offices. In the thirty-four elections with Green candidates that had been completed by August 31, fifteen Green candidates won the election; sixteen were defeated; and one seemed to win at first, lost on a recount (the issue involved the misspelling of John Schmidt's name on ten write-in ballots), and is now challenging the results in court; the other two sets of results were not available at the time of writing. As of September 2001, Feinstein's web site reported that there were ninety-two Greens in elected office in the United States.

In assessing public visibility, we need data that will let us separate Nader's visibility from that of the Greens. Nader was well known before he ran, but now he is well known (if not always approved of) as a presidential candidate. Probably many people know that Nader ran as a Green, but they may not know that the party has an independent existence. However, more visi-

Table 20.1   Green Candidates and Victories, Even Years, 1990–2000

Year	Number of Candidates	Yearly % Increase	Number of Victories	Yearly % Increase
1990	15	n/a	6	n/a
1992	98	553	15	150
1994	76	−22	14	−7
1996	82	8	19	36
1998	130	59	21	11
2000	274	111	35	67

Source: Compiled by the author from Mike Feinstein, "Green Party Election Results." Green Party of California State Clearinghouse, 2001, available at www.greens.org/elections (accessed December 2002).

bility is likely to come because of the increases in ballot access. Green parties now have the right to nominate candidates, either by primary or by convention, and have those candidates appear on the ballot in twenty-one states and the District of Columbia.[15] In contrast, at the beginning of 1999 the Greens had ballot status in only ten states. This more favorable ballot status, together with the influx of activists into the Greens during the campaign, may produce a surge in Green candidacies in the 2002 election.

Finally, the Nader campaign brought the Greens considerably closer to organizational unity. Under strong pressure from rank-and-file Greens, and conscious of the difficulty of winning public support for a movement torn by internal feuds, negotiators from the ASGP and GGPUSA met shortly after the election to draw up the "Boston Plan" for unity. The plan was quickly adopted by the ASGP. The GGPUSA, after months of debate, rejected the merger at its national meeting in July 2001, but lost many members as a result of the bitter dispute. At a national meeting in Santa Barbara, July 27–29, 2001, the ASGP voted to become the Green Party of the United States, and filed for recognition as such with the FEC.[16]

The different responses of the two organizations correspond to the nature of the "Boston Plan," which would have been essentially an ASGP victory. Having brought the Greens into the national spotlight with the Nader campaign, the ASGP had the upper hand, and most of the issues went its way. Technically, the ASGP was to have been replaced by a new organization, organized on somewhat different principles—mainly, a formal independent role for locals that do not feel themselves represented by their state parties— but the new organization would have had all of the essential features of the old, including membership based on voter registration. The GGPUSA, on the other hand, would have had to drop the word "party" from its name, and would have become essentially a caucus within the party. Whether this result should count as a success for "the Greens" depends on one's point of view. It was certainly a success for those ASGP activists who initiated the Nader campaign.

A final benefit for the Greens is that the visibility of the Nader campaign has made them the leading minor party on the left. As Collet and Hansen (2002) put it, they have "established Sartorian relevance." The New Party, the Labor Party, the Socialist Party, and the Workers World Party will continue to function, but young progressive activists looking for a way to get involved in electoral politics are likely to turn to the Greens.[17]

Green Costs. A 5 percent share of the vote for Nader, leading to Green Party entitlement to FEC general election matching funds in 2004, was widely proclaimed as a goal—not only by Nader and the Greens, but in the "Ivins Plan" promoted by *The Nation*.[18] Nader's vote (2.7 percent) fell far short of that goal.

However, with the benefit of hindsight we can ask whether the Greens were ready to handle the status a 5 percent vote for Nader would have given them. The fate of the Reform Party is instructive in this regard. Once Ross Perot withdrew from active candidacy, the party structure proved to be too weak to defend itself from a hostile takeover, while the FEC funds made it an extremely tempting target for just such a takeover. The Greens have faced takeover attempts on the local level, but have so far been able to contain them.[19] The Greens are stronger in organizational terms than the Reform Party ever was, because they were built from the bottom up. All the same, it may be that another four years of organizing may make them better able to handle $5 million in matching funds.

The new conventional wisdom of political scientists is that a party needs to attract ambitious politicians if it is to thrive and grow. John Aldrich (1995, 155) and Theodore Lowi and Joseph Romance (1998, 12) have argued this point convincingly in different contexts. The rational choice logic behind this argument is convincing, but a modification is needed. To thrive, a party must be able to maintain at least some of its core principles while ambitious politicians join it. Many members of the Liberty Party believed that the successor Free Soil Party compromised unacceptably on slavery, and many Free Soilers thought the same of the Republicans. Nevertheless, there was some historical continuity: The successor parties were widening the antislavery niche, not moving out of it. Pat Buchanan, in contrast, was able to move the Reform Party to a completely different—and far less tenable—point on the political continuum.

The perception that Nader's presence on the ticket caused Bush to win—a correct perception, as discussed earlier—also produced some costs. But for the most part these costs will be borne by Nader rather than by the Green Party. Democratic leaders and liberal lobbyists have heaped scorn on Nader, and declared that they will no longer join with him to work for progressive causes.[20] These threats, delivered in the throes of emotion, may not be carried out. Nader supporters are now the swing vote in several states, and the Democrats will need to woo them, not drive them away, if they hope to win the presidency in 2004 (Sifry 2000b). However, if the threats are carried out, while they would undermine Nader's personal influence as a lobbyist, they would also increase the Greens' appeal among that portion of the public that supported Nader's positions and saw the Democrats turning against them.

Future Prospects

The Greens now face the harsh reality of state electoral laws. To maintain their newly expanded ballot status they will have to nominate candidates for statewide office in many states where they barely existed before the

Nader campaign. They will be aided in this effort by the enthusiastic members, money, and visibility that the Nader campaign brought them. Perhaps there will also be an influx of talented candidates, perhaps even some disaffected major party politicians. The search for such candidates is now underway. At this point, with little data, the most probable outcome may be that the Greens will lose ballot access in some of the states where it is newly gained, but retain it in some others, while continuing to grow in those states where they were on the ballot before 2000.

Meanwhile, Nader embarked on a national speaking tour in the fall of 2001. The tour had been planned to focus on a set of "pro-democracy" reforms, but Nader seized the opportunity to speak out against the war in Afghanistan (which Greens have generally condemned). This condemnation of the war is not shared by most voters, but since both major parties support the war, the Greens may find new support among the minority who share this view.

As for 2004, it is really too early to say. Will Nader run again? Will other strong candidates join the Greens? Given the Democrats' endorsement of the war, a Green candidacy seems highly probable.

In the long run, the Greens probably have more potential for disrupting the two-party system than for winning the presidency. Nevertheless, they do need to get more votes in 2004 if they are to not fade away. If they can increase their vote to 8–10 percent, and the United States continues to elect presidents with no majority, ambitious politicians may begin to look for alternatives. The last time such a pattern developed was in the two decades before the Civil War, when the Liberty, Free Soil, and American Parties disrupted the political equilibrium, and thereby triggered the formation of the Republican Party. This change brought a new ideological dimension into force, and in due course, the end of slavery in America.

Notes

1. This organization should not be confused with the Committees of Correspondence for Democracy and Socialism, an organization, still in existence, of anti-Stalinist Marxists, many of whom were previously dissident members of the Communist Party of the USA. The two organizations are not related.

2. An additional possible choice would have been to seek the creation of a multiparty system in the United States. Since doing so would probably require a constitutional amendment to change the electoral system, such a strategy would have been less immediate. An excellent case for such a change is made by Amy (1993).

3. Collet (1997) treats the Greens as a postmaterialist party, but this characterization is open to debate, both because of shortcomings in Inglehart's conceptualization of postmaterialism, and because the Greens have incorporated many activists and many issue positions of the traditional left; see Berg 2000.

4. In 1996, Nader agreed to accept the nomination only on the condition that he and the

many nonprofit organizations associated with him not be subjected to the reporting requirements of the FEC; he believed that such reporting would be used to harass the nonprofits. For this reason, all money was raised and spent by state Green parties; there was no national staff or national advertising, and little national coordination. The Greens accepted this arrangement because they wanted the visibility a Nader campaign would bring them, and saw no better alternative. I shall not attempt to evaluate the wisdom of this choice here.

5. Micah Sifry's comments on an earlier draft are responsible for this and many other points.

6. The following paragraphs are drawn from personal observation.

7. The Nader 2000 organization ran a parallel series of campaign training sessions, led by paid staff, in another hotel. These were not issue debates, but instructions in how to raise money, handle press relations, and the like.

8. Except for McReynolds, all results in this and the following paragraph are taken from *Ballot Access News* 16, no. 10 (January 1, 2001); results for McReynolds are from the Socialist Party USA website, www.votesocialist.org (accessed December 2002).

9. Recalculated from exit-poll results reported on the CNN web page at www.cnn.com/ELECTION/2000/epolls/US/P000.html (accessed December 2002).

10. Association of State Green Parties, "ASGP Members and Affiliates," at www.greenparties.org/statelist.html (accessed September 2001).

11. Green Party of the U.S., "State Affiliation List," at www.greenpartyus.org/statelist.html (accessed September 2001).

12. Figures from *Ballot Access News* 14, no. 9 (December 8, 1999): 3; 14, no. 9 (December 5, 2000), at www.ballot-access.org. Comparison is made with 1998, rather than with the previous presidential election, because Green registration was higher in 1998.

13. Green Party of California State Clearinghouse 2001, "Green Party Election Results" at www.greens.org/elections (accessed December 2002).

14. Audie Bock was elected to the California State Assembly as a Green in a 1999 special election, but later left the party to seek reelection as an independent. To the best of my knowledge, she is the only Green yet elected to a state legislature.

15. The states are Alaska, California, Colorado, Delaware, Florida, Hawaii, Iowa, Maine, Massachusetts, Michigan, Minnesota, Montana, Nevada, New Mexico, New York, Oregon, Rhode Island, South Carolina, Texas, Utah, and Wisconsin. From *Ballot Access News* 14, no. 12 (March 6, 1999) and 16, no. 11 (February 1, 2001), at www.ballot-access.org/2001/0201.html (accessed December 2002).

16. Green Party of the United States, "Greens Create National Party," July 30, 2001, press release, at www.greenpartyus.org/press/pr_07_30_01.html.

17. As always, the situation would change radically if several unions were to give active support to the Labor Party, and particularly if the Labor Party were to nominate and campaign for candidates. As always, this is not likely to happen.

18. *The Nation* wanted Gore to win, but wanted the Greens to get matching funds; consequently it urged its readers to vote for Gore if they lived in electorally competitive states, but to vote for Nader if they lived in states certain to be won by either Gore or Bush.

19. On August 8, 2001, it was reported that Republican Party operatives had contributed money to the Washington state legislative campaign of Young S. Han, and had organized a "Green" nominating convention for the purpose of running Michael Jepson, who had no history as a Green, for another local office. In both cases the presumed intent was to draw votes from the Democratic candidate. Han returned the money, and the Greens denounced the maneuvers and demanded that Jepson withdraw from the race. Green Party of the United States, "Greens Reject Republican Money, Challenge Democrats to Support Instant Runoff Voting (IRV)," August 10, 2001, press release available at www.greenpartyus.org/press/pr_08_10_01.html (accessed December 2002).

20. See, for example, the *Christian Science Monitor,* November 15, 2000.

21

Ross Perot Is Alive and Well and Living in the Republican Party: Major Party Co-optation of the Perot Movement and the Reform Party

Ronald B. Rapoport and Walter J. Stone

In perusing the standard postelection books on the 2000 election, one searches in vain for references to the Perot movement, its role in the result, or its long-term effects on American politics. The implosion of the Reform Party merits mention for its sideshow value rather than for any meaningful legacy to the party system.

Why this is the case is not completely clear. In part it might be attributable to the strong personality of Perot and his enormous wealth, which focused attention on the leader rather than his movement, and in part it can be attributed to the movement's unusual nature, which transformed itself into a political party in time for the 1996 election and then became the object of a hostile takeover by Pat Buchanan in the 2000 campaign.

Here we focus on another reason: The fact that the Perot movement had its major effect not through the Reform Party (which was founded in 1996), but through its impact on the Republican Party and its fortunes, beginning with the 1994 elections. Coverage of the drama (as well as the dramatis personae) surrounding this movement and party has obscured the important effect that Perot and his followers have had on bringing the Republican Party into parity at the congressional level, in enhancing Republican support at the presidential level, and in mobilizing new activists into the Republican Party. It may be tempting to view a candidacy such as Ross Perot's in 1992 as an aberration in a candidate-centered age, and with no particular consequence for the two-party system once he disappeared. But we show that the effect of Perot's campaign was lasting and significant. Although it manifested itself first and most significantly in 1994, it remained significant in every campaign through the 2000 election—eight years after Perot's first appearance as a presidential candidate.

The Dynamic of Third Parties

Part of the difficulty in understanding the Perot movement compared with other third parties is that it did not quite follow the expected pattern (Green and Herrnson 2002). We refer to the tendency of "major" third-party movements to emerge in a single election and immediately disappear, as the "dynamic of third parties." Or as Richard Hofstadter (1955, 97) observed, "Third parties are like bees; once they have stung, they die."[1] This dynamic applies primarily to third-party movements that attract a substantial share of the popular vote—over 5 percent is a good guideline—rather than parties such as the Natural Law, Libertarian, or Socialist Labor parties that regularly attract minuscule vote shares, but persist from election to election. Why do "successful" third parties quickly die? The degree of success of the party or candidate signals the depth and breadth of discontent in the electorate, and alerts the two major parties to the political implications of their failure. The larger the vote the candidate receives, the greater the incentive the two parties have to respond. As Mazmanian (1974, 143) put it: "Usually after a strong showing by a minor party, at least one of the major parties shifts its position, adopting the third party's rhetoric if not the core of its programs. Consequently, by the following election the third-party constituency . . . has a major party more sympathetic to its demands." Hence the "dynamic of third parties": the more successful they are, the quicker they die (Stone and Rapoport 2001).

But, while Perot may have "stung" the two parties in 1992 by attracting almost 20 percent of the popular vote, he certainly did not immediately "die." In fact, he ran again in 1996 under the banner of the newly created Reform Party, and won more than 8 percent of the popular vote. In so doing, he became the first third-party candidate to win more than 5 percent of the popular vote in consecutive elections since the rise of the Republican Party in the 1850s. Indeed, with the guarantee of federal funds for the Reform Party campaign in 2000, there was a realistic possibility that the Reform Party might continue to defy the "dynamics of third parties" and remain on the scene for the foreseeable future. Such hopes proved to be overly optimistic, and the Reform Party nominee Pat Buchanan received only about 1 percent of the vote in 2000 and was easily eclipsed among third-party candidates by Green Party nominee Ralph Nader. (For an account of the Reform Party in 2000, see Green and Binning 2002.)

Despite the fact that Perot's political "death" was more prolonged than those of previous third-party candidates, we argue that the fundamental logic of the dynamic of third parties still applies (Stone and Rapoport 2001). In fact, by the time of the 1994 election, the normal co-optation by the major parties of third-party issues and supporters had already taken place on two of three issue clusters that Perot emphasized in 1992. As a result of this co-optation of two of the central issues in Perot's 1992 campaign, the Reform Party was already handicapped at its inception in 1996. Its demise was almost inevitable, unless it could mobilize on the basis of its remaining, albeit limited, appeal. Even though Perot received a substantial vote in 1996, his decline in support between 1992 and 1996 was greater than the vote share of all but a handful of third parties since the Civil War. In any case, significant long-term effects of the Perot movement were already manifested in the 1994 Republican takeover of Congress, and these effects have continued through the 2000 elections.

Major Party Responses to Perot's 1992 Success

The dynamic of third parties is, of course, well known to both major parties. After a showing such as that of Perot's in 1992, we would expect the major parties to try to attract his followers by adopting his core issue positions as much as possible. Although the Republicans were more successful in appealing to Perot supporters (as we will show), Democrats also attempted to appeal to Perot supporters. On February 15, 1993, less than a month after his inauguration, Clinton prepared to address the budget deficit. Because Clinton clearly understood the importance of Perot's response, he called Perot the day of his address to Congress and spoke with him for about fifteen minutes (Richter 1993). Although Clinton was not successful in eliciting Perot's full support, in a speech in Florida on February 20, Perot agreed with Clinton that tax increases were needed to balance the deficit. Perot also argued, however, that such tax increases must be accompanied by passage of a Balanced Budget Amendment, about which Perot had reversed his earlier opposition (Oliphant 1993), a cut in congressional salaries, benefits, and perks, and campaign finance reform. Further, he felt that the administration had not gone far enough on budget cuts. He demanded that the Clinton White House "give us the details on spending cuts" and "tell us precisely when they will occur" (*Associated Press* 1993, 9). Although there was some response from Perot supporters to Clinton's appeal, it was the Republicans who were most successful in attracting Perot's supporters.

The Republican strategy came into play as soon as the new Clinton administration had taken office. Almost immediately, the Republican Party, especially the House Republicans under the leadership of Newt Gingrich, began courting Ross Perot and his supporters.[2] After some initial resistance to this approach from Bob Dole, the Republican leader in the U.S. Senate, and Haley Barbour, the chair of the Republican National Committee, both were on board by the early summer of 1993.

There were several reasons why Republicans were in a better position to appeal to Perot voters than the Democrats. Perot supporters were distrustful of those in power in Washington (Gillespie 1993; Gold 1995; McCann, Rapoport, and Stone 1999). Because Republicans were in the minority in the House and Senate and the Democrats also controlled the presidency under Bill Clinton, the Republicans could play to that distrust by their criticisms of the Democratic government. In addition, Newt Gingrich and several other Republican congressional leaders went so far as to join United We Stand America, Perot's political advocacy group.

Specific issue appeals also helped the Republicans. The Gore-Perot debate on NAFTA and the perception that Clinton had reversed himself on the issue, and the Clinton health plan debacle and Perot's attacks on it, gave the Republicans a realistic opportunity to capture the bulk of the Perot vote in 1994. These were all important to Republican support in 1994 since Perot was not himself on the ballot, nor had he started the Reform Party or recruited candidates to run on his behalf. Thus, the Republicans benefited from their positive appeal to Perot supporters and residual dissatisfaction with the Democrats.

The clearest evidence of the Republican bid for support from the legions of Perot supporters is found in the Contract with America, a set of common legislative and policy commitments offered by the Republican Party and its House candidates in 1994. The need for such a "contract" was strongly endorsed by Perot in the final pages of his 1992 election manifesto, *United We Stand America*. There he sets forth a "Checklist for All Federal Candidates." This idea "about getting a contract of issues that candidates would have to sign in order to get an endorsement . . . was transferred to the Republicans, and of course, Perot was delighted by it" (Clay Mulford, in Posner 1996, 331).

The Contract with America emphasized issues of a balanced budget amendment, limited American commitment to internationalism, term limits, and congressional reform, all issues emphasized by Ross Perot in his 1992 campaign. Just as notably, the Contract omitted reference to Republican priorities such as stopping abortion and promoting free trade. These issues united the Republican base, but were strongly opposed by the pivotal Perot constituency. As Barry Jackson, staff director of the Republican House Conference, pointed out, "The Contract was carefully targeted toward people we wanted to bring back into the fold—Perot voters that had been alienated" (quoted in Gimpel 1996, 25). In addition, Newt Gingrich and other Republican leaders were skillful political entrepreneurs able to make the case that their party was best suited to further the Perot agenda if elected to the majority, a plea embraced by Perot himself when he called on his supporters before the 1994 elections to "give the Republicans a majority in the House and Senate and say, all right, now, we're gonna let you guys have a turn at bat" (quoted in Schneider 1994).

In addition to the orchestrated effort to woo Perot and his supporters by the Republican national leadership, the Republican Party managed to concentrate its most experienced candidates in districts with the greatest levels of Perot supporters and, therefore, districts with the greatest opportunity for gain. We have found a clear relationship between the size of districts' 1992 Perot vote and the appearance of experienced Republican candidates in 1994. This effect holds up with controls for whether the seat was open in 1994, the partisan composition of the district, and whether the Republican candidate in 1992 was experienced. By our estimates, in 1994 the probability of an experienced Republican emerging in Democrat-held districts where Perot received only 5 percent of the vote in 1992 was about .06. On the other hand, the chances of an experienced candidate running in 1994 climbed to .32 in statistically equivalent districts where Perot won 30 percent of the vote in 1992. This indicates some combination of active recruiting by the national Republican Party and the strategic decisions of experienced potential House candidates who recognized that a substantial Perot vote created an opportunity for Republicans in 1994.

The effect of these appeals by the Republicans, in particular, was to gain a significant boost in support from 1992 Perot supporters. In 1992, exit polls showed Perot supporters splitting their votes almost equally between Democratic and Republican congressional campaigns. However, in 1994, Perot supporters voted Republican by a 2-1 majority. This 17 percent shift among almost 20 percent of the electorate resulted in a net gain of more than 3 percent of the total vote to the Republicans. In addition, Perot's activist constituency showed similar shifts toward the Republicans in campaign activity. In both 1988 and 1992, levels of activity among individuals who called Perot's 1-800 number in 1992 were almost identical for the two parties' congressional candidates, but in 1994, Republican activity was 50 percent greater than that of Democratic congressional candidates (Rapoport and Stone 2000).

Because Perot was off of the ballot in 1994, and had called for "giving the Republicans a chance," it was difficult at the time to assess the degree to which Republican support from the 1992 Perot contingent was a positive response to Perot's call for a Republican majority, or a successful co-optation of Perot issues by Republicans. The implications of the two alternative interpretations would be crucial to Perot's potential to remobilize his 1992 constituency when he reentered the electoral arena as a candidate in 1996, and important in determining whether the 1992 Perot campaign would influence American politics in the long term. Were major party co-optation successful, Perot would find it far more difficult to reestablish his level of support in 1996 than if the Republican success of 1994 revolved around his mobilization of his supporters on their behalf.

What expectations from the dynamic of third parties and the results from analysis of election returns can we bring to survey data of Perot supporters after 1992? Our general expectation is that both major parties will show some success in co-opting Perot issues as early as 1994. As a result, these same issues should emerge as more important determinants of major party support, making the Perot appeal far less attractive by 1996 than it had been earlier.

Although the process of co-optation may be common to both major parties, the success of each in appealing to Perot supporters need not be equivalent. Given the out-party status of the Republicans, their appeal on the more popular Perot issues, and Perot's endorsement of them, we expect to find Perot supporters moving disproportionately to support the Republican Party in the campaigns following the 1992 election.

In sum, our argument is that Perot's support declined because of co-optation by the major parties, and that this decline redounded disproportionately to the Republicans, helping them achieve parity with the Democrats in 2000 and beyond.

Data

To test our hypotheses, we use a panel survey of Perot supporters covering the life of the Perot movement and Reform Party. It began as a survey of potential Perot activists in September of 1992, with subsequent waves immediately after the election in 1992, after the election in 1994, immediately after the 1996 election, and immediately following the 2000 election. (For earlier reports of the survey, see Stone et al. 1999, and Partin et al. 1994, 1996.)

Not only are the response rates reasonably good (ranging from 50.3 percent to 69.0 percent across waves), but post-1992 nonrespondents do not differ on important 1992 variables from respondents. This extended panel allows us to assess how much respondents participated in the 1992 Perot movement and 1996 Reform Party campaign, as well as their participation in campaigns for major party candidates in 1992, 1994, 1996, and 2000. Because we have surveyed the same people over an eight-year period, we can monitor change and continuity at the individual level over the eight-year period in attitudes and behavior.

Our sample of potential Perot supporters is comprised of individuals who called the Perot 1-800 number in the spring of 1992. This is a more active and elite sample than simply one of voters, since all individuals had to take the initiative to call the number. Most of these (80 percent) followed up with some activity (including trying to persuade others to support Perot) on behalf of the campaign.

There are significant advantages to studying an activist sample in a study of party change. In both major parties and incipient third parties, activists play disproportionate roles in defining party positions and priorities and in selecting party nominees. Particularly in third parties, the development of a cadre of activists is crucial to party success (Lowi 1996) since they provide a stable base of support and of campaign workers. Furthermore, because activists have more coherent and stable ideological and issue views than rank-and-file voters (Converse 1964; Jennings 1992), they reflect and shape the party positions on a wide range of issues. In a new third party, without any long-standing bases of group support, activists are likely to be particularly important as a window into the core appeal of the new party and its ideological and issue bases.

The Dynamic of Third Parties and Survey Evidence: Co-optation

In our research on the Perot movement, we have identified three distinctive sources of Perot support in 1992: issues relating to the budget/taxation, political reform, and economic nationalism. All three of these differentiated Perot from the major parties, which did not emphasize them at all or did so to a much lesser degree than did Perot. If these issues were available to Perot because the major parties ignored or downplayed them, then, by definition, they should play far less of a role in predicting major party political activity, and should be either insignificant, negative, or only weakly related to support for the Republicans and Democrats in 1992.

In September 1992, we asked respondents for their views on two reform issues (term limits and a balanced budget amendment), two budget/tax issues (measured here by a gas tax and increased taxes for social security), and two economic nationalism issues (limiting imports and curtailing U.S. involvement overseas). For each question respondents were asked the degree to which they favored or opposed each proposal. If they "strongly favored" or "favored" the Perot position on both issues in an area they were categorized as high in support; if they "strongly favored" or "favored" one of the two issues they were categorized as medium; and if neither of the issues received their support, they were categorized as low. We assigned each respondent a score in each of the three issue areas in this manner.

Since these three areas were all important to Perot's appeal in 1992, our expectation is that we should find each of these affecting Perot activity in 1992. In addition, because the issues were not central to either of the major parties' campaigns, they should not affect support for either the Democratic or Republican parties in that year. Of the three sets of issues, Republicans most directly addressed reform issues after 1992 in the Contract with America and budget/tax issues were most directly addressed by Clinton's 1993 budget plan. If co-optation occurred following 1992, then we should find that by 1994, Republican activity should have become particularly correlated with reform issues, and Democrats might have gained on the tax dimensions of the budget issue, which they passed soon after the election and on which they won praise from Perot. If the two parties were successful in taking these issues away from Perot, then the impact of these issues on Perot support in both 1994 and after should decline.

The relationship of the major parties to issues of economic nationalism after 1992 is more ambiguous. Neither party addressed the protectionist and foreign involvement aspects together in ways consistent with the approach of Perot's campaign. Although many Democrats actually opposed NAFTA, it was Clinton who delivered the crucial votes that, combined with the overwhelming majority of the Republicans in the House, saw its passage. While ignoring trade in the Contract, the Republicans nonetheless failed to repudiate NAFTA or free trade. On the foreign involvement issue, however, the Republicans stood strong against Clinton's "foreign adventurism" in Haiti, which the Democrats strongly supported. As a result, neither party can be expected to capture this issue and we should expect to find its continued influence on Perot support even after 1994.

In order to assess the level of co-optation, we look at the effect of each dimension of 1992 Perot support on Perot activity, Democratic activity, and Republican activity in 1992 and then 1994 and thereafter. Our expectation is that the level of support for Perot issues translated into Perot support in 1992 (and not into support for the major parties), but that co-optation by the major parties between 1992 and 1994 led these same individuals to increase their support for the major parties in elections in 1994 and after, on those issues for which co-optation was successful. Correspondingly, the impact of these co-opted issues on Perot support should decline after 1994. In order to insure that it is issue positions that determine campaign activity for Perot (and after), and not campaign activity that shapes issue positions, we use attitudes derived from questions asked of respondents in the September wave of our 1992 survey to predict activity that we asked about in November 1992. We use the same independent variables (assessed in 1992) to predict Perot and major party activity in 1994, 1996, and 2000. Thus, we set a difficult task for ourselves in demanding that attitudes in 1992 explain activity in the elections of 1994–2000, up to eight years after the attitudes were measured.

We begin with an examination of Republican co-optation success. Reform issues (balanced budget amendment and term limits) provided a target of opportunity for Republicans in 1994. They had been on the same side of both issues as the Perot supporters, but in their 1992 platform had not given these issues the emphasis that Perot had given them, nor that they gave them in the Contract, nor in the 1996 Republican platform. Reform of Congress (including term limits for committee chairs) led off the Contract, but the first legislative initiative was the balanced budget amendment and the last of the ten proposals was term limits. Emphasizing these issues made a great deal of sense for the Republicans. If they could co-opt these issues they could appeal to a broad base within Perot's constituency. Almost 60 percent of our sample of potential Perot supporters endorsed both term limits and the balanced budget amendment (59.9 percent of actual Perot activists) and this level of support was twice as great as for either of the other two issue areas.

If the Republicans were successful in co-optation of reform issues, then we should see a significant shift between 1992 and 1994 in the relationship between issue positions and Republican support. Whereas those high on "reformism" in 1992 should not differ significantly in the number of Republican activities that they performed in 1992 from those who are lower, we should begin to find significant differences in Republican activity in 1994 and after based on level of support for reform issues.

In figure 21.1 we report the mean number of activities for Republican candidates in 1992, 1994, 1996, and 2000 for our sample of activists at each level of support for reform issues.[3] The results are very much in keeping with our hypothesis. The relationship between support for "reform issues" and activity for the Republicans increases markedly between 1992 and 1994. In 1992 those most supportive of reform issues perform about twice as many activities as those least supportive. In fact, the relationship between September 1992 attitudes and November 1992 activity is weak and fails the traditional test of statistical significance. But by 1994, the most reform-minded performed almost four and a half times the number of activities as the least reform-minded. By 1994, the correlation is almost four times as great as two years earlier and the statistical relationship is highly significant. Remarkably, continuing to use 1992 reform attitudes as predictors of 1996 and 2000 behavior, we continue to find highly significant relationships that far surpass those of 1992. In 1996 the most reform-minded perform more than four times as many activities as the least reform-minded, and in 2000 almost three times as many.[4]

While Perot supporters took cognizance of the Republicans' appeal on reform issues, they were also aware of what Democrats were doing. Democratic proposals for budget balancing through increased taxes came to play a much more important role in shaping responses to Democratic candidates in 1994 and after than they had in 1992. As figure 21.2 shows, in 1992 there was only a very small relationship between budget/tax issues attitudes and activity for the Democrats. Those supportive of both the gas tax and social security taxes performed, on average, .70 activities for Democratic candidates, compared with .52 for those failing to support either tax proposal. On the other hand, two years later, 1992 taxation issue attitudes had become much more closely tied to Democratic support. Supporters of both tax proposals now performed 1.14 activities for the Democrats, more than twice as many as those supporting neither proposal, who perform only .54 activities. Interestingly, by 1996 the issue is slightly more closely linked to Democrats,

Figure 21.1   Republican Campaign Activities, 1992–2000, by 1992 Level of Support for Reform Issues

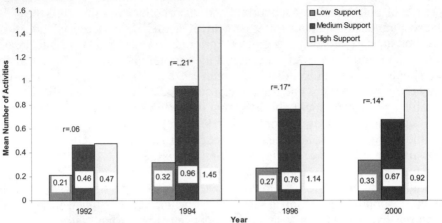

*Indicates correlation (r) is significant at p < .05.

with a ratio in Democratic activity of almost 3:1 between the strongest and the weakest supporters of tax increases on gasoline and on social security. In 2000—eight years after attitudes were assessed—1992 attitudes on the budget and taxes remain significantly related to Democratic activity, even though they had not been eight years before. Unfortunately for the Democrats, budget and taxation issues do not show the same level of support for Perot's position that reform issues did. Half as many potential Perot supporters supported neither of these initiatives as supported both of them. Still, the co-optation of these issues by the Democrats cut into Perot's ability to differentiate himself from the major parties and make unique appeals.

Both the Democratic and Republican parties were limited by their history and ideology from poaching on reform and budget and taxation issues, respectively. As a result, and as expected, "reform" attitudes do not impact the Democrats in a positive way, nor do "budget" attitudes impact the Republicans.

What does all of this mean for the Perot movement? To begin with, figure 21.3 shows that as support for Perot positions in all three issue areas increased in 1992, activity for Perot also increased significantly. Those most supportive of reform issues, economic nationalism issues, and budget issues show increases in mean Perot activities in 1992 of .79, .84, and .54, respectively. All three effects are statistically significant. However, by the time of the 1996 election, even with Perot running as an active candidate, both reform and budget issues were totally unrelated to Perot activity. On the other hand, although the absolute level of Perot activity dropped precipitously over

Figure 21.2 Democratic Campaign Activities, 1992–2000, by 1992 Level of Support for Budget/Taxation

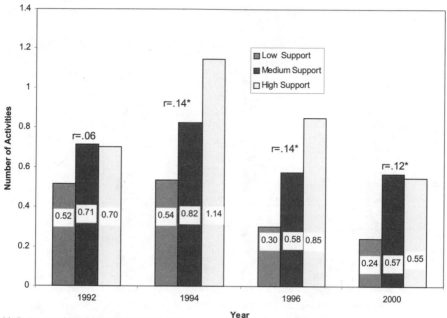

* Indicates correlation (r) is significant at p < .05.

the four years, economic nationalism attitudes remained significantly related to Perot activity. Supporters of both decreased military involvement and limiting imports (based on 1992 attitudes) performed almost three times as many activities in support of Perot in 1996 as those in support on neither issue. In fact, the same 1992 attitudes were *more* strongly related to Perot activity in 1996 than they were in 1992. Furthermore, economic nationalism was significantly related to neither Democratic nor Republican activity in 1996. Unfortunately for the future of the Perot movement, economic nationalism was insufficient to propel Perot's vote above the 8.5 percent he received on Election Day in 1996.

In sum, we have shown that the core issues in Perot's campaign were clearly associated with active support for Perot in 1992. However, the Democrats were able to co-opt the budget issue by taking up the cause of increasing taxes to balance the federal budget, and the Republicans were especially successful in raiding the Perot constituency by co-opting the reform issue. These efforts by the two major parties meant that after 1994, support for the issues they co-opted related more to activity in that party than to support for Perot.

Figure 21.3 Perot Activities in 1992 and 1996, by 1992 Level of Support for Perot Issue Clusters

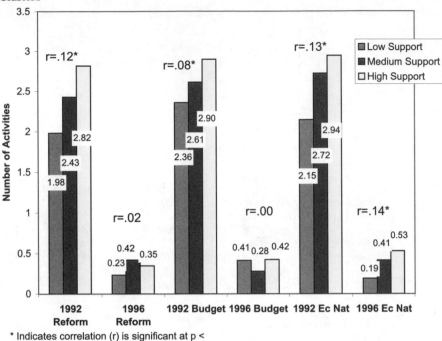

* Indicates correlation (r) is significant at p <

Perot Affect as the Stimulus for Republican Activity

In contrast to the major party co-optation hypothesis, there is another possible way to account for the rallying of Perot supporters to the Republican Party after 1992. Since Perot endorsed the Republicans for 1994, it is possible that the rallying was simply a response to his endorsement. By this account, the motivation was not issue appeals by the Republicans, but rather their leader's urging (an urging that Republicans could not necessarily count on after 1994).

If this hypothesis was correct, those most favorable to Perot in 1994 would be most likely to heed his request to work harder for the Republicans in 1994. In fact, however, those who rated Perot less positively (i.e., as either "Poor", "Below Average," or "Average") actually were more active on behalf of the Republicans than those who rated him more positively (i.e., "Above Average" or "Outstanding"). Although the difference is quite small (1.2 acts for Republicans among those less favorable to Perot, versus 1.1 on average for those more favorable to Perot), it is in the opposite direction to that predicted by the Perot mobilization hypothesis.

Even if co-optation had been successful for the major parties in 1994, it was done without Perot on the ballot. After the 1994 congressional elections, Perot still had two years in which to reclaim his supporters before he ran again in 1996. He failed to do so with either activists or with the mass electorate. This failure to remobilize the bulk of his constituency is important in both its results and its causes. It is important in its results because it produced a shift toward the Republicans that extended through the 2000 election. It is important in its causes because it further demonstrates that the seeds of the collapse were already in place by 1994.

Without denying the importance of Perot's strong showing relative to other third parties in 1996, the evidence for the decline in Perot support, particularly among his activist stratum, is undeniable. Based on the 1996 exit polls, Perot received votes from only a third of his 1992 supporters, while Dole got almost half of their votes (44 percent), with Clinton getting the other 22 percent. Had Perot attracted the same vote as in 1992, Clinton's margin over Dole would have increased by about 3.5 percent.

In our sample of supporter/activists the story is, if anything, even stronger. Only 25 percent of those who were active for Perot in 1992 were at all active in 1996. In fact, half again as many 1992 Perot activists were active for Dole-Kemp during the general election campaign as were active for Perot-Choate. These numbers indicate that there was a significant collapse of the Perot constituency between 1992 and 1996, and that it moved disproportionately toward the Republicans. This latter point is very much in keeping with our argument that Republican issue appeals provided a much stronger attraction than was the case for the Democrats. In 2000, the 8.5 percent of the electorate that had remained with Perot in 1996 split better than 2-1 for Bush, giving him the votes that allowed him to win the election.

Looking at the difference in total Republican and Democratic support (including congressional, presidential, and state and local races) among our potential Perot activists, we see a strong shift over the eight years of our survey. As figure 21.4 shows, in 1992, Perot activists were slightly more active on behalf of Democratic candidates than on behalf of Republican candidates. By 1994, however, these same Perot activists were doing significantly more for Republicans, and the difference remains significant through the 2000 elections, eight years after initial Perot activity and six years after the difference first appeared. Combined with the electoral shift to the Republicans from Perot voters, there can be little doubt that Perot's contribution to the electoral parity the Republicans achieved by 2000 was crucial.[6]

All of the foregoing suggests a classic co-optation process. Perot showed great success in 1992, and that success was highly correlated with three sets of issues: budget/taxation issues, reform issues, and economic nationalism. In the ensuing two years, two of these three issue clusters were co-opted by the major parties—reform by the Republicans and budget/taxation issues by

Figure 21.4 Mean of Differences in Activities for Republican versus Democratic Candidates among 1992 Perot Activitsts

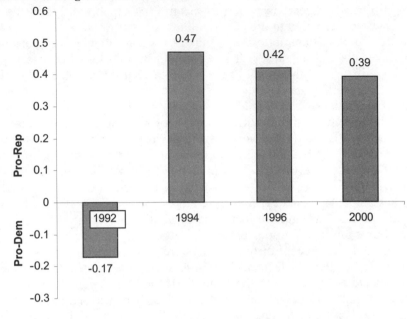

the Democrats. As a result, in 1994 and after, reform issues became correlated with Republican activity and budget/taxation issues with Democratic activity—while both ceased to be related to Perot activity. On the other hand, economic nationalism, which neither party really tried to co-opt, continued to have a significant impact (equal to that of 1992) on Perot activity.

The dynamic of third parties implies that a new third party is particularly vulnerable in the period after the election in which it first appears, and the more successful the party is in that first election, the greater its peril. The historic showing by Perot in 1992 created a golden opportunity for the Republicans to attract new supporters, an opportunity they exploited to win their own historic victory in 1994. This insight would mean that the eventual death of the Perot movement was rooted in the Republican victory in 1994, and that Perot faced a difficult, if not impossible, challenge in reclaiming the supporters he lost to the Republicans in 1994 when he ran again under the Reform Party banner in 1996.

To make our point, we need to show first that the Perot activists who increased their Republican activity in 1994 were the same individuals who were active for the Republicans when Perot reentered presidential politics in 1996—in other words, the 1992 Perot supporters who deserted Perot in 1996 were the same people who had already turned to the Republicans in 1994.

Of course it is possible that we are wrong and that Republican pickups from 1992 Perot supporters in 1996 came equally from those who had moved to the Republican party by 1994 and those who had not yet moved toward the Republicans by 1994, but who did so between 1994 and 1996.

Our focus here is on 1992 Perot supporters (those who were more active for Perot in 1992 than they were for the Republicans), since it is this group that Republicans needed to win over in order to broaden their appeal and undercut Perot's support. (This group comprises almost three-quarters of our sample of potential activists.)

The results support our expectation. Of all 1992 Perot activists, almost one-third (30.2 percent) increased their level of Republican activity in the 1992–1994 period. Of these 1992 Perot activists who increased their Republican activity in 1994, just about one half (49.4 percent) remained active for the Republicans in 1996. On the other hand, only one third as many (14.7 percent) 1992 Perot activists who did not increase their activity for Republicans in 1994 showed greater activity for Dole-Kemp in 1996 than for Perot-Choate (data not shown).

Our results, therefore, show that the shift to the Republicans in 1996 found its roots in increased Republican support in 1994. Those who increased their Republican support between 1992 and 1994 (with Perot off the ballot) tended to remain faithful to the Republicans when Perot reentered in 1996. Even though those increasing their Republican activity between 1992 and 1994 comprised less than one-third of the sample, they made up better than 60 percent of the individuals who moved from being Perot activists in 1992 to becoming Republican activists in 1996.

But what about 2000? Do we see a strong influence of the 1994 election on Republican activity six years later? Of the original pool of Perot supporters, is it those who shifted in 1994 that comprise the bulk of 2000 Republican activists? As we found for 1996, the answer continues to be yes. With Perot off of the ballot, we should expect greater major party activity in 2000 than we found in 1996, and that is certainly the case. But more important, almost two-thirds of 1992 Perot supporters who increased their Republican support between 1992 and 1994 were active for Republican candidates in 2000. This contrasts with only about one in five who had not already shifted toward the Republicans by 1994. Viewed another way, more than two-thirds of Perot activists who were Republican activists in 2000 had already moved toward the Republicans by 1994 (even though they comprised less than 30 percent of all 1992 Perot activists).

Conclusion

The 1992 Perot movement provides a recent example of a rare event in American electoral politics: a third party candidate who captures the nation's attention and attracts significant numbers of votes. In 1992, Perot bested every third-party candidate since 1912 by winning almost 19 percent of the popular vote. The appearance and success of Ross Perot in the 1992 election provide an unprecedented opportunity to study the dynamic of third parties by following his activist supporters through the next four national elections.

The dynamic of third parties anticipates significant change in the major party system following the appearance of a successful candidacy such as Perot's, because the Democratic and Republican parties have such powerful incentives to appeal to the third party's supporters. The Perot constituency offered three possible avenues of appeal to the major parties: reform, the federal budget and taxation, and economic nationalism issues. While the Democrats made a play for Perot supporters based on their attention to the budget/taxation issues, the Republicans were both better positioned and ultimately much more successful in attracting Perot voters and activists to their cause. They did this by appealing on the reform dimension of Perot support, especially in the Contract with America leading up to the 1994 elections.

Indeed, because of their success in co-opting the reform issue, the Republicans realized their own historic victory in 1994, just two years after Perot ran his insurgent campaign for president. In attracting a significant share of the 1992 Perot base to their cause in 1994, the Republicans sealed the doom of the Perot movement and the as yet unborn Reform Party. Perot was able to run again in 1996, thanks in large part to a generous subsidy from the Federal Elections Commission, but he had already lost much of his support to the Republicans, and he was largely unsuccessful in attracting new supporters. As a result, his vote declined sharply, although he was able to win 8.5 percent of the popular vote, still an impressive showing against the performance of other third-party candidates in American history. By 2000, the dynamic of third parties had taken its full effect, and the Perot movement along with the Reform Party it had spawned was dead.

Despite the fact that Perot was unsuccessful in building a lasting "third force" in American electoral politics, his legacy was an impressive change in the landscape of American politics and the two-party system. The result of his 1992 campaign was a Republican majority in both houses of Congress for the first time in forty years, and parity between the Republican and Democratic parties in presidential and congressional politics. Moreover, he succeeded in changing the debate on three core issues: reform, the federal budget, and economic nationalism. If the first two have been, perhaps temporarily, captured by the major parties, the third remains up for grabs. Pat Buchanan sought to capitalize on fears of globalization in his bid for the GOP nomination in 1996 and his own ill-fated Reform candidacy in 2000. Despite the failure of this issue to provide any traction in elections since 1992, we see it as a looming presence in American politics, which can be exploited in the future by a skilled candidate in either party (or in a new third party) if economic conditions deteriorate and public concern about foreign involvement increases. These are not, in our view, unlikely events in the next decade, and if they emerge we are likely to witness the effects of the unresolved agenda of the Perot movement reverberating through American electoral politics yet again.

Notes

This chapter is drawn in part from the authors' manuscript in preparation, *Party Change in America: Ross Perot and the Emergence of the Reform Party.*

1. We do not distinguish between candidacies such as John Anderson's in 1980 and Ross Perot's in 1992 that are "independent" of any party label, and those such as Robert LaFollette's in 1924 or George Wallace's in 1968 that have a party label.

2. Although the Contract with America was the most direct appeal to Perot supporters, the 1996 Republican platform also showed a clear nod in this direction, and a shift from 1992. The 1992 platform led off with family/society, followed by individual rights/safety. Sections on the economy and government reform followed. In 1996 the section on the economy (which now gave greater weight to balancing the budget) led off, followed by government reform. Family/society and individual rights/safety followed.

3. The number of activities measured is simply a count of the number of activities one carried out for Republican candidates for governor, senator, and representative in 1994. When we use only activities for Republican candidates for representative, the results are identical.

4. Although figure 21.1 shows only the bivariate relationship, the effects we find are independent of either traditional Republican support or spillover from other issues.

5. The Voter News Service (VNS) exit poll showed Bush receiving 61 percent from Perot's 1996 supporters, compared with 28 percent for Gore, 2 percent for Buchanan, and 8 percent for Nader; see members.cox.net/fweil/VNS2000National.html (accessed January 2001).

22

Toward a More Responsible Three-Party System: Deregulating American Democracy

Theodore J. Lowi

One of the best-kept secrets in American politics is that the two-party system has long been brain-dead—maintained by a life-support system that protects the established parties from rivals. The two-party system would collapse in an instant if the tubes were pulled and the IVs were cut. And until then, the dominant two parties will not, and cannot, reform a system in which they are the principal beneficiaries.

The extraordinary rise of Ross Perot in the 1992 election and the remarkable outburst of enthusiasm for his ill-defined alternative to the established parties removed all doubt about the viability of a broad-based third party. Poll after poll during the 1990s consistently showed a 60 percent favorable opinion base for a "third" party in America, and a most ingenious study by Walter Stone and Ronald Rapoport discovered that the 1994 Republican surprise victory in Congress, the surprisingly close electoral outcomes since 1994, and even the unexpected Bush victory in 2000 are "to be found in the changes in the party system rooted in the 1992 Perot movement" (Stone and Rapoport 2001, 50; see also chapter 21). They add in a footnote that "Perot was the first third-party candidate to attract more than 5 percent of the popular vote in two successive presidential elections since the Republican party first emerged in 1856" (Stone and Rapoport 2001, 57). It now falls to others to build on this base toward a more responsible three-party system.[1] But the impetus for reform is always scuttled by formidable defense mechanisms.

First, any suggestion of the possibility of a genuine third party receives the cold shoulder from the press and bored ridicule from academics. This reaction should surprise no one. Like the established parties themselves, social scientists are rarely given to innovation; they are almost always on the side of conventional wisdom, proven methodology, and the prevailing canon of their disciplines. Such defenses and ridicule are based on faith. Political scientists may call two-party doctrine a paradigm rather than canon, but they are no less loyal to it. With religious zeal, the high priests of the two-party system have preached the established faith and their students who became leading journalists, spread the two-party dogma to the great unwashed.

To the religion is added a great deal of scholarly analysis, advanced to explain why third parties so quickly disappear in face of a two-party system that is both natural and virtuous. Political scientists who hold this faith also believe that the traditional Anglo-Saxon electoral system—based on first-past-the-post, single-member districts—produces the two-party system by routinely discouraging new parties. They reason that since there can be only one victor in each district, even voters who strongly favor the candidate of a third or fourth party will ultimately vote for one of the two major candidates to avoid wasting their vote and also to avoid contributing to the victory of the least preferred of the major candidates. (This proposition has been elevated to the status of a physical law, called "Duverger's Law" after its most prominent purveyor.) A two-party system is the best of all possible worlds, they hold, because it produces automatic majorities, enabling the victorious party to govern effectively for its full term of office.

Interestingly enough, although many scholars present the two-party system as being inevitable, it has never been left to accomplish its wonders alone. It has been supplemented by primary, ballot, campaign finance, and electoral rules that are heavily biased against the formation and maintenance of anything other than the two-party system. And even with all of those legal life supports, two-party systems have prevailed in only a minority of all electoral districts in the United States since 1896. Most of the districts, from those that elect members of state legislatures up to the state as a whole in presidential elections, have in fact been dominated by one-party systems. During the past century, most of our larger cities and many counties, especially those governed by political machines, were admired by social scientists for their ability to overcome governmental fragmentation and integrate immigrants into electoral politics even as they preached the gospel of the two-party system. While crusading reformers attacked the machines, most political scientists continued to defend them, even while they criticized specific abuses. Although academics are often aware of the deficiencies and strengths of parties, their commitment to the present system prevents them from considering a new one.

It is now time for a frank, realistic discussion of alternatives. No amount of tinkering, adjustment, reorganization, or aggressive public relations campaigns can bring back to life a party system that, on its own, would surely have crumbled a long time ago and remains vibrant only in the hearts of party practitioners and political scientists. It is becoming increasingly clear that the usual scapegoats—divided government, campaign practices, scandals—are not the problem. The problem is, and always was, to be found within the two-party system itself.

The Constituent Function of American Parties

Much of the reluctance on the part of scholars to jettison myths surrounding the two-party system stems from a fundamental misconception regarding the true function of American parties. As I have argued elsewhere and at some length (Lowi 1975), parties perform a *constituent* or *constitutional* role in the American polity. Because this notion bears directly on my argument concerning the need for a responsible three-party system, a brief summary is in order.

By stating that parties perform constituent functions, I am not suggesting simply that they represent certain groups or individuals—all parties at least try to represent some segment of the public. Instead, I am using the term "constituent" in a much broader sense, meaning "necessary in the formation of the whole; forming; composing; making as an essential part." Constituent means that which constitutes. Constitution is the setting up of the way in which a political regime is organized and the laws that govern its organization. Parties have played a crucial role—intended or not—in "constituting" the American political regime by providing much of the organization and rules by which it is structured, staffed, and operated.

This view of party rests upon the distinction between constituent processes on the one hand and policy processes on the other. One the one hand, political parties may perform both constituent and policy functions; such parties have been labeled as "responsible." American parties have almost never been responsible, policy-making parties, and most reform efforts to make them so have failed. That includes, in particular, the 1950 report of the Committee on Political Parties of the American Political Science Association (Committee on Political Parties 1950). On the other hand, political parties may perform only constituent functions; such parties have been variously called "pragmatic" or "rational-efficient." American parties have nearly always been constituent parties, and attempts to improve their organizational capacity in this regard have often succeeded. Indeed, the genius of the American party system, if genius is the right word, is that it has split regime from policy, keeping the legitimacy of the government separate from the electoral consequences of governing.

One important effect of constituent parties has been the lack of development of American political institutions, even as society grew and modernized dramatically. A careful review of American history reveals several important regularities of the two-party system. First, the formation of new parties (or the dissolution or reorganization of existing ones) produces changes in the nature of the regime, while the functioning of established parties does not. In fact, the shift from new to established parties has been accompanied by a parallel shift in the effects of party, from liberal to conservative, from innovation to consolidation, or from change to resistance to change.

Second, new ideas and issues develop or redevelop parties, but parties, particularly established ones, rarely develop ideas or present new issues on their own. Party organizations are thus vehicles for changes in policy originating in other places; but they are not often the incubators of policy alternatives. Once a system of parties is established, the range and scope of policy discussion is set, until and unless some disturbance arises from other quarters.

Third, the major feature of the functioning of constituent parties has been the existence of competition, and not so much what the competition was about. The more dynamic and intense the level of competition, the more democratic the parties become, often in spite of themselves. But the more regularized and diffuse the competition, the more conservative the parties become. The key to understanding the two-party system, and the current necessity of a genuine third party, lies in understanding these regularities.

During the first party period, roughly from 1789 to 1840, parties served a liberating, democratic role.[2] To begin with, the new parties helped democratize the presidency. The first great organized effort to carry an opposition candidate, Thomas Jefferson, into office in the campaign of 1800 was a giant step toward the independent presidency—namely the pledging of electors. By such means the election of the president was decentralized and popularized by the parties. And the growth of parties directly checked or reversed tendencies toward a "fusion of powers" at the national level, mainly through the influence that the new parties exerted upon recruitment and succession of leaders.

The new parties also helped disperse national power by encouraging the formation of local organizations. The election of Andrew Jackson, the first rank "outsider," and the nominating, organizing, and campaigning of professional politicians around Martin Van Buren increased participation in the regime. The existence of vibrant organizations dedicated to the pursuit of many offices provided the raw material for opposition and debate. Grand alliances of these organizations made it possible to coordinate the activities of officeholders in a fragmented governmental system.

Finally, the new parties helped democratize the electorate. This effect is easiest to document by the sheer expansion of political activity at local levels. As a result of the expansion of organized political activity, individual involvement also spread greatly and mass participation in nominations and elections became highly visible at all levels of public office. The spread of political activity helped increase the size of the electorate and produced increasingly large turnouts. None of these consequences of the emerging parties were particularly policy-oriented, of course, but the process of party development linked elites to masses around the key issues of the day.

By the 1840s, however, the national party system seemed to pause in its development. Parties would henceforth monopolize all important elections, and party machinery would dominate, if not monopolize, all nominations. Parties would also monopolize the procedures and administration of Congress as well as virtually all of the state legislatures. The schemes of party organization and procedure were to remain about the same for decades to come. Parties no longer served a liberating or democratic role, but rather a maintaining, conservative one. Give or take a few exceptional moments, the two-party system has functioned this way ever since.

The tendencies of established parties were as nearly opposite to those of new parties as is possible in a dynamic, modernizing society. For one thing, the established parties contributed to the status quo in government structure. For example, they helped maintain the centrality of federalism, even as the national government and the Constitution expanded to meet the problems of a nationally integrated country. Political leaders, including members of Congress, developed a fundamental stake in the integrity of the state boundary because it was the largest unit for electoral office. This force has had a powerful impact on the substance of much important national legislation throughout the last century, from social insurance to environmental protection. The two major parties have participated in a silent conspiracy to prevent policy innovations from departing too far from eighteenth-century constitutional structure.

The established parties also made elective offices less democratic by resisting leadership change and policy innovation. From the courthouse to the White House, the parties have not of their own accord brought new elites to the fore or offered powerful checks on existing elites. Neither do they regularly bring new issues to the fore. It is unusual for the two major parties to take opposite stands on new controversies; it is much more common for new cleavages to develop *within* the existing parties, providing incentives to avoid cross-party controversies.

Finally, there is little evidence that partisan competition has a significant impact even on electoral mobilization. In many instances closely balanced parties appear to have actively resisted further democratization of the electorate. Expanding the franchise to new voters and mobilizing existing ones often threatens existing party coalitions, and thus established parties have reasons to ignore or actively oppose such expansions. Along these lines, established parties have an investment in existing social cleavages and no real interest in building a consensus across the myriad of ethnic, religious, and regional groupings that characterize American society.

Of course, there have been a few important instances since the 1840s when the established parties have been programmatic and innovative. At such times—most clearly in 1856–1860, 1896–1900, 1912–1914, and 1933–1935—significant differences appeared between the parties and they became innovative rather than conservative. Each period was ushered in by the "redevelopment" of one of the established parties after an earlier political disaster. Such reorganization made the party oligarchies more susceptible to direction from interest groups with strong policy commitments. Party leaders also became more susceptible to mass opinion, partly as the result of the mobilization of new social movements, but also due to increased competition from rivals. And in these periods, the appearance of a third party was a powerful factor in these changes. Of course, these third parties eventually faded, once the major parties stole their message and followers, and reestablished a new, conservative equilibrium.

The Two-Party Impasse

Back when the federal government was smaller and less important, the two-party system could carry out its constituent functions without much regard to ideology or policy. But with the New Deal and the rise of the welfare state, the federal government became increasingly vulnerable to ideological battles over policy. Even then, such problems were not particularly noticeable while the government and the economy were expanding, but in the early 1970s class and ideological conflicts began to emerge more starkly, and the two-party system was increasingly unable to offer productive competition.

Thus were born the familiar "wedge" issues—crime, welfare, prayer, economic regulation, social regulation, taxes, deficits, and anticommunism. No matter what position party leaders took on such issues, they were bound to alienate a substantial segment of their constituency. While the Democrats were the first to feel the cut of wedge issues, particularly concerning race, Republicans were soon to develop their own agonies over abortion, crime, foreign policy, and budget deficits. Wedge issues immobilized party leadership, and once parties are immobilized the government is itself immobilized.

Party leaders have responded to this gridlock not with renewed efforts to mobilize the electorate but with the strategy of scandal. An occasional exposure of genuine corruption is a healthy thing for a democracy, but when scandal becomes an alternative to issues, leaving the status quo basically unaltered, it is almost certain that all of the lights at the intersection are stuck on red. In fact, the use of scandal as a political strategy has been so effective that politicians have undermined themselves by demonstrating to the American people that the system itself is corrupt (Ginsberg and Shefter 1999).

The established parties have atrophied because both have been in power too long. In theory, a defeated party becomes vulnerable to new interests because it is weaker and therefore more willing to take risks. But for nearly forty years, *both parties have in effect been majority parties*. Since each party has controlled a branch of government for much of that time, neither is eager to settle major policy issues in the voting booth. Voters find it difficult to assess blame or praise, making accountability judgments and partisan affiliation difficult. A very important aspect of the corruption of leadership is the tacit contract between the two parties to avoid taking important issues to the voters and in general to avoid taking risks.

Even a brief look at the two established parties as they entered the twenty-first century reveals the urgency of the need for fundamental reform. The established parties do not lack for leadership, and with briefing books a foot thick and plenty of economists-for-rent, they certainly do not lack for programs. Here Ross Perot certainly was right: Washington is full of plans, good plans, which the two parties turn into useless parchment. The Republican and Democratic parties are immobilized by having to promise too many things to too many people.

Republicans say that they consider government to be the problem, not the solution. Yet, to attract enough voters to win elections, they have had to develop their own brand of conservative activism, which President George W. Bush has referred to as "compassionate conservatism." State and national efforts to put severe restrictions on abortion were already hardly the mark of a party that distrusts all government intervention. But they have gone well beyond that. The 2002 Republican amendments to the 1996 welfare reform laws (the Personal Responsibility and Work Opportunity Reconciliation Act, PRWORA) embody a national activism to the ultimate degree, adding new national standards for work in return for welfare eligibility, new requirements for identifying biological fathers, and added requirements and incentives for "marriage promotion." As welfare expert Gwendolyn Mink puts it, "The marriage vise and welfare policy directly contradicts the intimate decisional rights [established in *Loving v. Virginia*, 1967] that shifted the axis of marital decision making from government to adult individuals."[3] Bush's proposals included $100 million in "high performance bonus" points to promote "healthy marriages," requiring states to submit "marriage promotion plans" as a condition for receiving their Temporary Aid to Needy Families (TANF) grants as well as the bonus money. This is on top of the "illegitimacy bonus" provided under TANF 1996 provisions, providing extra money to states that achieve the greatest reductions in nonmarital births without increasing their abortion rates.

This Republican national activism succeeded in pulling the Democratic Party to the right. Democrats have always embraced national activism. But during the 1990s, national activism became dressed in Republican clothing, or, to change the metaphor, with Wendy's moving close to where McDonald's was already established. Although he tried during his first two years to restore a trace of Democratic Party policies of the 1930s and 1960s, Clinton, failing that, and then confronting the experience of 1994, became the last "Republican" president of the twentieth century. The Republicans hated

Clinton for stealing credit for their 1990s accomplishments, but of course, the Republicans had done the same in the 1969–1973 final triumph of Democratic Party policies, making Richard Nixon the last "Democratic" president of the twentieth century. The present two-party system continues to maintain its constituent function, insulating the regime from electoral vicissitudes. But has it succeeded too well? The tendency of the established two parties to preserve institutional structure, avoid divisive issues, and stifle electoral competition is too far advanced for easy reversal. Note, for one example, the fact that redistricting is more than ever a matter of incumbent protection. As a result of the redistricting that followed the 1990 census, 98 percent of the incumbents running for reelection won in 1998 and 2000. Though it is too early to tell at this writing, the redistricting that follows the 2000 census will probably be like its predecessors, with a series of 435 Incumbent Protection Acts. (Seven states get only one member of the House of Representatives, filled by a state-at-large election.) And, whether a cause or an effect, another sign of the shrinkage of democracy in our two-party system is electoral turnout in the midterm elections, dropping from an already historic low of 46.6 percent in 1970 to an average of 38.2 percent for the seven midterm elections between 1974 and 1998.

It is time for a new party system, a genuine alternative to the two old parties, to make electoral politics more competitive, as the original American parties did. A genuine third party that can last beyond one or two electoral cycles would shatter our two-party duopoly, would jump-start the development process, and would once again lead parties to embrace democracy rather than trying to avoid it.

The Real Impact of a Genuine Third Party

Predictably, defenders of the two-party system have devoted considerable energy to shooting down any suggestion that the status quo can be improved upon. They have produced all kinds of scenarios—a veritable parade of horrible examples. For instance, a third party could actually throw presidential elections into Congress, with the House of Representatives choosing the president and the Senate choosing the vice president. How horrible. Worse yet, if it managed to survive through two or more electoral cycles, a third party could hold the balance of power and, as a result, wield an influence far out of proportion to its electoral size. Indeed, it might, by its example, bring on a fourth or a fifth or even an "nth" party; and if one or more of these parties were represented by three, or four, or five, or six members of Congress, they could impose their extreme will on the majority. That of course assumes another horror, that the third party would not only produce a fourth and more, but that all of the parties other than the two major ones would be "extremist" parties. Far worse than that, representatives from third and other parties would inconvenience congressional leaders in their allocation of committee assignments.

There is some truth in all of these scenarios, but it is only natural that the high priests of two-party dogma would stress the horrible possibilities as though they were the only possibilities and were in fact inevitable outcomes. For the moment, however, let us look at the positive possibilities.

With three parties, no party needs to seek a majority or pretend that it is a majority. What a liberating effect this situation would have on party leaders and candidates, to go after constituencies composed of 34 percent rather than 51 percent of the voters. When 51 percent is needed, a party or candidate has to be all things to all people—going after about 80 percent of the voters to get the required 51 percent. A three-party system would be driven more by issues, precisely because parties fighting for smaller pluralities can be—and would virtually by nature be—clearer in their positions. American third parties have habitually presented constructive and innovative programs, which have then been ridiculed by leaders of the two major parties, who point out that third-party candidates can afford to be intelligent and bold since they cannot possibly win. But that is the point. In a three-party system, even the two major parties would have stronger incentives to be more clearly programmatic, since their goal would be more realistic and their constituency base would be smaller and simpler. Thus, each party could be a responsible party as well as a constituent party.

In the U.S. context, two factors help prevent the fragmentation that multipartyism produces elsewhere, as in Israel, the favorite horrible example. First, the American electoral system is not based on proportional representation. Any electoral system that allows a party garnering a small number of votes to send at least one representative to the legislature inevitably rewards fragmentation. Second, election of the chief executive provides incentives for splinter parties to coalesce behind one candidate. We are not a classic parliamentary system in which even a party that has elected only a few representatives can exert a disproportionate influence on the subsequent selection of the governing coalition.

Flowing directly from three-party competition, voting would increase, as would other forms of participation. Virtually our entire political experience tells us that more organized party competition produces more participation. And we already know that genuine three-party competition draws people into politics—not merely as voters but as petition gatherers, door knockers, envelope lickers, and $5 contributors—making the three-party system an antidote to the mass, "capital intensive" politics about which virtually everybody complains. Even defenders of the two-party system criticize the candidates' reliance on television, computerized voter lists, mass mailings, and phone banks—which dehumanize politics, discourage participation, replace discourse with ten-second sound bites, and reduce substantive alternatives to subliminal imagery and pictorial allusion. And the inordinate expense of this mass politics has led to a reliance on corporate money, particularly through political action committees (PACs), destroying any hope of collective party responsibility.

Experience teaches that new laws cannot eliminate these practices and their ramifications. Campaign finance reforms alone show that the feasible laws are ineffective and the effective laws are most probably unconstitutional. And many of the "unanticipated consequences" of these reforms (such as the mushrooming of the PACs after 1974) were either intended or were maintained after legal counsel learned how to manipulate them to the advantage of both major parties. Although a multiparty system would not immediately wipe out capital-intensive mass politics, it would immediately contribute to the easing of many of the pressures and incentives that produce its extremes, because third parties have to rely on labor-intensive politics. Third parties simply do not have the access to the kind of corporate financing that capital-intensive politics requires. But more than that, there is a spontaneity about an emerging party, literally as a social movement, that inspires people to come out from their private lives and cut short their escape into civic activity. All the recent palaver about civic engagement and social capital is a way of blaming the victims, when the blame for low political participation lies squarely with the party duopoly, all of whose incentives are to diminish the competitiveness of elections and the intrinsic rewards of political engagement.

Finally, the presence of a genuine third party in Congress would immediately parliamentarize the presidency. As noted above, once a third party proves it has staying power beyond one electoral cycle, it would increase the probability of presidential elections being settled in the House of Representatives. This immediately makes Congress rather than the masses the primary constituency of the presidency (see Lowi 1985, 208–212). Congress would not suddenly "have power over" the presidency. Congress has such power already: It has the power to make the laws and thus to give or take away the president's powers. It has the power to impeach. Thus the only added feature if Congress, with a third party, became the constituency of the president is that the president would have to engage Congress in constant discourse. This situation would change the presidency but would not diminish it. A skillful president could have even more power than now; the difference would be that he would have far less incentive to go over the head of Congress to build a mass following. And this prospect is to be contrasted with the reality of the current presidential situation, where the president faces two parties based loosely on artificial majorities, in which a president cannot depend on his own party to provide a consistent policy majority. A newly elected president can claim a mandate, but the closeness of elections renders that ridiculous, and even a decisive election does not convince many members of Congress to accept the principle of a mandate, even during the reputed honeymoon—which is in any case getting shorter and shorter. The point here is that a genuine third party is a liberating rather than a confining force. Just as the rise of the two-party system fundamentally altered the constitutional structure of our government appropriately for the nineteenth century, so a three-party system would alter the structure appropriately for the twenty-first century.

Actually a genuine third party with a few members of Congress would play the role of honest broker. It would hold the balance of power in many important and divisive issues, but there would be little fear of the tail wagging the dog because, unlike the highly fragmented systems elsewhere, Democrats and Republicans are ideologically close enough to cooperate with each other in any instance where the honest broker becomes a high-stakes playmaker. In other words, the presence of the third party delegation gives the president an alternative for bargaining, but if the third party raises its price too high it would simply give the president a greater incentive to bargain with the other major party. Finally, the presence of a third party in Congress would help lay to rest an important myth in the United States that policy issues are always binary, a matter of simple debate between the affirmative and the negative. The fact of the matter is that most issues, especially important issues, come in multiple sides, such that the simple affirmative versus negative in an adversary process is a result of a long and creative process of agenda making—the agreement on what to disagree about, or how a bill becomes a bill.

Eventually a three-party system would change the American regime. It would be a Third Republic, since, if we were true realists and enumerated our regimes, we would have to recognize that we have been living in a Second Republic for some decades. It is thus a change not to be feared. For example, it would not destroy the separation of powers and replace it with a Westminster or some other parliamentary fusion of powers. Rather, by making Congress the presidential constituency, the separation of powers would return to "the system of separated institutions sharing power," as Richard Neustadt put it so well over forty years ago (Neustadt 1960). Unfortunately, Neustadt was articulating this ideal at just about the time it was becoming something else, something I have termed "the absolute separation of powers" produced by the long stretches of divided government we have endured—90-plus percent of the time since 1980—in which each major party controls one electoral branch or chamber of government. If we honestly confront the pathologies and dysfunctions of the present Second Republic, we would not be nearly so apprehensive about the three-party alternative. A third party is not a governing party in the same sense of the two major parties. The most important goals of the third party within a two-party system is to put an end to the two-party system, to find a whole new calculus of voting and a whole new theory of representation.

Toward a Genuine Third Party

Since a three-party system requires a genuine third party, we will have to construct one. If we went with mainstream political science and conventional wisdom, there would no need for this effort, because all of the legal barriers and ideologically based opposition reduce the prospects well beyond acceptable probability. But accepting their assessment would be a self-fulfilling prophecy. In any case, and whatever the odds, laying out the scenario has considerable pedagogical value.

First and foremost, a third party must be a genuine political party, not a social movement, though a movement is a great base for such a party. This party must have powerful and attractive, movement-type leadership, but it must still be built from the bottom up. It cannot be a campaign for one election pretending to be a party, and it cannot be a party with only one candidate running at the top of the ticket without co-candidates below. It must have candidates for almost all of the offices on the ballot. It must also be an opportunistic party, oriented toward winning elections. The candidates must share some principles and policies, but there must also be flexibility in order to adapt to constituency and regional variations. In other words, the party cannot use the campaign simply as a sounding board for the few burning issues around which its members have organized.

Fusion Ballots. To do all these things, the third party must attract regular Democratic and Republican voters, and, *more importantly,* it must also attract Democratic and Republican candidates to run as candidates jointly on the new, third-party line. This practice of joint nomination, called fusion, was quite common in the late nineteenth century, when there were many third parties, and each tried to cooperate with the weaker of the two major parties in a kind of balance-of-power strategy. As Argersinger observes (1992, 56), "Fusion helped maintain a significant third party tradition by guaranteeing that dissenters' votes could be more than symbolic protest. . . . Most of the electoral victories normally attributed to the Grangers, the Independents, or Greenbackers in the 1870s and 1880s were a result of fusion . . . [with] Democrats." Later on, after Manhattan (New York County) consolidated with Brooklyn (Kings County), Queens, the Bronx, and Staten Island (Richmond County) to make the Greater City of New York as we recognize it today, fusion became the method whereby fragmentary third parties jointly nominated Republican candidates to provide Republican mayoral victories on three important occasions—John P. Mitchel, 1913; Fiorello LaGuardia, 1933, 1937–1941; and John Lindsay, 1965, 1969. (Mayor Giulaini was actually a genuine Republican, not a fusion candidate.) In the 1930s, various fragment parties of the left got together under the rubric of the American Labor Party and gave Republican LaGuardia enough independence to continue to force himself on the city's Republican Party, which had hoped to dump him in the 1937 reelection campaign.

All of this fusion was the great antidote for the "psychology of the wasted vote" from which wannabe third-party candidates and voters always suffer. However, with the rise of the Australian ballot, one state after another passed legislation prohibiting a candidate's name from being listed more than once on the now state-provided official ballot. Third-party experience in America tends to shrink dramatically thereafter (Argersinger 1992, chapter 6). In the current era, at least forty of the states prohibit fusion. Americans today take this for granted or hardly recognize it at all. But when states were first enacting antifusion legislation, its significance was very much appreciated. A contemporaneous Nebraska Supreme Court condemned the laws prohibiting fusion as an effort by the Republican Party to "use the Australian ballot as a 'scheme to put the voters in a straightjacket'" (Argersinger 1992, 57). Without the option of joint nomination, the minor party had the limited choice of either putting an obscure name on its ballot for a particular office or leaving that candidacy blank. Either way, it reduced drastically the ability of the minor party to poll the minimum percentage of the vote required by law to be recognized as a political party and thus be eligible for a place on the ballot for subsequent elections without having to go through an absolutely arduous last-minute petition process to get on the ballot.

As antifusion laws were adopted (especially following the Republican national sweep of 1896), third parties all went the way of the Kansas Populist Party, the South Dakota Populist Party, the South Dakota People's Party, the North Dakota Democratic Populists (and independents), and others, with especially devastating direct effects in the progressive states of the Midwest and West. After the successful culmination of the antifusion legislative movement, third parties continued to appear, but, as Argersinger (1992, 170) observes:

> With the exception of the Socialists, they were generally expressive rather than instrumental. Those with any great support were short-lived and often based on the appeal of a dominant personality. . . . [And] such parties rarely had, over time, the characteristics of late 19th century third parties: local organization, voter identification, mass support . . . and generalized regional strength.

Roosevelt (1912) and LaFollette (1924) come readily to mind, as do Dixiecrat Strom Thurmond and Progressive Henry Wallace (both 1948) and George Wallace (1968). John Anderson (1980) and Ross Perot (1992) were not really third-party candidates at all but merely bullet presidential candidates with or without a party name.

Ross Perot in 1996 was something of an exceptional case precisely because he took what had become a civic movement, United We Stand America, with its congeries of state chapters, and momentarily converted the movement into a Reform Party, with many of the United We Stand chapters becoming genuine units of a state party. Some of these in fact went so far as to put forward candidates for state and local office on the ballot along with Perot. Although Perot's presidential vote in 1996 dropped drastically below his 1992 percentage, his 8.5 percent was well above the minimum to qualify for the $12.6 million federal subsidy for the 2000 election and, with that plus the continued financial support from Perot, the Reform Party was able to hold together for one more electoral cycle. Another big boost came in 1998 with the election of Jesse Ventura as governor of Minnesota on the Reform ticket. This made Ventura and his Minnesota Reform Party a second and competing center. A struggle between Dallas (Perot headquarters) and Minnesota ensued, until early 2000, when Ventura resigned from the Reform Party, Donald Trump withdrew his candidacy, and the $12.6 million in federal funds went up for grabs between candidates Pat Buchanan and the perennial Natural Law candidate John Hagelin. The grant required an appeal to the Federal Election Commission, which handed down a verdict favorable to Buchanan just as Ralph Nader was receiving the nomination of the Green Party. Nader would ultimately do better than Buchanan (2.7 versus .43 percent of the vote), but not nearly well enough to meet the 5 percent vote requirement to qualify for the subsidy in 2004. Buchanan and Reform, Nader and Green: R.I.P. In mid-2002, Jesse Ventura hammered another nail into the coffin with his decision not to run for reelection.

This sad story will be taken down as further evidence that a third party in America is like a bee. It "stings once and dies," leaving the two-party system as the best of all possible worlds, providentially ordained (Hofstadter 1955, 97).

However, before this reaches the level of biblical truth, let us take a hypothetical look at the two-party system in a natural environment, without its legal safety net. Suppose Ross Perot were willing to set aside around $6 million for litigation against state election laws—just 10 percent of what he spent for his 1992 campaign. And we would be starting this game with two strikes against us, judging from *Timmons v. Twin Cities Area New Party* (117 S. Ct. 1364 [1997]), in which the Supreme Court held as valid the Minnesota state law prohibiting fusion, rejecting the argument of the small and inconsequential New Party that such a prohibition was a violation of First Amendment rights of speech and association. In fact, the Court went out of its way to validate the law, because the Minnesota Democratic Party and the Democratic candidate had indicated their willingness to accept the joint nomination of the New Party and thus appear on two lines on the ballot. However, the one strike left is important in that *Timmons* did get all the way to the

Supreme Court and had, in fact, won on First Amendment grounds in the Federal Court of Appeals, Eighth Circuit.

Thus, with one strike left, we can play a mental game of taking away the two-party system's legal safety net. Suits will be brought in several states by third-party leaders and candidates against ballot access laws, party eligibility laws, and, especially, apportionment and redistricting laws, mainly on the same First (and Fourteenth) Amendment grounds that got *Timmons* to the Supreme Court. In addition to the testimony of disappointed third-party candidates, the plaintiffs will draw "expert witnesses" from the prominent ranks of the American Political Science Association. Those same expert witnesses would also be relied upon by the defendant states and their two major parties.

We are already familiar with the testimony of the expert witnesses for the defense. In fact, their testimony was virtually summarized in brief in Chief Justice Rehnquist's opinion (for the 6-3 *Timmons* majority) that the states' interest in "protecting the integrity, fairness, and efficiency in their ballots" overrides First Amendment objections to the ban on fusion. That is, the state has a "compelling interest" in the integrity of ballots; moreover "[b]allots serve primarily to elect candidates, not as fora of political expression." Justice Stevens in his dissent (and for our plaintiffs) claimed vigorously that Minnesota's law places "an intolerable burden" on political expression and that the law "both intended to disadvantage minor parties and has had that effect." No political scientist worthy of the name could testify under oath that Justice Stevens was historically incorrect in his assertion that the negative effect of antifusion laws was intentional, and the preponderance of such testimony on this point could support new appeals from more than one circuit, with quite possible reversal of the *Timmons* case. Even the most ardent political science proponent of the two-party system would find it impossible to deny under oath the argument of the plaintiffs that "compelling interest" is anything more than the legal counsel of the two major parties acting as judges in their own cause. They cannot have it both ways: They cannot argue that the two-party system is natural and inevitable, and at the same time argue that the elaborate legal safety net is a compelling necessity for their maintenance. The witnesses for the plaintiffs can readily demonstrate that these laws are (1) patently intended to discriminate against minor parties, and (2) discriminatory in their application.

Single-Member Districts. Of far greater significance than fusion, however, is the constitutional status of the single-member district system. Many Americans believe that it is required by the Constitution; in fact it is totally silent on the matter and is concerned only with the number of representatives to the House of Representatives to be apportioned to each state. In 1842, Congress mandated the single-member district system nationwide for elections involving Representatives to the House. The law was reenacted after the Civil War with additional provisions requiring that districts be contiguous and as close as possible to equal in population. One obvious reason why Congress went to the trouble of reenacting the single-member district requirement was that multiple-member districts were very slow to disappear. In all the states during the nineteenth century, most members of Congress represented multiple-member districts (Klain 1955). Multiple-member districts were even slower to disappear in the states. In 1912, when the forty-eighth state entered the Union, multiple-member districts were still numerically dominant in legislatures in at least one-half of the states, and in 1955, 42 percent of the members of the state assemblies were elected from multi-member districts (Rosenthal 1981, 15). And by last count at the beginning of the 1990s, 64 percent of council members in U.S. cities were elected in at-large, multimember districts (MacManus 1991, 1012–1013).

We may take this short history as a "Brandeis brief" against the "compelling interest" theory that rationalizes bipartisan abuse of rule of law to protect a two-party system that did not depend upon the single-member district system for its existence—*but only for its protection*.[4] Here we have a patent case of intent to discriminate against new parties, which brings in the Equal Protection Clause as well as the First Amendment free speech and assembly provisions.

There is more, much more, to the case of the plaintiffs against state electoral districting laws, because on top of the evidence of intent to discriminate there is overwhelming evidence of discrimination by implementation and impact, so clear as to meet beyond question the standard set by the Supreme Court that "[a]ny law which is nondiscriminatory on its face may be applied in such a way as to violate the Equal Protection Clause." The standard was articulated in death penalty cases "where equal or lesser sentences were imposed on the elite, a harsher one on the minorities or members of the lower castes."[5] But minorities are not the only "lower castes," if caste can be defined as any grouping or class in a society to which is applied a separate system of law. And the standard set in *Furman* applies to realms other than capital punishment. Among these other realms, the most directly applicable is the "vote dilution" rule in state districting cases. As Chief Justice Earl Warren put it in one of his last opinions on the Supreme Court, "The right to vote can be affected by a dilution of voting power as well as by an absolute prohibition on casting a ballot."[6]

Granted, the particular concern of the federal courts and the Voting Rights Act was with dilution of the voting power of racial minorities. But the concept of dilution and the standard it set for impact on voting were not and are not intrinsically limited to racial minorities, and it would be the task of the plaintiffs and their expert witnesses to put this point across to the Court: In a single-member, first-past-the-post district, a minority is any recognizable category of voters who regularly vote for or prefer a candidate other than the one offered by the majority party. The most noteworthy example is of course the African American minority in a district where the majority party candidates are habitually not African American. But what of Democrats in a district where they are a consistent minority, or conversely where Republicans are a consistent minority? And what of the smaller but still more frustrated citizens who reject the candidates of both major parties and are faced with a Hobson's choice of "wasting" their vote on an unknown third candidate or for the candidate of the major party they dislike least. In an obscure Gilbert and Sullivan operetta, English colonial rulers teach the natives that "Yes is but another and a neater form of No!"

The single-member district colonizes the voters—going beyond vote dilution to vote negation.[7] Such a system as ours also discourages the *second* party whenever it consistently receives less than a plurality of the votes. All of this argument can be demonstrated in court, and can even be elicited from "hostile witnesses" whose expertise is normally used to defend and rationalize the single-member district system. They would be proud to admit that the single-member district system eliminates minority parties—that is what is called "Duverger's Law" and it is taken as the most hallowed example of a scientific proposition in political science. What they would have to add under oath is that, under the same conditions of minority status, the *second* party is also in grievous jeopardy of vote negation.

That is still not all there is to the "Brandeis brief" against the single-member district system. There is also a lot of history backing the complaint of the plaintiffs against the single-member district system. The single-member district was probably ideally suited for popular representation in the first century of the Republic. Since there was fear and distrust of democracy, a way out of representation by numbers and the "one-man-one-vote" method of representation was *geographic* representation. Madison was the first to see this point and to use it in defense of a national House of Representatives that would be "too small to possess a due knowledge of the interests of its constituents." Madison's answer was typically Madisonian—with a bit of Jefferson thrown in: For regulation of commerce and for taxation—the two most important "objects of federal legislation"—the "information required [will] be possessed in sufficient degree by a very few intelligent men. . . . Divide the largest state into ten or twelve districts and it will be found that there will be no peculiar local interest in either which will not be within the knowledge of the representative of the district."[8]

This argument made good sense all during the nineteenth century, when most districts were homogeneous, especially as regards the economic and fiscal issues Congress had to deal with. It was a form of "geographic representation of interests" right out of *Federalist #10* as well as *#56*, and it helps explain how Americans could be so complacent about the vast disparities of population size that would violate the standard of equal size established by law in the 1870s. Geographic representation also probably explains why Americans could be so complacent about partisan gerrymandering. But long before the malapportionment crisis forced a historic shift in Supreme Court jurisdiction in 1962 and adoption of the Voting Rights Act in 1965, geographic representation had become a horrible anachronism. Very few of the 435 congressional districts (not to speak of the thousands of state and local legislative districts) could be considered homogeneous with regard to anything. And even as states were put under court order to create districts that were closer to equal population size, there was no way possible to draw the lines to provide meaningful units of representation. With very few exceptions, modern American society has become far too heterogeneous to be districted.

Even the most perfect apportionment by population can only satisfy a single standard—equality of the weight of each vote. Although that was at first thought to be the sine qua non of good democratic representation, it was quickly shot down by the American confrontation with diversity, a compelling synonym for heterogeneity: *Jointly or severally, there is no way legislatures, courts, and parties, operating with the most high-powered computers, can deal with the problem of representation within the framework of the single-member district system.* The federal courts and the two major parties—or, more accurately, the judiciary as handmaiden to the two-party duopoly—have done their best to salvage the single-member district system at the risk of delegitimizing both the American judiciary and the principle of representative government: They tried to meet the problem with *benign gerrymandering*. The Supreme Court itself has practically abandoned any rule of law on representation or on affirmative action in order to give the two major parties leeway to work out "bipartisan" majority-minority districts, so that Democrats can add a few liberal Democratic African American members of Congress, while Republicans can draw district lines in such a way as to concentrate African Americans in one or two districts while negating their influence entirely in the remaining Republican/conservative districts. The Supreme Court did strike down one majority-minority district in North Carolina that was "so irregular on its face that it rationally can be viewed only as an effort to segregate the races for the purpose of voting."[9] In fact, it was beyond "irregular." The new district was so ridiculous that it could only have been designed by someone who desperately wanted to discredit all efforts at affirmative action with one reductio ad absurdum. Running in a very narrow strip for almost two hundred miles between Durham and Charlotte, North Carolina, it made the original salamander-shaped district (which, along with its perpetrator, Elbridge Gerry, gave the gerrymander its name) look downright rational, compact, and contiguous. It is very important to stress here by repetition that taking such liberties with minority electoral engineering can only have been permitted and encouraged by the Court because it was thought to be the only way to salvage the single-member district system now that, at least constitutionally, we cannot tolerate second-class citizenship.

Benign Alternatives. Since the two-party system with its enormous and detailed safety net, including the single-member district system, is and will remain an embarrassment to American democracy as well as a very real threat to the independence of the judiciary, the least we can do is consider alternatives. And when we compare the alternatives to the present situation, it moves from farce to tragedy, because the alternatives are so benign.

The first alternative is of course a two-party system *without* the legal and jurisprudential safety net. If we should succeed in our litigation against the biased electoral and party laws, then we would come to a true test of the mainstream political science catechism: If the two-party system is part of the nature of things, and if it is a logical consequence of the rational, Anglo-Saxon mentality of dualistic thinking, and if it performs so many functions vital to our democracy, then most cities, counties, and states would continue to have two-party systems. Thus, if the two-party system persists without the legal safety net, then we would have an honest two-party system resting on real rather than terribly artificial foundations. This eventually would also free political scientists from having to defend an artificial two-party system with distorted political realism, phony functionalism, and strained scientific objectivity.

If, on the other hand, our present system is, as I have been arguing for over twenty years, a mere artifact of the bipartisan abuse of the rule of law, then we are likely to get a new party system the minute all of those biased state and federal laws are wiped out. My first projection tells me that the Democratic and Republican Parties would remain the two most important parties, and in many states the two-party system might well persist, because it is already in place and there may be strong habits that continue to militate against a successful third party. But three- and four-party systems would fairly quickly develop in some cities and states as soon as the legal trash is swept away. The direct effect on national politics would come rather slowly, but it would come honestly, through increased voter turnout, expansion of electoral competition, intensification of the policy content of campaigns, drastic changes for the better in campaign timing and campaign finance, and an increased probability that some presidential elections would be settled in the House of Representatives—as already observed.[10] Sociological and agency representation would improve almost immediately. There is no guarantee that the presence of third-party members in the legislature would improve the policy-making process, but it could hardly be any worse.

Next, to the extent that the two-party system persists (with or without continued legal life supports) we need at least a new and improved system of voting so that the votes of persistent minorities are no longer negated. The simplest and most benign alternative to the plurality rule of winner-take-all, first-past-the-post is the *bipolar vote:* the power to vote "no" (Ferguson and Lowi 2001). Bipolar voting is instituted simply by legal provision of a negative vote to use as an alternative to a positive vote, and to assign that "no" vote the operational definition of subtraction—that is, negative 1. Beside the name of each candidate on the ballot there would be two boxes instead of one: a "yes" box to vote for a candidate [+ 1], and a "no" box to vote against that same candidate [− 1]. The voter would still have only a single vote to cast, but with bipolar voting, all positive and negative votes cast would be combined, the total for that candidate being the sum of the two. State laws would almost certainly vary in the precise endgame or decision rule. For example, the law could provide that if the two (or more) candidates for a given office turn up with net negative votes, that election would be held once again with a new slate of candidates. Or, some or all of the candidates could stay on the ballot, but would be required to participate in a runoff.

Bipolar voting elicits a fundamental and new piece of information from the voter as a sort of "legitimeter": it registers the relative measure of preference and also, albeit roughly, the absolute level of confidence in the candidates, the platforms, and the process.

In conventional, unipolar elections, someone always wins, no matter how odious the candidates or how feeble the turnout. What if we held an election and nobody came? Under present conditions, it wouldn't matter. If the electorate continued to shrink until candidates and their families and friends were the only voters, somebody would still get elected and hold office. In other words, we have fashioned a colonial electoral process, one that can function without us. Bipolar voting is the only workable scheme for remedying the situation.

The only existing alternative that comes close to bipolar voting is to give the voter the option of voting "none of the above" (NOTA). But there are three things wrong with it. First, as with third-party candidacies under present conditions, NOTA suffers from a severe case of "the wasted vote." Since NOTA votes do not directly figure in the margin of victory or defeat, highly negative passions will either result in true nonvotes, or become "yes" votes for the lesser of the remaining evils. Second, NOTA provides for no sensible procedure in the unlikely case that "none of the above" actually wins the most votes. (If NOTA votes were actually tallied, it would move closer to bipolar voting.) Finally, NOTA gives no boost to third- and other minor party candidates about whom all voters except a passionate minority are ignorant. NOTA turns out to be the lazy voter's protest.

Back to bipolar voting. Imagine an election in which the two leading candidates net respectively 100,083 versus 90,057 positive votes and 100,000 versus 90,000 negative votes. The first would have a plurality of net positive votes—83 beats 57. But even in America that result would be so embarrassing that it might stimulate the search for more satisfying choices.

And this result would be concrete evidence of electoral vulnerability, which is not only less evident in our present raw positive vote count, but also reflects upon the illegitimacy of the system. It is obvious that the bipolar vote would alter the very rationality of the electoral process.

But the very reasonableness of bipolar voting is its major flaw: It can soften some of the worst features of the single-member district system but cannot solve the problem, which is an embarrassment that becomes worse with every effort to save it by legislation, jurisprudence, or clever electoral engineering. The only saving alternative ultimately is to put an end to it, with reinstitution of the multiple-member district.

Since the single-member district will eventually be declared unconstitutional for the same reason that capital punishment was declared unconstitutional in 1972—that it cannot be applied fairly[11]—we can make it easier on today's Supreme Court by demonstrating that the immediate result and the inevitable alternative is not only acceptable but superior. The immediate result of such a Supreme Court decision would obviously be the multiple-member district. *Every seat allocated to a state would have to be elected at-large.*

With at-large elections, all members of Congress would have the same shared, statewide constituency. Candidates for Congress, including all of the incumbents, would be thrown together and would face a common problem. Take a state large enough to warrant ten seats. Every voter would get ten votes, and with no law forbidding it, all voters could spend their ten votes as they wished—with all ten going to a single candidate or with the ten votes spread across three or four preferred candidates, or with ten votes spent on ten separate candidates. In the formal arrangement of electoral things, this is called "cumulative voting." It is a version of Proportional Representation (PR) without the elaborate and complicated PR legislation involving computer-assisted (and disputable) "single transferable votes" and so forth. It is a very simple electoral system, virtually unregulated and free of administrative discretion (which, in electoral matters means discretion by party hacks holding administrative power). And cumulative voting can produce proportional representation along any lines of identifiable economic, social, class, racial, or other cleavage that happens to exist in a state. Of greatest relevance, it "can ensure that a politically cohesive minority will be able to elect candidates of its own choice, even where it is too dispersed to allow for the creation of minority-controlled single-member districts" (McDonald 1992, 83).

Such a simple system would obviously produce more "sociological representation" than we have ever had. That refers only to the proportional physical presence of identifiable minorities, without necessarily any improvement in genuine "agency representation." But, even so, it is not to be taken lightly. Physical presence within decision-making bodies has symbolic value and also can guarantee more transparency. But that is only a starter. In the next place, every member of Congress would have a broader vision of *what* is to be represented. The single-member constituency is not only narrow, it is, on average, artificial; as stressed earlier, few districts are sufficiently homogeneous to be representable as a unit. In contrast, the state is a meaningful unit. Third, minorities elected statewide are far less likely to be single-issue representatives, because members of these minorities (whether African American, or nonunion working class, or evangelical Christian) would be spread throughout the state rather than concentrated in single, isolated "ghettoized" communities.

Another virtue of the at-large, multimember alternative is that it encourages and fosters tighter party organization. This tendency begins with the nominating process—that is, just getting on the ballot as a candidate. At first, the at-large system would favor the two major parties. But they would be fairly quickly followed by one or more additional parties in order to enable independent candidates to cooperate in meeting even a nonbiased, minimal state standard for ballot access. The requirements set by the state for petitions to get on the ballot would of course be equal for all individuals and parties—that is, equal ballot access for the first time in modern history. Then, to have any chance at all in the statewide election, rationality would fairly quickly dictate a form of *list voting*, and that is what would foster and strengthen party organization—putting together a list of ten candidates under one banner, one ticket. The candidates on the same list—nominated by a party or a pre-party movement—would have enormously strong incentives to campaign together. And after a while, if not immediately, the party—as an institution—would become a meaningful programmatic organization, at least a common interest–bearing organization, and would have an organizational role as such in winning elections. Moreover, the ten (in this case) elected to Congress would have fairly strong incentives to work *as a state delegation*, regardless of party. And minorities within the delegation would have an enhanced influence on the state delegation positions and could still join with their minority counterparts from other states to enhance national party influence or to work together to exercise veto power or, lacking that, greater transparency in the larger public arena.

Finally, at-large representation would alleviate if not solve the problem of campaign finance. No new legislation would be needed, and most of the existing legislation could be dispensed with. Under present conditions, all incumbents and their opposition candidates are forced to rely largely upon their own efforts to raise at least the threshold level of finance—enough to justify additional and closer to adequate financing from relevant PACs, party soft money, and largess from senior congressional barons who target the millions of excess dollars they collect personally and through their own personal PACs. In contrast, at-large election, especially when reinforced by less voting, takes away the "prisoners' dilemma," or should I say the "candidates' dilemma." As long as the perverse incentives exist, no law is going to stop the money deluge and the derangement of constituency accountability. Elimination of the single-member district system would put an end to the plutocracy without destroying the parties. Soft money—given to the state party to support the entire state party lists—can become good and ethical money.[12]

Deregulating Democracy. This future of multimember districts with multiparty systems is not so difficult to imagine as a replacement for the outmoded two-party system if we put it in the context of constitutionalism and deregulation. The two-party system and its vast legal life-support system is an embarrassment to the American Constitution and the Republic for which it stands. Key members of the Supreme Court have been participating in a constitutional travesty for years, based upon a narrative of the history of American democracy that is an invention of the discipline of political science.

If we add to that the current political fashion favoring deregulation, the case should be clinched, because my rhetoric of "legal life supports" and "safety nets" is simply a metaphoric and, I hope, dramatized version of government paternalism. An impressionistic survey of New York and Alabama state codes revealed that there are more laws on the institution of elections and parties than on the institution of marriage and the family. Between courts, legislatures, and party-selected electoral officials, the democracy that American political science has espoused for its century of existence is a paternalistic, state-sponsored democracy. *It is time to deregulate American politics, letting it take whatever form it will.* If we are the free country we believe ourselves to be, we should reject sponsored democracy in favor of spontaneous democracy. Walt Whitman was trying to convey that lesson to us in 1871: "[Democracy] is a great word, whose history . . . remains unwritten, because that history has yet to be enacted."[13]

Notes

1. The reference here and in the title is inspired by the famous 1950 American Political Science Association report, "Toward a More Responsible Two-Party System" (Committee on Political Parties 1950).

2. This corresponds to the "first party system" (1790s–1850) and most of the "second party system" (1815–1856), as these are periodized by party historians (see McCormick 1986).

3. "From Welfare to Wedlock: Marriage Promotion and Poor Mothers' Inequality," Draft, prepared for *The Journal of Political Economy of the Good Society* (April 2002) 2. Quoted by permission.

4. The reference is to Louis D. Brandeis' innovative use of social science in legal argument, first employed in *Muller v. Oregon,* 208 U.S. 412 (1908).

5. *Furman v. Georgia,* 408 U.S. 238 (1972).

6. *Allen v. State Board of Elections,* 393 U.S. 544 (1969).

7. For more on this issue, which is as goofy as fiction, see Ferguson and Lowi 2001.

8. *Federalist #10* (Madison [1787] 1941).

9. *Shaw v. Reno,* 509 U.S. 630 (1993).

10. This argument is carried out more in detail in Lowi 2001.

11. *Furman v. Georgia,* 408 U.S. 238 (1972).

12. Although many assertions made here can be challenged, one in particular needs to be put to rest, and that is the judicial attack on at-large methods of electing representatives. In 1969, the Supreme Court used the Voting Rights Act to invalidate as racially discriminatory a Mississippi law converting a single-member district method of electing county supervisors to an at-large method. This was the first case to use the "minority dilution" standard rather than a vote suppression standard, and the case was also hailed for recognizing that electoral *systems,* as well as voting procedures, can be discriminatory (*Allen v. State Board of Elections,* 393 U.S. 544 [1969]. But this case, along with many other cases involving at-large election conversion, was patently racially discriminatory, by intent of the state of Mississippi. Civil rights lawyers fought at-large conversions in many other of the same sort of instances where the intent and the effect were race-conscious efforts at vote dilution, because the move to the at-large procedure tended to expand the boundaries of the principality to include the all-white suburbs. No multimember districts can be genuinely proportionate if the percentage of any minority is cut in half or below by the redefinition of the district. But in a state where African Americans constitute over 35 percent of a population whose boundaries cannot be expanded to dilute that size of a minority, it would in fact weigh 35 percent in a statewide election, whereas it would weigh 0 percent in all of those districts in which they are a permanent yet distinguishable minority in a winner-take-all, single-member district system of representation. For the best treatment of multimember districts, cumulative voting, and the issues of civil rights and representation associated with them, see Lani Guinier, "The Triumph of Tokenism: The Voting Rights Act and the Theory of Black Electoral Success," *Michigan Law Review* (March 1991), 1077–1154. For a thorough evaluation of the consequences of majority-minority districts, see Mingus Mapps, unpublished doctoral dissertation, Cornell University, 2002.

13. Walt Whitman, *Democratic Vistas* [edited by Floyd Stovall]. In *Prose Works, 1892* (New York: New York University Press, 1963–1964), 393.

References

Abramowitz, Alan, John McGlennon, and Ronald Rapoport. 1986. "An Analysis of State Party Activists." In *The Life of the Parties*. Alan Abramowitz, John McGlennon, and Ronald Rapoport, eds. Lexington, Ky.: University Press of Kentucky.

Abramowitz, Alan I., and Kyle L. Saunders. 1998. "Ideological Realignment in the U.S. Electorate." *Journal of Politics* 60: 634–52.

Abramson, J. 1998. "Political Parties Channel Millions to 'Issue' Attacks." *New York Times,* October 14: A1.

Abramson, Paul R., John H. Aldrich, and David W. Rohde. 1998. *Change and Continuity in the 1996 Elections*. Washington, D.C.: CQ Press.

Affigne, Tony, and John Rensenbrink. 1994. "Now Is a Decisive Moment in Evolution of U.S. Greens." *Green Horizon* 3: 6–7, 12.

Agranoff, Robert. 1972. *The New Style in Election Campaigns*. Boston, Mass.: Holbrook Press.

Aldrich, John H. 1995. *Why Parties? The Origin and Transformation of Party Politics in America*. Chicago: University of Chicago Press.

———. 1999. "Political Parties in Critical Eras." *American Politics Quarterly* 27: 9–32.

———. 2000. "Southern Parties in State and Nation." *Journal of Politics* 62: 643–670.

Aldrich, John H., Mark M. Berger, and David W. Rohde. 1999. "The Historical Variability in Conditional Party Government, 1877–1986." Paper presented at the Conference on the History of Congress, Stanford University.

Aldrich, John H., and Richard G. Niemi. 1995. "The Sixth American Party System: Electoral Change, 1952–1992." In *Broken Contract: Changing Relationships between Americans and Their Government.*, Stephen C. Craig, cd. Boulder, Colo.: Westview, 87–109.

Aldrich, John H., and David W. Rohde. 1998. "Measuring Conditional Party Government." Paper presented at the Annual Meeting of the Midwest Political Science Association, Chicago.

Allen, Mike, and Ruth Marcus. 2001. "GOP Missteps Helped Jeffords to Leave the Party." *Washington Post National Weekly Edition,* May 28–June 3: 7.

Alvarez, Lizette. 2001a. "Man in the News: James Merrill Jeffords, A Longtime Maverick." *New York Times,* May 25: A19.

———. 2001b. "New Chairmen Shift Priorities for the Senate." *New York Times,* May 26: A1 and A9.

Amy, Douglas J. 1993. *Real Choices/New Voices: The Case for Proportional Representation Elections in the United States*. New York: Columbia University Press.

Ansolabehere, Stephen, and James M. Snyder. 2000. "Soft Money, Hard Money, Strong Parties." *Columbia Law Review* 100: 598–619.

Ansolabehere, Stephen, and Shanto Iyengar. 1995. *Going Negative: How Political Advertisements Shrink and Polarize the Electorate*. New York: Free Press.

Ansolabehere, Stephen, Roy Behr, and Shanto Iyengar. 1993. *The Media Game: American Politics in the Television Age.* New York: Macmillan Publishing.

Appleton, Andrew M., and Daniel Ward. 1996. "How We Are Doing: Party Leaders Evaluate Performance of the 1994 Elections." In *The State of the Parties: The Changing Role of Contemporary American Parties.* 2d ed. John C. Green and Daniel M. Shea, eds. Lanham, Md.: Rowman & Littlefield, 125–139.

Argersinger, Peter. 1992. *Structure, Process, and Party: Essays in American Political History.* Armonk, N.Y.: M.E. Sharpe.

Arterton, Christopher F. 1982. "Political Money and Party Strength." In *The Future of American Political Parties: The Challenge of Governance.* Joel L. Fleishman, ed. Englewood Cliffs, N.J.: Prentice-Hall.

Associated Press. 1993. "Perot Pushes for Continued Focus on Debt." *Christian Science Monitor,* February 22: 9.

Austen-Smith, David. 1995. "Campaign Contributions and Access." *American Political Science Review* 89: 566–581.

Axelrod, Robert. 1972. "Where the Votes Come From: An Analysis of Electoral Coalitions, 1952–1968." *American Political Science Review* 66: 11–20.

Baer, Denise L. 1993. "Who Has the Body? Party Institutionalization and Theories of Party Organization." *American Review of Politics* 14: 1–38.

Baer, Denise L., and Davis A. Bositis. 1988. *Elite Cadres and Party Coalitions.* Westport, Conn.: Greenwood Press.

———. 1993. *Politics and Linkage in a Democratic Society.* Englewood Cliffs, N.J.: Prentice-Hall.

Baer, Denise L., and Julie A. Dolan. 1994. "Intimate Connections: Political Interests and Group Activity in State and Local Parties." *American Review of Politics* 15: 257–289.

Bagehot, Walter. [1867] 1928. *The English Constitution.* London: Oxford University Press.

Balkin, Jack M. 2001. "*Bush v. Gore* and the Boundary between Law and Politics." *Yale Law Journal* 110: 1407–1458.

Ballot Access News. 2002 "Minor Party and Independent Vote for Top Offices is Best Mid-term Result since 1934." *Ballot Access News* 18: 1.

Bartels, Larry M. 2000. "Partisanship and Voting Behavior, 1952–1996." *American Journal of Political Science* 44: 35–50.

Baumgartner, Jeff. 2002. "Digeo Goes Two-for-Two with S-A Deal." *Communication Engineering and Design Magazine,* July 15.

Beck, Paul Allen. 1974. "A Socialization Theory of Partisan Realignment." In *The Politics of Future Citizens.* Richard G. Niemi, ed. San Francisco: Jossey-Bass, 199–219.

———. 1977. "Partisan Dealignment in the Post-War South." *American Political Science Review* 71: 477–96.

———. 1979. "The Electoral Cycle and Patterns of American Politics." *British Journal of Political Science* 9: 129–56.

———. 1982. "Realignment Begins? The Republican Surge in Florida." *American Politics Quarterly* 10: 421–38.

———. 1992. "Party Realignment in America: The View from the States." In *Party Realignment in the American States.* Maureen Moakley, ed. Columbus: The Ohio State University Press, 259–78.

Bell, Daniel. 1962. *The End of Ideology.* New York: Collier Books.

————. 1973. *The Coming of Post-industrial Society.* New York: Basic Books.

Bensel, Richard F. 1990. *Yankee Leviathan: The Origins of Central State Authority in America, 1859–1877.* New York: Cambridge University Press.

Berelson, Bernard R., Paul F. Lazarsfeld, and William N. McPhee. 1954. *Voting.* Chicago: University of Chicago Press.

Berg, John C. 1995. "Prospects for More Parties in the United States by the Year 2000." Paper presented at the Conference on Parties in the Year 2000. Manchester, U.K.

————. 1998. "Beyond a Third Party: The Other Minor Parties in the 1996 Elections." In *The State of the Parties: The Changing Role of Contemporary American Parties.* 3d ed. John C. Green and Daniel M. Shea, eds. Lanham, Md.: Rowman & Littlefield, 212–29.

————. 1999a. "Green Liberty: Minor Parties and Realignment in the 1840s and the 1990s." American Politics Group. Cambridge University U.K.

————. 1999b. "Realignment, Minor Parties, and Economic Restructuring in the U.S. Today: A Marxist Account." American Political Science Association. Atlanta.

————. 2000. "State Green Parties in the USA: New Postmaterialist Wine or Old Wine in New Bottles?" American Politics Group. Keele, U.K.

Berke, Richard L. 1998a. "Lewinsky Issue Inspires Theme for GOP Ads." *New York Times,* September 2: A22.

————. 1998b. "Gleeful Democrats Assail Ads by G.O.P. on Clinton Scandal." *New York Times,* October 29: A1.

————. 2001a. "Campaign Finance Overhaul May Enhance Influence of Big PACs." *New York Times,* April 2.

————. 2001b. "Moderate Democrats Seek Unity and a Leader." *New York Times,* July 17: A17.

Bernard, Richard M., and Bradley R. Rice, eds. 1985. *Sunbelt Cities: Politics and Growth Since World War II.* Austin: University of Texas Press.

Bettelheim, Adriel. 2001. "New Chairmen and Agendas." *CQ Weekly Report* May 26: 1216–35.

Bibby, John F. 1981. "Party Renewal in the National Republican Party." In *Party Renewal in America.* Gerald Pomper, ed. New York: Praeger.

————. 1990. "Party Organization at the State Level." In *The Parties Respond: Changes in the American Party System.* Sandy Maisel, ed. Boulder, Colo.: Westview Press.

————. 1998. "State Party Organizations: Coping and Adapting to Candidate-Centered Politics and Nationalization." In *The Parties Respond.* 3d ed. L. Sandy Maisel, ed. Boulder, Colo.: Westview Press, 23–49.

————. 2000. *Politics, Parties, and Elections in America.* Stanford, Conn.: Wadsworth.

Biersack, Robert. 1996. "The Nationalization of Party Finance, 1992–1994." In *The State of the Parties: The Changing Role of Contemporary American Parties.* 2d ed. John C. Green and Daniel M. Shea, eds. Lanham, Md.: Rowman & Littlefield.

Biersack, Robert, and Melanie Haskell. 1999. "Spitting on the Umpire: Political Parties, the Federal Election Campaign Act, and the 1996 Campaigns." In *Financing the 1996 Election.* John C. Green, ed. Armonk, N.Y.: M.E. Sharpe, 155–186.

Binder, Sarah A. 1999. "The Dynamics of Legislative Gridlock, 1947–96." *American Political Science Review* 93: 519–33.

Binning, William C., Melanie J. Blumberg, and John C. Green. 1995. "Change Comes to Steeltown: Local Political Parties as Instruments of Power." Paper presented at the annual meeting of the American Political Science Association, Chicago.

———. 1996. "Change Comes to Youngstown: Local Political Parties as Instruments of Power." In *The State of the Parties: The Changing Role of Contemporary American Parties*. 2d ed. John C. Green and Daniel M. Shea, eds. Lanham, Md.: Rowman & Littlefield, 197–213.

Black, Earl, and Merle Black. 1987. *Politics and Society in the South*. Cambridge, Mass.: Harvard University Press.

———. 1992. *The Vital South*. Cambridge, Mass.: Harvard University Press.

Blumberg, Melanie J., William C. Binning, and John C. Green. 1997. "The Grassroots Matter: The Coordinated Campaign in a Battleground State." Paper presented at The State of the Parties: 1996 & Beyond. Ray C. Bliss Institute of Applied Politics, University of Akron.

———. 1999. "Do the Grassroots Matter? The Coordinated Campaign in a Battleground State." In *The State of the Parties: The Changing Role of Contemporary American Parties*. 3rd ed. John C. Green and Daniel M. Shea, eds. Lanham, Md.: Rowman & Littlefield, 154–167.

———. 2001. "No Mo[mentum] in Ohio: Local Parties and the 2000 Presidential Campaign." Paper presented at The State of the Parties: 2000 & Beyond. Ray C. Bliss Institute of Applied Politics, University of Akron.

Boerner, Gerald, Grace Boerner, David McGill, Patricia Skalnik, and Paul Verdugo. 2000. "Elements of Effective Web Pages." *Syllabus,* April.

Bogue, Allan G. 1994. "Legislative Government in the United States Congress, 1800–1900." In *Parties and Politics in American History: A Reader*. L. Sandy Maisel and William G. Shade, eds. New York: Garland Publishing.

Bonafede, Dom. 1981. "For the Democratic Party, It's a Time for Rebuilding and Seeking New Ideas." *National Journal,* February 21, 317–320.

Brady, David W., Joseph Cooper, and Patricia A. Hurley. 1979. "The Decline of Party in the U.S. House of Representatives, 1887–1968." *Legislative Studies Quarterly* 4: 381–407.

Brennan, Mary C. 1995. *Turning Right in the Sixties: The Conservative Capture of the GOP*. Chapel Hill: University of North Carolina Press.

Brennan Center for Justice. 2000a. "Bush Campaign Spending Increases; Draws Even with Gore." Press Release. September 19. Available at www.brennancenter.org/presscenter/pressrelease_20000919.html (accessed December 2002).

———. 2000b. "Candidates Come to Strategic Fork in California: Bush Spending More on TV Ads There Than in Any Other State, While Gore TV Campaign Remains Dark." Press Release. October 30. Available at www.brennancenter.org/presscenter/pressrelease_2000_1030cmag.html (accessed December 2002).

———. 2000c. "2000 Presidential Race First in Modern History Where Political Parties Spend More on TV Ads Than Candidates." Press release. December 11. Available at www.brennancenter.org/presscenter/pressrelease_2000_1211cmag.html (accessed December 2002).

———. 2001. *Buying Time 2000*. New York: Brennan Center for Justice.

Bridges, Amy. 1986. "Becoming American: The Working Classes in the United States before the Civil War." In *Working-Class Formation: Nineteenth-Century Patterns in Western Europe and the United States.* Ira Katznelson and Aristide R. Zolberg, eds. Princeton, N.J.: Princeton University Press, 187–192.

———. 1994. "Creating Cultures of Reform." *Studies in American Political Development* 8: 1–23.

———. 1997. *Morning Glories: Municipal Reform in the Southwest.* Princeton, N.J.: Princeton University Press.

Briffault, Richard. 2000. "The Political Parties and Campaign Finance Reform." *Columbia Law Review* 100: 620–666.

Broder, David S. 1971. *The Party's Over: The Failure of Politics in America.* New York: Harper and Row.

———. 2001. "Reform: The Doubt . . ." *Washington Post,* April 3: A21.

———. 2002. "'Accidental' No More." *Washington Post Weekly Edition,* November 11–17, 4.

Bruce, John M., John A. Clark, and John H. Kessel. 1991. "Advocacy Politics in Presidential Parties." *American Political Science Review* 85: 1089–1106.

Bruzios, Christopher. 1990. "Democratic and Republican Party Activists and Followers." *Polity* 22: 581–601.

Bryce, James. 1891. *The American Commonwealth.* Chicago: Sergel.

Budge, Ian. 1993. "Parties, Programs, and Policies: A Comparative and Theoretical Perspective." *American Review of Politics* 14: 696.

Budge, Ian, and Hans Keman. 1990. *Parties and Democracy.* Oxford: Oxford University Press.

Budge, Ian, and Richard I. Hofferbert. 1990. "Mandates and Policy Outputs: U.S. Party Platforms and Federal Expenditures." *American Political Science Review* 84: 111–32.

Buell, Emmett H., and John S. Jackson. 1991. "The National Conventions: Diminished but Still Important in a Primary Dominated Process." In *Nominating the President.* Emmett H. Buell and Lee Sigelman, eds. Knoxville, Tenn.: University of Tennessee Press.

Burnham, Walter Dean. 1970. *Critical Elections and the Mainsprings of American Politics.* New York: Norton.

———. 1996. "Realignment Lives: The 1994 Earthquake and Its Implications." In *The Clinton Presidency: First Appraisals.* Colin Campbell and Bert A. Rockman, eds. Chatham, N.J.: Chatham House, 363–95.

Butler, R. Lawrence. 2001. "Explaining Party Strength in the House of Representatives, 1789–1998." Paper presented at the annual meeting of the Midwest Political Science Association, Chicago.

Campaigns and Elections. 1998. "Independent Expenditures and Issue Advocacy: Tips for PACs and Associations That Want to Play." *Campaigns & Elections* 26: 62, 68.

Campbell, Angus, Philip E. Converse, Warren E. Miller, and Donald E. Stokes. 1960. *The American Voter.* New York: Wiley.

———. 1966. *Elections and the Political Order.* New York: Wiley.

Capital Eye. 2001. "The Bottom Line in 2000." *Capital Eye* 8: 1, 5.

Carmines, Edward G., and James A. Stimson. 1989. *Issue Evolution: Race and the Transformation of American Politics.* Princeton, N.J.: Princeton University Press.

Carter, Dan T. 1995. *The Politics of Rage: George Wallace, the Origins of the New Conservatism, and the Transformation of American Politics.* New York: Simon and Schuster.

Ceaser, James W., and Andrew E. Busch. 1997. *Losing to Win.* Lanham, Md.: Rowman & Littlefield.

———. 2001. *The Perfect Tie: The True Story of the 2000 Presidential Election.* Lanham, Md.: Rowman & Littlefield.

Chambers, William Nisbet, and Walter Dean Burnham. eds. 1975. *The American Party Systems: Stages of Development.* 2d ed. London: Oxford University Press.

Clark, Terry N., Seymour Martin Lipset, and Michael Rempel. 1993. "The Declining Political Significance of Class." *International Sociology* 8: 293–316.

Clymer, Adam. 2001. "New Senate Chief Can Look to Past in Charting Course." *New York Times,* June 7: A26.

Coleman, John J. 1994. "The Resurgence of Party Organization? A Dissent from the New Orthodoxy." In *The State of the Parties: The Changing Role of Contemporary American Parties.* Daniel M. Shea and John C. Green, eds. Lanham, Md.: Rowman & Littlefield.

———. 1996a. *Party Decline in America: Policy, Politics, and the Fiscal State.* Princeton, N.J.: Princeton University Press.

———. 1996b. "Resurgent or Just Busy? Party Organizations in Contemporary America." In *The State of the Parties: The Changing Role of Contemporary American Parties.* 2d ed. John C. Green and Daniel M. Shea, eds. Lanham, Md.: Rowman & Littlefield, 367–384.

———. 1999a. "Party Images and Candidate-Centered Campaigns in 1996: What's Money Got to Do With It?" In *The State of the Parties: The Changing Role of Contemporary American Parties.* 3d ed. John C. Green and Daniel M. Shea, eds. Lanham, Md.: Rowman & Littlefield, 337–354.

———. 1999b. "Unified Government, Divided Government, and Party Responsiveness." *American Political Science Review* 93: 821–35.

Collet, Christian. 1997. "Taking the 'Abnormal' Route: Backgrounds, Beliefs, and Political Activities of Minor Party Candidates." In *Multiparty Politics in America.* Paul S. Herrnson and John C. Green, eds. Lanham, Md.: Rowman & Littlefield, 103–124.

Collet, Christian, and Jerrold R. Hansen. 2002. "Sharing the Spoils: Ralph Nader, the Green Party, and the Elections of 2000." In *Multiparty Politics in America.* 2d ed. Paul S. Herrnson and John C. Green, eds. Lanham, Md.: Rowman & Littlefield.

Committee on Political Parties. American Political Science Association. 1950. "Toward a More Responsible Two-Party System." *American Political Science Review* 44: Supplement.

Common Cause. 1996. "Statement of Common Cause President Ann McBride at News Conference Asking for Independent Counsel to Investigate Campaign Finance Activities of Clinton, Dole Campaigns." Press release. October 9.

———. 1998. "Party Soft Money." Washington, D.C.: Common Cause.

Conniff, Ruth. 2000. "The Illusion of Inclusion." *The Progressive,* September. Available at www.progressive.org/conn0900.html (accessed January 2001).

———. 2001. "Et Tu, Feingold." *The Progressive,* March. Available at www.progressive.org/conn0301.html (accessed January 2001).

Converse, Philip E. 1964. "The Nature of Belief Systems in Mass Publics." In *Ideology and Discontent*. David Apter, ed. Glencoe: Free Press.

———. 1966. "The Concept of the Normal Vote." In *Elections and the Political Order*. Angus Campbell, Philip E. Converse, Warren E. Miller, and Donald E. Stokes, eds. New York: Wiley, 9–39.

Converse, Philip E., and Gregory B. Markus. 1979. "*Plus ca change* . . . : The New CPS Election Study Panel." *American Political Science Review* 73: 32–49.

Corrado, Anthony. 1997a. "Financing the 1996 Elections." In *The Election of 1996*. Gerald M. Pomper, ed. Chatham, N.J.: Chatham House Publishers, 135–72.

———. 1997b. "Party Soft Money." In *Campaign Finance Reform: A Sourcebook*. Anthony Corrado et al., eds. Washington, D.C.: Brookings.

———. 2001. "Financing the 2000 Elections." In *The Election of 2000*. Gerald M. Pomper, ed. New York: Chatham House.

———. 2002. "Financing the 2000 Presidential General Election." In *Financing the 2000 Election*. David B. Magleby, ed. Washington, D.C.: Brookings.

Corrado, Anthony, Thomas E. Mann, Daniel R. Ortiz, Trevor Potter, and Frank J. Sorauf. 1997. *Campaign Finance Reform: A Sourcebook*. Washington, D.C.: Brookings.

Cotter, Cornelius P., James L. Gibson, John F. Bibby, and Robert J. Huckshorn. 1984. *Party Organizations in American Politics*. New York: Praeger.

Cox, Gary W., and Mathew D. McCubbins. 1993. *Legislative Leviathan: Party Government in the House*. Berkeley: University of California Press.

Craig, Stephen C. 1996. "The Angry Voter: Politics and Popular Discontent in the 1990s." In *The Broken Contract: Changing Relationships between Americans and Their Government*. Stephen Craig, ed. Boulder, Colo.: Westview, 46–66.

Crane, Edward H. 1999. "The GOP: Slouching toward Irrelevance." *Cato Policy Report* 21 (3). Available at www.cato.org/pubs/policy_report/v21n3/crane.html (accessed January 2001).

Crotty, William J. 1969. "The Quest for Scientific Meaning in Analyses of Political Parties." In *A Methodological Primer for Political Science*. Robert T. Golembiewski, William A. Welsh, and William Crotty, eds. Chicago: Rand McNally.

———. 1984. *American Parties in Decline*. 2d ed. Boston, Mass.: Little Brown.

Danzinger, Sheldon, and Peter Gottschalk. 1995. *America Unequal*. Cambridge, Mass.: Harvard University Press.

David, Paul T. 1992. "The APSA Committee on Political Parties: Some Reconsiderations of Its Work and Significance." *Perspectives on Political Science* 21: 70–79.

David, Paul T., Ralph M. Goldman, and Richard C. Bain. 1960. *The Politics of National Party Conventions*. Washington, D.C.: Brookings.

Davidson, Rodger H., and Walter J. Oleszek. 2000. *Congress and Its Members*. 7th ed. Washington, D.C.: CQ Press.

Democracy Online Project. 2000. "Online Campaigning: A Primer." The George Washington University Graduate School of Political Management. Washington, D.C.

Diamond, E., and G. Geller. 1995. "Will Press Coverage be Virtual in the Online Political World?" *National Journal*, 27: 37.

Dionne, E. J. Jr. 1991. *Why Americans Hate Politics*. New York: Simon & Schuster.

———. 1997. *They Only Look Dead*. New York: Touchstone.

———. 2001. ". . . and the Delay." *Washington Post,* April 3: A21.

Dionne, E. J. Jr. and William Kristol, eds. 2001. *Bush v. Gore: The Court Cases and the Commentary*. Washington, D.C.: Brookings.

Donovan, Beth. 1993. "Soft Money's Reach: Grass-Roots Politics Thrive on Donations That Reformers Decry as 'Sewer-Money.'" *CQ Weekly Report,* May 15: 1197.

Downs, Anthony. 1957. *An Economic Theory of Democracy.* New York: Harper.

Doyle, Kenneth P. 2000a. "Democrats Justify Issue Ad Campaign Despite Gore's March Challenge to Bush." *BNA Money and Politics Report.* June 7.

———. 2000b. "GOP Responds to Democratic Ads with Ad on Bush Social Security Plan." *BNA Money and Politics Report.* June 13.

Drew, Elizabeth. 2000. *The Corruption of American Politics*. Woodstock, N.Y.: Overlook Press.

Drier, Peter, John Mollenkopf, and Todd Swanstrom. 2001. *Place Matters*. Lawrence, Kans.: University Press of Kansas.

Driscoll, Amy. 2001. "Review Finds Bush Won Despite Miami Recount." *Washington Post,* February 26: A4.

Dulio, David A. 2001. *For Better or Worse? How Political Consultants Are Changing Elections in the United States*. Ph.D. dissertation, American University.

Dulio, David A., and Robin Kolodny. 2001. "Political Parties and Political Consultants: Creating Alliances for Electoral Success." Paper presented at the Western Political Science Association Convention, Las Vegas, Nev.

Duverger, Maurice. [1951] 1954. *Political Parties: Their Organization and Activity in the Modern State*. Barbara North and Robert North, trans. London: Methuen.

———. 1986. "Duverger's Law: Forty Years Later." In *Electoral Laws and Their Consequences*. Bernard Grofman and Arend Lijphart, eds. New York: Agathon.

Dwyre, Diana. 1994. "Party Strategy and Political Reality: The Distribution of Congressional Campaign Committee Resources." In *The State of the Parties: The Changing Role of Contemporary American Parties*. Daniel M. Shea and John C. Green, eds. Lanham, Md.: Rowman & Littlefield.

———. 1996. "Spinning Straw into Gold: Soft Money and U.S. House Elections." *Legislative Studies Quarterly* 21: 409–24.

Dwyre, Diana, and Jeffrey M. Stonecash. 1992. "Where's the Party? Changing State Party Organizations." *American Politics Quarterly* 20: 326–344.

Dwyre, Diana, and Robin Kolodny. 2002. "Throwing Out the Rule Book: Party Financing of the 2000 Elections." In *Financing the 2000 Election*. David Magleby, ed. Washington, D.C.: Brookings.

Edsall, Thomas B. 2001. "Surveying the Battlefield." *Washington Post,* July 8.

Edsall, Thomas Byrne, and Mary D. Edsall. 1991. *Chain Reaction: The Impact of Race, Rights, and Taxes on American Politics*. New York: Norton.

Edwards, George C. III, Andrew Barrett, and Jeffrey Peake. 1997. "The Legislative Impact of Divided Government." *American Journal of Political Science* 41: 545–63.

Ehrenhalt, Alan. 1991. *The United States of Ambition: Politicians, Power, and the Pursuit of Office*. New York: Times Books.

Eilperin, Juliet. 1999. "Speaker-to-Be Hastert Vows Civility and Unity for House." *Washington Post,* January 6: A8.

———. 2001. "Supreme Court's Ruling a Boost for Democrats." *Washington Post,* June 26: A8.

Eldersveld, Samuel J. 1964. *Political Parties: A Behavioral Analysis.* Chicago: Rand McNally.

———. 1982. *Political Parties in American Society.* New York: Basic Books.

Eldersveld, Samuel J., and Hanes Walton, Jr. 2000. *Political Parties in American Society.* 2d ed. Boston: Bedford/St. Martins.

Epstein, Leon D. 1956. "British Mass Parties in Comparison with American Parties." *Political Science Quarterly* 71: 97–125.

———. 1967. *Political Parties in Western Democracies.* New York: Praeger.

———. 1986. *Political Parties in the American Mold.* Madison, Wis.: University of Wisconsin Press.

Erie, Steven P. 1988. *Rainbow's End: Irish-Americans and the Dilemmas of Urban Machine Politics, 1840–1985.* Berkeley: University of California Press.

Erikson, Robert S., Gerald C. Wright, and John P. McIver. 1993. *Statehouse Democracy.* New York: Cambridge University Press.

Falling through the Net: Toward Digital Inclusion. 2000. U.S. Department of Commerce. Available at www.ntia.doc.gov/ntiahome/fttn00/contents00.html (accessed December 2002).

Farmer, Rick, John David Rausch Jr., and John C. Green. 2002. *The Test of Time: Coping with Legislative Term Limits.* Lanham, Md.: Lexington Books.

Federal Election Commission (FEC). 1998a. "Proposed Audit Report on the Clinton/Gore '96 Primary Committee, Inc.—Media Advertisements Paid for by the Democratic National Committee." Memorandum to Robert J. Costa from Lawrence Noble et al. October 27.

———. 1998b. *Report of the Audit Division on Clinton/Gore '96 Primary Committee, Inc.* Washington, D.C.: Federal Election Commission.

———. 1998c. *Report of the Audit Division on the Dole for President Committee, Inc.* Washington, D.C.: Federal Election Commission.

———. 2000a. "FEC Announces 2000 Presidential Spending Limits." Press release. March 1.

———. 2000b. *Financial Control and Compliance Manual for Presidential Primary Candidates Receiving Public Funding.* Washington, D.C.: Federal Election Commission. April revision.

———. 2001. "FEC Reports Increase in Party Fundraising for 2000." Press release. May 15.

Feingold, Russell D. 1998. "Representative Democracy versus Corporate Democracy: How Soft Money Erodes the Principle of 'One Person, One Vote.'" *Harvard Journal on Legislation* 35: 377–386.

Ferguson, Daniel, and Theodore Lowi. 2001. "Reforming American Electoral Politics: Let's Take 'No' for an Answer." *PS: Political Science & Politics* 34: 277–280.

Fiorina, Morris P. 1981. *Retrospective Voting in American National Elections.* New Haven, Conn.: Yale University Press.

Fishel, Jeff. 1985. *Presidents and Promises.* Washington, D.C.: CQ Press.

Fitts, Michael. 2001. "Back to the Future: The Enduring Dilemmas Revealed in the Supreme Court's Treatment of Political Parties." In *The U.S. Supreme Court and the Electoral Process.* David K. Ryden, ed. Washington, D.C.: Georgetown University Press.

Flanigan, William H., and Nancy H. Zingale. 1998. *Political Behavior of the American Electorate.* 9th ed. Washington, D.C.: CQ Press.

Foner, Eric. 2001. "Partisanship Rules." *The Nation* 1: 6–7.

Ford, Henry Jones. 1914. *The Rise and Growth of American Politics.* New York: Macmillan.

Fossey, Richard. 1998. "The Dizzying Growth of the Federal Student Loan Program." In *Condemning Students to Debt: College Loans and Public Policy.* Richard Fossey and Mark Bateman, eds. New York: Teachers College Press.

Francia, Peter L., John P. Frendreis, Alan R. Gitelson, and Paul S. Herrnson. 1999. "Getting the Green, Fighting on the Ground, and Plotting Strategy: Labor's Campaign Activities in State and Federal Elections." Paper presented at the annual meeting of the American Political Science Association, Atlanta.

Frantzich, Stephen E. 1989. *Political Parties in the Technological Age.* New York: Longman.

Freeman, Jo. 1986. "The Political Culture of Democratic and Republican Parties." *Political Science Quarterly* 101: 327–56.

Frendreis, John P., James L. Gibson, and Laura L. Vertz. 1990. "The Electoral Relevance of Local Party Organizations." *American Political Science Review* 84: 225–235.

———. 1995. "Local Political Parties and Legislative Races." Paper presented at the Party Politics in the Year 2000 Conference, Manchester, England.

———. 1999. "Local Parties in the 1990s: Spokes in a Candidate-Centered Wheel." In *The State of the Parties* 3d ed. John C. Green and Daniel M. Shea, eds. Lanham, Md.: Rowman & Littlefield.

Frendreis, John P., and Alan R. Gitelson. 1993. "Local Political Parties in an Age of Change." *American Review of Politics* 14: 533–547.

Frendreis, John P., Alan R. Gitelson, Gregory Flemming, and Anne Layzell. 1996. "Local Political Parties and Legislative Races in 1992 and 1994." In *The State of the Parties.* 2d ed. John C. Green and Daniel M. Shea, eds. Lanham, Md.: Rowman & Littlefield, 149–62.

Friedenberg, Robert V. 1997. *Communication Consultants in Political Campaigns: Ballot Box Warriors.* Westport, Conn.: Praeger.

Frymer, Paul. 1999. *Uneasy Alliances: Race and Party Competition in America.* Princeton, N.J.: Princeton University Press.

Fund, John. 2001. "Unintended Consequences." *Wall Street Journal,* March 23.

Gainsborough, Juliet. 2000. *Fenced Off.* Washington, D.C.: Georgetown University Press.

Gallup News Service. 2001. "Gallup Poll Topics, A–Z: Supreme Court." September 17. Available at www.gallup.com/poll/topics (accessed December 2002).

Gerring, John. 1998. *Party Ideologies in America, 1828–1996.* New York: Cambridge University Press.

———. 1999. "Culture versus Economics: An American Dilemma." *Social Science History* 23: 129–72.

Gibson, James L., and Susan E. Scarrow. 1993. "State and Local Party Organizations in American Politics." In *American Political Parties: A Reader.* Eric M. Uslaner, ed. Itasca, IL: F. E. Peacock Publishers.

Gibson, James L., Cornelius P. Cotter, John F. Bibby, and Robert J. Huckshorn. 1983.

"Assessing Party Organizational Strength." *American Journal of Political Science* 27: 193–222.

Gibson, Rachel, and Stephen Ward. 2000. "A Proposed Methodology for Studying the Function and Effectiveness of Party and Candidate Web Sites." *Social Science Computer Review* 18: 301–319.

Gierzynski, Anthony. 1992. *Legislative Campaign Committees in the American States.* Lexington, Ky.: The University Press of Kentucky.

Gierzynski, Anthony, and David Breaux. 1991. "Money and Votes in State Legislative Elections." *Legislative Studies Quarterly* 16: 203–217.

———. 1998. "The Financing Role of Parties." In *Campaign Finance in State Legislative Elections.* Joel A. Thompson and Gary F. Moncrief, eds. Washington, D.C.: CQ Press, 188–206.

Gillespie, J. D. 1993. *Politics at the Periphery: Third Parties in Two-Party America.* Columbia, S.C.: University of South Carolina Press.

Gimpel, James G. 1996. *Legislating the Revolution.* Boston: Allyn & Bacon.

———. 1999. *Separate Destinations: Migration, Immigration, and the Politics of Places.* Ann Arbor, Mich.: The University of Michigan Press.

Ginsberg, Benjamin, and Martin Shefter. 1990. *Politics by Other Means: The Declining Importance of Elections in America.* New York: Basic Books.

———. 1999. *Politics by Other Means: Politicians, Prosecutors, and the Press from Watergate to White Water.* Rev. ed. New York: Norton.

Glasgow, Garrett. 2000a. "The Efficiency of Congressional Campaign Committee Contributions in House Elections." Paper delivered at the Annual Meeting of the American Political Science Association, Washington, D.C.

———. 2000b. "Strategic Distribution of Party Resources, 1997–1998." Paper prepared for the Annual Meeting of the Midwest Political Science Association, Chicago.

Gold, H. J. 1995. "Third Party Voting in Presidential Elections: A Study of Perot, Anderson, and Wallace." *Political Research Quarterly* 48: 775–794.

Goldman, Ralph M. 1994. "Who Speaks for the Political Parties? Or Martin Van Buren, Where Are You When We Need You?" In *The State of the Parties: The Changing Role of Contemporary American Parties.* Daniel M. Shea and John C Green, eds. Lanham Md.: Rowman & Littlefield.

Goldstein, Amy, and Dana Milbank. 2001. "Now, Real Bipartisanship?" *Washington Post National Weekly Edition,* May 28–June 3: 6.

Green, John C. 1999. "Whither the Parties? The Volatile Nineties and the Future of the Party System." *American Politics Quarterly* 27: 4–8.

Green, John C., ed. 1994. *Politics, Professionalism, and Power: Modern Party Organization and the Legacy of Ray C. Bliss.* Lanham, Md.: University Press of America.

Green, John C., and William Binning. 2002. "The Rise and Decline of the Reform Party, 1992–2000." In *Multiparty Politics in America.* 2d ed. Paul S. Herrnson and John C. Green, eds. Lanham, Md.: Rowman & Littlefield, 99–124.

Green, John C., and James L. Guth. 1991. "Who is Right and Who is Left? Activist Coalitions in the Reagan Era." In *Do Elections Matter?* Benjamin Ginsberg and Alan Stone, eds. 2d ed. Armonk, N.Y.: M.E. Sharpe, 32–56.

Green, John C., James L. Guth, Lyman A. Kellstedt, and Corwin E. Smidt. 2001. *How the Faithful Voted.* Washington D.C.: Ethics and Public Policy Center.

Green, John C., and Paul S. Herrnson. 2002. *Responsible Partisanship: The Evolution of American Parties Since 1950*. Lawrence, Kans.: University of Kansas Press.

Green, John C., John S. Jackson, and Nancy L. Clayton, 1999. "Issue Networks and Party Elites in 1996." In *The State of the Parties* 3d ed. John C. Green and Daniel M. Shea, eds. Lanham, Md.: Rowman & Littlefield, 105–119.

Green, John C., and Daniel M. Shea. 1996. *The State of the Parties: The Changing Role of Contemporary American Parties*. 2d ed. Lanham, Md.: Rowman & Littlefield.

———. 1999a. "New Terrains and Past Battlegrounds in American Political Party Scholarship." *Southeastern Political Review* 24: 251–72.

———. 1999b. *The State of the Parties: The Changing Role of Contemporary American Parties*. 3d ed. Lanham, Md.: Rowman & Littlefield.

Greenhouse, Linda. 2000. "Another Kind of Bitter Split." *New York Times,* December 15.

Greer, J., and M. LaPoine. 1999. "Meaningful Discourse or Cyber-Fluff? An Analysis of Gubernatorial Campaign Web Sites throughout the 1998 Election Cycle." Paper presented at the International Communications Association Conference, San Francisco.

Gurin, Patricia, Shirley Hatchett, and James S. Jackson. 1989. *Hope and Independence: Blacks' Response to Electoral and Party Politics*. New York: Russell Sage.

Hacker, Andrew. 1991. "Playing the Racial Card." *New York Review of Books,* October 24: 14–18.

Halbfinger, David M., and Jim Yardley. 2002. "Vote Solidifies Shift of South to the G.O.P." *New York Times,* November 7: A1, B2.

Hale, Jon F. 1994. "The Democratic Leadership Council: Institutionalizing Party Faction." In *The State of the Parties*. Daniel Shea and John Green, eds. Lanham, Md.: Rowman & Littlefield, 249–63.

Hall, Richard L., and Frank W. Wayman. 1990. "Buying Time: Moneyed Interests and the Mobilization of Bias in Congressional Committees." *American Political Science Review* 84: 797–820.

Harvey, Anna L. 1998. *Votes without Leverage: Women in American Electoral Politics, 1920–1970*. New York: Cambridge University Press.

Hasen, Richard L. 2000. "Shrink Missouri, Campaign Finance, and 'The Thing That Wouldn't Leave.'" Paper delivered at the American Political Science Association Annual Meeting, Washington, D.C.

Hawkins, Howie. 1996. "Third Parties: Independent Progressive Politics." *Z Magazine* 9: 15–20.

Heard, Alexander. 1960. *The Costs of Democracy*. Chapel Hill, N.C.: University of North Carolina Press.

Hearn, James C. 1998. "The Growing Loan Orientation in Federal Aid Policy: A Historical Perspective." In *Condemning Students to Debt: College Loans and Public Policy*. Richard Fossey and Mark Bateman, eds. New York: Teachers College Press, 47–75.

Heldman, Caroline E. 1996. "The Coordinated Campaign: Party Builder or Stumbling Block?" Paper presented at the Annual Meeting of the Midwest Political Science Association, Chicago.

Helpren, D. H. 1996. "Communication at the Crossroads: Using the World Wide Web to

Distribute Political Information to the Public." Paper presented at the International Communication Association, Chicago.

Herring, E. Pendleton. 1940. *The Politics of Democracy: American Parties in Action.* New York: Norton.

Herrnson, Paul S. 1988. *Party Campaigning in the 1980s.* Cambridge, Mass.: Harvard University Press.

———. 1989. "National Party Decision Making, Strategies, and Resource Distribution in Congressional Elections." *Western Political Science Quarterly* 42: 301–323.

———. 1990. "Reemergent National Party Organizations." In *The Parties Respond: Changes in the American Party System.* L. Sandy Maisel, ed. Boulder, Colo.: Westview Press.

———. 1992a. "Campaign Professionalism and Fundraising in Congressional Elections." *Journal of Politics* 54: 859–870.

———. 1992b. "Why the United States Does Not Have Responsible Parties." *Perspectives on Political Science* 21: 91–98.

———. 1994. "The Revitalization of National Party Organizations." In *The Parties Respond: Changes in the American Party System.* 2d ed. L. Sandy Maisel, ed. Boulder, Colo.: Westview Press.

———. 1998. *Congressional Elections: Campaigning at Home and in Washington.* 2d ed. Washington, D.C.: CQ Press.

———. 2000a. "The Campaign Assessment and Candidate Outreach Project." College Park, Md.: The Center for American Politics and Citizenship.

———. 2000b. *Congressional Elections: Campaigning at Home and in Washington.* Washington, D.C.: CQ Press.

———. 2001. "The Congressional Elections." In *The Election of 2000.* Gerald M. Pomper, ed. New York: Chatham House.

Herrnson, Paul S., and Diana Dwyre. 1999. "Party Issue Advocacy in Congressional Election Campaigns." In *The State of the Parties.* 3d ed. John C. Green and Daniel M. Shea, eds. Lanham, Md.: Rowman & Littlefield, 86–104.

Herrnson, Paul S., and John C. Green, eds. 1997. *Multiparty Politics in America.* Lanham, Md.: Rowman & Littlefield.

———. 2002. *Multiparty Politics in America.* 2d ed. Lanham, Md.: Rowman & Littlefield.

Herrnson, Paul, and David Menefee-Libey. 1990. "The Dynamics of Party Organizational Development." *Midsouth Political Science Journal* 11: 3–30.

Hertzberg, Hendrik. 2000. "Eppur Si Muove." *The New Yorker,* December 25: 55–56.

Hertzke, Allen D. 1993. *Echoes of Discontent.* Washington, D.C.: CQ Press.

Hetherington, Marc J. 2001. "Resurgent Mass Partisanship: The Role of Elite Polarization." *American Political Science Review* 95: 619–31.

Hibbs, Douglas A., Jr. 1987. *The American Political Economy: Macroeconomics and Electoral Politics.* Cambridge, Mass.: Harvard University Press.

Hodgson, Godfrey. 1996. *The World Turned Right Side Up.* Boston: Mariner Books.

Hofferbert, Richard I. 1993. "Society, Party, and Policy, Party Programs as Mechanisms of Mediation." Paper prepared for the annual meeting of the American Political Science Association, Chicago.

Hofstadter, Richard. 1955. *The Age of Reform: From Bryan to FDR.* New York, Vintage Books.

Hutcheson, Ron. 2002. "Bush Meets 40% of Campaign Goals." *Akron Beacon Journal,* January 20: A1.

Inglehart, Ronald. 1971. "The Silent Revolution in Europe." *American Political Science Review* 65: 991–1017.

———. 1977. *The Silent Revolution: Changing Values and Political Styles among Western Publics.* Princeton, N.J.: Princeton University Press.

Inglehart, Ronald, and Arvam Hochstein. 1972. "Alignment and Dealignment of the Electorate in France and the U.S." *Comparative Political Studies* 5: 343–72.

Ireland, Emilienne, and Phil Tajitsu Nash. 1999. "Campaign 2000: Parties Vie for Internet Dominance." *Campaigns and Elections,* October.

Issacharoff, Samuel. 2001. "Private Parties with Public Purposes: Political Parties, Associational Freedoms, and Partisan Competition." *Columbia Law Review* 101: 274–313.

Jackman, Mary, and Robert Jackman. 1983. *Class Awareness in the United States.* Berkeley: University of California Press.

Jackson, Brooks. 1990. *Honest Graft.* Rev. edition. Washington, D.C.: Farragut Publishing.

Jackson, John S. 1992. "The Party-as-Organization: Party Elites and Party Reforms in Presidential Nominations and Conventions." In *Challenges to Party Government.* John Kenneth White and Jerome M. Mileur, eds. Carbondale, Ill.: Southern Illinois University. 63–83.

Jackson, John S., Barbara L. Brown, and David Bositis. 1982. "Herbert McClosky and Friends Revisited." *American Politics Quarterly* 10: 158–80.

Jackson, John S., and Nancy Clayton. 1996. "Leaders and Followers: Major Party Elites, Identifiers, and Issues, 1980–1992." In *The State of the Parties.* John C. Green and Daniel M. Shea, eds. 2d ed. Lanham, Md.: Rowman & Littlefield, 328–351.

Jacobson, Gary C. 1980. *Money in Congressional Elections.* New Haven, Conn.: Yale University.

Jacobson, Gary C. 1985/1986. "Party Organization and Distribution of Campaign Resources: Republicans and Democrats in 1982." *Political Science Quarterly* 100: 603–625.

James, Karen, and Jeffrey D. Sadow. 1997. "Utilization of the World Wide Web as a Communicator of Campaign Information." Paper presented at the American Political Science Association, Washington, D.C.

James, Scott C. 1992. "A Party System Perspective on the Interstate Commerce Act of 1887: The Democracy, Electoral College Competition, and the Politics of Coalition Maintenance." *Studies in American Political Development* 6: 163–200.

Jehl, Douglas. 2001. "March 11–17; Switch on Carbon Dioxide." *New York Times,* March 18: D4.

Jennings, M. Kent. 1992. "Ideological Thinking Among Mass Publics and Political Elites." *Public Opinion Quarterly* 56: 419–441.

Jensen, Richard. 1971. *The Winning of the Midwest, 1888–1896.* Chicago: University of Chicago Press.

———. 1981. "Party Coalitions and the Search for Modern Values: 1820–1970." In *Party Coalitions in the 1980s.* Seymour M. Lipset, ed. San Francisco: Institute for Contemporary Studies.

Jewell, Malcolm E., and David M. Olson. 1978. *American State Political Parties and Elections*. Homewood, Ill.: Dorsey Press.

Jones, Charles O. 1994. *The Presidency in a Separated System*. Washington, D.C.: The Brookings Institution Press.

———. 1996. "The Separated System." *Society* 33: 18–23.

Jones, Jeffrey M. 2001. "Opinion of U.S. Supreme Court Has Become More Politicized." *Gallup News Service*, 3 January. Available at www.gallup.com/poll/topics (accessed December 2002).

Judis, John B. 2000. "Why W. Won't Stop an Emerging Democratic Majority." *The New Republic*. Available at www.thenewrepublic.com/110600/judis110600.html (accessed December 2002).

Judis, John B., and Ruy Teixeira. 2002. *The Emerging Democratic Majority*. New York: Scribner.

Kamarck, Elaine Ciulla. 2002. "Political Campaigning on the Internet: Business as Usual?" In *Governance.com: Democracy in the Information Age*. Elaine Ciulla Kamarck and Joseph S. Nye Jr., eds. Washington, D.C.: The Brookings Institution Press.

Kane, Paul. 2001. "Lott Not Missing 'Pain in the Neck.'" *Roll Call*, July 16: 1, 34.

Katz, Richard S. 1986. "Party Government: A Rationalistic Conception." In *The Future of Party Government*. Volume 1: *Visions and Realities of Party Government*. Francis G. Castles and Rudolf Wildenmann, eds. New York: Walter de Gruyter.

Kaufman, Karen M., and John R. Petrocik. 1999. "The Changing Politics of American Men: Understanding the Sources of the Gender Gap." *American Journal of Political Science* 43: 864–887.

Kayden, Xandra, and Eddie Mahe, Jr. 1985. *The Party Goes On: The Persistence of the Two-Party System*. New York: Basic Books.

———. 1993. "Back from the Depths: Party Resurgence." In *American Political Parties: A Reader*. Eric M. Uslaner, ed. Itasca, Ill.: F.E. Peacock Publishers.

Kazin, Michael. 1995. *The Populist Persuasion*. New York: Basic Books.

Keller, Amy. 2002. "Dear Voter: Direct Mail Expected to Boom in Wake of Campaign Reform." *Roll Call*, April 29: 11, 18.

Kelley, Stanley, Jr. 1956. *Professional Public Relations and Political Power*. Baltimore, Md.: Johns Hopkins University Press.

Kennedy, Randall. 2001. "Contempt of Court." *The American Prospect*, January 12: 15–17.

Key, V. O., Jr. 1942. *Politics, Parties, and Pressure Groups*. New York: Thomas Y. Crowell.

———. 1949. *Southern Politics in State and Nation*. New York: Alfred A. Knopf.

———. 1955. "A Theory of Critical Elections." *Journal of Politics* 21: 198–210.

———. 1956. *American State Politics: An Introduction*. New York: Knopf.

———. 1959. "Secular Realignment and the Party System." *Journal of Politics* 21: 198–210.

Kinsley, Michael. 1981. "The Party of FDR, JFK, and 2,500 Commodity Speculators: The Shame of the Democrats." *The New Republic*, July 29. Available at www.thenewrepublic.com/archive (accessed December 2002).

Kirkpatrick, Evron M. 1971. "'Toward a More Responsible Two-Party System: Political

Science, Policy Science, or Pseudo-Science?" *American Political Science Review* 65: 965–90.

Kirkpatrick, Jean J. 1976. *The New Presidential Elite: Men and Women in National Politics.* New York: Russell Sage Foundation.

Klain, Marcus. 1955. "A New Look at the Constituencies: The Need for a Recount and a Reappraisal." *American Political Science Review* 49: 1105–1119.

Klain, Ronald A. 2001. "How Democrats Can Use *Bush v. Gore.*" *Washington Post,* March 22: A29.

Kleppner, Paul. 1970. *The Cross of Culture: A Social Analysis of Midwestern Politics, 1850–1900.* New York: Free Press.

Klingemann, Hans-Dieter, Richard Hofferbert, and Ian Budge. 1994. *Parties, Policies, and Democracy.* Boulder, Colo.: Westview Press.

Kolodny, Robin. 1998. *Pursuing Majorities: Congressional Campaign Committees in American Politics.* Norman, Okla.: University of Oklahoma Press.

———. 2000. "Electoral Partnerships: Political Consultants and Political Parties." In *Campaign Warriors: Political Consultants in Elections.* James A. Thurber and Candice J. Nelson, eds. Washington, D.C.: The Brookings Institution Press.

Kolodny, Robin, and David A. Dulio. 2001. "Where the Money Goes: Party Spending in Congressional Elections." Paper presented at the annual meeting of the Midwest Political Science Association, Chicago.

Kolodny, Robin, and Diana Dwyre. 1998. "Party-Orchestrated Activities for Legislative Party Goals: Campaigns for Majorities in the U.S. House of Representatives in the 1990s." *Party Politics* 4: 275–295.

Kolodny, Robin, and Angela Logan. 1998. "Political Consultants and the Extension of Party Goals." *PS: Political Science and Politics* 31: 155–159.

Koltz, Robert. 2001. "Internet Politics: A Survey of Practices." In *Communication in U.S. Elections: New Agendas.* Roderick P. Hart and Daron R. Shaw, eds. New York: Rowman & Littlefield.

Krasno, Jonathan, and Daniel E. Seltz. 2000. *Buying Time: Television Advertising in the 1998 Congressional Elections.* New York: Brennan Center.

Krehbiel, Keith. 2000. "Party Discipline and Measures of Partisanship." *American Journal of Political Science* 44: 212–227.

Labaton, Stephen. 1996. "Dole's Campaign Nears Limit on Spending for the Primaries." *New York Times,* March 22.

Ladd, Everett Carll. 1984. "Is Election '84 Really a Class Struggle?" *Public Opinion* April/May: 41–51.

Ladd, Everett Carll. 1991. "On the Uselessness of Realignment." In *The End of Realignment?* Byron E. Shafer, ed. Madison, Wis.: University of Wisconsin Press.

———. 1998. "Nobody's Buying." *The New Democrat.* January/February: 10–12.

Ladd, Everett Carll, and Charles Hadley. 1975. *Transformations of the American Party System.* New York: Norton.

Ladd, Everett Carll, Charles Hadley, and Lauriston King. 1971. "A New Political Realignment?" *The Public Interest* 23: 46–63.

Lancaster, John. 2001. "The Uniter." *Washington Post National Weekly Edition,* April 16–22: 6–7.

Langbein, Laura I. 1986. "Money and Access: Some Empirical Evidence." *Journal of Politics* 48: 1052–1062.

La Raja, Raymond J. 2001. *American Political Parties in the Era of Soft Money*. Ph.D. dissertation., University of California, Berkeley.

La Raja, Raymond J., and Karen Pogoda. 2000. "Soft Money Spending by State Parties: Where Does It Really Go?" Institute of Governmental Studies and Citizens Research Foundation Working Paper.

Lee, Christopher. 2002. "Republicans Make Historic Gains in Statehouses." *Washington Post,* November 7.

Leege, David C., and Lyman A. Kellstedt, eds. 1993. *Rediscovering the Religious Factor in American Politics*. Armonk, N.Y.: Sharpe.

Lehmann, Chris. 1997. "In the End: Cynical and Proud." *New York Times,* May 12: 40.

Lemann, Nicholas. 1991. *The Promised Land*. New York: Knopf.

Lentz, Jacob. 2002. *Electing Jesse Ventura: A Third-Party Success Story*. Boulder, Colo.: Lynne Rienner.

Levison, Andrew. 2001. "Who Lost the Working Class?" *The Nation*. Available at www .thenation.com/doc (accessed January 2001).

Lieber, Francis. 1938. *The Manual of Political Ethics*. Philadelphia, Pa.: Lippincott & Co.

Lipset, Seymour Martin. 1981. *Political Man*. Exp. Edition. Baltimore: Johns Hopkins.

Lipset, Seymour Martin, and Stein Rokkan, eds. 1967. *Party Systems and Voter Alignments*. New York: Free Press.

Livingston, William S. 1976. "Britain and America: The Institutionalization of Accountability." *Journal of Politics* 38: 878–894.

Loomis, Burdett. 2001. "Senate Leaders, Minority Voices: From Dirksen to Daschle." In *The Continuous Senate*. Colton C. Campbell and Nicol C. Rae, eds. Lanham, Md.: Rowman & Littlefield.

Lowi, Theodore J. 1975. "Party, Policy, and Constitution in America." In *The American Party Systems: Stages of Political Development*. 2d ed. William N. Chambers and Walter Dean Burnham, eds. New York: Oxford University Press.

———. 1985. *The Personal President*. Ithaca, N.Y.: Cornell University Press.

———. 1996. "Toward a Responsible Three-Party System: Prospects and Obstacles." In *The State of the Parties*. 2d ed. John C. Green and Daniel M. Shea, eds. Lanham, Md.: Rowman & Littlefield, 42–60.

———. 2001. "Political Parties and the Future State of the Union." In *Decline or Resurgence?* Jeffrey Cohen, Richard Fleisher, and Paul Kantor, eds. Washington, D.C.: CQ Press, 229–240.

Lowi, Theodore J., and Joseph Romance. 1998. *A Republic of Parties? Debating the Two-Party System*. Lanham, Md.: Rowman & Littlefield.

Lublin, David. 1997. *The Paradox of Representation: Racial Gerrymandering and Minority Interests in Congress*. Princeton, N.J.: Princeton University Press.

MacManus, Susan. 1991. "Single-Member Districts." In *Political Parties and Elections in the United States: An Encyclopedia*. L. Sandy Maisel, ed. New York: Garland Publishing.

Maddox, William S., and Stuart A. Lilie. 1984. *Beyond Liberal and Conservative*. Washington, D.C.: Cato Institute.

Madison, James. [1787] 1941. *The Federalist*. New York: Modern Library.

Magleby, David, ed. 1998. *Outside Money: Soft Money and Issue Advocacy in the 1998 Congressional Elections*. New York: Rowman & Littlefield.

————. 2000a. "Election Advocacy: Soft Money and Issue Advocacy in the 2000 Congressional Elections." Report issued by the Center for the Study of Elections and Democracy at Brigham Young University.

————. 2000b. "Interest-Group Election Ads." In *Outside Money: Soft Money and Issue Advocacy in the 1998 Congressional Elections*. David B, Magleby, ed. Lanham, Md.: Rowman & Littlefield.

————. 2001a. *Dictum without Data: The Myth of Issue Advocacy and Party Building*. Provo, Utah: Center for the Study of Elections and Democracy, Brigham Young University.

————. 2001b. *Election Advocacy: Soft Money and Issue Advocacy in the 2000 Congressional Elections*. Provo, Utah: Center for the Study of Elections and Democracy, Brigham Young University.

Magleby, David, and Marianne Holt. 1999. "The Long Shadow of Soft Money and Issue Advocacy Ads." *Campaigns and Elections* (May): 22–27.

Magleby, David B., Kelly D. Patterson, and James A. Thurber. 2002. "Campaign Consultants and Responsible Party Government." In *Responsible Partisanship? The Evolution of American Political Parties Since 1950*. John C. Green and Paul S. Herrnson, eds. Lawrence, Kans.: University of Kansas Press.

Magnet, Myron. 1993. *The Dream and the Nightmare: The Sixties Legacy to the Underclass*. New York: William Morrow.

Maisel, L. Sandy. 1999. *Parties and Elections in America*. Lanham, Md.: Rowman & Littlefield.

Maisel, L. Sandy, and John F. Bibby. 2000. "Elections Laws and Party Rules: Contributions to A Strong Party Role?" Paper presented at the Annual Meeting of the American Political Science Association, Boston.

Malbin, Michael J., and Thomas L. Gais. 1998. *The Day after Reform: Sobering Campaign Finance Lessons from the American States*. Albany, N.Y.: Rockefeller Institute Press.

Mann, Thomas E., and Norman J. Ornstein. 2002. "Campaign Finance Critics Pushing Myths—Not Reality" Washington, D.C.: The Brookings Institution Press.

Mansfield, Harvey J. 2001. *The Chronicle of Higher Education,* January 5, BB: 15–16.

Marcus, Ruth, and Juliet Eilperin. 2001. "Campaign Bill Could Shift Power Away from Parties." *Washington Post,* April 1: A1.

Margolis, Michael, and David Resnick. 2000. *Politics as Usual: The Cyberspace "Revolution."* Thousand Oaks, Calif.: Sage.

————. 2001. "Does the Internet Level the Playing Field for Minor Parties and Their Candidates? Do We Really Want It To?" Paper presented at the Midwest Political Science Association, Chicago.

Margolis, Michael, David Resnick, and Joel D. Wolfe. 1999. "Party Competition on the Internet in the United States and Britain." In *Harvard International Journal of Press/Politics* 4: 24–47.

Matthews, Donald R. 1960. *U.S. Senators and Their World*. New York: Vintage.

Matthews, Donald R., and James W. Prothro. 1966. *Negroes and the New Southern Politics*. New York: Harcourt, Brace, and World.

Maveety, Nancy. 1991. *Representation Rights and the Burger Years*. Ann Arbor, Mich.: University of Michigan Press.

————. 2001. "Representation Rights and the Rehnquist Years: The Viability of the 'Community of Interest' Approach." In *The U.S. Supreme Court and the Electoral Process*. David K. Ryden, ed. Washington, D.C.: Georgetown University Press.

Mayer, William. 1995. *In Pursuit of the White House.* Chatham, N.J.: Chatham House.

———. 1998. "Mass Partisanship, 1946–1996." In *Partisan Approaches to Postwar American Politics.* Byron E. Shafer, ed. Chatham, N.J.: Chatham House.

———. 2001. "The Presidential Nominations." In *The Election of 2000.* Gerald M. Pomper, ed. New York: Chatham House.

Mayhew, David R. 1986. *Placing Parties in American Politics: Organization, Electoral Settings, and Government Activity in the Twentieth Century.* Princeton, N.J.: Princeton University Press.

———. 1991. *Divided We Govern: Party Control, Lawmaking, and Investigations, 1946–1990.* New Haven: Yale University Press.

Mazmanian, D. A. 1974. *Third Parties in Presidential Elections.* Washington, D.C.: Brookings.

McCann, James. A., Ronald B. Rapoport, and Walter J. Stone. 1999. "Heeding the Call: An Assessment of Mobilization into Ross Perot's 1992 Presidential Campaign." *American Journal of Political Science* 43: 1–28.

McClosky, Herbert, Paul Hoffman, and Rosemary O'Hara. 1960. "Issue Conflict and Consensus among Party Leaders and Followers." *American Political Science Review* 54: 406–427.

———. 1964. "Consensus and Ideology in American Politics." *American Political Science Review* 58: 361–382.

McConnell, Mitch. 2001. "In Defense of Soft Money." *New York Times,* April 4.

McCormick, Richard L. 1986. *The Party Period and Public Policy: American Politics from the Age of Jackson to the Progressive Era.* New York: Oxford University Press.

McDonald, Laughlin. 1992. "The 1982 Amendments of Section 2 and Minority Representation." In *Controversies in Minority Voting.* Bernard Grofman and Chandler Davidson, eds. Washington, D.C.: The Brookings Institution Press, 83.

McGerr, Michael E. 1986. *The Decline of Popular Politics: The American North, 1865–1928.* New York: Oxford University Press.

McWilliams, Wilson Cavey. 2000. *Beyond the Politics of Disappointment: American Elections, 1980–1998.* Chatham, N.J.: Chatham House.

Meeker, Mary, and Chris DePuy. 1996. *The Internet Report.* Harper Collins.

Menefee-Libey, David. 2000. *The Triumph of Campaign-Centered Politics.* New York: Chatham House.

Merzer, Martin. 2001. "Review Shows Ballots Say Bush." *Miami Herald,* April 4. Available from cgi.herald.com/cgibin/ (accessed September 2002).

Michels, Robert. 1962. *Political Parties: A Sociological Study of the Oligarchical Tendencies of Modern Democracy.* New York: Collier Books.

Milbank, Dana. 2001. "White House Stays Focused on Political Goals." *Washington Post,* April 22.

Milbank, Dana, and Mike Allen. 2002. "Bush Wins in Overtime." *Washington Post Weekly Edition,* November 11–17: 10.

Milkis, Sidney M. 1993. *The President and the Parties: The Transformation of the American Party System Since the New Deal.* New York: Oxford University Press.

Miller, Warren E. 1988. *Without Consent.* Lexington, Ky.: University of Kentucky Press.

Miller, Warren E., Barbara G. Farah, and M. Kent Jennings. 1986. *Parties in Transition: A Longitudinal Study of Party Elites and Party Supporters.* New York: Russell Sage Foundation.

Miller, Warren E., and the National Election Studies. 1999. *American National Election Studies Cumulative Data File, 1948–1998 [Computer File].* 10th ICPSR version. Ann Arbor, Mich.: University of Michigan, Center for Political Studies [producer] and Inter-university Consortium for Political and Social Research [distributor].

Miller, Warren E., and J. Merrill Shanks. 1996. *The New American Voter.* Cambridge, Mass.: Harvard University Press.

Mills, Karen M. 2001. "Congressional Apportionment." U.S. Department of Commerce, Economics and Statistics Administration, U.S. Census Bureau, C2KBR/01-7.

Mintz, John, and Dan Keating. 2001. "Florida Ballot Spoilage Likelier for Blacks: Voting Machines, Confusion Cited." *Washington Post,* December 3: A1.

Miroff, Bruce, Raymond Seidelman, and Todd Swanstrom. 1998. *The Democratic Debate: An Introduction to American Politics.* New York: Houghton Mifflin.

Mitchell, Alison. 1998. "House G.O.P. Content to Make Ripples." *New York Times,* March 11: A14.

———. 2001. "New Senate Leader Urges 'Principled Compromise' As Democrats Take Over." *New York Times,* June 7: A26.

Moncrief, Gary F. 1998. "Candidate Spending in State Legislative Races." In *Campaign Finance in State Legislative Elections.* Joel A. Thompson and Gary F. Moncrief, eds. Washington, D.C.: CQ Press.

Monroe, Alan D., and Brian A. Bernardoni. 1995. "The Republican 'Contract' with America: A New Direction for American Parties?" Paper presented at the Annual Meeting of the Southern Political Science Association.

Moore, David W. 2001. "Little Change in Philosophy Among Rank-and-File Republicans in Past Eight Years." Gallup Reports, June 1. Available at www.gallup.com/results/topics (accessed December 2002).

Moran, Brendan. 2002. "Two Way TV Make Play For U.S." Available at www.techtv.com/news/computing (accessed December 2002).

Morehouse, Sarah M. 2000. "State Parties. Independent Partners: The Money Relationship." Paper presented at the Annual Meeting of the American Political Science Association, Washington, D.C.

Morin, Richard, and Claudia Dean. 2001. "Generational Differences." *Washington Post,* June 19.

Mortenson, Thomas G. 1995. "Educational Attainment by Family Income, 1970–1994." *Postsecondary Education Opportunity* 41: 1–8.

Mundy, A. 1995. "Presidential Hopefuls Are Bypassing the Pundits and the Press by Putting Up Their Own Web Sites." *Mediaweek* 5, 27.

Murray, Charles. 1984. *Losing Ground.* New York: Basic Books.

Myers, D. D. 1993. "New Technology and the 1992 Clinton Presidential Campaign." *American Behavioral Scientist* 37: 181–184.

Nather, David, and Adriel Bettelheim. 2001. "Moderates and Mavericks Hold Key to 107th Congress." *CQ Weekly Report,* January 6, 49–51.

National Journal. 2000a. "RNC Attacks Gore's 'Litmus Test.'" January 11.

———. 2000b. "RNC Chides Gore's 'Litmus Test'." January 24.

————. 2000c. "Dems Fire First with Health Care Spot." June 8.

————. 2000d. "RNC Adds Bush to Commercial." June 15.

————. 2000e. "Dems Care Enough to Send the Very Best." June 19.

————. 2000f. "RNC Really Getting This Message Across." June 19.

————. 2000g. "DNC Touts Gore's Victims' Rights Plan." July 13.

————. 2000h. "Bush Backs Higher Education Standards in RNC Ad Buy." July 18.

————. 2000i. "Dems Pick Apart Cheney, GOP Convention." August 1.

————. 2000j. "Dems Say Their Drug Plan Is Better." September 5.

Natural Law Party. 1992. *Proven Solutions to America's Problems: Natural Law Party Platform.* Fairfield, Iowa: Natural Law Party.

Neustadt, Richard E. 1960. *Presidential Power.* New York: Wiley.

The New Republic. 2000. "Unsafe Harbor." 25 December: 9.

New York Times. 1990. "The Growth of Suburbs." September 11: A20.

New York Times. 2002. "Portrait of the Electorate: The Voters." Available at www.nytimes.com/library/politics/elect-port-vote.html (accessed December 2002).

Nichols, John. 2000. "Nader: Fast in the Stretch." *The Nation,* November 20.

Nichols, Stephen M., David C. Kimball, and Paul Allen Beck. 1999. "Voter Turnout in the 1996 Elections: Resuming the Downward Spiral?" In *Reelection 1996.* Herbert F. Weisberg and Janet M. Box-Steffensmeier, eds. Chappaqua, N.Y.: Chatham House, 23–44.

Niquette, Mark. 1996. "Mahoning County Stands Tall among Ohio Dems." *The Vindicator,* November 13: B1–B2.

Nisbet, Robert A. 1959. "The Decline and Fall of Social Class." *The Pacific Sociological Review* 2: 11–17.

Oliphant, Thomas. 1993. "Perot Takes the Easy Way Out." *Boston Globe,* Feburary 14: A7.

Ornstein, Norman J. 2001. "Time to Dispel Some Myths about McCain-Feingold." *Roll Call* 12 April. Available at www.rollcall.com/pages/columns/ornstein (accessed December 2002).

Ostrogorski, M. 1964. *Democracy and Organization of Political Parties.* Garden City, N.Y.: Doubleday.

Owens, John E. 1997. "The Return of Party Government in the U.S. House of Representatives: Central Leadership-Committee Relations in the 104th Congress." *British Journal of Political Science* 27: 247–271.

Oxman, Neil. 2001. Principal, The Campaign Group. Telephone interview by Robin Kolodny, January 23.

Page, Benjamin. 1978. *Choices and Echoes in Presidential Elections.* Chicago: University of Chicago Press.

Parks, Daniel J. 2001a. "It's the Day of the Centrist As Bush Tax Cut Takes a Hit." *CQ Weekly Report,* April 7: 768–774.

————. 2001b. "An Unassuming Authority." *CQ Weekly Report,* May 26: 1212–1213.

Partin, Randall W., Lori M. Weber, Ronald B. Rapoport, and Walter J. Stone. 1994. "Sources of Activism in the 1992 Perot Campaign." In *The State of the Parties.* Daniel M. Shea and John C. Green, eds. Lanham, Md.: Rowman & Littlefield.

Partin, Randall W., Lori M. Weber, Ronald B. Rapoport, and Walter J. Stone. 1996. "Perot Activists in 1992 and 1994: Sources of Activism." In *The State of the Par-*

ties, 2d ed. John C. Green and Daniel M. Shea, eds. Lanham, Md.: Rowman & Littlefield.

Patterson, Kelly, and Amy Bice. 1997. "Political Parties, Candidates, and Presidential Campaigns: 1952–1996." Paper prepared for delivery at the Annual Meeting of the American Political Science Association, Washington, D.C.

Peabody, Robert L. 1976. *Leadership in Congress.* Boston: Little, Brown.

Peniston, Bradley. 1996. "Politicians Caught in a Web: Going Online Could Bring New Life to the Local Democratic Process." *The Capital,* January 14.

Pennock, J. Roland. 1952. "Responsiveness, Responsibility, and Majority Rule." *American Political Science Review* 46: 790–807.

Persily, Nathaniel. 2001. "The Legal Regulation of Party Nomination Methods: *California Democratic Party v. Jones,* John McCain and Beyond." Paper delivered at the Annual Meeting of the American Political Science Association, Washington, D.C.

Petracca, Mark P. 1989. "Political Consultants and Democratic Governance." in *PS: Political Science and Politics* 22: 11–14.

Petrocik, John R. 1981. *Party Coalitions: Realignments and the Decline of the New Deal Party System.* Chicago: University of Chicago Press.

Pew Research Center. 2001. "Economic Inequality Seen as Rising, Boom Bypasses Poor." Released June. Available at www.people-press.org/june01rpt.htm (accessed December 2002).

Phillips, Kevin. 1970. *The Emerging Republican Majority.* New York: Anchor.

Pildes, Richard H. 2001. "Democracy and Disorder." In *The Vote: Bush, Gore, and the Supreme Court.* Cass R. Sunstein and Richard A. Epstein, eds. Chicago: University of Chicago Press, 140–164.

Polling Report. 2001. September 17. Available at www.pollingreport.com/institut.htm. (accessed December 2002).

Polsby, Nelson W. 1983. *The Consequences of Party Reform.* New York: Oxford University Press.

Pomper, Gerald M. 1970. *Elections in America.* New York: Dodd, Mead.

———. 1971. "Toward a More Responsible Two-Party System? What, Again?" *Journal of Politics* 33: 918.

———. 1998. "The Alleged Decline of American Parties." In *Politicians and Party Politics.* John Geer, ed. Baltimore: Johns Hopkins University Press.

———. 1999. "Parliamentary Government in the United States?" In *The State of the Parties.* 3d ed. John C. Green and Daniel M. Shea, eds. Lanham, Md.: Rowman & Littlefield.

Pomper, Gerald M., with Susan L. Lederman. 1980. *Elections in America.* 2d ed. New York: Longman, 1980.

Ponnuru, Ramesh. 1998. "Racial Politics." *National Review,* December 21. Available at www.nationalreview.com/document (accessed December 2002)..

———. 2001. "Lefty Nation: What the Trends Portend." *National Review,* April 16. Available at www.nationalreview.com/document (accessed December 2002).

Poole, Keith T., and Howard Rosenthal. 1996. *Congress: A Political-Economic History of Roll Call Voting.* New York: Oxford University Press.

Posner, Gerald. 1996. *Citizen Perot: His Life and Times.* New York: Random House.

Potter, Trevor. 1997. "Issue Advocacy and Express Advocacy." In *Campaign Finance Reform: A Sourcebook.* Anthony Corrado et al., eds. Washington, D.C.: Brookings.

Price, David. 1984. *Bringing Back the Parties*. Washington, D.C.: CQ Press.

Prothro, James W., and Charles W. Griggs. 1960. "Fundamental Principles of Democracy: Bases of Agreement and Disagreement." *Journal of Politics* 22: 276–294.

Puopolos, Sonia "Tita." 2001. "The Web and U.S. Senatorial Campaigns 2000." *American Behavioral Scientist* 44: 2030–2047.

Putnam, Robert D. 2000. *Bowling Alone: The Collapse and Revival of American Community*. New York: Simon and Schuster.

Rae, Nicol C. 1989. *The Decline and Fall of the Liberal Republicans from 1952 to the Present*. New York: Oxford University Press.

Rae, Nicol C., and Colton C. Campbell. 2001. "Party Politics and Ideology in the Contemporary Senate." In *The Contentious Senate*. Colton C. Campbell and Nicol C. Rae, eds. Lanham, Md.: Rowman & Littlefield, 1–18.

Rankin, Starlene. 2001. "G/GPUSA Secretary's Report, June 2000–January 2001." *Green Bulletin*—E-mail Version Part 2 (January).

Ranney, Austin. 1951. "Toward a More Responsible Two-Party System: A Commentary." *American Political Science Review* 45: 488–499.

———. 1954. *The Doctrine of Responsible Party Government*. Urbana: University of Illinois Press.

———. 1975. *Curing the Mischiefs of Faction*. Berkeley: University of California Press.

———. 1990. "Broadcasting, Narrowcasting, and Politics." In *The New American Political System*. 2d ed. Anthony King, ed. Washington, D.C.: American Enterprise Institute.

Ranney, Austin, and Willmore Kendall. 1956. *Democracy and the American Party System*. New York: Harcourt, Brace.

Rapoport, Ronald B. and Walter. J. Stone. 2000. "Third Party Success and Major Party Response: Ross Perot and the Reform Party." European Consortium for Political Research, Joint Sessions, Copenhagen.

Reichley, A. James. 2002. *Faith in Politics*. Washington, D.C.: Brookings.

———. 2000. *The Life of the Parties: A History of American Political Parties*. Rev. ed. Lanham, Md.: Rowman & Littlefield.

———. 1996. "The Future of the American Two-Party System after 1994." In *The State of the Parties: The Changing Role of Contemporary American Parties*. 2d ed. John C. Green and Daniel M. Shea, eds. Lanham, Md.: Rowman & Littlefield.

Republican National Committee. 1996. "RNC Announces $20 Million TV Advertising Campaign." Press release. May 16.

Rensenbrink, John. 1999. *Against All Odds: The Green Transformation of American Politics*. Raymond, Maine: Leopold Press.

Reynolds, John F. 1988. *Testing Democracy: Electoral Behavior and Progressive Reform in New Jersey, 1880–1920*. Chapel Hill: University of North Carolina Press.

Rice, Stewart A. 1928. *Quantitative Methods in Politics*. New York: Knopf.

Richter, Paul. 1993. "President, Perot Confer Before Address," *Los Angeles Times,* February 18: A27.

Riker, William. 1982. "The Two-Party System and Duverger's Law." *American Political Science Review* 76: 753–766.

———. 1986. "Duverger's Law Revisited." In *Electoral Laws and Their Consequences*. Bernard Grofman and Arend Lijphart, eds. New York: Agathon Press.

Ritter, Gretchen. 1997. *Goldbugs and Greenbacks: The Antimonopoly Tradition and the Politics of Finance in America, 1865–1896.* New York: Cambridge University Press.

Rohde, David W. 1991. *Parties and Leaders in the Postreform House.* Chicago: University of Chicago Press.

Rosen, Jeffrey. 2001. "The Supreme Court Commits Suicide." *The New Republic,* December 25: 18.

Rosenbaum, David E. 2001. "Bush's Tax Plan Gets Lift in House, but Senate Balks." *New York Times,* May 5: A1, A14.

Rosenstone, Steven J., and John Mark Hansen. 1993. *Mobilization, Participation, and Democracy in America.* New York: Macmillan.

Rosenthal, Alan. 1981. *Legislative Life: People, Process, and Performance in the States.* New York: Harper & Row.

Rudolph, Thomas J. 1999. "Corporate and Labor PAC Contributions in House Elections: Measuring the Effects of Majority Party Status." *Journal of Politics* 61: 195–206.

Ryden, David K. 2000. "The U.S. Supreme Court, the Electoral Process, and the Quest for Representation: An Overview." In *The U.S. Supreme Court and the Electoral Process.* David K. Ryden, ed. Washington, D.C.: Georgetown University Press.

———. 2001. "To Curb Parties or to Court Them? Seeking a Constitutional Framework for Campaign Finance Reform." In *The U.S. Supreme Court and the Electoral Process.* David K. Ryden, ed. Washington, D.C.: Georgetown University Press.

Sabato, Larry J. 1981. *The Rise of Political Consultants: New Ways of Winning Elections.* New York: Basic Books.

———. 1988. *The Party's Just Begun: Shaping Political Parties for America's Future.* Glenview, Ill.: Little, Brown.

Saleton, William. 2001. "The Money Jungle." *Slate,* 21 March.

Salmore, Stephen A., and Barbara G. Salmore. 1985. *Candidates, Parties, and Campaigns: Electoral Politics in America.* Washington, D.C.: CQ Press.

———. 1996. "The Transformation of State Electoral Politics." In *The State of the States.* Carl E. Van Horn, ed. Washington, D.C.: CQ Press.

Samuelson, Robert J. 2001. "Prohibition is Back." *Washington Post,* April 11: A27.

Scammon, Richard M., and Ben J. Wattenberg. 1970. *The Real Majority.* New York: Coward-McCann.

Schattschneider, E. E. 1942. *Party Government.* New York: Holt, Rinehart, and Winston.

———. 1960. *The Semisovereign People: A Realist's View of Democracy in America.* New York: Holt, Reinhart, and Winston.

Schenker, Jennifer L. 1999. "Talk-Back Television." *Time,* March 30.

Schlesinger, Arthur M., Jr. 1986. *The Cycles of American History.* Boston: Houghton Mifflin.

Schlesinger, Joseph A. 1985. "The New American Political Party." *American Political Science Review* 79: 1152–1169.

———. 1991. *Political Parties and the Winning of Office.* Ann Arbor, Mich.: University of Michigan Press.

Schneider, William. 1987. "The New Shape of American Politics." *Atlantic Monthly,* January: 39–54.

———. 1992. "The Suburban Century Begins." *Atlantic Monthly,* July: 33–44.

————. 1994. "Ross Perot Uses His Leverage to Influence the GOP." *CNN: Inside Politics.*

Seelye, Katharine Q. 2001. "Senate Republicans Step Out and Democrats Jump In." *New York Times,* May 25: A1, A18.

Seligson, Dan. 2001a. "Florida Adopts Sweeping Voting Reforms." *Stateline.org.* May 4. Available at www.stateline.org (accessed December 2002).

————. 2001b. "Election Reform Drive Brings Little Change." *Stateline.org.* September 7. Available at www.stateline.org (accessed December 2002).

Selnow, Gary W. 1998. *Electronic Whistle-Stops: The Impact of the Internet on American Politics.* Westport, Conn.: Praeger.

Shafer, Byron E., ed. 1991. *The End of Realignment? Interpreting American Electoral Eras.* Madison, Wis.: University of Wisconsin Press.

Shapiro, Isaac, Robert Greenstein, and Wendell Primus. 2001. "Pathbreaking CBO Study Shows Dramatic Increases in Income Disparities in 1980s and 1990s." Center on Budget and Policy Priorities, Washington, D.C.

Shaw, Carolyn. 1996. "Has President Clinton Fulfilled His Campaign Promises?" Paper prepared for the Annual Meeting of the American Political Science Association, San Francisco.

Shea, Daniel M. 1995. *Transforming Democracy: Legislative Campaign Committees and Political Parties.* Albany: State University of New York Press.

————. 1999. "The Passing of Realignment and the Advent of the 'Base-Less' Party System." *American Politics Quarterly* 27: 33–57.

Shea, Daniel M., and John C. Green. 1994. *The State of the Parties: The Changing Role of Contemporary American Parties.* Lanham, Md.: Rowman & Littlefield.

Shenon, Philip. 2001. "Lott Steps Aside, Making a Pledge of Cooperation." *New York Times,* June 8: A19.

Shogren, Elizabeth. 2001. "Campaign 2000: Focus Shifts from Voters to Donors." *Los Angeles Times,* March 15.

Sifry, Micah L. 2000a. "Nader's No Ventura, but . . ." *NewsForChange,* October 31. Available from www.newsforchange.com/articles (accessed December 2002).

————. 2000b. "What Went Wrong for Ralph?" *NewsForChange,* November 28. Available from www.newsforchange.com/articles (accessed December 2002).

————. 2002. *Spoiling for a Fight: Third Party Politics in America.* New York: Routledge.

Silbey, Joel H. 1984. "'The Salt of the Nation': Political Parties in Ante-bellum America." In *Political Parties and the Modern State.* Richard L. McCormick, ed. New Brunswick, N.J.: Rutgers University Press.

————. 1991. "Beyond Realignment and Realignment Theory: American Political Years, 1789–1989." In *The End of Realignment.* Byron E. Shafer, ed. Madison, Wis.: University of Wisconsin Press, 3–23.

Simon, Roger. 2001. *Divided We Stand: How Al Gore Beat George Bush and Lost the Presidency.* New York: Crown Publishers.

Sinclair, Barbara. 2001. "The Senate Leadership Dilemma: Passing Bills and Pursuing Partisan Advantage in a Nonmajoritarian Chamber." In *The Contentious Senate.* Colton C. Campbell and Nicol C. Rae, eds. Lanham, Md.: Rowman & Littlefield, 65–89.

Skerry, Peter. 1993. *Mexican Americans: The Ambivalent Minority.* New York: The Free Press.

Skiba, Katherine. 1995. "Cyberstump." *Milwaukee Journal Sentinel,* December 3.

Skowronek, Stephen. 1982. *Building a New American State: The Expansion of National Administrative Capacities.* Cambridge, Mass.: Cambridge University Press.

Smith, Rogers. 1993. "Beyond Tocqueville, Myrdal, and Hartz: The Multiple Traditions in America." *American Political Science Review* 87: 549–566.

Smith, Steven S. 1993. "Forces of Change in Senate Party Leadership and Organization." *Congress Reconsidered.* 5th ed. Lawrence C. Dodd and Bruce I. Oppenheimer, eds. Washington, D.C.: CQ Press, 259–290.

Sorauf, Frank J. 1964. *Political Parties in the American System.* Boston: Little, Brown.

———. 1975. "Political Parties and Political Analysis." In *The American Party Systems: Stages of Political Development.* 2d ed. William N. Chambers and Walter Dean Burnham, eds. New York: Oxford University Press.

———. 1980. "Political Parties and Political Action Committees: Two Life Cycles." *Arizona Law Review* 22: 446–450.

———. 1992. *Inside Campaign Finance.* New Haven: Yale University.

———. 2000. "Money, Power, and Responsibility: The Major Political Parties Fifty Years Later." Paper presented at the Annual Meeting of the American Political Science Association, Washington, D.C.

Stanley, Harold W., and Richard G. Niemi. 2001. "Partisanship, Party Coalitions, and Group Support, 1952–2000." Paper presented at the Annual Meeting of the American Political Science Association, San Francisco.

———. 1999. "Party Coalitions in Transition: Partisanship and Group Support, 1952–96." In *Reelection 1996.* Herbert F. Weisberg and Janet M. Box-Steffensmeier, eds. Chappaqua, N.Y.: Chatham House, 162–181.

Stevenson, Richard W., and Michael R. Kagay. 1998. "Republicans' Image Eroding Fast, Poll Shows." *New York Times,* December 19: B5.

Stone, Brad. 1996. "Politics '96." *Internet World,* November.

Stone, Walter J., and Ronald B. Rapoport. 1997. "A Candidate-Centered Perspective on Party Responsiveness: Nomination Activists and the Process of Party Change." In *The Parties Respond.* L. S. Maisel, ed. Boulder, Colo.: Westview Press.

———. 2001. "It's Perot Stupid! The Legacy of the 1992 Perot Movement in the Major Party System, 1992–2000." *PS: Political Science and Politics* 34: 49–58.

Stonecash, Jeffrey M. 2000. *Class and Party in American Politics.* Boulder, Colo.: Westview Press.

———. 2001. "The Trend That Never Happened: Incumbent Vote Percentages in House Elections." Department of Political Science, Maxwell School, Syracuse University.

Stone, Walter J., Ronald B. Rapoport, Patricia A. Jaramillo, and Lori M. Weber. 1999. "The Activist Base of the Reform Party in 1996: Problems and Prospects." In *The State of the Parties,* 3d ed. John C. Green and Daniel M. Shea, eds. Lanham, Md.: Rowman & Littlefield.

Stonecash, Jeffrey M., Mark D. Brewer, and Mack D. Mariani. 2002a. "Northern Democrats and Polarization in the U.S. House." *Legislative Studies Quarterly* 27: 423–444.

———. 2002b. *Diverging Parties: Social Change, Realignment, and Party Polarization.* Boulder, Colo.: Westview Press.

Sullivan, J. F. 1995. "Politics, Journalism and the Net" *Nieman Reports* 49: 4.

Sundquist, James L. 1982. *Dynamics of the Party System.* Rev. ed. Washington, D.C.: Brookings.

Suro, Roberto. 1998. *Strangers among Us: How Latino Immigration is Transforming America.* New York: Alfred A. Knopf.

Swindell, Bill. 2001. "Grassley, Baucus Stick Together on Tax Bill." *Congressional Quarterly Weekly Report,* May 12: 1052.

Tackett, Michael. 1995. "Internet Changes Ways of Politics." *The Times Picayune,* June 4.

Tate, Katherine. 1993. *From Protest to Politics: The New Black Voters in American Elections.* Cambridge, Mass.: Harvard University Press.

Taylor, Andrew. 2001a. "Senate GOP to Share Power." *Congressional Quarterly Weekly Report,* January 6: 21–22.

———. 2001b. "The Outlook for Bush's Cabinet Nominations." *Congressional Quarterly Weekly Report,* January 6: 67.

———. 2001c. "Shakeup in the Senate." *Congressional Quarterly Weekly Report,* May 26: 1208–1211.

Taylor, Humphrey. 2002. "Internet Penetration at 66% of Adults (137 Million) Nationwide: 55% of Adults Now Online from Home and 30% Online at work." HarrisInteractive. Available at www.harrisinteractive.com/harris_poll (accessed December 2002).

Thompson, J. W. Cassie, and M. Jewell. 1994. "A Sacred Cow or Just a Lot of Bull: Party and PAC Money in State Legislative Elections." *Political Research Quarterly* 47: 223–237.

Thurber, James A. 2000. "Introduction to the Study of Campaign Consultants." In *Campaign Warriors: Political Consultants in Elections.* James A. Thurber and Candice J. Nelson, eds. Washington, D.C.: The Brookings Institution Press.

———. ed. 2001. *The Battle for Congress: Consultants, Candidates, and Voters.* Washington, D.C.: Brookings.

Thurber, James A., Candice J. Nelson, and David A. Dulio. 2000. "Portrait of Campaign Consultants." In *Campaign Warriors: Political Consultants in Elections.* James A. Thurber and Candice J. Nelson, eds. Washington, D.C.: The Brookings Institution Press.

Tokar, Brian. 1992. *The Green Alternative: Creating an Ecological Future.* San Pedro, Calif.: R. & E. Miles.

Trish, Barbara. 1994. "Party Integration in Indiana and Ohio: The 1988 and 1992 Presidential Contests." *The American Review of Politics* 15: 235–256.

Turner, Julius. 1951. "Responsible Parties: A Dissent from the Floor." *American Political Science Review* 45: 143–152.

Van Buren, Martin. 1967. *Inquiry into the Origins and Course of Political Parties in the United States.* New York: Kelley.

Van Natta, Don, Jr. 2000. "The 2000 Campaign: The War Chest; GOP Plans Year of Raising Money and Reaching Out." *New York Times,* January 17.

Victor, Kirk. 2001a. "Independent's Day." *National Journal,* May 26: 1570–1574.

———. 2001b. "Rebel Revival." *National Journal,* July 7: 2150–2155.

———. 2001c. "McCain's Evolution." *National Journal,* August 4: 2464–2471.

Wallison, Peter J. 2001. "It's Not Corruption, It's Politics." *Washington Post,* June 3: B01.

Washington Post Staff. 2001. *Deadlock: The Inside Story of America's Closest Election.* New York: Public Affairs.

Wattenberg, Ben J. 1995. *Values Matter Most.* Washington, D.C.: Regnery.

Wattenberg, Martin P. 1984. *The Decline of American Political Parties, 1952–1980.* Cambridge, Mass.: Harvard University Press.

———. 1991. *The Rise of Candidate-Centered Politics.* Cambridge, Mass.: Harvard University Press.

———. 1996. *The Decline of American Political Parties, 1952–1994.* Cambridge, Mass.: Harvard University Press.

———. 1998. *The Decline of American Political Parties, 1952–1996.* Cambridge, Mass.: Harvard University Press.

Weare, Christopher, and Wan-Ying Lin. 2000. "Content Analysis of the World Wide Web: Opportunities and Challenges." *Social Science Computer Review* 18 (Fall): 272–292.

Weinberg, Daniel H. 1996. "A Brief Look at Postwar U.S. Income Inequality." Current Population Reports, June, P60–191. Washington, D.C.: U.S. Census Bureau.

Weisberg, Herbert, and Timothy Hill. 2001. "The Succession Presidential Election of 2000: The Battle of the Legacies." Paper presented at the Annual Meeting of the American Political Science Association, San Francisco.

West, Darrell M. 2000. *Checkbook Democracy: How Money Corrupts Political Campaigns.* Boston: Northeastern University Press.

White, John K. 1992. "Responsible Party Government in America." *Perspectives on Political Science* 21: 80–90.

———. 2002. *Values Divide: American Politics and Culture in Transition.* New York: Chatham House.

White, John Kenneth, and Jerome M. Mileur, eds. 1992. *Challenges to Party Government.* Carbondale, Ill.: Southern Illinois University.

White, John Kenneth, and Daniel M. Shea. 2000. *New Party Politics: From Jefferson and Hamilton to the Information Age.* Boston: Bedford/St. Martin's.

Wilcox, Clyde. 1995. *The Latest American Revolution?* New York: St. Martin's Press.

Wilensky, Harold L. 1966. "Class, Class Consciousness, and American Workers." In *Labor in a Changing America.* William Haber, ed. New York: Basic Books, 12–28.

Wilson, Woodrow. 1885. *Congressional Government.* Boston: Houghton-Mifflin.

Woodward, Bob, and Ruth Marcus. 1997. "Papers Show Use of DNC Ads to Help Clinton." *Washington Post,* September 18: A1.

Index

About the Contributors

Sarah Barclay is a research associate for The Pew Charitable Trusts–Colby College Coalition to Promote Civic Dialogue on Campaign Finance Reform Project.

Paul Allen Beck is professor of political science and department chair at The Ohio State University. He is the coauthor of *Party Politics in America* (9th edition, 2002). His most recent research, coauthored articles on the role of parties, discussion networks and the media in presidential elections, appears in the *American Political Science Review,* the *American Journal of Political Science* and the *Journal of Politics.*

John C. Berg is professor of government and director of the graduate program in professional politics at Suffolk University. He is the author of *Unequal Struggle: Class, Gender, Race, and Power in the U.S. Congress* (1994).

Nathan S. Bigelow is a Ph.D. student at the University of Maryland, College Park.

William Binning is professor and chair of political science at Youngstown State University. His most recent writing has been on Ohio politics.

Melanie J. Blumberg is assistant professor of political science at California University of Pennsylvania. She studies political parties, local politics, and Congressional elections.

R. Lawrence Butler is assistant professor of political science at Rowan University. He earned a Ph.D. at Princeton University, where he studied Congress, political parties, and other American political institutions.

John J. Coleman is professor of political science at the University of Wisconsin, Madison. He is the author of *Party Decline in America: Policy, Politics, and the Fiscal State,* and articles on political parties, elections, campaign finance, Congress, and the presidency in scholarly journals and books.

Anthony Corrado is professor of government at Colby College and is the author of a number of books and articles on campaign finance. He is the principal investigator for The Pew Charitable Trusts–Colby College Coalition to Promote Civic Dialogue on Campaign Finance Reform Project.

David A. Dulio is assistant professor of political science at Oakland University. During 2001–2002 he served as an American Political Science Association Congressional Fellow in the office of the U.S. House of Representatives Republican Conference for Rep. J. C. Watts. He is coeditor of *Crowded Airwaves: Campaign Advertising in Elections* (2000) and *Shades of Gray: Perspectives on Campaign Ethics* (2002).

Diana Dwyre is associate professor of political science at California State University, Chico. She has published a number of articles and chapters on the financing of congressional elections. She was the 1998 American Political Science Association Congressional Fellowship Steiger Fellow. Her recent publications include *Legislative Labyrinth: Congress and Campaign Finance Reform* (with Victoria A. Farrar-Myers, 2001).

Rick Farmer is assistant professor of political science at the University of Akron and a fellow in the Ray C. Bliss Institute of Applied Politics. He has written and taught in the areas of campaigns and elections, political parties, and term limits.

Rich Fender is a graduate of Kent State University.

Peter L. Francia is a research fellow and program coordinator for the Center for American Politics and Citizenship at the University of Maryland, College Park. He has written articles and book chapters on campaign finance, political parties, and the political activities of labor unions, corporations, and women's organizations. His work has appeared in *Social Science Quarterly, American Politics Research,* and *Women & Politics.*

John P. Frendreis is professor of political science and associate vice president for planning and analysis at Loyola University Chicago. His areas of scholarly expertise include American politics, with special emphasis on political parties and elections, and his publications include two books and articles in numerous journals, including *American Political Science Review, American Journal of Politics, Journal of Politics, Political Research Quarterly,* and *Polity.* His current research includes a multiyear, multistate study of the role of local political parties in state legislative elections.

Alan R. Gitelson is professor of political science at Loyola University Chicago. His recent publications include *American Elections: The Rules Matter* (with Robert L. Dudley) and "Testing Spatial Models of Electoral Competition" (with John P. Frendreis, Shannon Jenkins, and Douglas D. Roscoe), *Legislative Studies Quarterly,* 2002.

Heitor Gouvêa is a research associate for The Pew Charitable Trusts–Colby College Coalition to Promote Civic Dialogue on Campaign Finance Reform Project.

John C. Green is professor of political science and director of the Ray C. Bliss Institute of Applied Politics at the University of Akron. His most recent publication is the edited volume *Multiparty Politics in America,* second edition (2002).

Paul S. Herrnson is director of the Center for American Politics and Citizenship and professor of government and politics at the University of Maryland, College Park. He is the author of *Congressional Elections: Campaigning at Home and in Washington* and *Party Campaigning in the 1980s.* He is editor or coeditor of several volumes, including *Playing Hardball: Campaigning for the U.S. Congress* and *Campaigns and Elections: Contemporary Case Studies.*

John S. Jackson was formerly Interim Chancellor and vice chancellor for academic affairs at Southern Illinois University at Carbondale. He is currently visiting professor at the Public Policy Institute at SIUC. His most recent book, *The Politics of Presidential Elections* (2000), was coauthored with William Crotty.

Malcolm E. Jewell is a retired political science professor at the University of Kentucky, where he specialized in state politics and legislatures. In addition to books coauthored with Sarah Morehouse, he is coauthor of two books on Kentucky politics and the Kentucky legislature, and a book on legislative leadership.

Robin Kolodny is associate professor of political science at Temple University and was an American Political Science Association Congressional Fellow during the first session of the 104th Congress. She is the author of *Pursuing Majorities: Congressional Campaign Committees in American Politics* (1998) and other works on American parties in comparative perspective.

Raymond J. La Raja is assistant professor of political science at the University of Massachusetts, Amherst. His Ph.D. dissertation—written for the University of California, Berkeley—was entitled "American Political Parties in the Era of Soft Money." La Raja is the author or coauthor of more than a half-dozen scholarly articles about party funding and he serves as an academic advisor to the Campaign Finance Institute in Washington, D.C.

Theodore J. Lowi is the John L. Senior Professor of American Institutions at Cornell University.

Sarah M. Morehouse is professor emerita of political science at the University of Connecticut. She is the author of *The Governor as Party Leader* (1998) and coauthor with Malcolm Jewell of *Political Parties and Elections in American States* (2001) and *State Politics, Parties and Policy,* second edition (2003).

Gerald M. Pomper is Board of Governors Professor of Political Science (emeritus) at Rutgers University. He is the author of numerous books and articles on American parties and elections. They include *Passions and Interests: Political Party Concepts of American Democracy,* a quadrennial series on the national elections from 1976 to 2000, and the forthcoming *Ordinary Heroes and American Democracy.*

Ronald B. Rapoport is the John Marshall Professor of Government at the College of William & Mary. He is coeditor of *The Life of the Parties: A Study of Presidential Activists* (1993).

A. James Reichley is a senior fellow in the graduate public policy institute at Georgetown University. His most recent books are *The Values Connection* (2001) and *Faith in Politics* (2002).

David K. Ryden is an assistant professor of political science at Hope College and an attorney. He is the author of *Representation in Crisis: The Constitution, Interest Groups, and Political Parties* (1996).

Larry Schwab is professor of political science at John Carroll University. He is the author of *Changing Patterns of Congressional Politics, The Impact of Congressional Reapportionment and Redistricting,* and *The Illusion of a Conservative Reagan Revolution.*

Daniel M. Shea is associate professor of political science and director of the Center for Political Participation at Allegheny College. He has written and edited a number of books on parties and elections, including *Transform-*

ing Democracy (1995), *Campaign Craft* (1996, 2001), *The State of the Parties* (with John C. Green, 1994, 1996, 1999) and *New Party Politics* (with John K. White, 2001).

Walter J. Stone is professor of political science at the University of California, Davis. He recently completed a term as editor of the *Political Research Quarterly.*

Jeffrey M. Stonecash is professor and chair of political science at the Maxwell School, Syracuse University. His research focuses on political parties, their electoral bases, and their roles in shaping public policy debates. He has published in journals such as *American Political Science Review, American Politics Quarterly, Legislative Studies Quarterly, Political Behavior*, and *Political Research Quarterly*. His most recent books are *Class and Party in American Politics* (2000) and *Diverging Parties* (2002).

James A. Thurber is professor of government and director of the Center for Congressional and Presidential Studies at American University. He is coeditor of *Campaigns and Elections American Style* (1995) and coeditor of *Crowded Airwaves: Campaign Advertising in Elections* (2000). Thurber is also principal investigator on the Pew Charitable Trusts' Improving Campaign Conduct project.